STUDENT
The Push Guide to Money 2005
SURVIVAL

by Johnny Rich and Alice Tarleton

Second edition

Project Editor: Ruth Bushi
Additional research: Veronica Bain, Vasiliki Proiou
Special thanks to: Nicole Linhardt-Rich, James Rabson, Sarah Robertson, Nick Tatman

Published by: Nelson Thornes Ltd

Push Online: www.nelsonthornes.com/push

Push
...like it is

First edition published in 2001

Second edition published in 2004 by:
Nelson Thornes Ltd
Delta Place
27 Bath Road
CHELTENHAM
GL53 7TH
United Kingdom

04 05 06 07 08 / 10 9 8 7 6 5 4 3 2 1

A catalogue record for this book is available from the British Library

ISBN 0 7487 9028 4

Page make-up by Softwin

Printed and bound in Spain by GraphyCems

Note from Push

All our facts and figures were correct when we went to press (or to the best of our knowledge after a lot of checking), so if anything's changed in the meantime or it's just wrong, we're really cut up about it and very sorry, but we take absolutely no responsibility for it. Blame someone else, but let us know, okay? Cheers.

A few of the tips are illegal and are intended for amusement value only. Of course, Push would never seriously suggest doing anything against the law. If you want to get in trouble, that's your look-out, but don't go blaming us.

Contents

So, you think you can afford to be a student?

Introduction

What's this book about?

This book is about a tenner.

£9.95 to be precise, unless you've managed to get it discounted – in which case, good luck to you. That's the student spirit. Shave whatever you can off the price, whenever you can.

The irony of asking you to cough up for a book about how poor you're going to be as a student isn't lost on us, but the idea is that your ten quid investment now will pay you back hundreds of times, over your student career and beyond.

This guide will help you choose a university you can afford (they're not all the same), will help you maximise your income as a student and minimise your outgoings. And then, when you end up in debt – and you will – it'll help you manage it.

All that for less than price of a chart CD. Can't say fairer than that, guvnor.

The guide is divided into seven parts…

Part 1: So, you think you can afford to be a student?

This section is a general introduction to all things dosh-related.

The chapter you're reading now sums up the rest of the book. So, if you're already trying to save money by not buying a copy for yourself, you can read this chapter in the shop and decide if it's worth it.

The following chapter will talk about how the whole nightmare issue of money could, and indeed should, influence students' choice of university in the first place. From university to university, costs are more wide and varied than the effects of a hot curry on the digestive system – from average rents three times higher in some places than others to beer at half the price. See **Chapter 2**.

Part 2: How much will you have?

The next part of the book is about students' income and is quite disproportionately large considering how little money there is to talk about.

We break down the income into every likely source – not to mention some that are either less likely or best avoided.

There are so many exceptions to the rules that you could write a book about it (which is why Push has), but basically the income sources are as follows:

AWARDS AND GRANTS

Local Education Authorities (LEAs – local government, basically) give most students at least some money in the form of 'awards' that pay towards the cost of their course.

The amount students receive depends on all sorts of factors, the most important of which is how much money their parents have (unless they're already all grown up).

Before you get too excited, students don't see the money. It goes straight to the university.

There's also a bit of extra dosh available – not a lot, mind – in the form of grants. These go to students with special needs or from the poorest families and are more plentiful if you come from Scotland or Wales.

See **Chapter 3** and **Chapter 8**.

STUDENT LOANS

There's a Government-financed system, run by the Student Loans Company, under which students can borrow money cheaply to live on while they're studying and pay it back once they've got a job.

The amount students can borrow, like the awards, is down to how much their folks earn.

See **Chapter 4**.

PARENTS

If the LEAs decide students' parents can afford it, then the parents are expected to shell out to their offspring, not only to make up any shortfall in the course costs because they didn't get a maximum award, but also to help out with the students' living costs.

Not every parent, however, is able (or occasionally even willing) to afford it. But no one can force them and, although the system is designed to help students whose parents can't, some end up with even less money than they're supposed to.

On the other hand, some parents are more generous and are so proud of their kids going off to study, they either give or lend them more money. It's alright for some…

See **Chapter 5**.

BANKS

Most students rely pretty heavily on the black hole known as their bank account, not just as a place to keep the money they don't have, but as a potential source of more.

Whether they use it to tide over almost inevitable cash flow problems or to supplement their income, students usually make use of the free overdraft limits and favourable terms offered by most banks to students. Then, when they graduate, they have to pay it back.

See **Chapter 6**.

PAID WORK

Most students either have a part-time job while they're studying or look for temporary work during the vacations. Either way, working for a living while trying to study for a degree has its pros and cons.

Quite a few students – those on 'sandwich' courses – do a job as part of their studies, killing two birds with one sandwich. It's not as crazy as it sounds – they're usually on a work placement as part of their training for a career.

See **Chapter 7**.

1

BURSARIES, SCHOLARSHIPS, SPONSORSHIPS AND GRANTS

The next best thing to money for nothing is money for very little. There are all sorts of bursaries, scholarships and grants available to students, offered by charities, organisations and even by universities themselves for students who're hard up, especially talented or in some other way exceptional or deserving.

Meanwhile, some students are sponsored to study, usually by businesses or organisations that want to employ them either during their studies or on completion. Often the student has to make some sort of commitment to the company or organisation to get the dough.

See **Chapter 8**.

OTHER SOURCES

We also run down the other potential money pots – pretty much everything short of selling a kidney (not advisable) – and tell you the hows, whys and why nots.

For example there are 'access-to-learning' funds, you could sell or pawn stuff, become a landlord or borrow from friends, relatives, on credit cards and from loan sharks.

See **Chapter 9**.

Part 3: Tuition fees

There's so much fuss and so much fear about tuition fees that they get a section all to themselves.

At the moment, most students only ever pay a small proportion of what it actually costs to run their degree course, to employ staff to teach it and to put books in the library and sherry in the fridge in the vice-chancellor's office.

Until 2006, the student's contribution will be capped at about £1,150, but they don't all have to pay all of it.

For about a third of students, their contribution is met by the local education authorities after they've looked at the student's parents' income and totted up how much to contribute (as an award, see above).

Another third pay the full whack. Currently £1,150.

Almost all the rest pay something in between, again depending on their parents' ability to add to the pot.

From 2006, the rules will change with the introduction of so-called 'top up fees'. For new students (not those who're already studying) tuition fees will vary from university to university and from course to course. They will also almost certainly be higher – up to £3,000 a year – but no one will have to pay a penny until after they've graduated.

It's complicated stuff, but **Part 3** lays out the rules and regulations, whys and wherefores of who pays for what, when and how, both at the moment and in years to come. See **Chapter 10**.

Part 4: Where does it all go?
One way or another, at the end of the day, after they've paid any tuition fees they may owe, most students can reckon on having between £3,250 and £7,200 each year that they've begged, borrowed or earned.

So where does that money go?

Part 4 provides a breakdown of the wallet leaks, how they vary from place to place and how to keep them down without living like a nun.

Chapter 11 looks at the main expenses – the roof over your head, the food in your belly, the bills, the clothes, travel costs, books, biros, computers, insurance, night club admissions and the beer.

> Have a household kitty for shopping and bills. Everyone puts in equally. Then shop, cook and eat with your housemates. It works out cheaper, not only because buying in bulk is cheaper than for one, but also because everyone's competing to get their money's worth so they eat at home more often which is cheaper.

Then there are the hidden extras – the costs that bugger up the budget – such as the cost of getting settled in, of Christmas and birthdays and trips backpacking in Borneo or tanning in Tenerife. See **Chapter 12**.

1

Part 5: Finance for real people

Not everyone's an average case and because students are real people – or they look quite like them anyhow – we look at all the special cases out there.

Chapter 13 does money for the masses – including postgrads, mature students, overseas students, part-timers, student parents and students with disabilities

Part 6: The Push Guide to Penny Pinching

Chapter 14 lays it on the line, then it picks up the line and shows you how to make both ends of it meet with *Push's* own guide to living on a budget.

When it comes to students, finance is a four-lettered word and that word is 'debt'.

That's how they fund themselves – by borrowing.

And when you borrow money, somebody usually wants it back. And when they want it back, they want interest. What's so interesting about it? Good question.

Chapter 15 is a guide to handling debt, living off someone else's money, and how to pay it back.

Part 7: In the back

So you can choose the right university for your pocket – and exclusive to *The Push Guides* – **Chapter 16** dishes the dirt on the real costs of being a student at every university in the UK.

And finally, there's a list of useful contacts and sources of further information in print, on the web and on the blower.

So, is it worth it?

Given that volunteering to be a student is equivalent to volunteering to be poor for at least three years while mates from school are out there earning a wage, is it worth it?

Some might say poverty is what student life is all about – getting by cheaply, putting up with squalor and somehow learning to make the most of it.

There's some truth to that. Learning how to live on less money than you'd like is something most people have to do sometime – although getting by as a student is a pretty extreme way of learning it. Nevertheless, along with the sex, the drugs and the rock'n'roll, it's part of the wider education that you get along with a university degree (fortunately at no extra cost).

But the sad fact is that many students end up quitting their courses for no other reason than simply not being able to manage on their limited means.

In fact, nearly 16% of students flunk university. That's one in six. Most people think it won't be them. One in six are wrong.

Of course, not all of them flunk because of money. Far from it. But for almost all of them, poverty is another nail in the coffin and many of them wouldn't give up if it weren't costing them so much money.

Yet there *are* effective ways of minimising debts while maximising your enjoyment of the whole university experience.

It is just a matter of striking the right balance through careful budgeting and cost-cutting (which doesn't have to be as boring or as puritanical as it sounds).

And in the long term, there is a huge gain to be had.

Apart from anything else, what else would you do with the money anyway?

You get intellectual stimulation, access to cheap but kicking night clubs, inexpensive bars, some of the country's best leisure and sporting facilities, memories you'll never forget and, finally, letters after your name if you last the distance.

Being a student for three or four years is worth tens of thousands of anyone's money – if only to put off for another few years the rat race, the mortgage, the 2.4 kids and the slow march to retirement and death.

Not convinced?

Okay, let's get hard-nosed and financial about this now.

Your degree will cost you the following:
- **The debt you end up with when you graduate – currently running at around £13,000, but let's say £15,000 by the time you get through the system.**
- **The money you could have earned during your years as a student minus any money you do earn as a student. For**

1

the average 18, 19 or 20-year-old in full-time employment, that's about £10,000 to start with, rising yearly, but let's be generous and say £13,000 a year. Take off the money students earn on average – this can vary a lot depending on whether they work in term-time, holidays or both, but let's stay on the safe side and say a couple of grand – and that's about £37,000.

Therefore, the total cost – using the harshest measure – is £52,000 (although it's not as if you actually have to pay that money or would have had it if you hadn't gone to university).

Nevertheless, financially, what do you get for your investment?
- You will have greater earning power. A few years after graduation, most degree-holders are earning more than people of the same age without a degree. Graduates aged 21-30 earn around £5,600 a year more than non-graduates of the same age.
- Your income will rise more rapidly and steeply. Most starting salaries advertised for graduates are at least £12,000 – more in the London area, usually averaging something like £18,500. Promotional prospects are far greater.
- One in five big graduate employers offer starting salaries of more than £25,000.
- On average, a graduate earns 50% more than someone without a degree.
- Your chances of ever being unemployed will be cut in half.
- You'll have a wider range of career options open to you, whatever your subject.
- Conservatively, a graduate is expected to pull in £120,000 more over their working life than someone who went out to work with two A levels. In fact, according to the Government, a graduate will earn an average of £400,000 more over their working life than someone who didn't go to university.

In other words, apart from nearly an 800% index-linked return on your investment, you have added security.

Financial case closed, Push thinks.

Chapter Two

Choosing a university

Not all universities are the same

So many applicants are told, 'It doesn't matter where you choose. You'll have a good time wherever you go.'

Along with feeding pigs' brains to cattle, pitching a five-a-side primary school team against Real Madrid and standing anywhere near a paddling pool while being videotaped, this is one of the world's stupidest ideas.

Not all universities are the same and evidence suggests that students who choose their university using the dart-in-a-map method (aka the Clearing system) are more likely to be among the one in six students who drops out or fails.

That goes ditto for choosing a course.

There's no such thing as the country's best university, nor even the cheapest, and there's no such thing as the best course.

It depends on you, on what you want from student life, what you want to study, how you want to study it and, since you're unlikely to work for more than eight hours a day, what you want to do the other two-thirds of your time.

After you've chosen your course, there are still thousands of factors you could consider when choosing a university. Location, atmosphere, accommodation, welfare arrangements and the facilities and opportunities for entertainments, social life and sports to name but a few.

There are so many that we at Push just felt we had to provide a couple of books on the subject: *The Push Guide to Choosing a University*, to give the low-down on how to make the choice, and *The Push Guide to Which University* to give you the information about every UK university to help you decide.

But one of the most important factors when choosing a university or a degree is money.

Not only will your costs vary depending on where you are, but so too will your opportunities for finding extra income. In this chapter we run the gamut, showing the choices you face and saying why, frankly, my dear, we think you *should* give a damn.

In **Part 7**, we also break down some of these variations university by university, so when you're choosing your university in the first place, you can stack the odds in your favour when it comes to stashing the cash and dodging the debts.

Maximising income

Maximise your income and you're in a better position to minimise your debt.

We'll go into more detail about all the possible sources of income in **Part 2**, but in the meantime, here are a few tips on how to squeeze out a few extra pennies by picking the right course for you at the right place.

AWARDS AND GRANTS
As a rule, the level of your award doesn't depend on where you go, but on what your parents earn. But student finance is a world where there are exceptions to every rule – except the rule that there are exceptions to every rule.

For Scottish students studying at Scottish universities, there's a different and more generous system of funding. It doesn't mean they're loaded or anything, just that none of them has to contribute anything to their tuition fees while they're students (although they may have to pay a bit more than £2,000 when they graduate). For more details, see **Chapter 3**.

The effect is that for Scottish students, choosing an English university is like choosing a more expensive brand of toilet roll –

either brand gets the job done, it's just that the more expensive option has to do something quite special to your rear end to be worth the extra cost.

STUDENT LOANS

Similar rules apply to student loans as to awards – what matters is not your choice of university, but your parents' money-making. But, of course, there are exceptions. Two of them.

The first is that students in London qualify for bigger loans than everyone else, because London's so damned expensive. At the moment they get nearly £1,000 more, but whether that makes up for the extra expense is doubtful.

If, however, you've boiled your choice down to, say, Oxford Brookes University, Brighton University and Goldsmiths College London, the little bit extra may make all the difference because it's not actually that much cheaper to live in Oxford or Brighton than in London (especially not South East London, where Goldsmiths is located).

The second exception applies to students who live with their parents. They're entitled to less generous loans than everyone else because, it's assumed, parents aren't going to charge their kids rent while they're students, so their costs will be lower.

> When you've been out on the razz, you always buy food from the chip-shop on the way home. If you find you're too full of beer to eat them or pass out first, just put the cold chips under the grill the next day until they're hot. They'll taste even better than when you bought them.
> Jenny Blyth, University of St Andrews

As it happens, living at home can work out a lot cheaper – not only is rent usually free, but bills are thrown in, the fridge is stocked, there's a washing machine and you don't have to shell out if you want access to things like TVs or DVD players. You might even be able to borrow the car. Of course, not every home has all these freebies thrown in, but the standard of facilities in most parents' houses is better than in most students'.

The bad news is, of course, that although it may work out cheaper to live at home, it cramps your choice. You can only pick a university within commuting distance.

For some people – an increasing proportion – the saving is worth it. For most, however, not only would it cramp their choice, but living at home would cramp their style, too. Unless your parents are more understanding than multilingual Samaritans, it's hardly part of the full monty traditional student experience.

For more details, see **Chapter 4**.

PARENTS

If your parents are contributing to your costs, they may expect a say in where and what you study.

In an ideal world, they'd be more than willing and able to indulge your every whim, whatever it may be. Sad to say, in case you hadn't noticed, student finance is not an ideal world and if you can butter them up by choosing a course and/or a university that might make them especially happy, well, then you might want to factor it into your decision.

Push isn't saying that if they pay, they get to say. On the contrary, it's your call and it has to be right for you.

It's just that, all else being equal, there are times to diss parents – the time when you expect them to fork out for something is not one of them. If only to keep them sweet, ask them if they've got any thoughts (then ignore them if you want).

For more details, see **Chapter 5**.

BANKS

If you treat it right, a student's bank can be a like a little pot of gold at the end of the rainbow. A *very* little pot of gold, admittedly, and they'll want the money back eventually, but in the meantime they're very handy.

Banks, however, have more patience with some students than with others and it's not all down to how nice you are.

They cut medical students quite a bit of slack, for instance, letting them run up debts like mice run up clocks. It makes economic sense to them, because those students are more likely to be safe bets financially.

Similarly, it can make economic sense to you to choose a course that's going to hit pay dirt one day.

You should bear this in mind not only when choosing your course, but even when choosing your university.

Some universities are more successful than others at getting students into jobs. (Their employment stats are in **Chapter 16**.) Almost every university has a careers service, but in some places it consists of little more than a cleaner who occasionally reads the job ads, while at other universities there's a busy team of highly trained careers experts with excellent links to industry and a nice line in skills training.

It's students with that kind of back-up that banks like to lend money to.

For more details, see **Chapter 6**.

WORK

Not every university offers the same opportunities for part-time work and if you're likely to need part-time work to make ends meet, it's worth thinking about this as you choose your university.

In big cities it's not too hard to find an endless stream of student-friendly jobs, but the more remote you get, the tougher the job hunt gets.

At the end of each academic year, sell the books you no longer need to someone in the year below. They'll pay less than the full price and you'll get some of your money back — everyone's a winner.

Certain places have a particular blossoming of casual work ideal for strapped-for-cash students, particularly the coastal resorts like Brighton and Bournemouth. Meanwhile, tourist punters flock to St Andrews for the golf – and while caddying is a lot tougher than it looks, there's always the possibility of serving whiskies at the nineteenth hole.

In order to help students track down suitable jobs and to make sure they're not whipped like slaves when they find them, many universities (more usually the students' unions, in fact) run 'jobshops' – employment agencies, basically.

Invariably, one of the biggest local employers of students is the university itself or the students' union, who take students on to do everything from being nightclub bouncers and working behind bars to looking after conference guests and phoning ex-students and asking them for money. But, again, different universities have different needs for cheap labour.

A lot of students look for work during their vacations as well as, or instead of, taking part-time jobs during term. Again, the choice of university makes a difference.

Not every university has the same length breaks, for instance. An extra week or two – at, say, £150 a week – might make the difference between a week in Ibiza in the summer or spending it stacking shelves in Tesco. But don't be fooled into thinking that the eight-week terms at Oxbridge leave more than half the year for earning. Like many universities, they set enough work over the vacations to keep you almost as busy as during term-time.

Then there are certain courses which, if you choose them, can scupper your earning potential faster than poisoning your boss.

Medicine, for instance, might be a sure-fire money magnet in the long term but, while studying, students not only have less time off over the summer, they don't even have the same time off during the day or at weekends.

Students on sandwich courses, on the other hand, have just about the easiest time of it. They have work placements that not only count towards their course, but which almost always pay them decent money too. Don't get me wrong, they still end up in debt – just not up to their necks in it.

For more details on paid work, see **Chapter 7**.

SPONSORSHIP

Short subject, as there's not a whole lot of sponsorship money out there – not any more. Mostly, it comes with strings attached and among those strings is what course you choose and where you choose to do it.

Virtually the only courses that attract sponsorship are the ones where employers have real trouble recruiting talent. They tend to be hard-line sciences, technical subjects (such as engineering) or vocational courses. Don't even bother looking for sponsorship to do philosophy, English literature or sociology.

If you're likely to be in the running course-wise, check out which universities have good reputations with big employers and with industry.

Again, it's sandwich courses that are the best way to earn while you learn and many of them are similar to the old sponsorships in many ways, but involve more guaranteed rewards for the employer.

A 'thick' sandwich course might involve a deal with an employer where you work for them for, say, a couple of summer vacations during your course, as well as during your placement year and then you carry on working for them when you graduate.

For more details, see **Chapter 8**.

BURSARIES AND SCHOLARSHIPS

Most bursaries and the like are only available at one university and some universities have a lot more than others. Since most of them are endowments from charities and ex-students, the longer an institution has been around, the more likely it is to have stocked up on the goodies. This may be something to think about when making your choice.

For more details, see **Chapter 8**.

ACCESS TO LEARNING FUNDS

If you find yourself in deep financial doo-doo as a student, there may be help available.

Every university has an 'Access to Learning Fund' (or 'Financial Contingency Fund' in Wales) which is supposed to support students so they can afford to study. But each university decides its own rules about how it's going to hand it out – in general the idea is that it should go to students from backgrounds with little tradition of higher education or with specific financial needs. If that's likely to be you, you might want to make enquiries before applying, although be warned that these hand-outs are meant to be a last-resort. The fund is intended to help the desperately hard-up in times of particular crisis, not to subsidise every blagger that fancies a bit of extra cash.

For more details, see **Chapter 9**.

Minimising costs

It's not just the income that varies from university to university.

In fact, bumping up your student income by choosing the right university and the right course is peanuts compared to the coconuts you can save by choosing a university where the costs are lower.

The differences can run into thousands of quid without even trying.

TUITION FEES
Until 2006, tuition fees will be capped at a little over a grand, with discounts for people from cash-strapped families. Unless you're Scottish and want to go to a Scottish university (see above), there's not much you can do to reduce your contribution to these tuition fees (apart from persuading your parents to earn less, which, ultimately, would be self-defeating).

However, there is a risk that your choice of university might make your fees even higher.

Universities are responsible for collecting the fees and how and when they do it is up to them. Some charge fees if you pay late – sometimes as much as £50, regardless of whether it's your fault – which may not be much to them, but it may be a week's rent to you.

Some universities let you set up direct debits (which, while they're not cheaper, can be simpler) and they even offer small discounts if you do.

Then there's Buckingham University, which is a special case. It's a private university where the students pay all their own tuition costs and so their fees are usually several times what you'd pay at most institutions.

If, however, there's any reason why you'd have to pay in full anyway (you're not an EU citizen, for instance), then it can work out cheaper because Buckingham crams what would normally be a three-year course into just two years. And guess what: three-quarters of Buckingham's students are, indeed, overseas students.

If you're starting university after 2006, tuition fees will be higher – up to £3,000 a year – and different universities will be able to charge different amounts for different courses. Exactly how it's all going to work in practice is still a little sketchy, but you may well be able to save yourself a pretty penny in fees by shopping around.

While most courses will almost certainly charge the full three grand, some won't, particularly any that are having trouble getting student bums on lecture hall seats. Those that often don't attract enough applicants include some of the weirder courses and some of the hardcore sciences, such as physics and maths.

However, these new fees won't – unlike the current ones – be paid until after you graduate. So although you might want to think twice about saddling yourself with any kind of debt, it's also in your interest to choose a course that offers a better chance of earning a healthy salary with which to pay back the cash.

In the long-run, a more expensive course could end up being a better investment than a bargain basement cheapo option you didn't really fancy in the first place. But, if you were thinking anyway of a course that might be offered in the universities' equivalent of a bargain bucket, it will be worth shopping around.

For more details on tuition fees, see **Chapter 10**.

RENT

Most of your income – or quite often all of it – goes on rent.

Of course, not everywhere costs the same. In London it's not uncommon for students to pay rents as high as £100 a week – or £5,200 a year. Students in London may get about £950 more than everybody else, but that still means that before they've so much as sat down to their first lecture, their balance sheet is already in the red to the tune of about £150.

At the other end of the scale, in Hull, Teesside and Northern Ireland, it's perfectly possible to find somewhere decent to live for under £35 a week. Even without the extra bit of London loan, that means you've got an extra £2,430 a year to spend.

This is one of the reasons why choosing the right location is such a big deal – but it also makes a difference what you get for your money and how likely you are to be able to live in university housing (which usually works out cheaper). At some universities, more than two-thirds of the students live in. At others it's only a handful of overseas students and students with special needs.

The gaping hole that rent takes out of student finance is the reason why so many students now decide to stay with their parents (see above).

For more details, see **Chapter 11**.

LIVING EXPENSES

You wouldn't have thought that the cost of things like food, clothes and bills would vary that much from place to place, would you? And, sure, if you buy your clothes in chain stores and your food in supermarkets, the differences aren't that great.

If you're wise, however, your shopping habits will be different. Markets are often cheaper (and for clothes, way cooler), but not every university is in a town that has markets – or, at least, not anything decent.

In London, for instance, Camden market offers very fine gear at perfectly reasonable prices. Similarly, there's so much competition between food shops that you can almost always find better prices if you know where to look.

The problem is that places like Camden market are just too damn cool. You go to save a few quid on threads and end up splashing out a couple of hundred on half a dozen tops, some DMs and a lava lamp.

As for bills, they're not the same all over. In Exeter or Bournemouth, for instance, you can expect mild winters and hot summers – compared to Aberdeen, at any rate. And if for six months of the year you need to have the heating on full blast before you can poke a toe out from under the duvet, your bills are going to rocket.

For more details, see **Chapter 11**.

TRAVEL

Obviously, the further you go from home, the more it's likely to cost – although it depends how you get there.

Buses and coaches are the cheapest way to travel, but not everywhere's on a route and if it's a ten-hour trip, then you may want to think about the train – or even a plane. With no-frills airlines like easyJet, flying's often not only the fastest, but also the skinflint's way to get about, but beware airports miles from anywhere with only an expensive train line or taxi to get you where you need to be.

Indeed, that last bit of the journey is often the killer. Lampeter is about 20 miles from the nearest train station, so a taxi will add twenty smackers to the cost of any trip. (There is a bus, which costs £3.50, if you fancy lugging your bags on to it.) Fortunately, National Express now stops at the University, but it takes a while to get there.

London, for once, is on average the cheapest place to get to – but once you're there, getting around town is as ridiculously expensive as a diamond encrusted nasal hair trimmer. Travel in the capital often drains another £18 a week from a student's budget.

But at least London has night buses. After a night out in Newcastle, Sunderland University students have to dig deep for a ten-mile taxi-trip.

In Manchester, on the other hand, the city is compact enough that you can get from campus to the nightclubs and back to the student ghettos all on foot. (Or, failing that, by tram or bike.)

God had students in mind when she created bikes. Around many universities pedestrians walk in fear of being hit by oncoming two-wheelers. But at others it's just too bumpy, too spread out or just too expensive to keep replacing bikes every time they cycle off on their own.

It's very rare that cars are the answer – they're dirty things that cost a packet to buy, a packet to maintain and a packet to fill with fuel. Not to mention parking (oops, mentioned it). But at some universities – particularly the more remote – they're the most practical way to get about.

For more details, see **Chapter 11**.

ACADEMIC COSTS

You wear out more than a few pencils during the course of a degree. Apart from pens, paper and Winnie the Pooh pencil-cases, students have to find the money for books, floppy disks and specialist materials like paints for art students, flash calculators for mathematicians and lab coats for chemists.

Your choice of course affects these academic costs as much as your choice of location, but both factors make costs swing like pants in the breeze.

In this respect, art is just about the most expensive course you can do – all those oil paints and canvasses don't come cheap – but it's far from the only one with costs attached. Archaeology, for instance, means getting down and dirty with the digging once in a while. And no one's going to be falling over themselves to pay for your field trip costs.

All courses have some costs – think ahead to work out what they might be. If in doubt, ask the university department before you apply.

Meanwhile, different courses have different demands for books. On an English course, for example, you need loads of books, but most of them are quite cheap and you might find quite a few of them second-hand (if your university has a second-hand bookshop, that is). For biology, it may only be a few books a year, but they all cost a limb. For law, you not only need *lots* of books, but they're all almost criminally expensive.

At least when you've finished with your biology books you can flog them to next year's students. English students may not want to give up their Austens and Ackroyds. As for computer studies students, their books will be out of date by the time they've got them out of the bookshop anyhow.

But, Push hears you cry, why buy books? Isn't that what the library's for?

It should be, but some university libraries are less well stocked than a fish farm in a drought. Oxford and Cambridge, on the other hand, both have copyright libraries which means they get a free copy of every single book published in the UK (including this one).

Even if they do have the book, your university's library may have annoyingly short opening hours and you may find that the book you want can't be borrowed – that's when students spend hours, and pounds, standing by the photocopier. Libraries vary big-time and a bad one not only costs you money, but can stunt your study too.

As for computers, the good news is that students get free internet access from university computers. If they can get access to the computers, that is. Most universities don't have enough computers (Let's be honest, how many would ever be enough?) and sometimes they're slower than a Virgin Train, but the level of availability – how many and when – varies more than the weather at Wimbledon.

Of course, all students would like to have their own computer, but don't count on being able to save up for one. If the university's provisions are good enough, you can sidestep the issue and save money.

For more details, see **Chapter 11**.

ENTERTAINMENTS AND LEISURE

The standard and style of entertainments will vary hugely depending on where you go, not to mention the cost.

For example, some university bars are no cheaper than the pub next door. In the case of Imperial College, however, the pub next door is in one of London's classiest areas (South Kensington) and a pint there won't leave you with change from £2.50. In the college bar, however, it's almost half the price.

That shouldn't be a temptation to drink twice as much (students get pretty practised at nursing the same pint all night) – but at least it means that if you do, you'll have one fewer reason to regret it in the morning.

It's important to pick a university with the right spread of distractions for you (see Chapter 11). **If big name DJs and dance music are your scene, your social life may cost you more if you end up somewhere like the Courtauld Institute, which has little more than the occasional school disco. You'll end up going to non-student venues and paying non-student prices.**

If, on the other hand, you're a junkie for indie bands who can't let a gig go by, you may want to avoid Leeds Metropolitan, where the calendar of events will empty your pocket faster than a hole.

> Never buy your own drinks. Invest in a Wonderbra and practise smiling alluringly. I covered the cost of my holiday in Spain exclusively by being treated to drinks.
> Francoise, University of Edinburgh

Most universities have student balls (I'm talking about the ones with fancy frocks and penguin suits, okay?), but at some of the posh universities they're a big deal and you feel a bit left out if you don't go to at least one or two a year. But they can set you back the best part of the cost of a dirty weekend in Paris. Tickets alone can cost upward of £70 and on top of that there's the outfit, drinks and a hangover cure.

It's not just the cost of entertainments that vary – whatever you're into, if your university caters for it, you could save major-league money. (Well, a bit anyway.)

For example, sailing's not exactly a sport for anyone short of a bob. You need a boat for starters. If your university has a sailing club, chances are it's because they've got something to sail, so you could be saving yourself the cost of a yacht. Okay, so maybe you wouldn't have bought one, but at least it allows you to carry on sailing.

The same is true of photography, another expensive hobby, where a university darkroom could save you a fair whack.

For more details, see **Chapter 11**.

INSURANCE

Insurance looks simple enough. Endsleigh, for instance, has a flat rate premium for student rooms in halls of residence, whatever university they choose.

That's all very well, so long as you're in halls. If you're not living in university housing, all insurance companies charge premiums for high crime areas that are so huge it's almost as bad as being robbed (but only *almost* – so don't try to penny pinch by not being insured).

Where can you afford to go?

Money is a big bubble of worry in the gut for most students most of the time.

By choosing a university carefully, they can at least deflate that bubble to the size of a small football.

Different universities cost different amounts, even if the fees are the same.

Living in college usually works out cheaper than renting your own place, but not every university gives you the chance (and only a very few let you live in for your whole degree).

Local costs like travel, entertainments and shopping vary, as do different lifestyles that affect what you spend your money on and therefore how much of it you have.

On average a student outside London needs around £6,400 a year to live on after they've paid their fees. That leaves a shortfall of about £2,300 a year compared to the maximum student loan.

It's no surprise, then, that the average student has an extra debt of about £1,000 from commercial sources such as overdrafts and credit cards.

London students tend to have the highest debts on average, but the strange thing is that it's not just costs that affect the level of student debt. A whole bunch of factors drag it around like a rat on a string. Apart from simple costs, here are some of them (but bear in mind they often cancel each other out):

Keeping it lower:
- **A high proportion of students living in;**
- **Good general level of facilities;**
- **Campus universities;**
- **Being in a town or city;**
- **Being in a cheap part of the country;**
- **Collegiate universities;**
- **Smaller universities and colleges;**
- **Availability of paid work locally.**

Sending it up:
- **A high proportion of students renting privately;**
- **A truly kicking nightlife;**
- **Middle-class universities (where students don't panic about debt so much) – except collegiate universities;**
- **Poor choice of shops;**
- **Being in an expensive town – especially London.**

When choosing a university, you could do a lot worse than eliminate anywhere that you decide you simply can't afford.

What you can't afford to do is make the wrong decision. If you drop out, you quite probably won't be able to afford to go back. Unless you drop out quickly, you will almost certainly lose a year's funding – that's a year's student loan, a year's award and possibly even the Government's contribution to your tuition costs for a year. In other words, there's funding for you

to do a degree, but if you screw up somehow along the way,
you may well be paying privately for any extra years it takes.

Yet another good reason to choose the right university in the first
place.

1

Taking a Year Out

Most universities are quite chuffed if you decide to take a year out
(aka 'a gap year'). As far as they're concerned, you'll probably arrive
at university a bit more mature and rounded and ready to be a
responsible student. They may or may not be right.

But they don't want you to take a year *off*. That's why people call
it 'a year *out*'.

A year spent with the cast of assorted Aussie soaps and
miscellaneous sofa cushions is not what anyone has in mind.

The universities hope you'll broaden yourself somehow (mentally,
that is – becoming physically wider is only good for goalkeepers).
They imagine you'll go travelling, do voluntary work or get work
experience – you know, something horribly worthwhile.

However, these worthwhile things are, strangely enough, the
most worthwhile things you can do. They're fun and mind-expanding
and, if in your first week in the hall bar you can talk about camping
under the stars in the Kalahari or squatting in trees scheduled for
destruction for a new bypass, it'll make you a damn site more
interesting than the geeks comparing A Level results and bizarre
coincidences involving UCAS codes.

> Phone your parents regularly and get them
> to call you back. You don't want the only
> time you speak to them to be when either
> they call you or you're asking them for
> money. What's worse than the fact that
> it's tacky is that it looks tacky too.

What's this got to do with money and student survival?
There's another worthwhile activity to add to the list: earning money.

Work experience is all very well, but the problem is that it usually
falls into one of three categories.

Firstly, the genuinely helpful experience that pays nothing – sometimes even less than nothing because you get charged for it or at least have to pay your own expenses.

Secondly, the completely useless experience that pays nothing. Really, how much experience do you need to make tea and lick stamps?

And finally, the completely useless experience that at least pays decent bucks. This is more usually known not as 'work experience', but more simply as 'work'.

Getting a job may allow you to put a bit aside for the lean years ahead as a student and, if you've got all year to save, you might even notch up a few grand if you really try.

If you live at home while working your way through your gap year, your parents may well not expect any rent or contribution to the family finances – especially if you point out that you're saving up so that you won't always have to turn to them for help once you're a student. (Don't push that argument too hard, though – in the end it may not be true.)

You may decide, however, that you've got all your life to spend working. Your gap year is your one chance to do some serious budget travelling. The problem is that even *budget* travelling may not fit your budget. Which is another good reason to work for at least part of the year and save up enough for a few classic year out adventures.

A good compromise could be working abroad – usually doable in the EU if you can speak a few words of another language, or in a host of English-speaking countries thanks to organisations such as BUNAC. This way you get to earn some cash in an interesting part of the world, although there's likely to be equally interesting diversions on which to blow the lot.

With a little preparation, at the very least you can make sure you don't turn up at university with a big hole in the bank before you've even started to rack up your student debts.

Long-term benefits

Any work experience at all, anything from shelf-stacking to fruit-packing, is useful in improving your employability.

The fact that you've turned up every day, done what you're told and basically put up with it proves that you understand the crappier side of working for a living. Employers like to know that you can hold down a job and so any experience is better then none.

So, while your eyes may be on the money at the end of the week, you may do yourself some financial good in the longer term. If you're more likely to get a job and more likely to keep it, you're also more likely to get a higher wage and have a more secure future.

While that fact may not help directly with cash in the medium term, it should give you some comfort as the debts double and the bank balance bottoms out.

PART 2 2

How much will you have?

Chapter Three

Awards, grants and assessments

Briefly, what's an 'award'?

You've probably heard of student grants in the same way people talk about four-star petrol, space hoppers and bands getting to the top of the charts because they're good and not because they're hyped. All these things, however, are long-distant memories, fading like red knickers in a whites wash.

Well, almost. Just to confuse matters, a new, smaller grant – the Higher Education Grant, of which more in **Chapter 8** – will be doled out from 2004. But this young whippersnapper is a pale imitation of its forbears and only available to students from the poorest families. Student grants in the old sense – a big fat cheque to buy all the pints of beer and Smiths records you could want – are still extinct as a dead parrot.

If someone who went to university ten, five or even two years ago starts trying to explain to you how the whole funding system works, just tune out for a while. It's all changed. Forget mandatory grants, mortgage-style loans – all that stuff.

The good news is that about two-thirds of UK students still qualify for what is now called an 'award' for their first degree.

The bad news is they never see a penny of it, because the cheque goes straight to the university to pay for part of their tuition costs. The rest is paid mostly by the Government and most students have to pay something themselves in the form of tuition fees (up to a maximum of £1,150 a year). But more on fees in **Chapter 10**.

Even if you get the maximum award available, that's all it covers: part of the tuition fees. The two issues – awards and tuition fees – are basically two sides of the same coin (or, in this case, cheque).

Whether you get an award, and how much, depends on what your parents earn. They take into account things like whether your folks have to fork out for a brother or sister at university too. But when it comes down to it, the more they earn, the less you get.

2

If you're over a certain age and earning for yourself, they'll do the sums based on your own money.

Basically, they look at whatever might be available to you.

Once you've been accepted by a university, to sort out your award you'll need to get in touch with your local education authority (LEA) in England or Wales, the Student Awards Agency for Scotland, or the Department of Education for Northern Ireland. This is so they can assess your parents' income and so they know who to pay, when and for what. If you're in doubt about who to call, try asking your school, college, local library or local council. And don't forget to do it or else you could end up paying for it all yourself.

Explain that again, but in more detail

LEAs

Local Education Authorities – or LEAs as we'll call them – are the guys responsible for handling the whole awards deal for undergraduate degrees.

In Scotland, it's slightly different. Instead of an LEA, it's a body called the Student Awards Agency for Scotland (SAAS). And in Northern Ireland, it's the Education and Library Boards (ELBs). But to make matters simpler (and, let's face it, it could do with it), we'll just call them all LEAs, okay?

Whichever, LEAs (or things very much like them) do an **Income Assessment** for each student to tot up who gets what and then they pay it out.

The relevant LEA for you is the one that's in charge of education for the area where you normally live before you start your course.

WILL I GET ANYTHING?

That depends on whether you meet certain conditions:

Where you live

You've got to be a **home student** which means you must have been 'ordinarily resident' in the British Isles for three years immediately before the start of your course.

You don't have to worry about going travelling in a gap year or long holidays or even your parents working abroad. It's the 'ordinarily resident' thing that counts.

On top of that, your home should be in England, Wales, Scotland or Northern Ireland on the first day of the academic year in which your course starts. That means 1 September for courses starting in the Autumn term, 1 January for courses starting in the Spring term and 1 April for those starting in the Summer term.

You must also have 'settled status' – for example, if you were born in the UK (and are therefore considered a British citizen) but have lived abroad for a number of years, they might not count you as a 'home' student.

If there's any doubt, give your LEA a bell and they'll advise you.

Whether you've studied before

The Government only pays for you to do the whole higher education thing once. So, if you've taken a higher education course before, at university or college, either in the UK or even outside the UK, but with financial help from UK or EU public funds, then you may not be entitled to a second bite at the academic cherry.

You're likely to be okay if you dropped out before the start of the second academic year or had a very good reason for leaving, but you'll probably need to explain yourself. The various rules and regulations on this are more convoluted than a Russian novel and, since the decisions come down to individual judgements by the LEAs, the best thing is to give them a call if you think there might be a problem.

This does, however, highlight an important aspect of going to university: it's vital to pick the right university and course for you as an individual. If it doesn't work out – either you don't settle in, you can't afford to carry on or you just don't enjoy it – then you could end up paying heavily for a second chance.

For more on making the right choices, see **Chapter 2** and take a look at *The Push Guide to Choosing a University*.

What you study

LEAs only have to fund students to do certain types of course. That includes all first degrees and quite a lot else, but certain art, drama and dance students ought to read the small print in particular and, again, if in doubt, give the LEA a call.

Anyway, the courses the LEA will cough up for are:

- Full-time first degrees (eg. BA, BSc or BEd), including sandwich courses
- In particular cases, part-time courses of initial teacher training
- A Foundation Degree
- A Diploma of Higher Education (DipHE)
- A Higher National Diploma (HND)
- A Higher National Certificate (HNC)
- Part-time courses (except the Open University PGCE) which are at least one year (and don't take more than twice as long as doing the course full-time) are eligible for a grant of up to £575 to help pay the fees and up to £250 to live on
- A Postgraduate Certificate of Education (PGCE) or other postgrad initial teacher training course which qualifies you as a teacher. Also, various other qualifications that qualify you as a teacher such as a level 4 NVQ if you take it at the same time as a first degree, a DipHE or an HND. Some teacher training courses also get extra money, not necessarily from the LEA – but more about that later.
- A course which prepares for a professional examination higher than GCE level, Scottish Higher, National Certificate or National Diploma
- A foundation year which forms part of one of the courses listed above.

There are also certain courses where students don't have to contribute anything to their tuition costs anyway, so there's no need for LEAs to make awards, but we'll look more at these later (see **Chapter 10** on tuition fees).

Where you study

It's not just what course you study, but where you study it.

It has to be a publicly-funded UK university or college (i.e. not the University of Buckingham). Or a group of schools that's taking part in the School Centred Initial Teacher Training (SCITT) scheme. Or it has to be a specified private institution, where the fee support will be a bit lower – £1,075 – but won't be income-tested. If it doesn't fall into any of these categories, you'll almost certainly have to dig deep.

Your age

Actually, so long as you pass all the other conditions, it doesn't matter how old you are.

The only difference age makes is how likely you are still to be depending on your folks for your up-keep. Once you're not, the LEA checks out your own income (or even your husband's or wife's) instead of theirs, but if that's likely to be lower, then it might work out in your favour and qualify you for an award.

For more on being classified as an **independent student**, see below.

HOW MUCH *MIGHT* THEY GIVE ME?

The LEA won't actually give *you* anything. Not personally.

However, they will assess your family's income to work out how much they're willing to give your university or college to contribute towards the costs of your tuition.

At most, they'll pay all your tuition fees – that's £1,150 per year (at this year's levels, but it'll keep going up approximately in line with inflation, usually by £25 per year). About a third of students get that much. They're students from poorer families where, after a few allowances, the income is under about £21,475 a year.

Another third of students get the smallest possible amount from the LEA – i.e. no contribution at all. They're the ones whose folks earn more than £31,973 a year and, in theory at least, the parents end up paying the £1,150.

The students in between get something in between.

The same assessment that the LEAs perform is used by the Student Loans Company to work out how much they'll be willing to lend you. (More on loans in **Chapter 4**.)

From 2006, upfront fees are going out the window for new students (see **Chapter 10**), but awards will linger on. Students from poorer families will still get an award towards the first £1,200 of the fees, meaning they have less to pay back after graduation than their richer counterparts. But for those starting before 2006, the old system will still apply.

2

SO, HOW MUCH SHOULD I EXPECT?

LEAs all work to the same rules when deciding who to help and by how much.

There's a standard application form which asks you, among other things, all about your parents' salaries. Even if you're earning, unless you're an 'independent student' (see below), they're not generally worried about your own income.

From what you tell them on the form, the LEA works out your parents' **residual income** – in other words, what they have left after various allowances. But if you want to work out for yourself roughly what you'll get, it's best to play it safe and estimate on the low side. So forget about the allowances for now and just add your parents' gross incomes for last year (i.e. before tax and national insurance were taken off) and check out how you stand using the table:

Your parents' residual income	LEA Award
Below £21,475	Full fee of £1,150
£21,475	£1,105
For every £9.50 over £21,475	Subtract £1
£23,000	£945
£26,000	£628
£29,000	£312
£31,973 and above	Zilch

As usual, the calculations only really work if you happen to be a bog standard case, which almost no one is. However, the LEAs do look at each case individually.

So here are just a few factors that fudge those figures:

Brothers and sisters

If your parents have other offspring to support, their residual income is reckoned to be £1,000 lower for each one. If, however, they also happen to be in higher education at the same time as you, then it gets even more complicated. Normally, the LEA works out the parents' total contribution then shares it equally between all the student children. But as with all good rules, there can be exceptions and so it's best to check the specifics with your LEA.

Changes in circumstances

If the situation changes for whatever reason – your dad loses his job, your mum gets a whacking great pay rise, they get divorced, your sister goes to university and so on – then your LEA needs to take another look at the sums.

You only have to apply once to get on the books, as it were, but once you're there, the LEA will review the situation every year.

Parents without the blood tie

Guardians' incomes don't count when the LEA is doing its assessment, but adoptive parents do.

Divorce

Try to persuade your parents to get divorced or at least to separate – that way the LEA only counts the salary of the one you live with. But they'll have to remain celibate for the ruse to work – the LEA will take the salary of this parent's partner or new husband or wife into account.

Independent students

Independent students are students who the LEA reckons aren't supported by their parents, so they don't bother with what the parents earn but instead assess the student's own stack.

If that's less than the parents', the student might find themselves more likely to get a bigger award. But to see yourself classified as an **independent student**, it's not good enough just to say your parents can't or won't help out.

You have to prove that, by the date your course is due to start, you'll match at least one of the criteria:

- You'll be over 25
- You'll be married (and have a certificate to prove it – a Zanzibar beach ritual involving beads is unlikely to cut it)

How much will you have?

- You'll have been supporting yourself for the last three years or more – including being unemployed, caring for a child or doing a training scheme (and again, you'll need documents to prove it)
- Or they're dead (murder is rarely worthwhile – *Push* would advise against it).

It's not automatic, but you also stand a good chance of being treated as independent if you're in care (or were until you were 18), you're permanently estranged from your parents, your parents can't be traced or if they're abroad and contacting them might put them in jeopardy (such as if you're a refugee).

If you're classed as independent, then the LEA looks at your own income, which, while you're studying, is not likely to be all that big anyway. What's more they won't bother themselves about certain bits of income like NHS bursaries and casual or part-time work during term-time or in vacations.

Single independent students with incomes of less than £10,000 won't have to contribute at all. Those earning £10,000 will have to contribute £45, then there's an extra £1 contribution for every £9.50 over £10,000.

If your income is under £15,200, you'll be able to get the full HE grant (see **Chapter 8**).

Married students

If you're thinking of getting married, do the sums first. If your financé – oops, sorry – fiancé(e) is less well-off than your parents, go ahead as soon as possible.

But if they're quite rich, hold off till at least two years from the end of your course. Apart from the fact that university is a great place to meet people, if your husband or wife has enough residual income, the LEA will look at that instead of your parents.

Of course, if they're *really* rich, marry them and get them to support you through your studies.

If the LEA does decide to assess your spouse, they'll use the same assessment method and rules as when they're assessing parents.

How do I apply?

IF I'M NOT GOING TO GET ANY MONEY, DO I NEED TO APPLY?

However rich you or your parents are, however lazy you may be, however much you hate filling in forms, you still have to apply to your LEA for an award – even if you know you're not going to get one.

If you don't, you may end up having to pay your entire course costs – around £4,500 a year – instead of the regular full contribution of £1,150.

ALRIGHT, HOW DO I APPLY THEN?

There are two possibilities: old-fashioned application on paper (possibly filled out with an inkwell and quill) or the whizzy new-fangled online application at www.studentfinancedirect.co.uk.

If you go down the online route, you'll fill out a condensed form, which will then be sent back to you to check, sign and send back to the LEA. Push reckons this system might well be the most straightforward, if only to minimise the amount of paper that'll arrive through your letterbox. However, the website is a recent invention and, as Push goes to press, it's struggling with technical problems, so it's probably worth checking which form of application your school or LEA recommends before filling anything out.

On the next couple of pages, there's Push's handy guide to what to do and when, but the general rule is annoyingly trite: 'Don't delay, do it today'. (You can hate the slogan, but the sentiment's sound.) This guide is based on old-fashioned, paper-based applications. The website will include any specific instructions you need and the basic application process will be roughly the same.

Live on campus or near wherever you need to go everyday for your studies.

STEP 1: Getting started

What to do:

Contact your LEA for an application form (PN1) if they haven't already sent you one or download it from www.dfes.gov.uk/studentsupport/formsandguides.

When to do it:

If you haven't got a form by March of the year when you want to start you course (i.e. Year 13), get one. In fact, you might as well do it sooner or, at least, as soon as possible after applying for your course. You shouldn't wait till you've had your place confirmed or even until you get an offer.

Why do it?

You need to fill in the form so they can assess your financial situation. There's a separate, optional section to fill out if you want to apply for a loan.

Anything else?

Your LEA is the one for where you live, not where you'll be studying. Your school, college, local library or local council can help you find the contact details if necessary or they may even be able to give you the form themselves.

STEP 2: The LEA checks your eligibility and works out how much cash to give you

What to do:

Complete and return the form.

When to do it:

The form itself will tell you the deadline. If you don't want to apply for the income-assessed portion (e.g. help with your fees or a bigger loan), you can skip several sections but need to submit your form earlier – probably by the end of April. If you do want to apply for the income-assessed stuff, you have until around July 2. Don't only meet these deadlines. Get the form in as long before as you can. Don't just leave it in a drawer and forget about it till the last minute. The sooner you do it, the sooner you'll know what your financial situation's going to be and the sooner you'll get your money (including your student loan). What's more, if there are any problems, you'll have time to sort them out. (The absolute deadline is nine months after the first day of the academic year when you start your course – after that you've missed your chance. But don't even dream of leaving it that late. Get it in before you even start. *Now*. I think we've made our point.)

Why do it?

This is a no-brainer – if you don't fill out the form, you won't be able to apply for any financial support and may end up having to pay full tuition fees. You can also use this form to indicate whether you want to claim various bits of support for students with kids of their own (see **Chapter 13** for more information).

Anything else?

Make sure you fill everything in carefully.

Only choose not to be assessed if you absolutely know your parents earn way too much for you to get anything and you really can't be arsed filling in any more forms.

Fill out the loan request section if you want a loan (see step 3).

STEP 3: Apply for a loan

What to do:

Fill out the support request form at the end of the PN1 form.

When to do it:

At the same time you fill out PN1 – see Step 2 for details of the deadlines.

2

Why do it?

To get a student loan, which is likely to be your main source of student income and is probably worth applying for even if you think you're too rich to need it. This part of the form is very short, so there's no excuse for leaving it out.

Anything else?

You can choose whether you want to apply for the maximum loan allowed to you or specify a (lower) amount. You could ask for a higher amount, but there's little point as you're not going to get it. Push recommends just ticking the box to ask for the maximum amount as you never know when the cash is going to come in handy.

Sainsbury's, Tesco and some of the other supermarkets offer loyalty cards with money-off vouchers if you spend enough. Apart from making sure you collect your own, ask your parents if you can have theirs too. (But don't buy stuff you don't need, just because you've got a money-off voucher.)

If all goes to plan, you should get a letter showing the amount of support you'll get about six weeks after you returned the form.

WHAT IF I AM NOT SATISFIED?

Good question. What if the LEA takes forever, turns you down for an award unfairly or palms you off with less than you reckon you deserve?

LEAs do cock up from time to time. It's only natural. Forms fall down the backs of radiators or the LEA reads one too many noughts in somebody's salary. There's no need to panic or give them a hard time about it though, start off with a simple polite phone call. That's usually enough to sort it out.

But if it isn't, get the name of someone at the LEA to whom you can complain and put it in writing, stating clearly why you think you've had a bum rap and tell them you're giving them, say, 21 days to respond. Wait 21 days and then phone again if you haven't heard. Be polite, but be firm.

It's also possible the LEA will be nice as pie and deal with your case more efficiently than you thought possible, but makes a decision about your case that just doesn't seem fair. Many things that don't seem fair are in fact perfectly legitimate, but you may occasionally have grounds to seek a second opinion – ask the LEA for their advice and for details of any appeals procedure.

Once you're at university or have even been offered a place, if you're having problems with your LEA you can get help from the university's students' union. (Phone the university and just ask to be put through to the students' union welfare department.)

Alternatively, most universities and colleges have student funding and/or welfare departments too. Either that department or the students' union will usually take up your case with the LEA and answer any questions you've got about what might have gone wrong and how to fix it.

Don't jump straight to conclusions about it all having gone pear-shaped. It's a pear-shaped system and confusion is pretty much par for the course. Rather than rushing in to complain, always feel free to phone the LEA to ask questions or just to check on progress.

In fact, call the LEA about anything you like – how to fill in the forms, whether you're likely to be eligible, how to remove egg stains from a silk blouse – okay, maybe not about the stains, but they're there to help and they should treat everyone as an individual case.

Frequently asked questions

If I have my own savings, will I have to declare them?

If you want to apply for the means-tested elements of support, you'll have to estimate your gross taxable income for the year to come. This income includes all money you earn or receive that you pay tax on, except for any part-time or holiday jobs you do during your course. There are a few other sources they won't worry about either – the forms make it pretty clear and, if you're still not sure, ask.

If you have savings and investments and don't expect to earn more than your personal allowance in the tax year (currently £4,615 which doesn't include any loans), arrange for your interest to be paid without tax being deducted (see **Chapter 7** for more on tax). Then you won't have to claim it back.

2

What courses *don't* get any financial help?

Basically everyone gets one chance to take a degree or equivalent qualification, but only one. That means that students don't normally get Government funding for any of the following, although there's often another source you can try (for more info, see **Chapter 13**):

- **Postgraduate courses, including NVQ Level 5:** Unless they're training to be teachers (PGCEs or similar), postgrads either have to pay for themselves or get funding from the British Council, one of the research councils, their employer or some other organisation.
- **Any nursing or midwifery course:** Instead, students get a non-income-assessed NHS bursary or a special award for health services.
- **Access or conversion courses** which prepare students to take a higher education course.
- **Further education courses** like A Levels, AS Levels, Scottish Highers, NVQs, GNVQs, most BTEC courses, City and Guilds and so on. Funding for these is a whole different system – talk to the LEA.

What if I don't live in the UK?

Then it depends where you do live. If you normally live in any EU country other than the UK, you should be able to get assessed for help with your tuition fees (but you won't qualify for a student loan). It's down to individual circumstances, though.

For starters, contact the LEA that covers the university or college where you want to study.

And what if I don't live in the EU?

In this case, you're an international student (aka 'overseas student') and you're going to have to fund your course costs all by yourself or apply in your own country for whatever educational funding may be available. What's more, you're going to have to pay the full cost of your course (starting at around £4,000 a year), not just the £1,150 contribution.

See **Chapter 13** for more on international students.

What if I drop out and want to get back in?
Sometimes students avoid flunking altogether by repeating a year or dropping out of one university and starting again somewhere else.

Most LEAs won't support you financially for a repeated year, especially not if they reckon it's your fault. Reasons for it being considered 'your fault' might include not liking the university you chose, hitting the financial rocks or getting drunk and missing all your lectures. They might be more lenient if you're sick.

The policy on all this varies from one LEA to another, however, so if it looks like you may have to flunk, first check out how they'll react and, if it's likely to be a no-no, try to hang in there.

If you do want to repeat a year, you'll probably have to pay tuition fees for the time you're repeating and it may be not just the £1,150 contribution, but the whole whack (the same as an international student).

You might well get an extra year's student loan though – for all the good that'll do you.

The message is: choose your university carefully in the first place (see **Chapter 2**) and don't screw up when you get there by either not budgeting your money or by being a complete dosser. So long as you do that, no one can blame you and you'll avoid the worst of the financial rough justice for flunking.

Still confused?

Fair enough.

Read the DfES booklet 'Financial Support for Higher Education Students'. Call their information line on 0800 731 9133 for a copy. It's free.

Unfortunately, it'll make even less sense than this chapter.

So try completing as much of the application forms as you can, phoning up as you go along whenever you need to.

For general questions about finance and applying, call the Student Loans Company's Customer Support Office on 08456 077577. For more detailed questions about your entitlement to help, try the DfES helpline on (01325) 392822. Or just ring your LEA.

So long as you get the money, no one complains and you don't lie on the forms, it doesn't matter if the detail is clear as vomit in a toilet bowl.

There's a veritable library of suggested reading and recommended websites near the back of the book.

Spend as little money as you can by buying supermarket's own economy brands. People may think you're cheap, but at least the cash will last longer.
James Williamson, Bishop's Stortford College

Student loans

Briefly, what's a 'student loan'?

Awards take care of part of a student's tuition costs (see Chapter 3), **but they're only a paddle in the pool of payments compared to the full-on skinny dip of living expenses.**

And, just as awards cover part of the cost of tuition, student loans cover part of a student's cost of living – 'maintenance costs', as the jargon has it.

The student loan is split into two parts. Everyone who qualifies for anything gets three-quarters of the full loan – that's between about £2,400 and £3,800 a year depending on where they're living and studying.

They can only borrow the second part – the other quarter – if their LEA decides that they need it after they've assessed the students' parents' income. Again, it's like the awards (see **Chapter 3**) – the more the parents are getting, the less the students get and the more the parents are expected to cough up.

Depending on how much their folks earn, students can borrow up to a further £1,260 a year.

Most students – all UK undergraduates on full-time courses – qualify for at least the first three-quarters (75%) which they receive from the Student Loans Company (SLC), a name so imaginative and obscure it's a shock that anyone ever works out what they do.

Student loans have to be repaid, of course. That's in the nature of a loan. But students don't have to even start settling up until they've got a job earning more than £15,000 (although, if they've got other debts to settle – as they usually do – fifteen grand doesn't leave much room to live the high life). If they never earn that much, they're off the hook.

In addition to the pretty soft repayment terms, the interest *is* fairly cushy too. Contrary to popular belief, there is interest on student loans – in other words, they do want more back than they lent you – but it's pegged to inflation and, relatively speaking, it doesn't really get much lower than that.

Even the maximum loan (which assumes your folks won't be able to spare a penny) is rarely enough, so students almost invariably rely on hand-outs from parents, paid work or borrowing from banks on top of what they're lent by the SLC.

From 2006, loans are being increased to cover tuition fees as well as living costs. Students won't actually get any more hard cash to spend, but instead of having to pay tuition fees while at university, they will have to repay the cost of their fees (up to £3,000 for each year of study) along with their maintenance loan (the money they're lent to live on) after graduation. But, so long as you start your degree before September 2006, the old system will apply: you'll have (probably) lower fees to pay, but you'll have to hand over the readies up front, and your loan will cover living costs only.

Explain that again, but in more detail

For students, debt is not something to avoid. It's something to accept as a fact of life and which you simply try to keep to a minimum.

In the long term, students are likely to land better jobs, with better pay and, eventually, their student debts will either be paid off or written off. That's only the *average* scenario, however, and there are some for whom the legacy of debt is harder to shift than an elephant with no legs.

For anyone at all, starting a career with a debt hanging over you like a concrete cloud isn't ideal and some students feel that the burden of borrowing just isn't fair given what they ultimately contribute to the economy. But most just feel that, by their age, they don't want to have to rely on their parents for money or to have to cross their finger every time they try to use the cash machine.

It's certainly debatable whether it's a good idea to fund our higher education system by forcing millions of young people so far into the red that wearing green becomes painful. And, indeed, it is much debated. But that's not what this book's for. If you think it's unfair, you can campaign all you like, blow up Parliament and moon the Queen – but, like it or lump it, that's the score for the time being. Deal with it. Push tells you how.

A large part of a student's debt will usually be owed to the Government, who skulk around behind the **Student Loans Company (SLC)**, funding the whole operation but keeping it out of smelling distance. It's the SLC that does the lending.

WHAT ARE STUDENT LOANS FOR?

The Government-funded student loans available from the SLC are most students' main source of income to cover the costs of living – somewhere to live, something to eat, something to wear, books, travel, beer money and maybe the odd Ferrari from any left-overs.

It's only 'income' in the sense of being money available to them, not in the sense of it being their money, because, of course, they have to pay it back eventually. Along with any awards from the LEAs, student loans come under the umbrella term 'student support'.

Students don't _have to_ apply for student loans (not even in the way that they should for LEA awards) – but don't try to be a hero, the one student in the country who makes it through university without borrowing. Unless you start off rich, it's not possible.

Even if you do have more money than a premiership footballer, you should still try to get a loan. If you don't need it, dump it into a high yield account and earn more interest than you have to pay. Should be worth a few hundred quid over eight years.

Unfortunately, that's not an option for most students. Student loans are an inevitable necessity rather than a fall-back option. They're what you've got to live on.

If you're having second thoughts about the whole idea of student life, check back at the reasons why it's worth it at the end of **Chapter 1**.

DEBT IS INEVITABLE – SO WHAT'S THE GOOD NEWS?

The good news is the terms. They're better than almost any personal loan. Students get pretty good deals from banks (see **Chapter 6**), but even *they* are rarely as good as this.

See **Paying it back** later in this chapter for details.

WILL I BE ABLE TO GET A STUDENT LOAN?

Most students can. In fact, all students under 50 are entitled to apply, if they normally live in the UK and are doing a full-time course lasting at least a year and ending in a first degree, a higher diploma or one of the other eligible qualifications (basically the same courses that might qualify for an award – see **Chapter 3** for more details).

Even if you're over 50 and under 54, you can still receive an award so long as you intend (or say that you intend) to go back to work after studying.

You won't be able to get a loan, however, if you're not a UK student. Not even our Euro-cousins.

> Complain, a lot, whenever you get a bum deal or anything that's off. Apart from the fact that you can't afford the waste, you'll often get more than just a replacement. Some companies will give you your money back and/or coupons too, effectively meaning you get what you bought for free.

HOW MUCH *MIGHT* THEY GIVE ME?

Every year, the Government bumps up the maximum available loan – good news as far as having access to cash is concerned, but not so good given that it means students' debts are snowballing every year, if not avalanching.

Currently, the most anyone can borrow in a year is £5,050, but most students can't get anything like that much. It all depends on the following factors…

Where you live and study

Students living at home (with their parents) aren't allowed to borrow so much, because it's reckoned that they either don't pay rent or that it's a darn sight cheaper and comes with a tray-full and a laundry-load of extras.

On the other hand, living in London is more expensive than most places and so students whose courses are based in the capital are entitled to borrow more (although for most students, it's not enough extra to cover the additional costs and they end up even further in debt).

What you study

The course has to be eligible – which means it has to be on the list of courses for which LEAs pay awards (see **Chapter 3**). It doesn't matter if you don't actually *get* an award because you don't qualify for some reason, so long as the course does.

If you're doing some weird qualification and you're worried about not getting a loan, give the SLC a call. As they used to say on the ads, it's good to talk.

> **Apply to your LEA before going to university even if you don't think you'll qualify for any financial support. After all, you may be wrong — but, more importantly, if you don't, you may end up having to pay more.**

Which year of your course you're in

In your final year, you're not entitled to quite as much. The same goes for courses that last only one year.

The theory is that in most years you'll need the loan to see you through the summer, but in your final year you're free to start work the day after you leave university.

This cuts both ways because, while you're a student, you're not able to get any unemployment benefit – oops, 'job seekers' allowance' – but the day after you leave university, if you're not marching into your new job you can get down to the dole office and sign on.

How much you and your family are expected to contribute

If you're eligible for any loan, you're eligible for at least 75% of the full amount that anyone in the same situation could get (not forgetting the factors above).

The other 25% is based on the assessment of your family's income that the LEA does when deciding whether to give you an award (see **Chapter 3**).

2

The length of your course and academic year

If your course is longer than average – such as most medical degrees – then they'll lend you a bit more.

If the course itself lasts longer than 30 term-time weeks in any year, then you get into the zone. Once you're in, then you're eligible for an extra loan allowance for each additional week up to 45 weeks. After 45, the SLC says 'what the hell' and just calls it a whole year, basing the amount on 52 weeks.

Whatever you get for the extra weeks is worked out on essentially the same terms as what you'd get if you and your course hadn't made it into the zone.

SO, HOW MUCH SHOULD I EXPECT?

It starts with your LEA (see **Chapter 3**). There'll be a student support request form to send off with your PN1 (that's the form they use to calculate how much support you're eligible for). You need to fill out the form to show you want a loan and indicate how much you want to borrow. In the summer, you'll get a 'final notice of entitlement', which should make it clear how much you're actually likely to get.

Even if the LEA decides that you're not going to get anything towards your tuition, it doesn't mean you won't get a student loan. It just means you'll only be able to borrow the first part of the loan – i.e. 75% of what someone else in the same situation but with poorer parents could get.

Here are the amounts you might be able to borrow in the academic year 2004/2005. It'll be going up each year (probably) in line with inflation.

The columns labelled as the 'first part' are the 75% that almost everyone gets.

The second part is means-tested, in other words, it depends on your family's fortune (well, their income anyway) and so the columns labelled 'maximum' are only available to those whose parents earn under £21,475 a year. If they earn between £21,475 and £31,973, you should be able to borrow something between the two amounts.

Students living and studying:	Full year		Final year		For each extra week (over 30 in one year)
	First part (75%)	Maximum	First part 75%)	Maximum	
In London	£3,790	£5,050	£3,285	£4,380	£94
Elsewhere	£3,070	£4,095	£2,665	£3,555	£73
At parental home	£2,430	£3,240	£2,125	£2,830	£49

HOW AND WHEN DO I GET THE MONEY?

Usually you get it in three instalments – one at around the beginning of each term, but occasionally the money comes in two payments or even just one (but only, as a rule, if you've applied after the beginning of the academic year). The SLC will send you a schedule to let you know when they'll cough up and how much.

The SLC also usually transfers the money directly into your bank or building society account. That robs you, unfortunately, of the elation of holding a stonking great cheque in your sweaty paw.

It's not that the SLC doesn't trust you with your money, but direct payments in instalments does help avoid the feelings of recklessness that might overcome even the most normal student when confronted with the ability to pump nearly three grand into their bank account.

Even when it's only a thousand, don't be tempted to splurge on a cruise in the Bahamas, a half-tonne bar of chocolate or a dead cert in the 2:30 at Newmarket. That money's gotta last. That's why you should have a budget (see **Chapter 14**) – to scare yourself into appreciating the truly tiny amount you really have.

How do I apply?

Make sure you fill out the right bit (the support request section) of the form PN1 and get it back to the LEA by the start of July (or the end of April if you're sure you don't want the means-tested bits of support). Full details of what's required are in **Chapter 3** and the sooner you get cracking, the better.

Even if you've applied in plenty of time, until you get the wonga in your hands, it's best to be sceptical about it turning up promptly.

The same is true even if you don't apply till after you've started your course (which you're allowed to do if you enjoy the financial equivalent of walking on hot coals). Leaving it till you're really skint is like waiting till your clothes have all rotted before buying new ones – you're going to have to go out there naked. It's the same with money – you don't want to end up unable to buy food because you're waiting for the SLC's bureaucracy machine to clunk its way through to issuing your loan. Better to apply early, before you're truly broke and leave yourself enough of the folding stuff to cover you till the loan arrives.

Nonetheless, you can still apply for your student loan anytime up to one month before the end of the academic year. Each year you need to apply again and if you don't apply in any year for some reason, you can still apply again the next year (but you can't apply retrospectively for a year's loan you didn't ask for at the time).

Paying it back

A loan wouldn't be a loan if they didn't want it back and although you don't need to worry about it while you're still a student, it's just as well to know the score so you know what to expect later and they don't have to send the boys round.

WHEN YOU HAVE TO REPAY

You don't have to pay back a penny until after you've finished your course (or dropped out). In fact, not until the April afterwards – usually a whole nine months later.

You also don't have to pay until you've got a job that pays £15,000 a year.

The SLC will send you a statement every year between September and November. Then they'll send you an interim statement to let you know how your account stands just before you're due to start repaying. Once you've started making repayments, they'll keep you up-to-date with a statement at the end of every tax year.

HOW YOU REPAY

'How can they just take money from my salary?', you may well ask. Because the SLC is in cahoots with the taxman, that's how.

Using your National Insurance number, the Inland Revenue will charge your employer the repayments and, come the April after graduating, they'll just take it out of your pay along with your income tax and your national insurance contributions. Your pay statement each month will show how much they've lifted.

If you're self-employed, of course, you have no 'salary' as such and no employer for them to deal with. But then, you have to let the Inland Revenue know what you've earned each year anyway (on a tax self-assessment form) and you pay your tax later. They'll just ask for the loan repayments then as well.

Every year in September, until you've paid off your debts, the SLC will send you a schedule to show you how you're doing. They'll also let you know if you need to pay more or less per month over the next year, depending on how much interest they're charging you.

This whole conspiratorial alliance with the Inland Revenue only applies to loans issued after 1998 – so-called 'income-contingent loans'. So if someone older than that tries to tell you how it works based on their personal experience, bear in mind they're probably talking out of the wrong orifice, because their experience isn't relevant.

Save all your coppers and 5p coins and put them in a jar. They always come in handy at the end of term when you're completely broke. It's amazing how much you can collect.
Jenny Blyth, University of St Andrews

HOW MUCH WILL I HAVE TO REPAY?

It depends on what you're earning, but it's worked out as 9% of anything you earn over fifteen grand. Basically it's a pretty small slice of your pay packet. The table shows how it works out.

Income each year	Repayment as a percentage of income	Monthly repayment
£15,000	0%	£0
£16,000	0.6%	£7.50
£18,000	1.5%	£22.50
£20,000	2.3%	£37.50
£23,000	3.1%	£60.00
£25,000	3.6%	£75.00
£30,000	4.5%	£112.50
£35,000	5.1%	£150.00

If your salary goes up, your repayments go up and, obviously, you keep making your monthly repayments until you've given back everything you borrowed, but then there's a bit extra too – the interest. (So called because interest is what makes banks interested in giving anyone money.)

WHAT INTEREST WILL THEY CHARGE?

The interest rate on student loans is linked to inflation, so in 'real' terms the amount you ultimately pay back may be more than the amount you borrowed, but it's an equivalent amount nonetheless.

In other words, if you borrowed enough for 2,000 pints of Stella, 2,000 packets of peanuts and 500 cheese and bacon toasties, by the time you come to repay it, you'll only have to give back the cost of the same again, please, barman.

At the moment the rate is hovering at around 3.1% a year.

They start adding the interest from the day you get your first loan payment and annual statements each September after graduation show you the interest charged.

HOW LONG WILL IT TAKE TO REPAY?

That depends on how much you borrowed in the first place and how quickly you're able to pay it back which, in turn, depends on your income once you've graduated.

At the moment, an average student earning an average graduate salary should reckon on making repayments for at least a decade. But graduate debt is shooting up faster than a greyhound with a rocket strapped on its back and debts are likely to take even longer to repay in future. Go to www.slc.co.uk for a handy on-line calculator that lets you tap in a few of your details for a more accurate estimate – although even this can only be an estimate.

In the meantime, the monthly repayments are such a small percentage of your income that, unless you stretch your bank balance to the point where cheques become rubber, you'll hardly notice the effect on your income. Compared to some of the other monthly salary-guzzlers once you've graduated – income tax, council tax, rent or mortgage, bills, other direct debits and so on – student loan repayments are just another fly on the windscreen.

If you do want to pay more each month or shell out one big lump sum to get yourself out of debt sooner, no one's going to stop you. Just contact the SLC. Plenty of graduates do it, especially if they begin to earn a tidy package, but if you're in a position to pay off debts, pay off any others first because, if you're paying interest at all, you won't be borrowing more cheaply than this.

The new tuition fees – that's the ones of up to £3,000 a year that won't have to be paid back until after graduation – will send debts rocketing through the roof when they hit the first generation of students who start in 2006. Depending which course and university they choose, students whose families earn too much money to qualify for an award towards the fees could face an extra £9,000 in fee-debt – that's on top of what they're borrowing to live on (the maintenance loan). That means these superdebts could take nearly twice as long to repay as the current students' debts.

WHAT IF I CAN'T PAY?

Some graduates don't find a job immediately after they leave university. Some go on to do more studying – postgraduate courses and the like. Some pack their bags and go travelling. And some are unemployed – it's not common and it usually doesn't last, but it happens.

If it happens to you, you can 'defer' your repayments.

Likewise, if your income is under the point at which repayments kick in (£15,000) or if it *was* higher but drops below, repayments get postponed until you're making a bit more.

However, all the time you're not paying back, the amount you owe will carry on growing because of the interest.

2

CAN YOU GET AWAY WITHOUT REPAYING IT?

There are only four ways to get out of paying back your student loan or any part of it that you still owe:

- If you get to retirement age (65) first
- If you never earn more than the minimum salary threshold (£15,000)
- If you become permanently disabled
- If you die.

You may also get cut loose if you take up a career in teaching certain shortage subjects that qualify you for the repayment of teachers' loans scheme – see **Chapter 13** for more details.

It may not look easy to get out of it, but it's still better than most loans – most lenders wouldn't let a little thing like death stand in the way of getting their money back.

Nonetheless, you won't be able to avoid starting to repay when they ask you to on the basis of some flimsy excuse. If your salary's still more modest than a bashful nun or you don't get a salary at all, then fair enough – but otherwise forget about dodging the system.

It may not sound like the most foolproof scheme in the world, but trying to cheat the taxman is like giving yourself an enema with battery acid – it's something you don't even want to try.

Not only will tax evasion land you in jail, it's also a pretty despicable way to behave towards other students who need your taxes to pay for the chances you've had.

If you change your address, your name, your bank account or anything else relevant, you need to let the SLC know. Ultimately, there's no point running from them. There's nowhere to hide.

They may not be into horses' heads in beds, but they'll be willing enough to use the legal thumbscrews if you get shifty and, unless you have a completely fair case, they'll wipe the floor with your sorry ass.

Frequently asked questions

I live in the UK but I'm doing part of my course abroad – will I get a loan?

Yes, if your study abroad is a necessary part of your course. Most language degrees involve some time abroad and that's covered.

The maximum amounts are currently £5,000 or £4,350 if it's your final year that you're spending abroad. If you're spending less than eight consecutive weeks abroad, you'll get the same amount of loan as if you were spending the whole year studying in the UK.

However, if your course is studied abroad entirely, the SLC probably won't pay out anything. If in doubt, ask your LEA.

I've finished my degree. I'm off travelling. Do I still have to repay my loan?

You need to let the SLC know what you're doing and they'll tell you where you stand.

It's in your interests to tell them as soon as possible because it's your responsibility to have them allow you to defer your repayments. If you just scoot off without getting your deferment authorised, you could have some serious explaining to do and some big payments to make when you come back.

If you're going travelling and won't be working, deferment shouldn't be too big a problem because you'll be under the fifteen grand income threshold for repayments anyway.

If, however, you'll be living outside the UK tax system and will be earning above the threshold, you'll need to make repayments direct to the SLC and not the Inland Revenue. You'll need to provide evidence of your (expected) income for the financial year so they can calculate how much you should give them each month.

If I'm away, can anyone else talk to the SLC about my loan on my behalf?

Afraid not.

It's a legal thing. The Data Protection Act means the SLC can't discuss it with anyone – not parents, not partners, not even your employer (they tell them no more than how much they want out of your salary each month).

The only way round it is to write a Power of Attorney letter to the SLC authorising them to release information to a named individual. Giving somebody Power of Attorney means they have the legal right to act on your behalf, so don't go giving it to anyone unless you trust them completely.

By the way, you can give someone Power of Attorney over your bank account, for example, but that doesn't mean they have the same power over anything else – that includes your student loan.

2

I only wanted to borrow part of my loan allowance at first. Can I get the rest now?

Yes, but you only get one chance to go back.

In other words, if you're entitled to £4,095 a year and you only apply for £1,000 at first, then you can go back for more later (up to the remaining £3,095), but you can't go back for another £1,000 and then another and then the final £1,095. Whatever you do, though, it won't affect how much you can get the next year.

To get a second amount in one year, you will need to get, believe it or not, *another* form – a Loan Adjustment form. Call the SLC on 0800 405010 and ask them to send you one.

If in any doubt about how much you need, it's pointless to try and keep your debts down to a minimum by applying for anything less than the full allowance.

If you think you might not need the money and you're frightened that just by having it in the bank, you'll spend it, just shove it in a separate savings account until you graduate and then pay it back to the SLC in a lump sum. At least you'll have earned some interest on it in the meantime.

Frankly, the chances are that you'll be more desperate for cash than you ever thought possible. The best way to keep your debts down is to minimise what you spend, not to minimise what you have available to spend.

What happens if I drop out or need to take some time out from my course?

If you drop out during the academic year, then that's it, you're cut off. You won't get any more loan instalments and you'll need to start paying your loan back starting from the April following the end of the academic year.

If you're away from your course for more than 60 days because you're sick or have personal problems, then you should let your university's Student Loans Administrator know as soon as possible. Usually, they'll make sure you continue to get your loan instalments so long as you don't actually drop out.

Can part-time students get student loans?

Nope. There are some grants available instead. To find out more, first read **Chapter 13**, but if that's not the answer to all your dreams, try calling the DfES information line on 0800 731 9133.

Part-time teacher training is treated differently and usually more generously, because the Government desperately wants more teachers.

I'm utterly skint. Can my future instalment(s) be brought forward?

No way, José.

The rules are the rules as far as the SLC is concerned.

If your pocket is really hurting, read what **Chapter 9** says about the Access to Learning Fund and then go ask your university's or students' union's Student Support Officer if you can get one.

I've received the full loan allowance. What if I still don't have enough money to get by?

Again, no dice.

Try the Access to Learning Fund (see **Chapter 9**), or singing in the street till people pay you money to stop.

Still confused?

The SLC are quite happy to answer questions and their helpline is mostly staffed by people with lovely Scottish accents, so try giving them a call (contact details at the back of the book). Or you can visit their website at www.slc.co.uk which is helpful, but doesn't have the accents.

Parents

What should you expect from your parents?

For most students, parents are an essential part of the financial equation.

It's not just that most students hope they might bung them the odd few quid here and there. The whole student funding system relies on the expectation that parents who can afford to help will actually do so.

Rather than the parents or even the students, however, it's the Government (through the LEAs) that, in effect, makes the official decision about what parents can or can't afford.

Well… the Government can decide whatever it likes, but ultimately, it's the parents who make the choice about whether to put their hands in their pockets at all. It's also up to them to decide, when they pull their hand out, how much they're clutching.

Many parents are so proud that any son or daughter of theirs is going off to university that they're only too pleased to fork out whatever they can.

Others want to know if there's some particular amount they're expected to provide – they don't want to give too much and make you into the big spender at the student bar, but nor do they want you to be so hard up you can't be a brilliant scholar.

Some parents, however, don't place the same importance on university as others (or as you). Or they think that by the time you get to 18, they shouldn't have to support you anymore. They might even think that not being supported after a certain age is an important part of your education.

And some parents – many, in fact – may want to help, and the Government may expect them to, but they have too many other financial commitments and simply can't afford it. (This is particularly likely if the family income drops for some reason.)

As far as the students are concerned, let's face it, most look at university as a chance to be independent and they find it more than a little frustrating and demeaning to have to rely on mummy and daddy for pocket money.

The new funding plans – that's the ones expected to come into force in 2006 – shift responsibility for paying fees from the parent to the graduate. Nevertheless, oldies with high enough incomes will still be expected to contribute to their offspring's living costs.

IS THERE A SPECIFIC AMOUNT I SHOULD EXPECT?

There is an amount that, as far as the Government is concerned, you should expect from your parents, but it's not as simple as that. Is it ever?

Before we can open the envelope to reveal that amount known as 'the **family contribution**', we need to explain the thinking behind it.

In theory, all students should end up with approximately the same amount of money at the end of the day. The idea is that students with rich parents shouldn't have a significantly better opportunity to study than students from poorer backgrounds. So the exact amount the folks are expected to fork out depends on what other money you're getting from awards and student loans and where you're living and studying.

Parents make up the difference between what you get from the LEAs and the SLC and the amount the Government thinks you need to live on for a year. In reality, unless you're some kind of economy freak, you can't actually live on what the Government thinks you need – but never mind, crap happens.

The idea is that if you receive a smaller loan allowance, it's because your parents can afford to make up the difference. Also, if you're getting a smaller loan, it means you won't be getting an award from your LEA either and so, if you start your course before September 2006, there'll be £1,150 in tuition fees to pay as well.

So, until 2006, the parental contribution is whatever amount is necessary first to top up your LEA award to £1,150, so you can pay any tuition fees, and then, if you didn't receive the full loan allowance, to top that up too.

If you start your course after the changes in 2006, it'll just be the living expenses your parents are expected to help out with (to bring you up to the level of the full loan allowance). They won't be expected to help out with the 'topped up' tuition fees as you don't have to shell out for them till after you're finished.

Whether your parents actually give (or lend) you that amount is up to you and them.

In 2002/3 the average student received £1,314 from their parents, an amount that had gone down 18% in real terms from the 1998/9 average parental hand-out. Mind you, a different survey found 85% of students got some help from their parents and 21% of these got more than £1,500 a term.

Very nice. The new Higher Education Grant (see **Chapter 8**) is also there to give an extra boost of up to £1,000 a year to students with parents at the lower end of the income spectrum.

Give up smoking.
Eugene Lewis, LSE

HOW MUCH SHOULD I EXPECT?

Once your LEA has completed its assessment of your parents' income, they'll not only let you know how much they're going to give you, how much loan you'll get, but what they think your parents' contribution should be.

At around the £21,475 mark, their income will start to affect your loan allowance and the more they earn, the less you'll be able to borrow till it hits 75% of the maximum loan available.

At the moment, for a student living away from their parents and not in London, the figures look like this:

Your parents' residual income	Parental contribution...		Total parental contribution (per year)
	...to fees	...to living expenses	
Below £21,475	£0	£0	£0
£21,475	£45	£0	£45
For every additional £9.50	£1 more	£0	£1 more
£23,000	£205	£0	£205
£25,000	£416	£0	£416
£29,000	£837	£0	£837
£31,973	£1,150	£0	Full tuition fees of £1,150
For every additional £9.50	£1,150	£1 more	Full tuition fees of £1,150 plus £1 more
£35,000	£1,150	£319	£1,469
£38,000	£1,150	£634	£1,784
£41,710	£1,150	£1,025	£2,175

The parent's contribution maxes out when the part for living expenses hits 25% of your maximum loan allowance (given where you're studying, living, what course you're doing, how many weeks in the year it runs and so on – see **Chapter 4**).

The absolute maximum that any parents are ever expected to contribute is £2,410 a year, for which not only would they have to be earning over £43,943 a year, but you'd also have to fall into all the most expensive categories of location, course and the rest of it.

There are various factors that affect the sums a bit, in particular whether you've got brothers or sisters, which is why it says 'residual' income above – i.e. the LEA only counts left-over money. Unfortunately, they also get to decide how much is left over.

So, if, for instance, you've got brothers or sisters still at school or, at any rate, dependent on your folks, then for each child, the LEA knocks £1,000 off the income before working out what your parents should contribute.

If they're at university or college too, then the LEA usually takes the total contribution from the table above and splits it between all the students in the family.

Case study quiz

Because this whole thing is just so much fun, here's a little quiz just for a laugh – a few examples with multiple choice answers.

Have a go. It'll either help you get your head round awards (see **Chapter 3**), student loans (see **Chapter 4**) and parental contributions or bore you senseless. Possibly both.

Send your answers on a postcard to someone who gives a damn.

2

CASE 1: NADIA NEEDSALOT

Nadia, 18, is from Northampton where her dad works down the last cheese-mine in the country earning £12,000 a year. Her mum does a part-time job painting the feathers on parrots at a nearby pet shop, putting another £5,000 a year into the family purse.

Nadia has been offered a place at the University of East London to do a degree in Nursery Rhyme Technology. She has no brothers or sisters and the course lasts a pretty standard 29 weeks in each year.

She applies to the LEA for an award contribution to her fees and sends off to the SLC for a student loan.

(1) What should Nadia expect by way of an annual award?

    (a) £45

    (b) £1,150

    (c) £1,150 plus a Higher Education Grant of £715

    (d) £1,150 plus a Higher Education Grant of £1,000

(2) What should she expect by way of a student loan for her first year?

    (a) £3,070

    (b) £3,790

    (c) £4,095

    (d) £5,050

(3) What should her parents expect to contribute each year?

    (a) Nothing

    (b) £45

    (c) £1,025

    (d) £1,260

CASE 2: LAWRENCE LOOT-LOADED

Lawrence, 17, is from Eton where he attends a local school. 'Pater' does something awfully important in the city – a banker, indeed, a right banker – and takes home a six-figure sum (all before the decimal point). Mumsy does jolly lovely things for charity.

Lawrence is off to St Andrews to study Imperial History with Capitalism.

His little sister Letitia is about to do her GCSEs.

(1) What should Lawrence expect by way of an annual award?
  (a) Nothing
  (b) £45
  (c) £1,150
  (d) £4,000

(2) What should he expect by way of a student loan for his first year?
  (a) Nothing
  (b) £3,070
  (c) £3,790
  (d) £4,095

(3) What should his parents expect to contribute each year?
  (a) £1,150
  (b) £2,175
  (c) £3,000
  (d) £3,333 and a Convertible Golf GTi

CASE 3: MAGGIE MIDEARNER

Maggie, 19, took a year out and saved up about £7,000 selling stress-removal kits to the team of Push researchers.

Maggie's dad ran off to sea with a primary school teacher named Albert when she was three. Her mum earns £25,000 a year in an animal sanctuary shaving badgers to make brushes, which keeps her too busy (and hairy) to find a new husband or non-furry partner.

Loving only-daughter that she is, Maggie has decided to live at home with her mum in Bolton during her degree course in Doll's House Architecture with Engineering in Lego.

(1) What should Maggie expect by way of an annual award?
- (a) Nothing
- (b) £416
- (c) £734
- (d) £1,150

(2) What should she expect by way of a student loan for her first year?
- (a) £2,430
- (b) £2,830
- (c) £3,240
- (d) £3,070

(3) What should her mother expect to contribute each year?
- (a) Nothing
- (b) £416 and free rent
- (c) £734 and free rent
- (d) £1,308, free rent and a badger

CASE 4: SIMON SIBLING

Simon, 18, lives in Liverpool and is one of eight offspring of Stella Sibling. The father is rumoured to be a Catholic Bishop, but only Stella knows for sure.

Stella has a private income of £35,000 a year from a mysterious Vatican-based trust fund.

All four of Simon's older brothers and sisters are already at university and Simon intends to join them doing Contraceptive Technology at Christ's College Cambridge.

(1) What should Simon expect by way of an annual award?
- (a) Nothing
- (b) £443
- (c) £920
- (d) £1,150

(2) What should he expect by way of a student loan for his first year?
- (a) £2,430
- (b) £2,665
- (c) £3,070
- (d) £4,095

(3) What should Stella expect to contribute to Simon each year?

    (a) Nothing

    (b) £230

    (c) £549

    (d) £1,152

ANSWERS

1 Nadia Needsalot

(1) Her award for fees should be the most you can get – £1,150 – because her parents earn less than £21,475 a year. In fact, they only earn £17,000, which means she's also entitled to a Higher Education Grant of £715. So the correct answer is (c).

(2) She'll be entitled to borrow the maximum for a student doing a full year, living away from home in London, which is (d) £5,050.

(3) The answer's (a). Her parents won't have to contribute a penny, which is just as well because it's hard to imagine that on £17,000 a year they'd find it easy.

2 Lawrence Loot-Loaded

(1) He won't get an award and will have to pay his own tuition fees of £1,150 (see **Chapter 10**). So the answer's (a). With an income that high, having another child won't make any real difference to what his parents have to fork out.

(2) His loan is (b) £3,070 – in other words, the first bit only which isn't means-tested...

(3) His parents, therefore, are expected to stump up only (b) £2,175 (£1,150 towards fees and £1,025 towards living costs), although we have our suspicions he may end up with a bit more.

> 10% of something you didn't want at full price isn't a saving, it's a waste of 90% of the cost.

3 Maggie Midearner

(1) Maggie's award should be around about (c) £734. That's £1,150 minus £45 (for the first £21,475 of her mum's income) minus £1

for each £9.50 over £21,475 (i.e. £371). So that's £1,150 – (£45 + £371) = £734. Maggie's own savings are irrelevant.

(2) She'll be able to borrow (c) £3,240. Since her mother's income is under £31,974, Maggie's entitled to the full loan allowance for anyone living at home.

(3) Her mum will be expected to fork out (b) £416 towards Maggie's tuition fees and, since she's living at home, she probably won't charge for rent.

4 Simon Sibling

(1) Simon's award should be around (c) £920. His situation is complicated by the hordes of brothers and sisters. Normally someone whose parents earn £35,000 – or even the £32,000 that's counted after knocking off £1,000 for each of the younger, dependent siblings – wouldn't get any award, but when Simon goes to Cambridge, his mum will have five kids at university and she can't be expected to pay £1,150 for each of them.

(2) For the same reason, Simon will be eligible for a full loan allowance of (d) £4,095.

(3) In total Stella will be contributing about £1,152 to her various kids' costs as students – but that's not the right answer, because her contribution is split between all her student kids by being divided into five. Therefore her contribution to Simon's costs will be about (b) £230.

SCORING

Give yourself a point for each correct answer. If you scored…
- More than 12: You cheated.
- 9 to 12: Have you thought of a career in the civil service?
- 5 to 8: Nice, nothing too showy.
- 2 to 4: Perhaps another look at the last few chapters, eh?
- 1 or 2: Debtsville, expect another visitor.

Borrowing from parents

There is a saying that goes something like, 'to find your place in the sun you must first escape the shade of the family tree'.

But when you're a student, all those hopeful delusions of independence and financial freedom will probably be shattered as, recovering from freshers week, you realise that all you have left is £19.63, seven slices of quickly greening bread and half a packet of Nurofen to last you the rest of the term.

Depending on what your LEA gleans from your income assessment form, parents who are expected to contribute to fees may well be expected to make further contributions towards your general living costs. But if they've already doled out said dosh and you've cheerfully frittered it away on copious ethanolic refreshment, post-pub kebabs and CDs, you could find yourself paying them a little cap-in-hand visit.

Of course, some students are fortunate enough to have wealthy/generous/understanding/indulgent (delete as applicable) parents who'll shower them with cash in times of financial embarrassment (let alone genuine monetary misery). Even if you fall into this fortunate category, you wouldn't want to take it for granted. You don't miss the water until the well runs dry, as another saying goes.

And for every student who can rely on their parents for hand-outs, there are dozens whose parents can't or (perhaps sensibly) won't.

If your parents *are* willing and able to help, **borrowing** rather than taking money from them seems like a sensible compromise – and who better to borrow from than parents?

They're not likely to charge you any interest, they won't come round and kneecap you if you miss the odd repayment and, sometimes – either deliberately or due to a touch of brain rot – they may actually forget about the loan altogether.

Just don't expect your parents to bale you out all the time. You don't want to be a scrounger all your life, do you?

Money management means learning to make your budget stretch, to economise wisely and to provide for yourself whenever you need extra cash.

Failing that, it means at least facing up to the consequences for yourself.

There's no question about the fact that university's a major financial challenge and seeing yourself through it is part of the education (and, luckily, there's no extra charge for that). A mission impossible, if you will. But, hey, you chose to accept it.

Parents, however, aren't completely ignorant of the fact that you'll be receiving less money than a fruit machine in a Methodist chapel. So it's comforting to know that they're only a (reverse charge) phone call away if you do make the odd cash-related cock-up.

If they have the money, most would probably much rather you borrowed from them than from anyone else.

And, if they do offer you a nice long-term interest-free loan, a churlish refusal during your spell as a cash-strapped student may be extremely poor timing. Especially if it means you'll only have to borrow the money elsewhere and borrow it more expensively. Just take it gratefully and gracefully and pay them back when you can.

Repaying this debt will probably be lowest on your list of priorities, but it's still a debt. Unless they have unequivocally reassured you that they don't want their money back (in which case, consider yourself a very fortunate person indeed), you should feel like a total heel if you go so far as to exploit your parents' generosity.

Whether they're giving you loans or hand-outs, it makes sense all round to establish exactly how much and how often they are planning on providing. Not only does it make you feel less like a charity case and more like a maintained asset, it also gives you a much clearer idea of how much cash you are likely to have to play with.

For their sake as much as yours, you may also do better simply not to ask for money every time.

Instead of hard cash, for instance, you might suggest they buy whatever you would have bought with the money – books, clothes, tinned food, coffee, bus or train tickets, travel cards, postage stamps (for all those summer job applications), phone cards or pre-pay mobile phone top-up credit (for calling them, natch). Quite apart from the fact that it may feel less embarrassing for all concerned if no actual money changes hands, it will reassure your folks that their money's going on stuff you actually need. (And to be fair, it does stop you spending it on stuff you don't.)

There's also a kind of halfway house. They can give you book tokens, clothes vouchers and the like. It's money really – it's just there's a limit on how you spend it.

They can be idiosyncratic old things, parents, and might choose to kit out your bedroom with Habitat goodies or whisk you away on a plush family holiday at their expense. Very nice this may be, so long as you're not too embittered by the struggle to eke out one tin of beans for ten poverty-stricken meals to thank them for their extravagant gestures. A few helpful hints can go a long way but remember that, ultimately, it's their money and up to them to spend as they see fit.

Why not get your parents to visit every now and then? They'll feel loved and needed, which is all very nice, but more importantly you can often get them to take you out for a slap-up meal. After surviving on an uninterrupted diet of baked beans on toast, pasta and tinned tomatoes, beer and burgers, your stomach will be grateful for some proper nutrition.

Parents may also consider getting a strictly 'emergency use' credit card or opening an emergency instant access account as a safety net, just in case. Stranger things have happened.

Depending on the idea behind a gesture like that, you will presumably not want to abuse it. Just having something like that, however, can lift from your shoulders the ever-present panic at being completely without money or any means of getting any.

Ultimately, not all parents are that much wealthier than their student offspring. They probably already don't feel overchuffed at the prospect of not being able to help you out.

If they can't afford to help, there's nothing to be gained by making them feel bad about it.

If, however, your parents genuinely can't help, the new Higher Education Grant system and the Access to Learning funds you can get from your university are there to provide the kind of just-in-case cushion other students get from their parents.

Banks

Do I need a bank account?

As a student you will need to make your bank your friend. And it will feel like cuddling up to a rabid dog.

Not that banks are nasty to students. It's just that most students are scared of talking to their bank because they owe them so much money and they know the bank has the power to cut off their cash supply.

In fact, most banks suck up to students like they were millionaires (because they hope one day that's exactly what they'll be – or, at any rate, they know they're likely to be richer than non-graduates). To entice students to open accounts, banks offer them freebies, good deals and, more importantly, free overdrafts.

Student loans are really only enough for those weird people whose powers of budgeting defy imagination. So borrowing from the bank is almost a necessity for students. Even the weird people may at least have cash flow difficulties.

Normally, if you want to borrow from a bank, they charge you for it, but for students (for as long as they remain students) the big banks offer interest-free overdrafts of up to £2,000 over your course. Some may even oblige with more, if you ask nicely.

The crunch comes, however, when you graduate. Unless you walk into a megabucks job, you'll have your student loan to pay off plus your bank overdraft and that's when the interest can start to rack up (although some banks offer helpfully slow repayment packages).

It's best to get chummy with your bank from the start. If you already have a good relationship with a bank, you might want to keep your account right where it is, though by all means switch to a student account to get the freebies.

Also, always let them know what your situation is, however bad it gets. They don't often cut students off if they're acting responsibly.

Bank deals explained

Banks speak a language of their own, invented by customer service experts in a secret underground facility beneath Alton Towers. At great personal risk, however, Push has acquired a black book containing translations of common terminology. Here are some extracts…

STUDENT ADVISERS

Most banks take apparently ordinary staff and specially train them to act as student advisers in their campus branches and/or those close to universities and colleges.

These advisers are under instructions to be sympathetic to the plight of students – many of them are recent graduates themselves so they will nod empathetically.

As the name 'advisers' suggests, not only do they nod, but they can also give advice about how to handle your cash flow situation, should you want it (or should they think you need it).

Although you'll probably never be swearing eternal love to one another, you should get to know your adviser pretty well and you should contact them whenever you want to change or discuss any aspect of your bank account (such as getting overdraft extensions) or if you have any specific money worries.

This isn't so they can snatch your plastic and cut it up before your eyes, but so they can work with you to make sure you have enough to live on without going too far into the red.

OVERDRAFTS

An overdraft is a minus amount of money in your account. So an 'overdraft limit' is the sum that your bank has decided you're allowed to take out of your account even though you haven't actually got any money in there.

An overdraft is usually denoted by the letters 'OD' on your bank statement. So, if the months go by and the amount in your account just seems to be growing, but there are these strange letters after the totals, start to worry.

'£700 OD' means that's what you owe them, not the other way around and so if you paid £150 into your account, you'd then be £550 OD. Or if you paid in £701, your balance would swell to the knee-buckling sum of £1 CR (CR standing for credit).

Most banks offer a free overdraft facility to students up to a certain limit. This means that, so long as you don't go over the limit, you won't get slapped with any unexpected charges.

Always get official confirmation from your bank of what your overdraft limit is and make sure that it's going to be enough. Depending on your year of study, the overdraft limit is usually between £750 and £2,000 (it grows as your student debts accumulate). If there's any danger that you're not going to be able to stick to the limit, you need to have a chat with your bank's student adviser to arrange an 'extension'.

A couple of don'ts... Don't wait till you're nearly at your limit before trying to arrange an extension, 'cos then you're stuffed if they say no. You should be able to do the maths and – on the basis of what's coming in (student loan payments and parental contributions) and what's going out (see **Chapter 14**) – work out whether your balance is going to drop below the limit. **They'll be more likely to help you if you're being all responsible about it**.

And **don't exceed your limit without getting authorisation to do so**. Your overdraft is then no longer free and you get hit with charges and fines. There'll be fines for going over the limit and for bouncing cheques (i.e. not honouring them) and they'll even charge you for sending you a letter to tell you that you're over your limit. Then they'll fine you because you can't pay the charges.

Worst of all, they'll charge interest. Interest rates on unauthorised overdrafts can be huge. In fact Push would say they were immoral if it weren't for the fact that an unauthorised overdraft is essentially taking their money without asking – so you started it.

While you're a student, your bank overdraft is the cheapest and easiest way of borrowing – cheaper even than student loans, because there's literally no interest on most authorised

student overdrafts while student loans rack up interest from day one.

However, overdrafts do have to be paid back eventually and the bank theoretically has the right to ask for the money at any time. After you've graduated, most start charging interest (although often not immediately) and it doesn't take long for overdrafts to become an expensive form of amusement.

So don't get complacent about your overdraft – it's certainly a lifeline for most students, but it's not an automatic right.

CHEQUE BOOKS

Most banks will give you a cheque book as part of your basic welcome pack when you open an account. They'll give you a paying-in book too, which will probably see less use.

The cheque book will be essential for paying rent, bills etc., but these days you won't need it for much else because you'll usually be able to use plastic. Nevertheless students are famous for writing cheques for a packet of crisps or a pint of milk when the cash machine has turned them down with the fateful familiar phrase: 'Insufficient funds. Refer to bank'.

There are several things to bear in mind before you get too chummy with your cheque book.

Just because you've written a cheque, it doesn't mean the bank will actually give the money to the person you gave the cheque to. The bank can 'bounce' it if you don't have enough money in your account – unless, that is, you show your 'cheque guarantee card' when you hand over the cheque (see below). They'll charge you for the privilege of bouncing your cheque and they can take your cheque card away and fine you if you start abusing it. As they say in chess, cheque mate.

So, once you've run out of dough, don't keep writing cheques.

When you write a cheque, the money doesn't 't leave your account immediately. Nor, if you ever find yourself in the happy position of paying in a cheque, does the money arrive immediately either (see 'Check your cheques' below).

This is because banks need time to allow the cheque to 'clear' (i.e. for the bank to decide whether to bounce it or not). Why, following the invention of the abacus, let alone the computer, it should take so long is one of the great mysteries of life, but there are those who suspect the banks dawdle on purpose so they can make a bit of extra interest while the money is in limbo.

However, the upshot is that you can't always trust your bank balance because there may be uncleared cheques. You may have spent money that hasn't yet disappeared from your account or, just because you've paid in a cheque, it doesn't necessarily mean you can get the cash out.

If you ask a cash machine for a bank balance, it usually gives you two amounts: the balance (how much there is potentially) and the available funds (how much they might actually let you have).

CHEQUE, DEBIT, CASH AND CREDIT CARDS

Most accounts come with at least one slice of plastic, but the cards themselves do different things. (Incidentally, make sure you sign the strip on the back.)

There are four main types of card and some cards can be more than one type at the same time.

Cheque guarantee cards

Most places won't accept a cheque unless you have a matching cheque guarantee card. By writing the number of your card on the back, they have a guarantee from the bank that they'll get their money without worrying whether you've got anything in your account or not.

Students' cards usually only guarantee cheques up to £50 or £100. They come in higher denominations, too, but banks don't trust students with those.

If you write a cheque and offer the card, make sure your balance can stand it. Otherwise you'll find yourself with an unauthorised overdraft and all the deluge of poo that entails (see above).

Debit cards

If you need a card to write a cheque, why bother with writing the cheque?

Sure enough, that's a debit card. You offer it. You sign. The money comes out of your account.

The shop (or whatever) can phone up to check whether your account can handle whatever payment you're trying to make although, since debit cards are also usually cheque guarantee cards, they usually won't bother if it's under the cheque limit. (Often the phone call is made automatically by the till.)

Cash cards

Slide it in a hole in the wall, punch in your PIN and get cash up to a daily limit or whatever your account can pay out.

PIN stands for 'personal identification number'. Please don't say 'PIN number'. It really bugs me. The word 'number' is redundant. Thanks.

Beware of charges for using another bank's cash machine. Most are happy to dole out the dough for each other for free, but not all. You can intend to take out a tenner and end up with £12.50 coming out of your account. Figure out first what fees apply. You'll be told to look out for a particular symbol such as the Switch, Link, Visa or Cirrus logos.

Credit cards

At first a credit card seems to work the same way as a debit card. You hand it over. You sign a slip. Everyone's happy.

In fact, they're not the same, because it doesn't matter how much money there is in your bank account if you're using a credit card. Instead the money is added to your credit account and you get a bill at the end of the month for everything you spent on the card.

You can either settle up then or pay a minimum payment and let the rest sit there. Bad idea. If you leave a balance unpaid on your credit card account, they'll charge interest on it and we're talking interesting levels of interest here. It's an expensive way of borrowing and not recommended for students without bottomless pockets.

More on credit cards in **Chapter 9**.

CAREER DEVELOPMENT LOANS

Career Development Loans (CDLs) are a Government-funded scheme to help people who are doing vocational training courses. The loans are offered by just three banks (Barclays, The Co-operative and The Royal Bank of Scotland) but most undergrads don't qualify anyway.

For more on CDLs, see **Chapter 9**.

ONLINE AND TELEPHONE BANKING

Internet banking is becoming increasingly popular and students can get in on the act as easily as anyone – not least because most universities provide free web access to all their students.

This means that rather than traipsing to your nearest branch and queuing up for hours behind someone with 4,317 pennies that need to be counted, instead you can sit at a terminal in the university library, picking your nose and avoiding the essay you're supposed to be writing.

Many students prefer to speak to someone, however, especially if they want to give excuses or get advice. But the internet banks have thought of that. Most offer a 24-hour telephone banking service (or at least a service beyond the usual nine to five).

Even so, the face-to-face contact of a student adviser who you recognise is still popular. It's up to you.

Also check the costs – there may be charges for banking down the wires.

DEFERMENT PERIOD

Slim Jim the Fence owes Joey the Knife £10,000. Joey gives him three days to come up with the money – that's a 'deferment period'.

To put it another way, it's a period of time that a bank gives you either to raise the funds to repay an overdraft or loan or, more usually, to find work.

When banks offer a deferment period, it tends to be more by way of a practical approach to debt management rather than a threat (as it is with Joey the Knife).

Rather than immediately snatching every penny you earn and landing you in as much financial crap as you endured as a student, a deferment period helps you settle into a job and ease your way into repayments. Banks usually give students a year or two (or even three) after they've graduated before giving them a hard time about repaying their overdraft. Meanwhile, however, they are charging interest on what you owe.

If a bank doesn't offer a deferment period to graduates, you may want to look elsewhere.

REPAYMENT HOLIDAYS

A repayment holiday is similar to a deferment period, but usually shorter – a matter of a few months.

It's a period when they'll let you off repayments while you're having a hard time, so long as you start paying again when you're out of the woods. It can be either before or after you've started repaying.

BANK LOANS

The difference between a loan and an overdraft is that an overdraft is simply what's not in your account, whereas a loan is an agreement to lend you a certain amount for a certain period on certain terms.

Most banks do offer loans to students, although some of them need to be paid back before graduation. That rules them out as a way of financing anything other than a particular expense that you know you'll be able to repay. Definitely not the right choice for students who foresee the financial swamp just getting deeper and swampier further down the line.

All loans are subject to various terms and conditions, however, so do some thorough investigation before applying.

For more on loans from banks, loan sharks and anyone else, see **Chapter 9**.

Which bank?

Of course, you've probably had a bank account since the tooth fairy gave you 10p for your first milky peg. But becoming a student gives you a great opportunity to review the situation.

Look out for special offers and incentives. And that's 'look out' in both senses of the phrase.

On the one hand, there are some enticing bribes out there. Free cash may sound good, but some of the discounts on books or travel could end up being of greater value after a few years.

On the other hand, it's not worth being duped by the offer of a cuddly Barney the Banking Bear if that means you're stuck with an :count that makes loan sharks look like kippers. Keep your eye on : long term.

The banks usually change their package every year and full ils aren't usually available until mid-June.

Most of them have now shut down the loophole whereby you could open five accounts, collect all the freebies and then close down the ones you don't need. They now require that you bank with them *exclusively* as part of the agreement when you join up.

You may already have a bank account you are quite happy with. In this case, let your bank manager know you are going to university and s/he will transfer your current account to a special student one and give you all the info you'll need – and, hopefully, shower you with perks.

Try to join up with a bank at least a few weeks before starting university to take full advantage of any offers (some are offered on a while-stocks-last basis). It'll also mean you avoid long queues at the bank at the beginning of term, you should get your plastic in plenty of time and you'll have a chance to get to know the bank's particular facilities and arrangements. Perhaps most importantly, it'll mean you can tell the SLC where to put your student loan.

THE DEALS

Following is a summary of what some of the big high street banks are offering for 2004/5, but the exact deals are likely to change from year to year. Remember, they're not only not the only banks, they're not even necessarily the best for students.

For example, check out student deals from Clydesdale, Abbey National, Nationwide, The Co-operative, Alliance & Leicester and Halifax (now also known as HBOS after its merger with Bank of Scotland). If you live or study in Ireland, try Bank of Ireland (NI) or Ulster Bank (NI).

There's also a bundle of banks on the internet now, including Smile (good interest rate when in credit), First Direct, Cahoot and Intelligent Finance, to name but a few.

Do your supermarket shopping on a Sunday or at the end of the day when things that could go off get marked down. Then don't forget to eat them before they do.

	Barclays	HSBC
Website	www.barclays.co.uk	www.ukpersonal.hsbc.co.uk
Phone	0800 400 100	0800 130 130 (Textphone: 0800 028 0126)
Freebies	£20 worth of Waterstone's and HMV vouchers. Additional discounts on Waterstone's and HMV vouchers throughout the year.	Free 5-year railcard or £50 cash, student insurance policy from £24 per year, BSM and Lonely Planet discounts.
What do you need to apply?	UCAS letter or student ID and one other official piece of ID showing name and address.	UCAS letter and confirmation of university place, plus additional proof of name and address, your last month's bank statement.
Interest on current account when in credit	0.1% AER	0.1% AER
The Full Deal	Easy online banking; Barclays Connect Card (debit, cash and cheque guarantee); cheque book; offers and discounts throughout the year; direct debit and standing order facilities; monthly statements.	£100 cheque guarantee and debit card; cheque book; direct debit facilities; monthly postal statements (if you want); internet and telephone banking.
Overdraft facility/Credit zone	Automatic interest-free buffer of £200 available on opening account. Up to a *further* £1,300 interest-free on request. £1,500 to £3,000 at a preferential interest rate of 8.9% EAR for as long as you need it. Interest rate over maximum authorised overdraft: 27.5% EAR.	Interest-free overdraft limits (until graduation): • 1st Year: £1,000 • 2nd Year: £1,250 • 3rd Year: £1,500 • 4th Year: £1,750 • 5th Year: £2,000 (certain courses only) Overdraft limit goes up each year only if you've proved you can manage it responsibly. Interest rate over maximum authorised overdraft: 14.8% EAR.
Student adviser	Student business officers in selected branches.	Student advisers in all student branches.

NatWest	Lloyds TSB	Royal Bank of Scotland
www.natwest.com	www.lloydstsb.com	www.royalbankscot.co.uk
0800 200 400	0845 3000 134	0800 100 0148
£40 in cash, or £55 if the account is opened at an on-campus branch.	National express coachcard, Eurolines coach vouchers, 10% off Blackwell's books bought online, entry into free prize draw to win up to £3,600, deals on Dial-a-Phone mobiles.	20% off selected books, discounts on CDs, DVDs, tapes, videos and games, 25% off concert tickets, 2 for 1 deals at more than 350 nightclubs.
Apply online, or UCAS or university letter, one form of official ID (e.g. a passport), confirmation of home and term-time addresses.	Unconditional offer letter or UCAS letter and one other official piece of ID showing name and address.	UCAS, SLC or university letter of offer or acceptance, piece of ID, last 3 months' bank statements.
0.1% AER	None	2.02% AER
Free online banking, if required; 24-hour freephone help-desk; NatWest Service Card; monthly statements.	Interest-free overdraft; free internet banking; electron, debit card or cashcard (£100 cheque guarantee); cheque book; telephone banking; credit card; monthly statements; computerised phone-bank express service; can be used abroad.	Student Royalties account has phone and internet banking, credit card, interest-free overdraft, cheque guarantee and debit card, cheque book, postal statements.
Interest-free prearranged overdrafts individually agreed with advisers, up to £2,000. Interest rate over maximum authorised overdraft: 17.81% EAR.	Interest-free overdraft limits: • 1st Year: up to £1,000 • 2nd Year: £1,250 • 3rd Year: £1,500 • 4th and 5th Year: up to £2,000 Interest rate over maximum authorised overdraft: 14.8% EAR.	Interest-free overdraft of up to £1,250 in 1st year, rising to up to £2,000 in 5th year. Interest rate over maximum authorised overdraft: 29.8% EAR.
All branches on or near campus have Student advisers.	Student and graduate telephone team or ask in branch.	Student advisers in some branches.

2

	Barclays	HSBC
Graduate loan & overdraft schemes	Option to transfer student overdraft of up to £3,000 at 15.6% APR. Graduate interest-free overdraft: • 1st Year: up to £1,500 • 2nd Year: up to £1,000 Graduate loan of up to £10,000 at 8.9% APR, with up to 3 months repayment holiday.	Up to £25,000 at 7.9% over up to 8 years. Graduate interest-free overdraft: • 1st Year: £1,500 • 2nd Year: £1,000 • 3rd Year: £500
Career development loan	From £300 to £8,000. Call 0800 60 900 60 for more details. Professional Studies Loan also available – up to £10,000 (£25,000 for full-time Law students). Enquire at local branch.	Postgraduate and Professional Studies Loan covers course fees and living expenses up to £5,000 (or two thirds of previous annual salary) each year. Call 0800 529 429 or apply at local branch for more details.
Insurance	Special deal negotiated for students. Cost depends on location and type of accommodation.	Special student package available with four levels of cover. Pick up leaflet from nearest branch or call 0800 277 377. Travel insurance available (for students aged 17 to 30) – for details call 0800 299 399.
Credit card	Student Barclaycard with credit limit up to £600 – additional benefits such as money-off vouchers. 17.9% APR.	Automatic credit limit of £500. Up to 8 weeks' interest-free credit when balance is paid in full.
Anything else?	Commission-free travel money, offers on software. Additional discounts on some items purchased with Student Barclaycard.	Automatic transfer to 3-year graduate service. 24-hour telephone banking. Internet banking. Commission-free foreign currency and travellers' cheques. Gap year service available.

NatWest	Lloyds TSB	Royal Bank of Scotland
Up to £15,000 for up to 7 years at 7.5%. Interest repayment holiday of 4-12 months. Graduate interest-free overdraft: • 1st Year: up to £2,000 • 2nd Year: £1,000 • 3rd Year: £500	Up to £10,000 over 5 years at 7.8%. Optional 4-month repayment holiday. Graduate loan protection scheme. Graduate interest-free overdraft: • 1st Year: up to £2,000 • 2nd Year: £1,500 • 3rd Year: £1,000	Interest-free overdraft of £2,000 until June after graduation, interest-free loan of up to £2,000 to pay overdraft. Graduate loan of up to £15,000 with up to 9 months deferred repayments (interest still charged), variable rate of 6.6% APR.
Professional Trainee Loans – borrow up to £20,000 for up to 10 years. MBA loan scheme.	Further education loan for current account customers taking professional courses e.g. doctor, dentist, lawyer, accountant – borrow up to £10,000 for up to 5 years, repayments can be delayed for 48 months, 9.9% APR	Special loans for healthcare and postgraduate law students of up to £15,000 – no repayments during study period, then up to 7 years to repay.
Student belongings insurance (call 0800 783 5657) and student travel insurance (0800 051 5051).	Insurance available online or enquire at local branch for deals.	20% discount off single-trip travel insurance, special policy for longer trips, student belongings new-for-old insurance cover.
Student Mastercard, 17.9% APR variable rate, up to 8 weeks' interest-free credit when balance is paid in full.	Can apply for personal credit card with limit of at least £500, up to 8 weeks' interest-free credit, 17.9% APR.	Up to 8 weeks' interest-free credit, 17.9% APR.
Car insurance and breakdown cover, has the most branches on campuses.	Fully comprehensive internet service for students and graduates. PhoneBank Express (automated phone service) and commission-free travel money.	Payment card protection, lost key retrieval service, 10% off selected holidays and travel, commission-free travel money.

2

Graduate packages

Postgrads have different needs of their banks. They're often meeting the whole cost of their course and their living expenses tend to be higher, but they also often stand to gain even more financially from their course than undergrad students.

Most banks have packages for postgrads, although not every student is able to get them. Like with undergraduate accounts, a nice fat interest-free overdraft can't hurt and you're more likely to need an extra loan on top. The information in the table above is subject to change and postgrads' situations vary, so it's worth popping in to your local branch to check what they can do for you specifically.

Learn to love your lender

PICKING A BANK

A quick summary then.

Faced with the fountain of freebies and the glut of goodies on offer from every high street bank, it's almost as hard to choose a bank as it was to choose a university.

They nearly all provide online and telephone banking services and most offer interest-fee prearranged overdrafts, preferential rates on loans and probably staff who'll perform sexual favours.

Don't get suckered by the gimmicks. It's worth shopping around to get the best banking deal you can.

Before deciding, you should get answers to the following questions:

- How much interest will you get on money in your account for the short period that you happen to be in credit (usually that's only for a few weeks after getting your first student loan instalment)? The interest is often so small you can't even fold it – making a separate savings account a wise move if you're ever likely be in the black.
- What's your maximum overdraft limit? And check it's interest-free.
- How quickly do they expect you to pay off your debts and when?

- How nasty are the charges they slap on you for unauthorised overdrafts? They *will* be nasty, but some are the stuff of nightmares.
- What are the facilities like, such as the number and location of cash machines? Is there or will there be a cash machine near where you go every day as a student (either on campus or wherever you're living)?
- Is there a branch somewhere convenient?
- If you can't get to a branch when it's open, what other banking services do they offer – such as over the phone or on the internet? What can and can't you do by phone or online?
- Do they charge anything if you use another bank's cash machine and if so how much?
- Do they offer specialist advice for students and graduates?
- How easy is it to set up and cancel standing orders and direct debits?
- If you care, how sound are they? For example, do they have shady connections in other countries propping up dictatorships that abuse human rights?
- What freebies do you get and what are they really worth to you?
- Do they offer student bank loans beyond overdrafts and on what terms?
- What support will they give you once you've graduated?

Other people – especially other students – may have useful tips. They may want to plug a particular bank to you or warn you off another one. Don't necessarily take what they say at face value, but a tip's a tip.

Besides, you may be able to get extra-special 'family loyalty' treatment if your parents recommend their own bank to you – ask them.

The top tip of all is to think about the long term. The freebies are all very well for as long as they last, but a relationship with a bank is something you enter for the long haul. Who's going to be offering you good deals in three years when you need to extend your overdraft for the ninety-third time?

Think about the practicalities, too – which banks are most convenient? That's when it gets down to individual choice. It's all very well being told by a friend about the great deals on offer from the Scilly Isles Bank, but it's no good if you're going to want a bit of face-to-face with someone and they're miles off the Cornish coast.

Make a list of your priorities and then find the bank that most closely matches your own individual criteria.

Ultimately, you'll be doing the bank a favour by opening an account with them. In a few years, you will no longer be a student with barely two coins to rub together, but an extravagantly wealthy graduate with years of fabulous earning power ahead of you. Or something.

STAYING FRIENDS WITH YOUR BANK MANAGER

Staying on your bank's good side is in your interests. Not only will they send you fewer stroppy letters (with the added insult of charging you for them), but you'll also get more out of them.

One of the best ways to keep in with the guys in suits is to practise sensible banking.

Safe sex is best until you're in a long-term relationship. Sensible banking is the same – don't try anything else till you've been sleeping with money for a while.

Here then are Push's top tips for sensible banking.

When in credit

Sensible banking doesn't mean leaving all your money in your bank account. It means doing the best for your money and your money will do its best for you. What's more, your bank will respect you for it.

For instance, take advantage of being in credit. It won't happen often or for long.

Try to buy your textbooks second-hand. They're cheaper and the good bits are probably already underlined.

When you're in credit – or should that be 'if' – don't keep all your student loan or other money in your student bank account. The rate of interest will probably pay out something like 10p a year for every hundred pounds.

Instead, transfer some of it into a separate savings account that you should keep on one side for any windfalls such as money you earn over the summer, birthday paydirt, inheritances from your long lost Aunt Maud, whatever.

Your bank manager knows that your student bank account is there for your short-term cash needs. That's why it has the overdraft facility. But just because the account might spend most of its time in the red, it doesn't mean that when you've got money your bank manager will expect you to keep more in your current account than you have to.

In fact, s/he'll probably be only too glad to open another account for you that pays interest, but that you won't be able to overdraw.

That way, while you've got money, you won't be losing out on the opportunity to make your money earn you more money. But be careful not to get stung with charges just because your money was in the wrong account.

Cash machines just give cash, they don't print it

Limit your cash withdrawals to one a week and don't be tempted to draw out more than you need. That will stop you blowing your budget without noticing, because you'll only ever be able to spend what you've got.

Most banks allow up to about £250 cash out per day (funds permitting, of course) – but your budget should see you taking out way less. Fifty quid is nearer the mark. On the other hand if you prefer paying for things with the genuine folding stuff and rarely use your debit card or cheques for purchases, then you may need a bit more.

Keep your balance

Keep a watchful eye on your balance and print out a mini-statement at least every few days to keep a check on any splashing out you may have inadvertently done on the plastic.

You'll get an official statement from the bank every month. Don't throw it away – read it, check it and look for mistakes. Even banks make them sometimes. (Point out the mistake, even if it's a bank error in your favour. Unfortunately this game doesn't work like Monopoly – when they realise, they'll want the money back, which may be tough if you've already spent it. Strangely enough, however, the mistakes are more usually tilted the other way.)

There may even be extra payments on your statement that you know nothing about. This may be a sign that someone's using your details fraudulently (which happens to most people at some point) – in which case you've got to let the bank know as soon as possible if not sooner, or you could end up footing the bill. Alternatively, it may be a sign that you're not keeping track of your spending – in which case, you should get a grip.

Pen pals
Keep a record of all correspondence from your bank and reply promptly to the letters – even the nasty ones. In fact, *especially* the nasty ones. Keep statements in a separate folder, as you may need proof of your poverty to claim emergency cash (see **Chapter 9**) in times of need.

Check your cheques
It's all too easy to use your debit card without realising you don't have enough overdraft left to cover it.

It's even easier with cheques, because you can forget about one you wrote some time ago, but then it gets cashed and the money disappears from your account when you least expect it.

So when you use a cheque to pay for something, bear in mind that it could take several days or even weeks to go through. Similarly, when you pay a cheque into your account, it will take a while to clear – three to four working days usually.

Don't be fooled into thinking you have more money than you actually do.

Ideally, you should keep a note of what you think your bank balance should be and compare it with your monthly statement when it arrives. In reality, that may be too much to expect from most people but, believe me, there are folks out there that do it. (And they're the ones in credit.)

> **Eat according to the season. Fruit and veg prices vary according to the time of year, so choose the fresh stuff according to what's cheapest.**

Know your limits
Because unauthorised overdraft charges are higher than an airliner on acid, never exceed the limit you've agreed with your bank and make sure you've had written confirmation from your bank of what your limit is.

Going over the limit is like being caught sleeping with someone else. Your bank may say they forgive you, but you'll always have this uneasy feeling that they don't really trust you. (And you're probably right.)

If you are having real trouble coping with the limit at its current level, talk to your bank's student adviser before it's too late. They can usually work something out.

2

Protect your plastic

Be very careful with your debit card (and extra careful with your credit card).

If you lose it or it gets stolen, report it immediately. Even if you think it's probably hidden somewhere and you don't want to have to wait for a new one to arrive by post, report it anyway. If it's used fraudulently by someone else, if the loss hasn't been reported you may find yourself at best doing some embarrassing explaining – and at worst, shelling out yourself.

Don't even think about 'kiting' – see **Chapter 9**.

Don't keep your chequebook and your cheque guarantee card together. If they're both stolen, you could have your entire account cleaned out.

Don't write your PIN down. Keep it to yourself and be careful that nobody's checking it out over your shoulder when you use the machine.

Beware the smiling shop assistant who chirpily asks whether you want cashback as you pay for your weekly shop. Unless you urgently need some readies and are positive there're no working cash machines in a several-mile radius, say no. It's all too easy to sink into a cashback-happy hole of grabbing extra cash each time you shop without ever having to look at your waning bank balance. But when you do check the figures – or the bailiffs come round or whatever – it'll be a nasty shock, believe us.

And never, ever, put your card behind the bar for a tab. You'll end up drinking more than you intended and every pisshead in the bar will be putting their drinks on your slate. You'll wake up feeling sick, skint and sorry.

Chapter Seven

2

Working for dough

Most students work at some point during their time at university or college.

Some of them even work at their studies – but never mind that, most do *paid* work for readies.

For some, it's the only way they can afford to do any travelling over the summer. For others, it's the only way they can justify more than one pint in the student bar. For all too many, however, it's the only way they can keep their finances from going into free-fall.

At any one time, 58% of students have regular part-time jobs to supplement their income during term-time. And the proportion is on the up. Five years ago, it was 47% that were juggling employment and studies.

Then there are the temp jobs in the vacations. All in all, 90% of students are thought to take paid work at some point.

THE PROS
Working for money has its advantages.

For starters, there's the money. Don't underestimate the importance of that.

Some jobs – however dull – offer a break from academic work. Sometimes the more mindless they are, the better.

And many have great little perks such as staff discounts (if you work in a shop) or free food and drink (if you work in catering).

There's also the fact that, quite apart from *making* money, most jobs – because they take up so much of your time – stop you doing anything that might involve *spending* money.

If you work behind a bar, for instance, you can't spend all your evenings on the other side of it handing over cash. What's more, you don't lose out entirely when it comes to socialising with the people who do spend all their time and money in there.

There's also the work experience. Most part-time or temporary student jobs may not quite be rungs on the career ladder, but there is the opportunity to work in a variety of different work environments, to meet new people and to learn new skills. It all adds horsepower to your CV.

2

Even if you're just pulling pints at your local bar or scanning barcodes at the supermarket, every little helps. It proves you can be relied on to show your face regularly and not hurl abuse at your boss or the customers. Both valuable assets in an employee and rarer than you might imagine.

Ultimately, having to work usually boosts a student's employability and therefore not only their present, but also their future, finances.

As more graduates turn out with work experience, employers get more choosy about what they expect from the top recruits. Whatever you can do to make yourself stand out as jobworthy is worthwhile.

Employers want all the buzzwords and phrases – highly developed communication and interpersonal skills, teamwork, ability to meeting deadlines, IT literacy, numeracy, the ability to stay calm in a crisis, initiative, managerial potential, quick and reasoned decision-making and a demonstrable analytical approach – all that waffle. Scary, but true.

Doing a job helps prove you've got at least some of them and, with luck, your degree does the rest.

Oh, and did we mention the money?

> **Hang on to receipts and guarantees. Things do break, but a free replacement or refund can ease the pain no end.**

THE CONS

Ideally, of course, students should spend every waking moment with their minds bent on the high ideas involved in their studies.

While it's not true that if you've got a job you can't possibly get a good degree, it is important to maintain your perspective.

You're doing the job to support your studies and your studies should come first. However, if your boss is more pushy than your tutor – and, since s/he is paying you, s/he probably will be – when it comes to a choice, it's often your studies that are left behind while you go out to work.

Universities usually recommend that students do no more than 15 hours work a week. Some institutions, particularly Scottish universities, say ten hours should be the maximum.

In reality, the average working student puts in 14 hours a week – which means some are doing far fewer hours, but some are doing far more. Two out of five students work for more than 15 hours a week, particularly those living in London or with parents.

This worker-ant lifestyle isn't doing their degrees any favours. Recent government research found 58% of students who worked regularly got 2:1s or first class degrees, compared with 71% of jobless students. The difference was even greater among students who'd got top A level grades.

It's sometimes hard to find a job that offers the right number of hours at the right times and which has the flexibility to let you rearrange your hours once in a while if you have a study commitment. Signing up with an agency that will give you work when you've got time for it without strings or fixed hours attached can be a good move, providing you can survive without a fixed wage each week.

It's not just class work that's important. Students have to make time for individual study – in fact, quite a bit of it. If it means missing an essay deadline or skipping a lecture or seminar, you shouldn't be going to work.

To put in the hours both studying and working for money, something's gotta give. Just make sure it's the right thing. There's no point finishing your degree without debt if you don't pass.

Then again, stressing about your debts isn't exactly conducive to good study, so there's a whole swings and roundabouts scenario going on here.

The solution for some people is to work full-time and study on a part-time basis. That's your call, but unless you've got a good job that you want to hang on to and you're in no hurry to get qualified, you might find yourself higher on the stress scale and not an whole lot better off, because you aren't eligible for the same support.

Oxbridge

At Oxford and Cambridge, the terms are shorter than usual – just eight weeks – and the level of academic intensity during that time is turned up a bit. They – and other universities with short terms – are a bit firmer about what students should and shouldn't do to make ends meet.

Term-time jobs get a big frown and, although you might get away with it if you keep quiet, if there's any hint of conflict with your studies it'll be a them-or-us situation. Oxford's Student Union reckons one in five students are holding down term-time jobs on the sly.

You'd have thought that longer vacations mean you could just make up the money doing full-time temp work. Afraid not. At Oxbridge, you tend to get almost as much work set between terms as during them – and if you don't, then you'll probably want to get ahead on next term's reading list while there's time.

Finding the time for more than a couple of hours of paid work a week isn't easy and anyway it's hard to find jobs with such minimal commitment of time. But on the up-side, Oxbridge students tend to have fewer financial problems – partly because nearly 50% went to private schools and partly because there's more student support funding floating around than in most other universities.

Finding a job

WHAT KIND OF WORK AM I MOST LIKELY TO FIND?

Clearly not every job is suitable for students. After all, most involve going to work during the day.

There are some obvious candidates, however – casual work in bars, restaurants and hotels (and catering in general), shops and supermarkets. Others that get a look in include childminding and care work, cleaning, warehouse jobs, market research and temporary office work.

If you fancy something a bit more unusual, how about life modelling for artists, being a teaching assistant, a

psychologist's guinea pig, telesales, DJing, taxi-driving, nightclub bouncing or exotic dancing.

Depending on what you're willing and able to do, there's really no such thing as a typical job.

It's worth trying to think of the jobs that don't require you to do much more than sit there, occasionally move about a bit doing stuff and then sit there again – night security, for instance, or baby-sitting (once the kid's in bed). You can use the time for study – or at least reading – and, bonus, you get paid for it.

JOBSHOPS AND JOB OPPS

Although they'd rather their students didn't have to work for money, most universities came to terms with the reality of the situation a while ago.

And if you can't beat 'em, join 'em.

Most universities now have a **jobshop** based on campus – basically a job agency that finds employment for students and finds students for employers. These are different from the university careers offices which try to find jobs for students once they've graduated (although the two are often combined into a single service). Jobshops find work during the vacations and, sometimes, part-time jobs during term.

Jobshops, however, do more than your bog standard temp agency – apart from anything else, they don't usually take a slice off your wage packet (or if they do, it's a smaller one than usual).

The difference for employers is that they specialise in students, which, to many of them, is a good thing. Students tend to be intelligent, keen, polite and, on average, no less reliable than anyone else. Most importantly, however, students are cheap.

Don't indulge in 'solvent abuse' — ie. teasing people because they're not in debt. It's not big and it's not clever. When it comes to student debt, you should be more proud of keeping it small than having a big one.

The difference for students is that jobshops specialise in jobs for students. The vacancies they've got tend to be the ones that have some flexibility over hours and where the boss understands some of the commitments students have to juggle.

Jobshops are in a good position to do a nice bit of matching. But their responsibilities usually go further. Often they'll exercise a cut-off point on wages.

For most people the minimum wage (as of October 2004) is £4.85 an hour, but for 18 to 21 year-olds, it's only £4.10 an hour. Many jobshops impose their own minimum – at least the legal minimum wage and sometimes higher – and they'll tell employers looking for slave labour to shove it.

Jobshops will also sometimes lay down the law on other things, such as better-than-minimum working conditions, holiday pay and so on. (Even part-time workers are entitled to paid leave.) How successful they are depends on how needy the local job market is.

One of the biggest local employers of students tends to be the university itself, which smacks just a tad of hypocrisy – but who's complaining?

Universities often need people to work in bars, shops, cafés and cafeterias, or cleaning rooms, doing admin work, looking after conference guests, serving drinks at functions, looking after new and prospective students, even phoning former students and asking them to donate generously to the vice-chancellor's retirement fund. All ideal work for students.

There are often still more jobs going at the students' union, which is the student-run organisation that usually manages most of the bars, shops, nightclubs and other non-academic services for students within the university. As often as not, it's the students' union that runs the jobshop and it employs students to do it.

Some universities are in areas so devoid of job opportunities that the jobshop doesn't even bother to try to find jobs for students off-campus and lists only vacancies on offer from the uni itself or the students' union.

Every jobshop operates slightly differently and some might just as well try to find Ann Widdecombe a date for Saturday night as try to find you a job. Either they're not very good at it or there just aren't the openings out there. (By 'openings' we mean job opportunities –

we're not talking about Ann Widdecombe any more, okay? Ugh, nasty thought.)

Flexible evening and weekend work is easier to come by in a large city than in a small town and it's often possible to get longer shifts during holidays or even go full-time if you're jammy.

If, however, you're at university in Smallsville, you'll probably want to head home for the holidays to find work. (Unless, of course, you come from Tinytown.)

Obviously, if it's not local work you're looking for, your university jobshop will be less use than a cricket bat in a snow storm. So, a few weeks before the end of term, get in touch with a few agencies or businesses near your home. That way you avoid the post-term flood of students.

Christmas is an especially good time to find shop work and summer is, of course, tourist season. Lots of big companies have summer vacation schemes, sometimes called internships (see below), of usually between four and eight weeks.

OTHER PLACES TO LOOK

Most student jobshops worth their salt come up with something within a few weeks if there's anything to come up with.

But what do you do if they draw a blank? Or there is no jobshop? Not even a vacancies noticeboard?

The local job centre may be able to help, but their main priority will be getting jobs for the unemployed, not (as they may see it) feathering the nest of students who're already sitting on a cosy little egg of a future.

> Tempting as it sounds to go and drink yourself to death each night, I suggest you only take a small amount of cash with you so you can't spend too much. Also, stick to drink soft drinks only — they're cheaper. Yeah, right — as if.
> James Williamson, Bishop's Stortford College

Local newspapers, employment agencies and even postcards in newsagents' windows may be a better bet. Some temping agencies specialise in finding short-term assignments for young people – the work tends to be menial, but if it's really crap you can turn it down. Sign up with more than one if the work is a bit thin on the ground.

Also, try the university's own bulletin – not the student newspaper, but whatever newsletter the authorities produce for staff (there probably is one, even if most students don't know about it). Or why not just barge into the uni's conference office and see what they've got.

Don't be afraid to go into a pub, a restaurant or a shop on spec and ask. What's the worst they can say? Remember to have your CV on hand and try something politer than, 'Oi, gi's a job'.

Even if the jobshop can't find you anything, they should be able to give you advice. And if there's no jobshop, the careers office might be turned on to a few ideas and opportunities.

Ultimately, if the regular avenues turn into dead-ends, it's important to try the alleys that other people haven't. Chances are there's a job going somewhere that someone's desperate to fill, it's just that they're not trying the right channels. If you can tune in to same channels, you may find you're the only person chasing the job.

Lateral thinking is called for.

If, for instance, it's coming up to Easter, think about who does a lot of business then. A quick phone call to Thornton's the chocolate egg-makers and you may find yourself helping them meet the extra demand (not to mention acquiring a revulsion to chocolate). Or, since the horse-racing and big sporting seasons are just getting under way around then, maybe the bookies will need someone numerate.

You can even advertise your own services – childminding, house cleaning, dog walking, gardening, DIY, GCSE tutoring, underpants scouring, etc. That's what the windows of newsagents and corner shops are for – those cards usually cost no more than a pound a week and in some supermarkets they're free.

Herd all your mates onto the same mobile tariff — it'll be cheaper in the long run. Some companies offer rewards for converting people.

And how about teaming up with a friend or two and offering yourselves as a multi-skilled 'student workforce'? (You could even start your own jobshop if there isn't one.) Back to cards in the shop windows, but this time, you're sharing the cost.

If you're offering services, however, a couple of things to bear in mind. You may find you need to provide references, to prove you can do what you're advertising and that you're reliable. It's also best if you can find someone to check out anyone you're working for.

With certain jobs, such as childminding, there may be legal dimensions that you're not aware of. A bit of babysitting's not a problem, but pretending to offer a full-scale crèche could land you in more than a pile of smelly nappies.

Get advice from the jobshops, careers service or the local Citizen's Advice Bureau if you're worried.

There are also some useful web addresses in the back of the book that are worth a surf.

HOW MUCH CAN I EARN?

Obviously it depends what you do. Students usually end up working in shops, pubs, bars and restaurants, and usually receive something like £5 to £6 an hour.

If they stick to the university's recommendation of no more than 15 hours a week, that should bring them an extra £75 to £90 a week, but there may be things like tax and National Insurance (NI) to worry about (see below).

If you did that every week, that would put about £4,000 into the right side of your budget equation, but the fact is that, one way or another, you're unlikely to do it for more than about seven months. Over the summer, you may well not be around and during May and June, you'll probably have exams to worry about which are definitely more important than paid work.

According to Government research, the average student gets just over £1,100 a year from paid work, not including anything earned in the long summer vacation. Although, as not all students work, those that do are likely to earn a bit more to compensate for those that earn diddly squat.

So, assuming you can find any work at all and assuming that it pays okay and assuming you can do it enough for hours

and weeks to make it worthwhile, then you could hope to earn about two grand a year as a student.

But don't rely on it when it comes to calculating your budget (see Chapter 14) **until you know what you're really likely to receive.**

2

Tips

Working in a restaurant, you might receive a lower basic wage (remember, it's illegal for them to offer less than £4.10 an hour), but there will probably be tips on top of that. If you're taking a job with tips, check out the employer's policy. Some places will let you keep your own. At others, they split them equally and, occasionally, you find a tosser boss who pockets the lot. Sometimes, the boss pockets only the tips on credit card slips and you get any cash.

Tips can double your wages but, of course, don't – we repeat, don't – forget you are supposed to pay tax and NI on tips too. Definitely, supposed to. Okay? So, we told you *not* to just keep shtum. Right? So long as we've got that straight.

Aiming high

If you're a risk-taker, there are opportunities to make a lot more money – but the risk is that you make less, nothing or even lose out.

For instance, there are selling jobs out there that are 'commission-only'. You get a cut of any sales you make. The problem is, if you make nothing, you get nothing.

It's a mug's game, really, but if you reckon you could sell toilet roll to a constipated deaf man with no arms (or, even tougher, advertising space to small businesses), you might just hit the jackpot and rake in a lot more than most students.

Other high-stakes games including starting your own business. There are plenty of eighties throw-back entrepreneurs out there paying their way through university with their wheeling and dealing skills.

Among the popular ideas are running club nights and events, hiring out evening dress to students for balls, launching magazines and selling second-hand designer gear.

As we said, these are the popular ideas – in other words, other people try them regularly and most fail. Make sure there's a market with a gap in it and minimise your potential to lose big-time.

Other avenues for work

UNPAID WORK AND WORK EXPERIENCE

It may sound crazy, but it might pay in the long run to consider working for nothing, especially if looking for paid work is proving harder than hunting for condoms in a convent.

Work experience

A week or two of unpaid work experience during your vacation doesn't cost you anything but effort and may prove to be a clincher if you're trying to get into something highly competitive when you graduate (such as advertising, the media or banking).

Apart from the obvious benefits for your CV, it may boost your morale and, if you make yourself genuinely useful, they may even think of you if anything that pays crops up. Ultimately, it beats chasing non-existent jobs.

Don't let any employer take advantage of you, though. Even if they don't pay you, they should at least give you expenses for travel and maybe even lunch.

Just a quick plug for *Push's* own scheme – our research team is made up high-flying students and recent graduates. We do pay, but we're the first to admit it's less than our researchers are worth.

Over the years, because we only skim off the cream of students, it's come to be a well-respected feather in your cap as far as employers are concerned – especially in publishing, market research and the media. So, if your cap could do with feathering, check out Push Online (www.push.co.uk).

Voluntary work

There are profound advantages to voluntary work that have much greater meaning than money. Spirituality. Inner peace. A sense of giving and knowledge that your life has touched others'.

You don't buy that hippy stuff? Okay. Try this…

Future potential employers will be very impressed by your obvious goodwill and determined spirit. I mean, volunteering is all very well, but when you're rapidly becoming a charity case yourself, you want to see some benefits.

Working for dough 103

But back to the hippy stuff. It really does make a difference to thousands of projects going on in developing countries, not to mention the countless projects all over the UK.

There's everything from conservation work (the National Trust, who look after historic monuments and land) to helping the disabled (the Winged Fellowship Trust), from animal welfare (the RSPCA, animal shelters and other organisations that Rolf Harris interferes with) to the elderly (Help the Aged, who are more than just a song by Pulp).

There are almost always restrictions and conditions involved with helping out any of these schemes and while some organisations will pay general maintenance and travel, don't rely on it. Many schemes (such as Earthwatch, who do cool conservation projects all over the world or i-to-I, who do work, volunteer or teaching projects) will even expect you to fork out big sums in order to be allowed to help.

> **Get condoms for free from the doctor or family planning clinic in advance. Your sex life is at its most expensive if you rely on slot machines in pubs and clubs.**

Even so, it's well worth investigating the options. It's another line on the CV and will give you an inner feeling of harmony, man.

Most students' unions have a Student Community Action group that does work with all sorts of local projects. Some are more active than others. Some are less active than lead.

INTERNSHIPS AND TRAINEE SCHEMES
Monica Lewinsky was an intern at the White House when she did not have sex with *that* man. But not every internship promises to teach you quite so many uses for a cigar.

The idea is that, by spending a certain period working in an environment, you get an idea of what goes on and how to do it. There may even be a certain amount of showing you the ropes, but as often as not an intern is a fancy word for a gofer (as in 'go fer a cup of coffee, milk and two sugars, please').

Still, an internship or trainee scheme – especially a genuine one – is not only useful work experience. Since they're usually in high demand, it's like having a neon sign on your CV. It may even be a first step towards getting yourself a proper job with the organisation.

Best of all, they're often paid – not brilliantly, but what do you expect?

You may find them advertised in your university careers advice centre and there are guidebooks that list them (though the information is out of date almost before they hit the bookshops). **The Step Project** matches undergraduates up with business or technology projects – details at the back of the book.

Getting a place could involve an in-depth interview or even a series of interviews (especially if there's a chance that they might end up giving you a job after graduation).

The big, corporate companies are always on the lookout for the next bright young thing, but it's often a case of hundreds of applicants for every vacancy.

FILLING THE GAP

Back in **Chapter 2**, we looked at the whole issue of taking a year out – the pros and cons. So this is just a reminder that rather than work as a student when you've got studying to do, there's always the possibility of working first.

There are dangers – the biggest of which is that you get hooked on the idea of having money and decide that you don't want to go back to education.

Alternatively, you may develop expensive tastes in the meantime – or if not exactly expensive, they may not be as cheap as they should be if you want to stay solvent as a student.

The other big danger is that you spend all year working in order to make life more comfortable as a student, yet you don't actually save anything. Or worse, you get a headstart in the debt race. What a waste of a gap year that would be.

If you're going to spend the year saving, then save. If not, then make the most of it. Travel the world, save the planet – and just make sure you don't get into debt before you start.

It is, of course, possible to travel *and* save. Just about. Find yourself a cushy job somewhere exotic, then have a whale of a time and come back tanned and flushed.

Meanwhile, back in Blighty, there are plenty of year out programmes that offer work, experience and even, sometimes, the possibility of earning a few knicker.

For example, there is an organisation called **The Year in Industry** that places gap year students with companies all over the UK, in jobs paying about £8,000 for the year minimum. Getting a temporary placement through this scheme can be a bit of a door-opener and may give you sound business awareness, confidence and practical skills before you even start your university course.

There are regional centres for The Year in Industry all over the place, which schools and colleges usually know about. Alternatively, write to them at the address in the back of this book. We've also listed contact details for a number of other gap year organisations, including BUNAC and Council Exchanges.

There are specialist organisations tailored for adventurous students interested in art, science, conservation projects, amateur dramatics, sporting activities, wilderness exploration, teaching... just about anything that floats your boat.

JOBS ABROAD

If you haven't gone for the Gap Year option and you have a serious case of wanderlust, remember you still have that gorgeous three-month summer holiday from the beginning of July to the end of September each and every year for the duration of your course.

And three months is plenty of time to organise a few weeks abroad, get yourself a cheap travel ticket and hop on a plane to a far-flung destination.

Backpacking and inter-railing are notoriously popular with plucky student adventurers and there's no shortage of cheap travel firms, advice books and organisations.

Assuming you can afford it.

However, if you've blown your loan months ago, maxed out the overdraft and can't afford a holiday, then you face three options. First off, don't go. Secondly, spend most of the summer working at some no-brain job and saving up for a week or two at the end.

Or thirdly, get a paid job abroad. You can work on a kibbutz, supervise children on a summer holiday camp, be a nanny or an au pair (even if you're a bloke, if you think you're hard enough), teach, pick fruit, help run a hotel, assist a new business venture, pan for gold…

If working abroad over the summer appeals to you, make enquiries well in advance and, if you want to join a particular scheme, apply as soon as possible (at least six months in advance) to beat the rush.

It's a big bonus if you can speak a second language. Failing that, try America, Australia or New Zealand (where they speak something that sounds vaguely like English).

If you are going to be travelling to a country where you either don't speak the lingo or it's a bit rusty, consider taking a language refresher course – even if it only gives you enough to get by. Many universities offer them cheap to their own students, but often only during term-time – so plan ahead.

You don't even have to have the cost of the airfare to get abroad. BUNAC (details in the back) have introduced a deal to give interest-free airfare loans to cash-strapped students, who can then pay the money back as and when they begin paid work overseas. If you get work on the Summer Camp USA and KAMP programmes then your flights are usually paid for.

Even if you get a deal like this, however, don't leave home without enough dough (or some means of getting cash – such as plastic) to cover you for at least your first month. It can take easily that long for your first pay cheque to come through. If you're going to have to rent somewhere to stay, take enough to cover not only the rent, but the deposit too.

Buy a return ticket (not just a one-way), so if things go pear-shaped – financially or otherwise – you can at least get home.

Working abroad presents a swamp of practical puddles. You need a visa to work in some countries. You may need injections. You may not be allowed to work at all. To get into Malawi, men must have hair shorter than collar length. Honestly.

Preparation is your safety net. Take plenty of passport photos for assorted forms and ID cards.

Talk to other students who've worked abroad. Ask them for tips and contacts. Even if you've no intention of getting in touch with their second cousin once removed who lives on the other side of the country you're heading to, it may come in handy to have their number. When you land in jail for inadvertently giving a rude hand gesture when you only meant to hail a cab, it's good to have someone to call.

At *Push*, of course, we have our own useful contacts for you. They're at the back of the book under 'Summer Work Abroad'.

Sandwich courses

Sandwich courses are nothing to do with bread and fillings unless they happen to be sandwich courses in catering.

It's a metaphor. The bread symbolises slices of academic study. The filling is job experience on a work placement. In order to fit in the filling, most sandwich degree courses are four years rather than three.

The metaphor doesn't always work so neatly, because although there are 'thick' sandwich courses that involve a year or two at university, a year in work and then another year back at university, many sandwich courses involve more than one layer of filling and in only six-month layers. They call these 'thin' sandwich courses, but if you think about it, maybe 'club' sandwich courses would be truer to the trope.

We're clearly too hung up on the food thing.

Basically, sandwich courses – thin, thick, club, toasted, whatever – are those that involve an industrial placement as a compulsory part of the course.

This can be the answer to every strapped student's woes, because they usually get paid for the working part of their course.

It's rarely as much as they'd get if they were doing the job as a fully paid-up employee, but that's what's in it for the employer. The student gets to do their course and the employer gets someone cheap but capable.

As a result, sandwich students tend to have fewer financial worries than most. Better still, sandwich courses also have a pretty good record of getting students into jobs when they graduate, quite often with a company where they did a placement.

It's not all pay day and high living, though. There are added expenses for sandwich students. For example, you'll probably have to own a couple of smart outfits and there'll be dry cleaning bills to pay (something students normally only have to cover when they throw up on someone's ball outfit).

Then there's the effect on fees, awards and loans to consider.

AWARDS AND TUITION FEES FOR SANDWICH COURSES

If a work placement takes up a full year of the course, at home or abroad, it'll cut the cost of your fees for that year in half – currently £575. That also means that, in turn, your LEA won't pay an award of more than £575 to cover it.

For anything less than a full year, the full fees will still be charged and the full award will still be available to those who're eligible.

The same rules apply about who's eligible for awards and fees and who's not. See **Chapter 3**.

STUDENT LOANS FOR SANDWICH COURSES

Students on sandwich courses get a reduced level of student loan for any year in which they spend more than half the year doing a paid placement. It's just under half the maximum available normally, but at least it's not means-tested.

YES

You don't have to be on a sandwich course to get a bite of this particular snack.

Back in the late seventies, Aberystwyth University introduced a highly successful scheme called YES – the **Year in Employment Scheme**, which gives non-sandwich students the opportunity to take a year out in a work placement – whatever their own degree course. And now, you don't have to be studying in Wales to do it.

There are over 100 different types of placement and they're more varied than a packet of M&Ms, with several of them being abroad and most of them paid. In fact, unless you're working for a voluntary organisation like a charity, most students on placements get between £9,000 and £15,000 a year.

That sure fills a hole in your bank balance.

The icing on the cake (or sandwich) for participating students, apart from the personal and career development prospects and the financial boost, is that they don't have to pay any tuition fees during the year.

Student tax guide

INCOME TAX

Taxes are like Alcatraz after lights out. Nobody escapes taxes.

That goes for students, same as everyone. The difference is that although students have to pay income tax, the amount is usually zero. The difference may be subtle, but paying nothing is not the same as escaping them.

Everyone gets a personal non-taxable allowance which is the amount you're allowed to earn before the Government starts taking a cut. Tax years run from April to April (don't ask why – it's something to do with medieval sheep markets) and for the tax year that ended 5 April 2004, the personal tax allowance was £4,615.

So if, between 6 April 2003 and 5 April 2004, you earned or received income above £4,615, you were supposed to pay income tax (we hope you did) – although you only have to pay tax on the amount above the allowance, not on the whole lot. The more you earn the more you pay, but at first it's only 10%.

Loans and awards don't count as income. Nor do scholarships or bursaries. So really, we're talking about what you receive from paid work and there aren't too many students doing full-time courses who'll be earning more than four-and-a-half grand in a year.

So if you get part-time work or a vacation job, make sure your boss knows you're a student. They should have the appropriate forms which you'll both need to fill in and sign – they're not complicated, for a change, although you'll need your National Insurance (NI) number.

For temp jobs, the relevant form is called a P38(S) and for term-time work it's a P46. Where they come up with these crazy names, we'll never know.

Once you've filled in the forms, tax shouldn't be taken out of your wages. If you don't, however, it'll be deducted automatically. All is not lost if this happens. You can claim back any tax that you needn't have paid from the Inland Revenue at the end of the tax year, but it's a bit of a hassle and it does mean it's in their account rather than yours in the meantime.

The students who are most likely to end up paying more than nothing in income tax are those doing work placements (usually as part of a sandwich course, see above).

What they receive from their employer is subject to tax, although there are sneaky get-out clauses for certain money earned by certain students meeting certain conditions.

It's one to check out with your students' union officer or Tax Office.

Students with savings or investments might also end up paying tax if the income generated takes them over the £4,615 threshold. And if they've got that much stashed away, why not?

If, however, you have smaller savings, get in touch with whoever is paying interest or returns on those investments and ask that the money be paid gross (i.e. without the tax being taken off before they give it to you). That'll save you claiming the money back.

And if you find you're getting near the threshold, let them know and they can start deducting the tax again. Otherwise you may have to pay a lump sum when the taxman finishes their calculations.

Taxes are one of those things that are a total headache in life. Few people ever get their head round them properly and even if they do, the Chancellor only goes and changes all the rules at the next Budget anyway.

At some time while you're a student, you will almost certainly need advice about either paying or claiming back tax. When those times come, your local tax office is there to help or you can visit www.inlandrevenue.gov.uk, where you might want to get hold of any or all of the following leaflets, each more thrilling than a night in the bath with Dale Winton, a loofa and a packet of ginger nuts:

- Income Tax and Students (IR60)
- Income Tax and School Leavers (IR33)
- Pay as you earn (PAYE) (IR34).

If you're small enough, buy clothes in the children's department. There's no VAT, so it's like January sales all year round.

There's also a handy student tax checker on the website, which lets you calculate whether you've paid too much tax and could be due a refund.

NATIONAL INSURANCE (NI)

NI is separate from tax although it's collected by the same people at the Inland Revenue. In theory it pays towards your state pension and so on. You can't opt out of it, so it feels pretty much the same as a tax.

It's taken out of your salary by your employer who then pays it to the Inland Revenue (along with a little bit extra they have to add).

It's not much and how much you pay is related to how much you earn. As with tax, earnings under a certain threshold are exempt and so it's unlikely many students will have to cough up.

Chapter Eight

Scholarships, sponsorships, bursaries and grants

Money for nothing

The problem with awards is they only pay towards tuition costs. The problem with loans is you have to pay them back. The problem with working for money is, well… working.

Wouldn't it be nice if you could get money for nothing?

It's not quite as crazy as it sounds. There are various ways of getting money, if not for nothing, for very little at least.

Scholarships, sponsorships, bursaries and grants (sounds like a firm of solicitors) are all different ways of putting the fun into funding. Well, okay, 'fun' may be pushing it, but at least they take away some of the misery.

You don't hear much about them because it's not as if there's an ocean of money flooding the universities. It's more like a puddle, with too many people jostling to suck it up through straws.

Nonetheless, this puddle is in fact worth many millions of quid a year. That's the kind of puddle Push wouldn't mind getting splashed by.

However, most of the deals are either incredibly competitive or so specific that most students can't apply anyway. They don't get much publicity because that would only mean even more students being disappointed about not getting money, money that they wouldn't have otherwise known was even on offer.

What this means, however, is that a little research on your part can go a long way. It's like a lottery that not many people know about. Even fewer can win, but just by finding out about

it at all, you've got through the first stage of filtering out the losers.

Hunting down these sources of funding can be time-consuming, but don't be put off – there are more educational charities, trust funds, foundations and other professional organisations in the UK than you can shake a stick at. Though why you'd want to is anyone's guess.

Most rule out almost everyone from even applying, which means you won't get too many bites at the cherry. But it also means that if you find one that doesn't rule you out before you start, you may be one of only a few applicants.

So how do you go about finding one? Start by getting in touch with some of the specialist organisations listed in the back of this book and taking a look at some of the recommended reading. But before you go and do all that, you'll want to read this chapter to know what it's all about.

SO WHAT ARE SCHOLARSHIPS, SPONSORSHIPS, BURSARIES AND GRANTS AND HOW DO THEY DIFFER?

Once upon a time, the word 'grant' followed the word 'student' like a devoted puppy. But since the funding system was shaken up way back in ancient history – the 1990s – there's been a grant drought. As we go to press, that's in the process of changing and a new Higher Education grant has been introduced to give a top-up of funds to students from low-income families (see below). It's not exactly the generous grant of days gone by, but it's a start.

Nowadays, these terms are all used fairly inexactly for various sources of free money. You can use one instead of the other, in pretty much the same way that there's no need to know which is Ant and which is Dec.

There are distinctions between them, but there's as much difference between individual bursary deals, for example, as there is between the whole categories of bursaries and scholarships. And a sponsorship deal may include bursaries and scholarships may have sponsors and so on.

Having said that you can't really tell the difference, that's exactly what we're now going to try to do, by laying down a few general rules. Just go a bit easy on us when we have to make wild, sweeping generalisations, okay?

So here are some brief explanations to kick us off, with more detailed dissections below:

Bursaries and grants

These are contributions of money given to a student that don't have to be repaid and don't require them to do anything special to get it. It may – in fact, usually does – have certain qualifying conditions, but that's all.

Like we said, money for nothing. Conditions attached, but no strings.

Sponsorships

Sponsorships come from companies or organisations who have something to gain from giving you money, but it may not be anything that they get from you personally. A sponsorship will often include a 'bursary' (told you it got messy) awarded during term-time while you're studying.

Your sponsor may expect you to work for them before, during or after your course. But then they may well pay you extra for that work anyway, so who's complaining?

The strings attached to sponsorship are of varying thickness and can often be untied in any case. Even students on NHS-funded courses, for example, don't have to work for the NHS when they finish their courses.

Scholarships

Broadly speaking, scholarships plug whoever gives them – like a sponsorship – while giving a financial pat on the back to the students who get them for their personal achievements. That's usually the main criteria for getting a scholarship – you've done well at something or you're likely to.

Scholarships don't usually involve any industrial or commercial training or trade-off for favours that come with a sponsorship, but they may not be entirely without other strings.

Bursaries and grants

We're about to invent another distinction that doesn't really exist – between standard and special bursaries.

By 'standard' bursaries, we mean ones that are pretty much open to everyone, so long as they meet the rigid conditions.

By 'special' bursaries, we mean ones that are exclusive to particular institutions or one-off arrangements that don't get easily slotted into boxes.

2

STANDARD BURSARIES

Depending on your age, where you're studying, where you live, your background, your status, your personal academic success, your choice of course and probably how often you finished your greens as a kid, you may well be entitled to one of a few standard bursaries.

The first one to get your head around is the Higher Education Grant, appearing for the first time in 2004. It's available to new undergraduates from low income families – that's £21,185 a year or less, to be precise.

Because the cash comes from the Government and is dependent on household income, it's time to get all technical and cast your eye over this table of income thresholds to check eligibility. If you need a reminder of the finer details of how this income assessment stuff works, cast your eye back over **Chapter 3** – it's basically the same.

Household income	Amount of HE grant
£0-£15,200	£1,000
£16,000	£873
£17,000	£715
£18,000	£556
£19,000	£397
£20,000	£238
£21,185	£50
Above £21,185	Zilch

Independent students are just as eligible for the grant as their dependent counterparts. The only thing that really matters is their income – if it's low enough, they qualify.

The table below has the lowdown on the grant plus a couple of other standard bursaries. These are only for medical courses of different types (see **Chapter 10** for the full list of eligible courses and more about the tuition fees involved). If you want an NHS bursary, it doesn't matter if you've already done a degree and received public funding for it, you'll still be eligible.

For other healthcare courses you might get a bursary, depending on whether you can afford it without one.

In some cases, by the way, if you get an NHS bursary, because it gives you money you don't have to repay, you won't be able to get a student loan as well.

Type of bursary	What is it?	Am I eligible?
Higher Education Grant	An award for new undergraduates from low-income households.	New full-time and sandwich students and part-time initial teacher training students who start their course in the 2004/5 academic year.
NHS bursary for health professional courses	Grants and allowances to help students on full- or part-time pre-registration health professional courses. For full details about the help available, call the NHS Student Grants Unit on 01253 655655 (England), 02920 261495 (Wales), 0131 476 8227(Scotland) or 02890 524726 (NI)	You must be accepted for an NHS-funded place. If you are not eligible for an NHS bursary, you may still be entitled to help from your LEA or university.
NHS bursary for medical and dental courses	Bursaries and help with tuition fees for the final years of study.	UK undergrads doing standard 5- or 6-year medical and dental courses (or those on years 2-4 of the four-year graduate entry programmes)

> If you're going out with mates, meet at
> home first, do most of your drinking
> there and then go out. The off licence is
> way cheaper than pubs and clubs.

If you want to find out more about careers in the NHS and getting financial help from them whilst studying, call their careers helpline on 0845 60 60 655 or visit www.nhscareers.nhs.uk.

There are also a host of bursaries and bungs for students with children and students with disabilities. Find out more about these in **Chapter 13**.

How much and how is it paid?	How do I apply?
Up to £1,000. The SLC will pay it in three instalments along with your loan.	Make sure you fill out all the forms to apply for the means-tested portion of an LEA award. Eligible students should receive the dosh automatically.
The NHS pays your tuition fees in full whether you're studying at degree or diploma level. Students studying at degree-level can only apply for a reduced rate student loan from their LEA. Other support for living expenses may be available.	If you are offered a place on an NHS-funded health-professional course, your college will tell the NHS Student Grants Unit (SGU). The SGU will then contact you directly with an application pack which you should return to them as soon as possible.
Depending on your specific course and place of study, you'll get your tuition fees covered for your fifth and sixth years of study. You'll also be eligible to apply for a reduced-rate student loan for those years.	

SPECIAL BURSARIES

Most special bursaries and the like are only available at a particular university and some universities have a lot more than others. Some are open to all students, while others will be restricted to high-fliers on a designated degree course.

In future (i.e. from 2006, when the whole funding malarkey is due for a vigorous shake-up) bursaries should become far more common as universities will have to provide more cash support for poorer students if they want to charge higher tuition fees. Venerable institutions such as Imperial College, Exeter and Cambridge universities have already thrown their hats into the ring with promises of £4,000 for the brightest paupers. You can bet they won't be the only ones to jump on the bursary bandwagon.

Things aren't quite that rosy just yet, but there's still a fair few special bursaries out there for the taking. Since most of them are endowments from charities and ex-students, the longer a university has been around, the more likely it is to have stocked up on the goodies. Something to think about when choosing where to study, perhaps.

Often the money has to be spent on something in particular, such as travel or research costs, but, hey, it's their money – at least it's you who gets to spend it.

The catch is that you usually have to meet the right criteria for whatever hand-out is on offer. These tend to fall into three categories – being good at something, being a particular type of person or doing a particular course. Occasionally, there's a fourth: behaving in a particular way. Often it's a mixture of any of them.

So, being good at something. (You see? The distinction between bursaries and scholarships is crumbling before our eyes.) The most obvious thing to be good at is studying and there are millions of pounds in awards, scholarships, prizes, studentships, grants and bursaries for the top brain-boxes – especially if they're brain-boxed in a particular subject and they're willing to study it.

But there's also cash available for sports heroes, musical maestros and so on.

Next, being a particular type of person. Pick from the following list: poor; religious; from a particular place (such as local to the university, local to whoever put down the money for the scholarship in the first place or from another country); a parent (preferably single); from an ethnic minority; a student with a disability; or a woman.

Then there's doing a particular course – which is self-explanatory.

And finally, there's behaving in a particular way. This might include not drinking (is it worth it?), agreeing to do missionary work or caddying at a golf course.

Some of these hand-outs can be worth thousands of quid. For example, the University of Aberdeen has an annual Entrance Bursary Scheme, under which an elite band of really brainy students get £1,000 a year during their undergraduate degree. As is often the case, the applications need to be in quite early (in this case, by the end of March in the year the students want to start).

These big bounties tend to be the hardest to get – so don't get over-excited, not least because there are others which are worthless, sorry that should read 'worth less'. For instance, the J B Cobb Scholarship (available only to students at Exeter University) is worth a grand total of £12 a year.

Still, better than nothing.

> Buy fresh food from greengrocers and market stalls. Not only are fruit and veg cheap and nutritious they're also cheaper from these places than supermarkets, often by as much as half.

Sponsorships

Once upon a time employers were so keen to get graduates on their payroll that they were willing to fund them throughout their degree course (or in some cases, higher national diplomas). Sometimes the students didn't even have to go and work for the sponsor afterwards.

That, unfortunately, was in the days when you could throw rocks at a dozen people between the ages of 21 and 25 and not expect to have stoned a single graduate.

Nowadays, like the crocodile and the coelacanth surviving everything evolution could chuck at them over the millennia, while there are still quite a few sponsorship deals left, they're the relics.

Depending on the deal, taking a sponsorship might be like selling your soul and, even though you may need the cash, you should always check what Satan's going rate is these days.

In any case, virtually the only courses that attract sponsorship are the ones where employers have real trouble recruiting talent. They tend to be hardcore sciences, technical subjects (such as engineering), business studies, and economics or vocational courses.

Don't even bother looking for sponsorship to do philosophy, English literature or sociology. There are some sources out there, but you might as well spend the amount of time it would take to find one earning money the traditional way.

WHAT'S IN IT FOR THE SPONSOR?

Sponsors don't do it just because they're being nice.

They have good commercial reasons and ultimately they hope to gain at least as much if not more from the deal than the student. Highly capable and skilled people with management potential are a limited commodity and sponsorship is a way of getting in there before the competitors. It's like jumping the queue at the deli counter because they're running out of taramasalata. Perhaps not.

While it may feel like a great personal compliment if you're jammy enough and smart enough to nab yourself a sponsor, they'll probably be just as chuffed to have nabbed you.

WHAT DOES A SPONSORSHIP INVOLVE?

Most sponsors expect students to work for them at some point before, during or after their course.

But it's rarely a form of bonded labour. Often they'll pay not only for the time you're studying, but give you a decent wage while you're working for them too. What's more, when you're working, the learning won't necessarily stop. Usually there's at least some element of on-the-job training.

This may sound suspiciously like a sandwich course and, sure enough, they're one of the most lucrative ways to earn while you

learn these days. For more on sandwich courses, see the whole
section on them in **Chapter 7**.

However, sometimes you work for your sponsor during your
summer breaks instead.

Either way, the employer-cum-sponsor gets a chance to train up
and check out its sponsored students while the student gets a shufty
at the company's culture and working environment at the same time.

Obviously, everyone's hoping the student will want to work for
the company and the company will want to employ the student when
they graduate – however, there's rarely either a guarantee of a job or
a requirement to work for them.

**Some students wouldn't want a sponsorship even if they
found one knocking at the door. It can make you feel like your
options are closing down around you faster than village post
offices. You'll have various commitments – such as giving up
your summer holiday to work – and it may all be a waste of
time if you decide you wouldn't want to work in that industry
anyway, let alone for that company.**

If you don't enjoy working for your sponsor, things could get
awkward. After all, you're going to feel obligated to them. You're not
going to want to turn round and say, 'You know you gave me that
huge bundle of notes? Well, thanks, but now I've got my degree I'm
going to take it elsewhere.' It's only natural.

> Buy a beer making kit. It'll save you
> money and occupy all that time you
> wouldn't have if you actually turned up
> to lectures.

But there's no need to feel bad. If there's no commitment to
them, don't sweat it. That's their look-out. You can bet that if the
tables were turned and you'd blithely spent your student years
thinking you'd waltz into their offices the day after graduation, but
they'd decided they didn't want you, they'd have no qualms about
slamming the door in your face.

Indeed, most companies will get tough if you don't keep your
side of the deal – whatever it may be. They might stop your

payments or demand you give them back what they've paid you if you don't agree to join them after graduating.

Things like that will be in the contract in the first place, so think about them before you sign on the dotted line. How picky they are will usually depend on how much they're sinking into you. Always check the small print and ask about anything that isn't clear as clean glass.

And even if you do change your mind and want to back out, sponsorship's often far from a dead loss anyway. It's almost unbeatable experience, it looks like gold dust on your CV and – with anything from a few hundred to a few thousand quid a year – the financial rewards can be sweet as honey-coated sugar cubes.

WHO MIGHT SPONSOR ME?

There are basically four roads to sponsorships:

Employers: Especially the big boys like investment banks, engineering businesses and legal or accountancy firms.

The Armed Forces: The Army, Navy, Royal Air Force and Royal Marines all offer sponsorship (although they call them 'bursaries') to potential officers while they're in higher education. They're sometimes called 'cadetships'.

Although the actual conditions vary according to the amount they give you and which service you join, they'll usually demand that your course must benefit them somehow and also benefit you somehow once you've joined them after graduation. So hairdressing's probably out then.

Don't go for a cadetship if you wouldn't have wanted to serve in the Armed Forces anyway, because if in the end you decide these delights – travelling the world, meeting interesting people, killing them – aren't for you, then you'll need the permission of your commanding officer to leave and they'll want all their money back in full.

Things vary according to which force you're interested in. Army undergraduate bursaries are usually worth about £1,000 a year, while Navy bursaries can be up to £4,000 for engineering hopefuls. Special packages are available for medical students.

Students on most undergraduate bursaries remain civilians throughout their degree, but would be expected to spend a bit of time in the holidays on military larks. There are other options, such as sponsorship from sixth form onwards or starting military training before going to university.

Enquire at your local Armed Forces careers office or surf on to www.mod.uk/careers for more information.

Professional bodies: Engineering students are the prime targets for many sponsors.

Universities: Usually on behalf of employers.

These groups will see a few students through their education with amounts of money that allow them to live in the lap of luxury compared to other students, but aren't that much in the real world.

Sure, it's partly about competitiveness in the capitalist world, but you might want to ask yourself why they're so desperate. Is it because people like you really are an emerald among a sea of tinned peas? Or is it that something is putting everyone else off?

IS IT WORTH APPLYING FOR SPONSORSHIP AND, IF SO, HOW?

In the words of the great Scotty: It's a long shot, Cap'n, but it might just work.

If you're more ambitious than a hedgehog trying to hump a shoebrush and better at your chosen subject than a Mastermind Champion on steroids, then you are in with a good chance, especially if your subject is one of the really sexy disciplines such as engineering. (Sexy to sponsors, that is.)

There are various books worth looking at that list the likely targets, but make sure you look at a recent edition as they go out of date quicker than boy bands. They're listed in the back of this book. Your school, college, library or careers office will probably have copies and may also have helpful suggestions.

The more you can home in on what you want, the quicker and easier it'll be to compile your list of potential sponsors. Check your facts, compare salary possibilities, investigate the pros and cons and, if possible, talk to other sponsored students to get the inside story.

Above all, ask yourself if you are the right kind of person for the potential sponsor and suitably committed to a future with them. Remember – although there's usually a get-out clause for both parties – choosing a sponsor is tantamount to choosing a career.

Sponsorship doesn't have to start from day one.

It might even start before your course. Sometimes a prospective student will be working for a regular employer one day and the next, they'll have hatched a plan out between them that s/he should go off to university for a few years and that the employer should pay.

Or you might be offered sponsorship following some work experience in the summer before your course starts, for example, or during a gap year. Another good reason for doing work experience.

But more often, sponsorships are set up during your course, often as part of the process of finding somewhere to do a placement.

Then, sometimes, you'll be doing a placement and it'll be working out very cosily and eventually it turns into a longer deal.

And sometimes, it's just a case of sponsor turning up towards the end of a student's university career and deciding they want to muscle in on a bit of the action. By then, they reckon, you've already proved your dedication to your course and they haven't had to shell out for your first few years. Nearly a third of sponsors limit their schemes to final-year students.

If you've already started your course, but you're still interested in a sponsorship deal, just ask at the university's careers service – they'll have contacts with employers and will be able to advise you. Some, by the way, have much more intimate relationships with employers, sponsors and business than others.

Indeed, some universities – Warwick, for instance – even have a Student Sponsorship Officer specialising in matchmaking those with the money to those who need it.

Most sponsors don't advertise – there's no need. So you'll probably have to try a speculative application or two (or ninety-two). And don't focus only on the 'big name' companies – the smaller ones may be better targets as they'll get fewer applicants (and generally they're friendlier places to work).

Companies local to your home town are often a good bet, especially if you know someone on the inside.

Your choice of course should come *before* your choice of sponsor. If you're keen to work for a particular company and they say that to qualify for a sponsorship you have to do molecular science, don't jump in to the molecular pond with both feet.

It's better to match a sponsor to a course than a course to a sponsor. After all, the sponsor might say no and you're stuck doing something you wouldn't have chosen. More than one in six students drops out or fails their course and for many of them, choosing the wrong course didn't help. Students who flunk are often in the deepest financial crap of all.

Most of the time, the exact course isn't the big clincher anyway. So long as you're in the right ball-park, they'll be more interested in whether you've got the drive, the business instinct and the commitment.

Sponsorship needs to suit you. It has to fit in with what you wanted to do anyway. Otherwise it's just a pain in the neck. For one thing it can make it tricky to change courses if you need to. It can tie you down to what you do and when you can do it. And you'll resent all of that if it's holding you back.

Eventually it stops being worth it for the money. After all, the most important thing is to enjoy being at university and to get the most out of it. If you end up changing course and your sponsor dumps you, so be it.

Bear in mind that for every sponsor, there are hundreds of other students probably as keen as you to take their dosh. If you want to be sponsored throughout your course, start sending applications as soon as your UCAS form's done.

Whatever you do, get in there early and keep your expectations realistic.

Also see the section on **Filling a Gap** in **Chapter 7** for details about **The Year in Industry scheme** – a kind of makeshift sandwich course programme.

ALTERNATIVES TO SPONSORSHIP

Employers wanting to bribe graduates these days often go for a more direct approach than traditional sponsorship – 'the golden hello' – where they pay thousands of quid to them just to join the company. Sometimes they offer to pay off your student debts.

In fact, even the Government's got in on the act offering to pay off student loans for graduates willing to become teachers in subjects where there are shortages (if they stick at it for a year or two).

A warning though: apart from teachers, it's usually only real high-flyers who get the dough from these deals and they're usually attached to very particular jobs.

Recently, a couple of top accountancy firms and management consultants have been doing it. But don't count on it though. They may not be offering it by the time you're ready and you may not get it anyway.

Scholarships

Scholarships reward students for being brilliant at sport, music, public speaking, writing – virtually anything you can think of. Even academic work.

When we say 'brilliant', in fact you only need to be better than – or even only as good as – anyone else who applies. Indeed it may well not even be an open competition, in which case the word 'competition' would be something of an overstatement.

Like special bursaries (see above), apart from being good at something, you'll normally have to fulfil various criteria. You may need to be under 18 on the third Sunday in August, the orphaned second daughter of a doctor or an ex-student of a certain school in Bognor and the proud owner of a pet rabbit called 'Chuckles'. Or something.

Some scholarships aren't fussy about how you spend the money and some are just for tuition costs – but others can get very particular about what they will and won't fund. For example, they may be for travel costs only or to study abroad, to fund some research, even to buy a musical instrument or sports kit. There are even scholarships that only cough up in book tokens. (What do they think this is? Blue Peter?)

As you'll probably have already realised, a lot of the nuts and bolts of bursaries can be screwed equally on to scholarships and, if they can't, you can be pretty sure that the sponsorships toolkit will work.

There are four fountains of funds when it comes to scholarships.

INSTITUTIONAL AID

Institutional aid comes in the shape of a gift to a student direct from the university or college's own funds, usually to promote some special facet of university life and/or study.

Your first point of reference should be the university prospectus, which may give you an idea of some of the awards on offer (or at least a contact name and address), but also keep an eye on department noticeboards once you've started studying.

PRIVATE FINANCIAL AID

Sometimes – when they're more fussed about getting good publicity than doing direct recruitment – companies opt to offer scholarships rather than sponsoring students.

These may or may not come with conditions about doing work for the company. Whether they do or not, a lot of the same advice about sponsorship applies (see above).

PHILANTHROPIC AID

Sometimes individuals, charities or trusts decree that students should benefit from a scholarship. Far more important than decreeing anything, they also stump up the lolly.

The reasons why are their own. Sometimes it's the parents of a former student who died that they want to commemorate. Sometimes it's an ex-student who's gone on to make their fortune and who wants to help others (or just gloat). Sometimes it's a tax dodge. Whatever the reasons, who cares? So long as they show you the money.

Most have an application deadline, but may still keep you waiting for months before responding. Before applying to any charity, it's worth making a few preliminary enquiries to find out what they're looking for and if your odds of getting any dosh are any better than a well-fattened cow's chance in a steakhouse.

Where to get the details

For starters, try your university's admissions office and ask them what they know about scholarships and how to apply. While you're at it, you might as well find out about bursaries and sponsorships too.

Failing that, you could try The Education Grants Advisory Service – or EGAS to its friends. It is one of a small number of organisations that offers advice to undergraduate students about which charities to contact for grants of any kind.

If you write to them with your details they'll then send you a list of likely names and addresses and a leaflet about the whole application process. For EGAS's contact details and further reading, see the back of the book.

Note that when it comes to financial help, most organisations try to help those who deserve it most. That usually means either those with the biggest financial challenges – single parents, disabled students and those from disadvantaged backgrounds – or those who show the most promise.

Chapter Nine

Other sources

When it comes to what you have to live on, all we've really heard about so far are loans and overdrafts (which you have to pay back), parental contributions (which they may not be willing or able to give), money from paid work (which you have to earn) and various grants such as bursaries and scholarships (which most students aren't likely to get).

Frankly, it's a pretty pathetic whip-round. Like the collection plate in a prison chapel, there'll be less at the end than when you started.

So where else does the debt-driven student turn?

Here are a few suggestions. Unfortunately, most of them are either only for the heroically hard-up or come with a day-glo health warning.

Access to Learning Fund

There is an official emergency fund given by the Government to universities to rescue students who find themselves up a certain creek without a paddle, life jacket or even a piece of driftwood. As of 2004, it is known as the Access to Learning Fund or the Financial Contingency Fund in Wales and replaces the hardship funds and loans scheme.

The Fund is open to all hard-up, full-time and part-time UK undergraduates – but because of limited availability, the money usually goes on a first-come, first-served basis. Even if you have a genuinely urgent case, you may still end up disappointed, particularly if you leave it till later on in the academic year to apply.

The amount of money that each university has to distribute depends partly on how many students they've got, but only partly – it also varies according to the students' backgrounds and so on. The universities are free to hand out the money as they see fit within certain guidelines. Some decide to help just a few people a lot, others prefer to help a lot of people just a little.

Generally they prioritise students from poorer backgrounds and those with particular difficulties – such as a disability or kids (those with kids may not appreciate the distinction). They also tend to favour students who've made it through to the final year of their course.

How do I apply?

There'll be a department of the university admin that deals with these funds – usually called something like 'Student Services'. If you can't find out who to ask, try the students' union welfare department.

Student Services (or whoever) will get you to fill out a form that details any money you have coming in, and evidence of just how broke you are.

They should give you a decision within a month, although if the situation's really extreme, they might let you know sooner and even let you have a cheque within a few days. That's not the norm, however, and it's better to apply before the situation becomes really desperate – it'll only have got worse by the time you see any money.

To get any money at all, you'll need to prove you're in financial 'hardship'. The definition of that is as fuzzy as a night on tequila, so the university is basically free to make it up as they go along. The main limiting factor is the amount they have to give out and how thinly they're likely to have to spread it.

Keep a pocket diary handy and make a note of everything that you spend with daily and weekly totals. This makes living frugally into a competition with yourself, as well as making you aware of where it's all going.

As a result, you may have to come up with some hard evidence to back up your case, because any money they give you won't be available for anyone else. You may well have to pull out rent books and bank statements and if there's a sorry trail of debits to Armani, Tiffany's and Le Manoir (or even French Connection, HMV and Pizza Hut), it won't help your case.

The funds are given to students in crisis, particularly if they've been hit with huge or unexpected expenses. The amount paid out, therefore, is often just enough to cover a particular bill. The funds are also intended to help those students who may be considering giving up their course because of financial problems, which might be worth bearing in mind if you're trying to concoct a convincing sob story.

Priority will also go to certain groups of students:

- Students with kids, especially lone parents
- Other mature students, especially those with existing financial commitments
- Students from low-income families
- Disabled students
- Students who have been in care
- Homeless students (or in shelter housing)
- Students in their final year.

That's not to say others can't apply. It might just take a bit more to convince the people in power of your worthiness for assistance.

If you need to, you can go back as often as you like in a year, but the university's patience may wear a bit thin and, once the fund runs dry, the stream won't start flowing again until the next academic year. All too often, the piggy bank's empty even before Christmas comes around.

Payments are usually given as grants, although occasionally you might get a short-term loan, for example to tide you over until some cash comes in from another source.

Your university student services will give you more information and let you know their own guidelines and policy (if they have one).

Borrowing from friends

As a rule. Don't do it. Ever.

Even if your friend happens to be one of those lucky bastards who takes out a student loan just so they can stick it in a high-interest account and reap the rewards after picking up the interest.

Even if your friend has recently won the lottery, lives in a castle in Hampshire, drives a Ferrari and shops in Harvey Nichols because the student discount shops are so frightfully common.

Even if your friend is a friend of royalty – in fact, even if they *are* royalty, *don't* borrow from them.

Just don't.

Unless – and this is just about the only exception – you really don't want them to be your friend any more. Because they won't be.

Every day that you're not paying them back, they'll be wondering whether you ever will. They'll be wondering whether you think they're a stupid sap that you've just managed to take for a ride, wondering whether you're really that selfish, wondering whether you're sleeping with their boyfriend/girlfriend too and wondering – no, not wondering – *telling* people that it's you who never washes up, who always leaves the milk out to go sour and always finishes the toilet roll without ever replacing it.

By then, paying them back won't make any difference.

There may well be times when friends will offer to help out. That's what friends are for.

Sometimes, you will have little choice but to accept, such as when you find yourself short of a bus fare at the end of the night or your housemate has done the shopping and you owe them for milk, bread and toilet roll but you can't get any money till next week.

Situations like these provide another exception to the rule. It's okay because (a) it's **short term** (the shorter the better – it starts to get dangerous after a few hours, literally), (b) they're only bunging you a few quid (the fewer the better) and (c) you'd do the same if the roles were reversed.

That's the crunch factor. **Ask yourself if you'd do the same if the roles were reversed. If you're in any doubt, forget it, put the shopping back on the shelves, whatever it takes.**

The other possible exception is when your friend can afford it easily and is not a student. (Although they must understand that you will continue to be poor for at least as long as you remain one yourself.)

Even then, proceed with extreme caution and follow the four cardinal rules of borrowing from friends:

- Make sure that both of you know exactly where you stand and that you make no promises or guarantees that you are either unable or don't fully intend to keep.
- Write an IOU. Ultimately, it will count for nothing other than reassurance that that you're as good as your word. The ritual return of an IOU (if carried out within sufficiently short time) symbolises the return of the relationship to a status quo.
- Always repay your debt fully, promptly and in accordance with your original promise. Oh and when you do, it doesn't hurt to buy a small gift. A drink will do, just something to show you appreciate your debt was more than just the money.
- Never *ask* to borrow money from a friend and don't be too ready to accept it if it's offered. (And don't insult their intelligence by dropping hints, either.)

These rules are good even after graduation, but while you're a student you should treat them as if they make the Ten Commandments look like the instructions on a packet of Pot Noodles.

Parents are one thing – they produced you and may even be impressed by your promises, however insincere, to pay them back.

But being in debt to a friend is something altogether more horrid to contemplate. It can break up friendships previously thought to be stronger than Carbon-60 (which makes mincemeat out of steel). That even includes boyfriends and girlfriends. People who you think you know well have strange and hidden feelings about money (especially if they haven't got much).

Likewise, if you're not prepared to borrow from a friend, don't lend to one either. Even if you trust your mate 100%, there is a good chance that you won't see the money again for a long time, if ever.

It's better just to give them money than lend it. And don't get your hopes up that they might give you some in return one day.

Credit, loans and sharks

There's a whole ocean of sharks out there and not all of them have fins. Whenever you borrow money, know the terms and conditions.

Know when they want it back and how much interest they'll be charging in the meantime. That applies whoever the lender is – your bank, the Student Loans Company, but especially any service not specifically designed for students and/or not recommended by your students' union. (If in doubt, ask the welfare department.)

Interest rates

Bear in mind that interest rates are almost invariably 'compound'. In other words, 10% a year on £1,000 may mean 'only' £100 in the first year, but it won't mean £300 after three years. In the second year, there'll be interest on the first year's interest and in the third year, interest on the interest, making £1,331 you have to pay back.

And that's if the interest is calculated annually. It may well be more often than that. If 10% annual interest is added monthly, for instance, you'd be looking at more like £1,348.18 after three years. If it's added daily, it'll be even higher.

Lenders all use terms like APR, AER and so on. They mean standard things. Don't worry about learning the distinctions, just understand what it means in real terms to you or suddenly a great-looking deal of 5% a month may mean you're paying over 85% a year.

SPECIALIST CREDIT AND LOAN COMPANIES

Be particularly wary of taking out a loan or borrowing money from any organisation that isn't specifically geared towards students. They might be kosher as bagels and chicken soup, but that doesn't mean that their deal will be right for the peculiar circumstances of being a student.

Basically, it's not usually a good idea. The interest rates are often high and you usually need to start repaying long before a student is likely to be ready to do so. The terms of these loans are rarely such that many students could deal with them.

Because students can't usually pay back within the terms of the loan, these companies don't usually want to lend to them anyway.

It's not worth it to them to charge you interest you can't pay. That's not how they make money. The best they'll be able to do is send round the bailiffs to take your stereo, your CD collection and your books (which probably won't cover the cost of the bailiffs). (You don't want to think about the worst they could do.)

They're only interested in people with a steady income to pay back what they borrow or people who can guarantee the loan with something worth taking if they need to.

If they're not bothered about such things – be afraid, be very afraid. Unsecured loans are costly as caviar and as risky as naked ferret-farming.

Even those companies that are prepared to lend to students won't offer as good a deal as the Student Loans Company and won't offer such a convenient repayment package. And if they claim to, be very suspicious – there can't be anything in it for them. It's only worthwhile to the SLC because the Government pays them.

SHORT-TERM EMERGENCY LOANS

If you aren't eligible for the access to learning fund (see above) or if you've already got it, but are still in deep crap, you may need a quick-fix solution.

Don't be tempted to turn to loan sharks and independent brokers. It's a rocky road to oblivion for anyone and students shouldn't even contemplate going there.

Go to your student welfare department and get advice. It probably won't come to it, but even if you have to drop out of university, it's better than working the rest of your life to pay sums some shark dreamt up when thinking about the population of China.

A PACK OF CARDS – CREDIT, CHARGE AND STORE CARDS

We're back on vaguely respectable ground here, but unless you're careful and responsible, the dangers are still big as a cockroach in your ice cream.

Cards, however, do have their plus points if used frugally.

They're convenient (especially over the phone or 'net) and, if you only spend what you can afford and always pay off what you owe on time, then you can actually use them as a way of keeping money in your account for as long as possible.

They're also very easy to use and for this reason alone should be treated with caution – the more accessible the credit, the faster the debts will snowball.

Credit cards

Britain is a nation of credit card fiends and students are no exception.

Credit cards can be used all over the UK and in many places abroad as well – most shops, supermarkets and restaurants – as well as for a wide variety of internet purchases.

Credit cards such as Mastercard and Visa are issued with a monthly spending limit that you mustn't exceed. (In fact, whatever purchase would send you over the brink may be denied if you try.) Like with overdrafts, it may be possible to get your limit bumped up a bit by asking nicely before you exceed it.

The interest rates for cards with the main student bank accounts tend to be between 15 and 30%, although these can change rapidly. Your own bank's credit card might not be the best deal for you, so shop around a bit.

Some charities, political parties and other organisations (even some universities) now offer their own cards, but these tend not to be designed for students, so check the terms.

Every month you'll get a statement, telling you exactly where you have used your flexible friend and the total damage. It'll also tell you the minimum you absolutely have to pay and by when.

If you pay the whole lot in one go you won't have to pay any interest on the balance. If you don't, however, the interest will grow on the balance like mould on a forgotten cheese sandwich.

Credit cards are ideal for short-term credit, but don't get carried away – when you first get one it can feel like free money, which it most certainly isn't. In the long-term it's a ridiculously expensive way of borrowing, but if you use your credit card in moderation you will probably find it is a good way to spread payments for essential purchases and it can help ease temporary cashflow problems.

But if those temporary problems don't get plugged, credit card debt can mount and mount until just the interest repayments alone are costing several hundred pounds a year.

Keep track of what you owe and always try to pay your bill in full. Most of all, don't develop swipe-happy habits.

Charge cards

Charge cards work in much the same way as credit cards, only you pay an annual fee for the privilege instead of paying any interest on money you owe.

The reason you don't pay interest is that you're not authorised to use the card unless you can pay off the whole debt each month. You usually have to set up a direct debit with your bank account, so they can just help themselves to the money when it's due.

The most common charge card is American Express (although they offer credit cards too – see above) and it's only really a way of spreading out your payments.

Store cards

Store cards also work in much the same way as credit cards, but you can only use them in one shop or chain of stores (or sometimes a group, e.g. a Dorothy Perkins card can be used in BHS).

> I set up accounts for different things —
> one for bills, one for travel funds etc.
> Whatever's left in my current account I
> can spend on goodies and I don't have to
> worry about not having any money to pay
> bills at the end of the month.
> Karen Baxter, London

Most stores will only issue you with a card subject to a satisfactory credit check. Nevertheless, plenty of shopaholic students would have little difficulty in getting one – or worse, several.

Before even thinking about a store card, answer the following questions honestly. Can you resist a skirt/shirt/other item of clothing if it's a bargain? If you owned four pairs of jeans, would you think you had enough? Do you think it's too much to own at least one album in the charts at any given time?

If the answer to *any* of questions was 'no', do yourself a favour – go nowhere near a store card till you're earning twenty grand plus.

Resist the sales patter, even if they're offering discounts and freebies to card holders. You often pay the extra in card charges or interest anyway and, in the case of many high street fashion outlets, students can get just as good a discount just by flashing proof that they're a student.

Store cards can be a famously sure-fire way to get up to your ears in debt in lightning time.

What's more, you'll find that most stores won't be too sympathetic to the plight of students who can't pay up. Eventually, they'll come down hard and send round bailiffs to take back what you bought and pretty much anything else they take a shine to in order to pay off the debt.

Superdebts

People who end up on *Trisha* with debts the size of telephone numbers usually managed it with the help of plastic and with credit and store cards in particular.

Having more than one card which gives you any kind of credit (as opposed to your bank debit card which transfers money straight out of your account) is like juggling sharp knives coated in oil, not least because some people are tempted to try the impossible and pay off one debt by putting it on another credit card. There's consolidation and then there's just plain stupidity.

See **Chapter 14** for advice on how to get the most out of your credit card without having a panic attack every time your statement arrives.

Kiting

'Kiting' is when someone reports their card as stolen and then in the short period of time between the report and the official recording of the incident (when the card is barred so that shops won't accept it), they go wild in the aisles. They hope they won't be held accountable for the purchases.

The banks and credit companies have wised up to this practice and there are way too many in-store cameras these days, so don't even think about it.

Kiting, and indeed any kind of credit card fraud, is a serious criminal offence that can lead to a massive fine and

black-listing at best, prosecution and jail at worst. To cap it all, it'll probably get you kicked out of university.

Back to the banks

OVERDRAFTS

As we said in **Chapter 6**, a bank overdraft is the cheapest and easiest type of student borrowing – cheaper even than the student loan, at least until they start charging you interest.

Once you've signed up and completed all the necessary forms, your bank should send you written confirmation of your authorised overdraft limit (anything up to about £2,000, but usually less, especially if you are a first year).

If at any point you think you're in danger of going over the limit, get in touch with them immediately. They'll make an individual judgement based on your circumstances as to whether they'll let you have more.

Their decision will in part depend on how well you've looked after your finances to date and how much you've kept them in the picture.

For example, HSBC's standard package means that they'll only increase your overdraft limit each year if you've demonstrated sound money management and have not abused the bank privileges. Barclays' package also provides an automatic 'buffer' of up to £200, but if you want more than that you'll need to complete an official overdraft application. NatWest say they are fairly accommodating about increasing overdraft limits, so long as the student approaches them for help in good time.

Although having an overdraft is the least expensive and most convenient way of borrowing, never get complacent about being in debt to a bank. Treat them as if they were holding the rug under you feet and they could tug whenever they like.

PERSONAL BANK LOANS

If your overdraft and the student loan just aren't going to cut it, you can arrange a personal loan with your bank.

You borrow an agreed amount over an agreed period and agree to repayments, which are usually agreed monthly amounts at an agreed rate of interest. There's a lot of agreeing to be done, so when choosing your bank check that they offer good terms for personal student loans.

Shop around, as it could save you money in the long run.

In general, banks are not the best bet for long-term borrowing for students – that would be overdrafts and student loans – but they're better than other money-lending companies.

LOAN ADVICE

Some people think that if they borrow small amounts from a wide variety of different places, spreading their debts around, this will somehow be better than borrowing larger amounts from one or two places. Then again, some people believe in alien abductions and that Elvis really is dead.

The more debtors you have, the greater the risk – better to stick with the student loan, the overdraft and, if absolutely necessary for specific situations, no more than one other reputable funding source (such as a student credit card for short-term cashflow shortfalls or a personal loan for a big single expense).

Any more than that and you will find it very difficult to keep track of your money and your borrowings, not to mention your repayments. If you fail to keep up repayments on just one loan, this could result in you being 'blacklisted' – which means the word goes round the credit companies, mortgage companies, banks, building societies, TV rental shops, hire purchase firms and probably the local pub that you're a financial leper who shouldn't be trusted.

There's no such thing as an official blacklist, but if you want credit, people have access to your 'credit history' and they'll all make similar judgements about a dodgy past. It can take years to rub the slur from your good name.

Never borrow more than you can realistically pay back and don't agree to anything that asks you to pay it back any sooner than you'll be able. It's all very well thinking you can worry about repayments later, but when they hit, they'll hit hard.

Some companies will offer to 'consolidate all your existing loans' into one big loan (with 'easy to manage' monthly repayments). The idea's okay, because it's better to have a single payment of a fixed amount taken out of your account at a certain time each month, rather than direct debits of various amounts flying at you throughout the month. In practice, however, they'll probably want a higher interest rate.

So keep to as few lines of debt as possible in the first place and 'consolidation' won't be necessary. If possible, stick to the student loan from the start – relatively speaking, the interest rate is microscopic.

For advice on how to make your student loan last and so avoid borrowing from other sources, see **Chapter 14**.

By the way, Elvis is alive and well and working for a branch of Lloyds TSB in Ormskirk.

CAREER DEVELOPMENT LOANS

Career Development Loans (CDLs) are a Government-funded scheme to help people who're doing vocational training courses. If it ain't vocational, then you won't qualify.

Most undergraduates don't qualify anyway because you can only get a CDL for a course that the LEA or NHS won't fund. (It doesn't matter if you don't get funding from your LEA, just whether the course qualifies.)

However, CDLs can be helpful for some postgrads and students doing courses of two years or shorter. (Or three years if it includes a year's work experience.) If the course lasts longer than that, you may still get a CDL to fund part of it.

The scheme is run through three of the high street banks: Barclays, The Co-operative and The Royal Bank of Scotland, who will lend between £300 and £8,000 to cover up to 80% of your course fees (or 100% if you've been unemployed for three months or more at the time you apply) plus any other necessary costs (books and materials). You can only get money for general living expenses if your course is full-time.

The Department for Education & Skills (DfES) is behind the scheme and they pay the interest on CDLs while you're training and for up to a month after you've finished.

Talk to all the banks offering CDLs before going with any one of them. You don't have to have an account with them already and they do offer slightly different terms and conditions. You can only apply to one bank in the first instance, though you are free to apply to the others if your application is rejected.

A free booklet is available about the Career Development Loans. See the contact details at the back of the book.

Benefits

We'll let you into a secret. When we were planning this book, we thought we'd write a whole chapter on benefits, but it took all of ten seconds to realise it would be a paper-wastingly short chapter.

Most students are basically excluded from most of the social security benefits system, not least housing benefits or dole (oops, Job Seekers' Allowance) during vacations.

However, there are exceptions both to the 'most students' part – students with kids, for instance, or with a disability can get support – and to the part about 'most benefits' – for example, there's help for students with prescription charges, not because they're students but because they're on a low income (if they are).

For more on special cases, see **Chapter 13**.

Council tax

Full-time students are usually exempt from council tax unless they have a second home. Your university will give you a certificate to send off to the local council to prove you're a student and that should be the end of it.

Tax credits

There may be some extra help for students with children through the tax credit system – see **Chapter 13**.

Barrel-scraping ideas

SELLING AND PAWNING STUFF

Some students, in their blind desperation, will take their most prized possession – a hi-fi, an electric guitar, a signed photograph of Justin Timberlake – down to the pawn shop and get as much as they possibly can for it.

The pawn shop acts like it doesn't want that tat, then buys it (usually at a fraction of what it's worth) and promises not to sell it for a while. If the student returns within that time and gives the pawnbroker back their money (plus a handsome interest, of course), then they can have their goods back. If not, they have to run the risk that the pawnbroker will sell it to someone else first.

Then there are other students, bless their hearts, who put an ad in the local paper or the local newsagent offering anything they own that might be worth a few quid.

These are desperation tactics and they should never be necessary.

If you're starting to see some of your precious 'luxury' items as a way of paying next month's rent or the watch your gran gave you for your 18th birthday begins in your head to resemble a good square meal, then you should get down to the bank or the students' union welfare department and discuss less drastic measures.

You should not have to give up the personal things you value just so you can afford to live. Even if you think you'll be able to buy them back eventually, it's not the answer to even the most urgent situation.

Other sources will lend you money more cheaply and without expecting you to give up your belongings before you're even supposed to repay the debt, let alone before you've failed to do so.

Of course, if you have an old pile of textbooks you don't need, a CD collection you no longer listen to, an unwanted Christmas pressie from Auntie Edna or any old junk you think you could flog, there are ways of swapping genuinely unwanted stuff for much more useful stuff – cash, for instance.

Most universities have a second-hand student bookshop, which will give you cash for your old textbooks. It can also be worth advertising your wares on department or students' union noticeboards, particularly if the books are still on the reading list for the up-and-coming year.

Amazon.co.uk lets you sell unwanted books and the like to other buyers for a small fee, or you may be able to make a pretty penny by auctioning just about anything you can think of on www.ebay.co.uk (apparently, they won't let you sell human organs). Also, check out the website www.studentswapshop.co.uk – or your university may have a special swap shop scheme of its own.

Just don't go getting rid of anything unless you're pretty sure you didn't want it anyway.

BEING A LANDLORD

Actually, it's not quite as crazy as it sounds.

Some parents are in a financial position to guarantee a mortgage and, by owning property, not only does the student get the ultimate in independent living for themselves, but while interest rates are low the mortgage payments may work out cheaper than rent.

Meanwhile, the student home-owner can now do the landlord thing and get a few other students in as housemates, charge them a going rent and maybe even wipe out their own contribution to the mortgage altogether. If they're really lucky, the property's value will go up and they can move out when they sell it, clearing their student debts with the tidy profit.

Sounds great, eh?

Unfortunately, it's full of pitfalls. Even the process of buying a property (rather than the property price itself) can cost more than a year's rent and it's a sackful of hassle too. Then there's finding the readies for furniture.

Also, once you own property, you can't complain to the landlord when the boiler blows up or the roof collapses. You could have a situation where you can't even live there yourself, let alone charge rent to anyone else, unless you find hundreds of quid to mend your plumbing.

Meanwhile, although being a live-in landlord isn't as bad as just being in it for the money, there's a bundle of red tape over contracts and safety and all the rest.

Finally, as they say in the small print, the value of your investment can go down as well as up.

Strictly for the wealthy or risk-junkies.

GAMBLING

Another one for the risk-junkies. And maybe the maths undergraduates, although most of them will have worked out that the odds are always stacked against the gambler.

Any money you spend on gambling, whether it's the lottery, scratch cards, horses, dogs, slot machines, poker or speculative share trading, should not be regarded as an investment and nor should any money you happen to win be regarded as income. You're too likely to lose it unless you never gamble again.

Gambling profits and loss belong strictly under the heading 'entertainments' in your budget (see Chapter 14**). If you gamble at all as a student, you gamble for fun and since gambling's most fun when there's real risk involved, you should consider it a source of fun you can't afford.**

There have been professional poker players on degree courses, but not as many as there have been students who've thrown away money they didn't have. Definitely not a source of income.

There is one exception to the above, but it hardly has the thrill of true gambling – premium bonds, which, if you want to buy yourself the dream of winning big are the cheapest way to do it because you can cash them in again.

If, however, you have enough money to leave in premium bonds for long enough to make it worth the effort, then you could find much better things to do with the cash that are far more likely to yield a decent return.

ILLEGAL ACTIVITIES

Now, of course, illegal activities are against the law. That goes without saying, so we're now regretting that we bothered to say it. However, for some students, simply being against the law doesn't seem to be enough motivation not to give them a try.

So if that doesn't convince you, remind yourself why you're at university in the first place. Breaking the law to get money to complete your studies is an utter waste of time because, if you get caught, you'll probably have your ill-gotten gains confiscated and be drummed out of university in double time. And the problem with assuming you won't get caught is that you can't be sure – you won't even have a clue – until it happens.

Some offences, busking without a licence, for instance, certainly don't seem too serious and tend not to carry jail sentences. What's more, until musical incompetence is classified as a crime, you're unlikely to get chucked out of the university for being hauled up in front of a magistrate for playing 'Blowing in the Wind' in the street.

If, however, you choose the wrong patch or your rendition is so bad that it has Bob Dylan leaping into his grave just so he can turn in it, then not only are you unlikely to make much money, but if you also end up with a fine it can undermine the whole purpose of the exercise.

Drug-dealing, however, is, if you'll excuse the expression, a much bigger deal.

We're not going to pretend there aren't students who do drugs. There are.

We're also not going to claim that there aren't a few students who start off just scoring for themselves and a couple of mates who quickly find they've got a lot more friends and a bigger bank balance. It happens, but don't let it be you.

Students have often been thrown out just for using drugs when they've been caught (and in a tight-knit community like a university, it's pretty easy to work out who's doing what). As for dealing, a university's sympathy will disappear faster than coke up a rock star's nostril and it will often be the university itself pushing the police to bring charges.

Then there's sex.

A few students – a very few – work in the sex industry and if they're okay with that and they're not breaking the law… well, that's their call. It is not, however, the best way to deal with financial problems. Other less risky occupations pay better and involve less hassle.

A lesbian student recently made just over £8,000 auctioning her virginity to avoid debts, but common sense and the amount of press coverage the act generated suggests this is the exception rather than the norm.

There may be good money to be made by young attractive people working for the less sleazy escort agencies and strip joints (as if any strip joint isn't sleazy). But the problem is not knowing what you're getting into.

Everything might look okay, but in any industry that hangs over the edge of legality, you're always too close for comfort. Whatever pleasant assurances you might be given to start with, you can't know that it's not going to go further than you'd like. Only when it does will you find out and by then you may find you're already in an uncomfortable, possibly even threatening, situation.

As for prostitution, the act itself is not illegal but soliciting is. It's also a dangerous environment involving enormous mental anguish for all but the most firm of purpose and medical dangers for everyone (not just those who don't practise safe sex).

Again, the fact that things are against the law shouldn't be your only deterrent. Common sense should tell you there are easier ways of getting by.

As a general rule, if you wouldn't be happy telling your mum, your friends, your tutor and your bank how you got your money, you should think seriously about whether you're not risking or giving up too much for the sake of too little.

2

ID PARADES

There is, however, one option that lets you brush with the underworld without actually doing anything illegal. The police are always on the lookout for willing volunteers to stand in a room with a suspect. Not just for fun, but to see if witnesses can pick out their man – or woman – from a handful of people who look similar.

```
Don't bother with dial-up internet access
at home. Either get a fixed monthly
tariff and share the cost with flatmates
or get your fix on campus for free.
```

Don't worry it the witness clocks you as the guilty party – it doesn't mean you'll be pounced on as an alternative suspect. Line-ups are a way of testing suspicions, not creating them out of nowhere.
You'll usually be paid at least £10, depending on how long you have to hang around for. Though unless you bear an uncanny resemblance to a lot of suspects (probably by looking as average as possible – there's likely to be more demand for 5ft 10in men with short dark hair than 8ft women with three legs and green dreadlocks), it won't be the most reliable source of income.

Check with your local police force for details of how to register.

BODY PARTS, ETC.

Many medical students (the male ones, naturally) are wankers. In that they do it for money and get paid for their product, as it were. The reason medical students tend to do it is that they tend to be near a sperm bank.

There's no reason, however, why generations of babies born to women who've gone for fertility treatment should all be the spawn of medical student tossers. Move aside, you trainee doctors, and let some others drop their seed into the gene pool.

Sperm donors don't tend to get much for their efforts – around £10 or £20 quid a pop as a rule – and you're not allowed to do it too regularly. Quite apart from rumoured damage to eyesight, they need to keep sperm counts up and don't want any particularly hairy-fisted individuals monopolising the market.

There's also a very real possibility that the future spawn of sperm donors will be able to find out the identity of the men who contributed half their chromosomes. Those making donations until April 2005 have the right to anonymity, but after that the law is set to change. So if the prospect of someone turning up twenty years down the line and claiming to be your son or daughter fills you with dread, it's probably best to give this one a miss.

Female students don't have the same opportunities. They're not currently allowed to sell eggs (although they can donate them) and while you can act as a surrogate mother you're only allowed to claim reasonable expenses for doing so. It's really not a means to pay your way through college.

Selling organs can't be recommended either. Unnecessary medical procedures tend to interfere with study and… oh yeah, there's some risk to your health.

More realistically, students might be tempted to take part in medical experiments, which is also not something to volunteer for unless you're very clear about the risks you face. While researchers conducting any such experiments are obliged to inform you of any known or likely risks, their enthusiasm, and indeed the fact that the experiments need to be done at all, mean that you shouldn't have too much faith.

You should have your own independent understanding of exactly what's involved and weigh up the risks on the basis of whether you would do it if it were for free. There's not enough money to make it worth it if you don't feel safe, although it's hard to imagine what would be enough.

Medical experiments usually involve testing treatment procedures and new drugs. The dangers should be obvious. However, not all research is so risky. Lots of research projects,

**particularly in psychology, involve nothing more hazardous to
volunteers than filling in questionnaires and doing aptitude
tests.**

Twins, particularly monozygotic twins – that's identical twins to
you – are especially in demand. But only if you can persuade your
twin to volunteer too.

Again the money's not big bucks, but if it's advancing human
understanding, why not? If your university has a psychology
department, go and offer your services. The worst that can happen is
they laugh at your suggestion and psychologically scar you forever.

2

PART 3 ⓷

Tuition fees

Paying for your course

Briefly, what are 'tuition fees'?

Higher education doesn't come cheap and somebody has to foot the bill to run the universities, to employ the lecturers, to put books and computers in the library and so on.

Who it should be, however, is a controversial matter.

Push has no opinion (or not one that doesn't involve obscenities) – we're only here to tell it like it is.

The system is set for an almighty shake-up from 2006, but it won't affect people who started university before that date. See 'Top up fees' below for details of what the post-apocalypse funding world might look like.

At the moment, the Government pays by far the biggest part of any student's tuition costs. They run into many thousands of quid per student per year and, even since the introduction of tuition fees, most students pay only a fraction of the bill.

Anyone who starts university before 2006 will be charged a fixed-rate fee of £1,150 a year.

Not every student has to pay the full whack, however. In fact, about a third don't have to pay any fees at all and about another third pay less than the full amount. It's only those who can afford it – or, more accurately, those whose parents can afford it – who have to cough up.

How much you have to pay is based on your parents' income, their situation (get them to divorce if you can – then only one salary counts), whether you've got brothers and sisters in higher education, how old you are, whether you're married or earning, whether you're from outside the EU and hundreds of other conditions and details that we either already went into in **Chapter 3** or we'll cover later in this chapter or, if they're special cases, in **Chapter 13**.

Strictly speaking, in fact, unmarried UK students under 25 without an income and living with their parents aren't usually expected to pay their tuition fees out of their own pocket – not at the moment. Even if the student is the one who actually hands over the cheque to the university, in theory their parents are supposed to be 'contributing' enough to pay the bill, whether it's over a grand or nothing at all (see **Chapter 4**).

Whatever your situation, how much you or your parents are supposed to pay is worked out by your LEA when you apply for an 'award' (see **Chapter 3**).

Explain that again, but in more detail

WHAT DOES A DEGREE COST?

Students don't normally have to pay the whole cost of their course – which is just as well since most undergraduate degrees come in at a cool four grand a year to run (at least).

That pays for the tutors, the admin staff, the heating and lighting of teaching rooms, the photocopying of course notes, the books and computers in the library, the rubber bands to go on the degree scrolls and so on. Where they start having to pay for high tech equipment and lots of rubber gloves – such as on clinical courses – the bill can be as much as twenty grand a year.

As we said, it's just as well it's not normally the student who pays it.

The bulk of the bill, usually at least two-thirds, is paid by the Government. Often it's actually paid by the LEA, but it's all coming from taxes in the end anyway.

WHAT DO STUDENTS PAY?

Until 1998, students rarely had to contribute anything. Now they have to contribute a bit and soon they will have to contribute a bit more.

At the moment, about two-thirds of students in England, Wales and Northern Ireland have to contribute something to the cost of their tuition – up to a current maximum of £1,150. This goes up in line with inflation, which has meant a £25 raise every year since 1998.

How much students are expected to shell out depends, in theory at least, on their ability to pay – or more to the point, their *parents'* ability to pay.

The idea is that rich students (or ones from richer backgrounds at any rate – rich students are few and far between) should pay what they can, but that poorer students shouldn't be put off the idea of university by the prospect of having to contribute.

WHAT ARE TUITION FEES AND HOW ARE THEY PAID?

Tuition fees are the yearly cost of a higher education course charged by the university and paid for by either:

  (a) your LEA;
  (b) you and/or your parents; or
  (c) a combination of (a) and (b).

The university shouldn't demand any other fees for admission, registration, graduation and so on, although don't expect the fees to include your own photocopying, say, or a replacement library card when you lose yours.

Whatever amount you have to pay, you'll have to pay it direct to your university. The exact arrangements for taking money off you vary from place to place, but, don't you worry, when it comes to getting their cash, it won't be something they'll leave you in any doubt about.

They may want the whole amount right at the beginning of the academic year, but most are pretty flexible and will accept it in monthly or termly instalments. It may be slightly cheaper to pay it in one go, depending on the university's preference – again, you can be pretty sure they'll let you know.

A house video or DVD player means endless nights of cheap entertainment. Just be sure to avoid fines by taking any rentals back on time.

They'll all have some kind of deadline after which they'll try various threats, such as a late payment fine, but ultimately, they'll just chuck you off the course if you don't pay up.

Some also try to persuade you to set up a direct debit (an automatic regular payment from your bank account), which can actually work out easier for you too. They may even try to charge an admin charge if you don't. But if your bank balance is erratic and you're skating on a thin and icy overdraft limit (see **Chapter 6**), you may prefer to handle the payments in a more hands-on way.

Meanwhile, your LEA (or equivalent) may be paying all or part of your fees if you're a UK or EU student (see **Chapter 3**).

They'll send their contribution direct to the university, so once you've got it sorted and they've confirmed to you whether they'll pay and how much, then you can leave it to the LEA and the university to work it out between themselves.

HOW MUCH WILL I HAVE TO PAY?

This is the flip side of the coin of LEA awards that we covered in **Chapter 3**. Take the total fee (currently £1,150) and subtract whatever the LEA's willing to cough up. That's your share.

It's also the flip side of the coin of parent contributions (see **Chapter 5**). (Hang on, this coin seems to have an unfeasible number of sides.) You only have to contribute to your tuition fees if your parents (or, under certain circumstances, if you) can afford it, so your share of the fees and your parents' contribution to them would normally be the same thing (although your parents might also be contributing to your living costs).

To decide how much your share of the tuition fees should be, your LEA assesses your parents' income and your status. Details are in **Chapter 3** (and, if you haven't already read **Chapter 3**, you've probably worked out that all this would be so much easier to follow if you had).

Basically, if your parents' residual income (i.e. after a few deductions and allowances) is under £21,475, you won't be paying anything. At £21,475, you'll be expected to pay £45 a year and for every extra £9.50 that they earn, you'll have to pay another pound a year. Until finally, when they're on £31,973 or more, you're paying the maximum annual contribution of £1,150.

For married students, they'll usually count your spouse's income instead of your parents' and, for single mature students and lone parents, the LEA will count your own income and you'd normally be entitled to additional help anyway (see **Chapter 13**).

Even if you're absolutely certain that you'll have to pay the full tuition fee or even if you might not have to but you're perfectly happy to pay £1,150 a year anyway, apply to your LEA anyway. It's not just because we take a sadistic pleasure in recommending that people fill in forms (although it is fun for us, and we do conduct pointless surveys at weekends as a hobby). It's because, **if you don't, the LEA won't know you're doing the course at all and won't know to pay the bulk of the course costs. You may end up paying them yourself**.

And, as we already said, that's usually at least £4,000 and sometimes as much as £20,000. A fair whack to have to cough up just for not bothering to fill in one fairly straightforward form.

SCOTTISH STUDENTS

Different funding arrangements apply under the Scottish parliament. **Scottish students studying in Scotland do not have to pay tuition fees.** However, they do have to pay a 'graduate endowment' of around £2,100 once they have graduated – this will be added to their loan repayments. Certain students, such as mature students, lone parents and disabled students, are let off this Graduate Endowment. See **Chapter 13** for more information.

WHO DOESN'T HAVE TO PAY TUITION FEES?

Apart from Scottish students at Scottish universities (see above) and the third of English, Welsh, Northern Irish and EU students who have all their fees paid for them, there are some students whose courses are considered too important to the rest of us for them to have to cough up anything themselves.

Basically, that means medics of various breeds and flavours and teachers.

In other words, UK and EU students on any of the following courses shouldn't have to pay a penny in fees:

- Postgraduate courses leading to qualified teacher status (e.g. PGCE)
- Chiropody

- Dental hygiene
- Dental therapy
- Dietetics
- Midwifery
- Most nursing courses
- Occupational Therapy
- Orthoptics
- Physiotherapy
- Prosthetics and orthotics (England only)
- Radiography
- Speech and language therapy

Undergrads training to be teachers – on BEd courses – need to watch out for this, because they'll have to fork out for fees along with everyone else. However, they may get a 'golden hello' – a lump sum when they actually become teachers (see 'Alternatives to sponsorship' in **Chapter 8**) – or, if they want to teach a subject in which there's a shortage, they might get extra funding under the 'secondary shortage subject scheme' (see **Chapter 13**).

If you fancy becoming a teacher – or the fact that you may have an easier financial time as a student may tip the balance for you – give the Teaching Information Line a shout on 0845 6000 991 (or the Welsh Teaching Information Line on 0845 6000 992).

See **Chapter 8** for more details on the NHS bursaries, which cover fees for the medical courses listed above.

It's possible to escape paying fees for one year only if you're studying abroad as part of the Erasmus scheme (see **Chapter 13**).

There are also a few people who get a grant of £560 towards their fees, which basically means they'll be billed £590 tops, rather than £1,150. The following qualify:

- Students on a sandwich course in an academic year involving less than 10 weeks of full-time study
- Students studying abroad as part of their course (i.e. not those doing an entire course abroad)
- Students in a final year which is ordinarily required to be completed after less than 15 weeks' attendance
- Students on a part-time ITT (initial teacher training) course involving less than the equivalent of 10 weeks of full-time study.

Frequently asked questions

What if I want to change my course or my university?
Talk about it first – to friends, to parents, to tutors, to the students' union welfare department, to people in the street, priests, radio talkshows – till you're either bored of the idea or absolutely convinced it's the right thing to do.

The reason you need to take such care is that it will affect you financially and there may be the most horrendous pile of red tape and administrative hassle to deal with.

But if you're more sure of yourself than a tabloid columnist with a bad idea, then:

- Tell your university what you've decided to do (generally it's easier to change courses than institutions).

- Tell your LEA. If they've paid out any money for your course, there is a good chance they'll want it back and it's you they'll expect it from. So the sooner you raise the subject with them, the better.

- Tell the Student Loans Company. As soon as you leave your course, you're liable to start paying back the loan unless you are going to reapply and start university again. (The SLC doesn't have to wait a few months, as they would after graduation, if you've left your course early.)

If you're lucky and tell everyone as soon as you've decided what you want to do and then keep everyone informed, then you may be able to transfer any support you're getting from one course to another, even if it's at a different university. If you don't have to drop back a year (or even, very occasionally, if you do), it may not lose you any funding at all. No guarantees though.

Your university – in fact, both universities if you're switching – must first agree to what you're intending to do and there are some standard restrictions on transfers. If you're on a course at a private university or college, you may have to pay extra tuition fees.

Usually, you're allowed one 'false start', which means you don't lose out too much if you drop out of the first course before starting the second year. You're likely to have an extra year's worth of debt and fees to contend with, of course, but you're unlikely to be penalised otherwise.

All other things being equal, you'll usually still be eligible for whatever amount of support you would have got for either the course you've moved from or the course you're moving to (whichever is longer and/or more expensive), but not both.

So, for example, if you switch from a three-year degree just at the start of the second year to a four year degree somewhere else, but you only have to go back to the beginning of the second year of your new course, then you may well not lose out. Your LEA and the SLC would have been happy enough to support you for four years of study if that's what you'd decided in the first place, so they probably wouldn't object to you doing it this way.

You'd have more of a problem if either they'd already coughed up for your second year at the university you don't like or if you had to go back to the start of the four-year course at your new university. In that case someone, somewhere would have to pay for more years' study than they would have otherwise and that someone is going to be you.

What's worse is that you may end up paying not only for your living expenses and your tuition fees but, unless you can persuade your LEA, you might end up paying all of the course costs for any extra years.

By the way, if you move into or out of London or either away from home or back in with your parents, then the loan rates will be changed accordingly.

What if I want to drop out?

If you really aren't happy at university and you're sure that a change of course or scene isn't the answer, naturally you have the option to drop out.

More than one in six students drops out or fails and, although it's rarely the only reason, financial hardship is often a contributing factor.

Jumping ship, however, may not be the answer to your financial problems. It could make matters worse. Indeed for some students, the debt looming over them is a reason to stay the course. Depending on when in the academic year you decide to bail out, your university may well charge you for the whole year and, depending on your particular arrangement, some LEAs may want their contribution towards your tuition paid back too.

You could end up with the worst of both worlds – not only might you have all the usual student debts, a university on your back for fees and an LEA chasing you for repayment of its contribution, but you won't even have the higher education qualification to show for it and the higher earning potential that brings.

What if I'm not from the UK or the EU?

Any UK university is going to expect full fees from you. That's not just the tuition fees charged to UK students (with the current maximum of £1,150 a year), but a price based on the total cost of your course – anything from a couple of thousand quid a year up to around twenty grand. They'll probably even want to make a bit of profit out of you.

Contact the university for details of overseas students' fees for individual courses.

There may be help from your government or other organisation in your own country.

The UK higher education system is considered to be of a pretty high standard and, since in some countries you'd have to pay all the costs anyway, it may work out cheaper and better to study here.

Top up fees

If you manage to get through the university doors before 2006, top up fees won't affect you at all. But the whole fee set-up will change if you start university in, or after, September 2006.

As _The Push Guide to Money_ goes to press, the new plans are wending their way through the last stages of the parliamentary process, which means the odd detail could still be tinkered with here and there. We'll publish any necessary updates on the free access area of Push Online (www.push.co.uk).

However, it looks pretty certain universities will be able to charge higher fees – up to £3,000 a year – from 2006.

They'll be able to charge lower fees as well, but most cash-conscious establishments won't want to. Most will decide that to offer a cheaper degree will make it *look* like there's something wrong with it. It may be that the only courses that are offered cheap are the ones they have difficulty filling otherwise. So there may be nothing wrong with them other than their popularity, but it's how it will *look* that's likely to matter. And if it makes marketing sense not to sell it cheap, who'd want to?

There are also occasional rumours of possible US-style fees of £15,000 a year, but there's no evidence – yet – that they'll become a reality on this side of the pond any time soon.

The other important thing to know about these new fees is that students won't actually have to pay them until after graduation. Instead, you'll have a big, fat loan – obese, in fact, as it'll be roughly twice the size of pre-2006 loan, which just covers living costs – to pay back once you're earning more than £15,000 a year.

This new arrangement is supposed to stop studious 18-year olds being reliant on their parents for cash. However, students from poorer families will get some extra help to try to make it easier for them to stomach the thought of all that debt.

> Be ruthless with everything you haven't worn/read/used for the past six months — sell it. Try e-bay online, a room sale or that old standby, a blanket on the pavement outside the English department lecture theatre.

Students who currently qualify for an award – ie. those who would get some or all of the £1,150 paid for them – will continue to get the same amount of help. So if you would have got the full tuition fee paid for you under the old system, you'll get the first £1,200 paid for you under the new system. (Because of inflation, they're assuming £1,150 will be have increased to £1,200 in 2006.) If you would have had to pay half of the old fees, you'll be let off paying £600 of the new fees.

Because the finer points are still being fleshed out (and they'll probably carry on fiddling with the arrangements right up to and after the new system starts), the whole caboodle is subject to change. So it's advisable to check Push Online (www.push.co.uk) or one of the Government sources listed in the back of the book for the latest.

In the meantime, this gives you an idea of how it will work if you're thinking of starting a course after September 2006. If you can, though, it will work out cheaper in the long run (although more expensive while you're actually studying) if, by the time you're reading this, there's still a chance to start your course sooner.

PART 4 4

Where does it all go?

Chapter Eleven

Where most of it goes

So, tell me again, how much will I have?

On average, students in 2004/5 should have between £3,250 and £7,200 a year to live on depending on whether they work part time, whether they live at home, whether they live in London and on how rich and/or generous their parents are. Of this, a large percentage isn't real income, it's a student loan but what the hell, at least it's money to spend.

You can add to that another possible thousand or so in overdrafts from the bank. Again, it's not income, but it's spendable and that's all that counts till you have to pay it back.

That comes at the end when, at the moment, students are on average between £9,000 and £14,000 in the red. That figure is not likely to be dropping. In fact, anyone going to university now ought to reckon on being at the top rather than the bottom of the scale by the time they finish.

And if you're planning to start in 2006 or later, you can add up to another £6,000, depending on what top up fees you'll have to pay and what help you'll get paying them (see **Chapter 10**).

The thing is that all this 'on average' business undermines a lot of specific advice and makes the prospect of hardship seem less real. You'll have to work out for yourself what you're likely to have. Helping you do that is what Part 2 of this book was all about.

If you think you can easily live on even £7,200 a year – pretty much top whack for a student – think again, pal. Get a grip or else you're going down big time.

Unless you're way off one end of the bell curve, getting by as a student will be as difficult as everyone says. They're not kidding. They're not boasting about how tough it is for them. Hardship is for real. For almost all students.

In 2002/3, for example (these are the most recent figures available), the average student had £5,513 to play – or rather *pay* – with. However, average total expenditure was £6,897 – the remainder being made up by savings, overdrafts, credit cards etc.

What are the main expenses, then?

The single biggest cost is accommodation. The roof over your head. It's expensive, but an essential.

The next biggest expense may be your tuition fees, depending on how much you have to pay. We'll leave that out of the equation for the time being. Just take a look at **Chapter 10** (and **Chapters 3** and **5**) if you haven't got fees sussed yet.

Other biggies are food, travel, academic costs (like books etc.), clothes and bills. All essentials too.

Your entertainment costs are among the top wallet wasters, too, and don't think they're not essential. You can't have a successful time at university if you're hating every minute of it because you're too stingy to allow yourself a penny for fun.

Think of it more as an investment in the wider education that university offers (the education that teaches you how to survive a 9am lecture with the hangover from hell). Or you can think of it as the wise purchase of a support mechanism (otherwise known as 'having friends').

The breakdown on average – again that phrase that tugs out the rug – goes something like this:

	Nationwide		In London	
	Annual Average	Percentage of total costs	Annual Average	Percentage of total costs
Rent/housing	£2,060	32.2%	£2,898	38.6%
Food	£1,074	21.7%	£1,074	14.3%
Leisure/ entertainments	£1,389	16.8%	£1,389	18.5%
Travel	£466	7.3%	£730	9.7%
Academic (books, photocopying, stationery, etc.)	£429	6.7%	£429	5.7%
Clothes	£406	6.3%	£406	5.4%
Household bills	£406	6.3%	£406	5.4%
Laundry/washing	£107	1.7%	£107	1.4%
Insurance	£61	0.9%	£76	1.0%
Total	£6,398		£7,515	

Region by region, the breakdown Push has calculated is something like this:

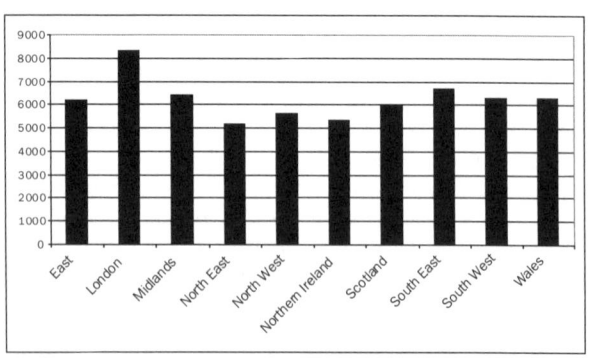

But remember that costs vary not only from one part of the country to another, but from one part of town to another or even within the same university depending on whether you're living in or out, which hall of residence you're in or which course you're on.

Perhaps the most useful way of looking at it is to think in terms of how it splits up what you've got. For people studying outside London, it looks something like this:

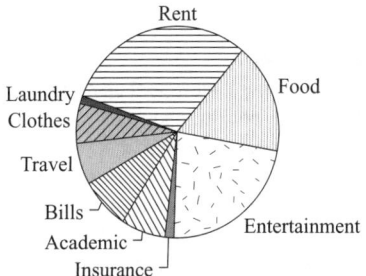

But for those in the Big Smoke, it's more like this:

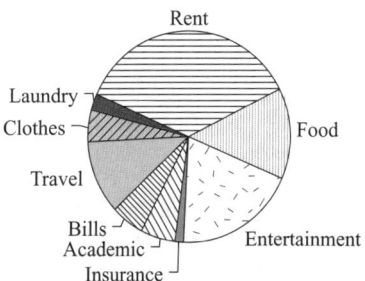

Having added them up, let's break the costs down.

In **Chapter 2**, we already covered the inside track on how exactly they vary from place to place and how you can stay solvent by choosing your university carefully. Here's a more general idea of where exactly so much money disappears so quickly.

Rent and housing

This is your biggest expense – it will eat up a whacking great proportion of your loan, perhaps about half your available income and it will account for about a third of what you spend in a year.

And, unless you are living with your parents or they have gone a step or two beyond the call of duty and actually bought a place for you, it's an expense that cannot really be avoided or minimised.

So be sure to make your dough work hard for you.

Accommodation costs vary enormously. Depending on location and what you look for, a student might normally expect to spend anything from £35 a week, for a very basic rented room in a student house, right up to £100 a week or even more for some catered or particularly flash digs.

In London, however, you might end up forking out nearly a hundred just to get the basic rented room that would be rock-bottom of the market anywhere else.

There are two basic alternatives for students – they break down into endless complicated subsets, but let's not spit in the Evian right now, okay?

Students can either live in or out. The 'in/out' bit refers to university accommodation – housing that belongs to your university or college or is at least managed by them. Or at least by someone else on their behalf. Told you it got complicated.

If you live out, you have to find your own accommodation, deal with your landlord personally and generally get involved in the whole homemaking business for yourself.

If you live in, the university will lay on all sorts of extra benefits. For example, there may be someone who empties your bin and runs a vacuum round the floor every once in a while. There may be a canteen, common room, a bar even. And, what's more, your bills will probably all be included in your rent.

As a rule, living in works out much cheaper. It depends on what the university is charging, but it's rare that once you've allowed for bills, meals and anything else they throw in, it works out on the wrong side of what's available locally.

Another benefit is that it's usually easier to manage your finances if you live in. Because bills are usually 'all in', you don't have to worry about brown envelopes landing on the doormat threatening to cut off your heating and light unless you pay the electricity bill. (What's worst is they'll probably pick the middle of *Eastenders* to throw the switch on you.)

You can't always live in. In fact, very few universities offer the chance to live in throughout your student career and besides, frantic fun though it often is, after a year of it, most students are more than happy to move out.

First years usually get dibs on whatever housing the university has and most students can live in for one year at least.

Living in may be cheaper, but it has its down side. In catered accommodation, you may also have to eat institutional food from time to time. And, depending on the exact arrangements, most students living on campus have to share limited bathroom and catering facilities with a large number of other students – which can be a strain, especially if you value sleep or privacy.

But, then again, what better way of getting to know a strange bunch of people than being stuck in an enclosed space with them for the entire academic year?

There are quite a few factors to consider when choosing where to live.

You may not always have total freedom to choose (especially if you live in, as you may simply be allocated whatever's going), which makes it all the more important to know what you want so you can get your money's worth from whatever's available.

Making the right call about housing – not just where you're going to live, by the way, but also who you are going to live with – is crucial. Most tenancies are for a full year and it's often expensive, inconvenient and tough to find anywhere better if you decide you want to move halfway through an academic year.

CHOOSING HOUSING: WHAT TO CONSIDER

The level of the rent

The cheapest is not always the best. It's just the cheapest.

There is no such thing as a good deal on a ten-foot-by-four-foot room that's cold, smelly and damp with rickety furniture and an infestation of rats.

It's far better to fork out a little extra each month for somewhere where you'll be able to sleep, study and just hang loose. If you can't, you'll only end up more miserable and no better off, because you'll be paying costs constantly for the bus to the library and for food and drink when you get there.

When choosing a place to live, sniff about like a dog in a meat-packer's. Try talking to someone who's lived there before or is living there now, just to get an idea of what you will be getting for your money. Ask about any hidden costs (such as a heating system that uses fuel, but seems incapable of producing heat) and get their opinion on how well – and how quickly – the landlord sorted out any problems they've had with the house.

This is another advantage of living in. Universities tend to look after their tenants better than most landlords and it's easier to find out the problems up front and (usually) easier too to get something done about them.

If you're living out, the more people you share with, the more the cost of the bills can be spread and the smaller your own proportion of the rent. There is the danger of increased tension amongst housemates, but more people can also mean that tensions are spread more thinly.

A huge factor in the amount of rent you actually pay is how long you're there.

Find out if you have to pay rent during the holidays. Most privately owned, off-campus accommodation requires that you do, but university digs usually have 30 to 38 week contracts that match the length of the terms.

Unless you absolutely have to, don't rent over the summer break. By not renting for more than the nine months of the year that you actually need, you might save yourself more than £500.

Private landlords are likely to want some of your cash over the holiday, but it's worth asking for a summer reduction (try for at least half price) if they don't offer one. And if you do have to pay rent over the holidays, there is nothing to stop you staying there and finding work rather than going home.

Before saying yes to any accommodation, calculate what it's going to cost you over the year. Multiply the weekly or monthly rent by how long you're actually going to live there and add appropriate amounts for anything that's not included (such as bills or furniture).

Do you have to share a room?
Students who live in sometimes have to share whether they want to or not.

If you do, your rent should be lower – a lot lower – not least to make up for the cost of having to get on pretty damn well with whoever you're sharing with.

Everyone needs their own space sometimes, so this is not a satisfactory option for most students, especially beer-swilling, chain-smoking hedonists who end up sharing with a younger version of Cliff Richard.

However, sharing isn't as common these days as it used to be, even in halls of residence. And if you state on your accommodation application that you do not want to share, you'll usually not have to.

Even those who do need to share are normally sent questionnaires by the university so they can make roommate matches as harmonious as possible. If one of these drops through your letterbox, make yourself sound as anti-social as possible. That way they'll probably have to put you on your own (or, failing that, with someone else pretending to be anti-social).

A word of warning: if you get into university through the Clearing system, you may end up dumped in whatever accommodation the university couldn't foist on anyone else. It's almost always safer to take a year out and apply again the following year. That way you can get your housing application in nice and early while the competition are still brushing up their A level revision skills.

If you live out, sharing may make more financial sense because, rather than just getting you a discount, it should actually halve the price.

Some landlords, however, especially if they're providing two beds in one room, charge per person, not for the room. It's immoral, crooked and there's nothing you can do about it.

Never share unless you know you can get on with your roommate. That goes for boyfriends and girlfriends too. Otherwise it can be like living in a room with no heating. You'll end up spending more because you can't spend time at home.

What's included?

When you're working out where to live, work out what's included in the cost. It's no good economising by renting a room at £30 a week if it doesn't include any bills or any furniture. By the time you've made the place habitable, you'll have forked out as much as somewhere twice the price.

If bills are included, expect to pay about 20% more than without. But check which bills are thrown in and which aren't. Push heard about someone who was told they wouldn't have to pay gas bills. Sure enough, they didn't – because there was no gas supply. The heating was electric and on a meter that gobbled coins like they were chocolate.

Run through the list to see what's included and what's not: electricity; water rates; gas; oil; coal/solid fuel. Most housing doesn't usually need more than water, electricity and, sometimes, gas – but check first.

It's highly unlikely you'll find anywhere where the phone bill is included and don't be impressed if they start talking about council tax. Most students don't have to pay any (see **Chapter 9**).

If you're living in, the price will almost always include all the bills (except the phone) and may include a cleaner, bed linen and sometimes even a TV (with licence).

Universities will frequently offer catered accommodation as an option (or even as the *only* option). They may charge you only for the food you eat, either like a cafeteria or as a flat charge for every meal, but it's also common for the food bill to be thrown in with your rent (not literally – you get it on a plate).

Catered accommodation is often around 50% more expensive and it can be a boon or a bane. Check out exactly what meals are provided (lunch usually isn't, nor evening meals at weekends). Also check the meal times. It's all very well having paid for breakfast or dinner (or tea or supper or whatever you want to call it), but not if breakfast is always finished before you get up and dinner's over by the time you get back from lectures.

Find out what other options remain when a meal isn't provided. **You don't want to get into a situation where every Sunday night you're ordering a takeaway because there's no meal provided and only a toaster where you can cook anything for yourself.**

Think too about the quality of the grub. Catered accommodation is often a bargain, because at least it's a nutritious square meal and it's already paid for – but if it's inedible, it's just more money down the pan. (All too often quite literally, if indirectly.)

Location

How far is your accommodation from the university? Or at least, how far is it from whatever part of the university you need to go to most regularly? Bear in mind that lots of universities are based on more than one site – sometime considerably more than spitting distance apart (unless you know anyone who can project a loogie more than five or ten miles).

If you're too far from the action, you're either going to be paying travel costs to get around or spending a lot of time walking and cycling.

> Forget about free flights to Ibiza: if you have a loyalty card with a supermarket and you're offered money off a shop, always take it. You'll rake up big savings over the year without feeling deprived.

If you can't find anywhere close (as is sometimes the case), what's the local transport like? Are there buses or trains and, if so, are they regular and do they operate until late into the night? If not, you'd better put taxis down as a pretty big item in your budget plans.

Obviously the closer, the better – another good reason for living in (although university housing isn't *always* where you'd like it to be).

Even if you're on or near campus, are you anywhere near other essential services such as shops, a cheap and friendly

pub, a supermarket, an Indian takeaway? Is it a popular student area – will the social scene be good? Again, if not, you'll spend half your time and/or money travelling.

What's the crime like in the area? Steer clear of anything too dodgy, even if the house itself seems pleasant enough. Mistakes like that can be false economies.

Facilities

You get what you pay for, so if you're getting a big, plush room with en suite bathroom, crystal chandeliers and shag-pile carpets, then expect to plunge deep into the debt pool.

In reality, of course, most student houses are notoriously bog standard (and often sub-standard), but occasionally you may be lucky enough to find hints of luxury. Don't laugh, but en suite shower rooms and toilets are becoming pretty much standard in newer housing.

Don't expect to get it for free, however.

If you're living out, most student houses come equipped with the basics, although if you want a washing machine, TV, VCR, sauna and so on, you'll have to make your own arrangements. (Oh, and if there's no plumbing for a washing machine, check that you won't have to carry your dirty kecks halfway across town to find the nearest launderette.)

You may well also need to provide your own kitchen equipment – everything from knives and forks to pots and pans. But not usually including the kitchen sink.

If you go in with a sizeable group of housemates, you may all want to chip in to buy or rent a microwave and/or a freezer if there isn't one provided. Renting one is usually pricier in the long-term (see below) and if you own it, you can at least sell it on to the next bunch of students when you leave. However, rental does avoid arguments about whose TV it is – especially if it gets nicked.

You should expect central heating, with fully functioning radiators in every main room. Your room should have, at the very least, a bed, a radiator, a desk, a chair and a wardrobe. Fashionably spartan rooms (Push believes the word is 'minimalist') are the norm and don't expect brand new spine-friendly mattresses or top quality furnishings. Expect orange carpet, purple curtains and brown walls.

4

Where does it all go?

It's up to you to give it your own personal makeover to make it feel as homely as possible, but ask the landlord's permission before doing anything expensive or permanent or you may end up paying again to reverse it. If they like your plan, they may pay for it.

RENTING TIPS FOR LIVING OUT

Most universities have an accommodation office that helps students find a suitable place to lay their weary head, but if there's high demand, they won't be able to do much more than help you realise a bit quicker how hard it is to find anywhere affordable.

If you aren't using the university's property service to find accommodation, at least get them to check out your tenancy agreement before you sign it. In fact, nag them with questions if anything to do with your living arrangements is bugging you.

Get your landlord/lady to give you confirmation that everything's in satisfactory working order (a boiler certificate, for example) *before* you sign anything and whenever something goes wrong pester them till they sort it out. Especially if it's dangerous or causing you expense. Tenants have rights and you shouldn't have to put up with faulty plumbing, blocked drains, a leaking roof or rising damp.

Make sure you get an inventory of everything that's there when you move in and make sure it doesn't have anything on it that isn't.

Your landlord will check it all when you leave and if there's anything missing, they'll charge you for it.

Before you move in, you'll have to pay usually a month's rent in advance plus a deposit. The deposit is usually the same as a month's rent (if it's more than two months, get suspicious) and it's there as protection for the landlord if you either trash the joint or do a runner. You won't normally have to pay a deposit if you live in college.

Despite what a shocking proportion of landlords seem to think, it's not there as a bonus for them to keep when you move out.

All things being well, you should get the deposit back at the end of the year. However, in the meantime, it can make a hole of several hundred quid in your bank balance.

Apart from checking the inventory, another way to protect yourself is to take photos of the place when you first move in –

especially if there's any dodgy decorating or anything broken. That way you can prove what's got worse while you've been there.

A reasonable amount of wear and tear shouldn't cost you your deposit, but specific breakages and party damage will. It's also not a deposit-losing offence if the roof falls in or the boiler blows up, unless it was clearly your fault. (So hide the elephant afterwards.)

When negotiating your tenancy, try to get the landlord to put the deposit in an account held jointly in your name and theirs. That way neither of you gets the money at the end of the year without the other party agreeing it's fair.

Never hand over any money (for deposits, retainers, rent or anything else) till everyone's happy with all the terms and conditions and has signed on the line. A verbal agreement is not good enough.

Don't be fooled by wily, charming or – worst of all – apparently vague landlords or property agencies: they're business people after your money. And it's not as if there's much to go around.

Don't give it to them until you know exactly what you will be getting and firmly believe it is right for you.

'The Young Ones' is not a documentary about student house-sharing and should not be regarded as a guide to student living. Cleanliness may not come naturally to you. It may not even be your top priority, but you don't want to get a call from the landlord saying they're popping by tomorrow if that's okay and then have to splash out on a professional house-cleaning crew in order to protect your deposit.

Nor do you want the place to become a health hazard, for that matter.

Speaking of surprise visits, depending on your contract, your landlord normally has to give you notice if they want to come round. But usually it's only 24 hours and, besides, it can be hard to say no in case they ask why.

Your landlord isn't usually allowed to put your rent up more than once a year, so if they try, tell them you won't pay the increase. Then don't. So long as you pay your old rent, they won't be able to do anything.

Read your tenancy contract and don't do anything you're not allowed to. Then you should be fine. And don't stand for any crap from your landlord that's not in the contract. Always be as friendly and polite as possible and only as rude and firm as necessary – that's the way.

Food

Food will probably take the next largest bite out of your budget.

It's perfectly feasible to eat healthily, sensibly and cheaply all at the same time, but students tend to concentrate most on the last of those three. Or they do until the pub closes and then they're more worried about eating fast.

As a result, students have a tendency to be junk food junkies. If you can't order it with fries or bung it in a microwave or a toaster, it's simply too much hassle for most. Okay, so we can't all be Jamie Oliver, but there are plenty of cookbooks on the market written specially for students.

Healthy eating on a budget is not as tedious as it sounds. In fact, learning to cook is one of the most useful skills you can acquire as a student (stuff all that computers and foreign languages nonsense). It's also the best way of keeping your costs down.

Take ready-made garlic bread for instance. Even the economy brand costs more than a quid. You can make your own for half the price in about the same time. Honestly. Try it. Mix garlic puree, butter, dried parsley, spread it in a French stick, slam it in the oven, 200°C, ten minutes. As Jamie would say, pukka.

The real key, however, is not to make your own versions of fast food, but to work with fresh ingredients. Fruit and veg are nutritious and a lot cheaper than meat or packet foods. Eating healthily is not only best for you – it works out relatively cheap and, once you've got into it, tastes damn fine too.

Here's another one for you. Get some vegetables (courgettes, tomatoes and peppers, say, with a bit of garlic), chop 'em up, bung the lot in the oven for 20 minutes with a little oil, salt, pepper and some herbs. Serve with pasta and cheese. Cracking nosh at next to nothing.

A lot of students go veggie (if they're not already), which, so long as you get a balanced diet, is healthier and cheaper. (Even *cutting down* on the dead flesh makes quite a difference.)

There's also the appeal of it being more sound. In fact, buying politically correct products is often no more expensive, especially if you know where to shop. Many student shops on university campuses stock a decent range of sound groceries from trade-fair choc to biodegradable washing powder that are cheaper and just as good as leading brands.

Organic foods do tend to be more expensive, however – at least for the moment. But even the organic products at the market can be cheaper than the stuff blasted with chemicals at the supermarket.

For packet foods, own brand stuff is almost always cheapest. Most supermarkets even have an own economy brand, which is really cheap. They're often not noticeably inferior, they just package it like that to make you feel good about spending more. Don't be fooled.

If you're spending more than about £40 a week on food, you're probably spending too much. (There's a proper budget plan in Chapter 14.**) Remember that your food budget isn't just what's on your supermarket receipt. Don't forget to count snacks, teas and coffees in the campus cafeteria and any takeaways.**

You can ignore eating out when working out the weekly food budget, so long as you remember to count it under your entertainment costs.

What you spend on grub is bound to depend on where you live, what you eat and how much, but set aside a realistic nosh dosh allowance and stick to it.

If you're lucky, your parents will pack you off to uni with a big box of basics: fruit juice and tinned goodies, coffee, tea, pasta and so on. But students cannot live on basics alone and this lot won't last long anyway.

Just remember that odd little snacks throughout the day do add up, so take the long route home from lectures, the one that avoids the coffee shops, the newsagent and the snack-crammed vending machine.

TOP TUCKER TIPS
An hour or two before closing, supermarkets mark down some of their goods, usually stuff that's heading fast towards its sell-by date.

Like hyenas to the waterhole, scavenging hoards of bargain-hungry students have been known to descend on Tesco of an evening in the hope of bagging a few half-price items. But make sure you eat them before they go off.

Also, look out for tins that are marked down because they're damaged. So long as you can still get a tin opener latched on, there's nothing wrong with the contents.

What's more, supermarkets always have various special offers going, but some are more special than others. Keep your eyes peeled for those that are actually worth something, especially 'bogofs' (buy one get one free).

Don't shop while you're hungry – you'll end up with twice as much stuff as you need in your basket.

Collect coupons from magazines, flyers or from the sides of packets – or anywhere so long as it cuts the price. Remember to take them with you when you go shopping.

On the other hand **don't buy stuff just because it's marked down or on special offer or you've got a coupon.** It's not enough that it's cheaper than usual. It's got to be cheaper than other things. A reduced price frozen pack of macaroni cheese is probably still three times the price of one you could make for yourself.

Most supermarkets (not Safeway or Asda) offer a loyalty card of some sort which in the end gives you money off. They're all a bit of a rip off, because presumably you end up paying for any loyalty card deals by paying higher prices in the first place, but that certainly doesn't mean you shouldn't use the system. Why should you be the one who pays extra for everyone else's discounts?

Don't over-order at restaurants – the 'eyes bigger than belly' syndrome. Of if you do, ask for a doggy bag.

If you're eating out, exploit all-you-can-eat buffets to an almost criminal degree. However, don't starve yourself so you can eat more. It doesn't work. We know a Warwick maths student who fasted for a day before gorging on ten pepperoni pizza slices and three servings of cold pasta salad for the bargain price of £4.99. He spent the evening with his head in the toilet bowl getting no nutritional value from his food whatsoever.

Any ready-made sandwiches that cost more than 50p are a con. You can make your own with whatever fillings you want for just a few pence.

Learn to cook before you leave home and don't try to save money by eating less or only eating plain pasta. Food is your fuel. Try putting lighter fluid in a Formula One car and you won't get top performance.

Team up with housemates to form a cooking syndicate. Cooking for one is expensive and, besides, a rota means that you only have the hassle of cooking once in a while. What's more, if you only know how to do spag bol, you might get to try someone else's speciality once in a while.

If a cooking syndicate doesn't appeal (it may turn out that your housemate's idea of *cordon bleu* is cremated bread with spaghetti hoops), how about cooking in bulk – make big casseroles that will last you a few days. Especially good if you've got a freezer and/or a microwave.

Remember to refrigerate leftovers, especially if they contain meat. Then remember to eat them before they go off.

Although eating like a veggie is a good option, even on a budget the devoted flesh-feeder doesn't have to give up sausages and bacon.

Rice, beans, lentils and pasta are words that most carnivores do not use very often, but they're a staple in most students' diet. They contain lots of carbs and goodness, they're very versatile and, when you get used to the taste, actually quite yummy.

University is not the time to get hooked on the Atkins Diet. All that meat, cheese and protein food doesn't come cheap. Unless a can of tuna a day is your idea of a satisfying menu, save cutting the carbs until you have the salary to treat yourself to fillet steaks and fresh mozzarella.

Household bills

To some students – if they've not lived away from home before – bills can come as a shock. (The electricity bill would be an electric shock, Push guesses.)

From the start, make an arrangement with your housemates to avoid future tension. Perhaps you could make a different person responsible for each bill and divide the costs equally between you from there. This is far better than putting all the bills in one person's name and leaving that poor sod to sort out all the payments. Especially if the poor sod is you.

Assuming you do split the bills fairly, they're likely to cost each person about £40 a week.

When you're living out, the bills that are likely to come dropping through the door are as follows:

TV Licence

If you have your own TV set or have bought or rented one with your housemates, you'll need to get a licence.

It's currently £121 for a colour telly, which isn't so bad if it's divided between several people. Dodgers are easily caught these days and it's definitely not worth risking the £1,000 fine and criminal conviction.

Telephone

Mobile-happy households may be able to cope just fine without an extra house phone bill to argue about. But if you do want a land line, make sure you get a good deal (perhaps one with an internet package included).

BT offers its 'Family & Friends' discount deal, among others. If you use the internet from home, make sure your ISP's number is down as your best friend. It may feel particularly sad to have the internet as your best friend, but forget pride, this is serious. It's about money.

Alternatively, it may be worth investing in an unlimited hours package (usually requiring a monthly fee) if you're not the only one in the house with a surf habit. Broadband deals are getting cheaper by the day and could end up saving valuable time if you don't fancy having the phone line tied up by the net. Check how long you're signing up for – anything that requires a minimum commitment that's longer than your academic year could prove to be a false economy.

BT is far from the only phone company around, so do a little research to find the best deal, especially if you make many international calls.

If you're sharing a line with housemates – which you probably will be – have a notepad by the phone on which everyone writes down all their outgoing calls. That way you can minimise the arguments when the bill comes. (Oh, and make sure you get itemised phone bills.)

Gas, electricity and other fuel

The costs will depend on how many of you are sharing, how many electrical appliances you have between you, how much you all enjoy steamy baths and warm rooms, and the time of year (rates will naturally be higher in winter).

Gas is generally a bit cheaper, but an efficient electric central heating system is cheaper than an old gas boiler.

In rural areas you may still find you need to use oil or solid fuels (such as coal). It's not common and they're a total pain in the butt – not too mention dirty, environmentally unfriendly and inconvenient when you run out of fuel.

See **Chapter 14** for tips on how to keep the bills down.

Water rates

Your landlord will often pay these for you, but find out where you stand because if they don't, just having running water will usually add between £200 and £300 a year to the household budget. Students are usually able to split the costs as housemates, but still, it's more money you haven't got.

Some houses now use water meters that measure exactly how much you use. Unless you're compulsively clean and take one hell of a lot of baths and do a load of washing every day, for students, these tend to work out cheaper.

Hire and rental fees

If you choose to rent kitchen appliances or entertainment equipment, it's best to go with a recognised outlet and look out for student deals at branches in university towns.

There are plenty of budget rental shops, but some of them are a bit suspect and their kit often has a tendency to break down on an exhaustingly regular basis.

Average rental for a washing machine (or washer/drier) runs at around £12 to £20 a month. Compared to going to the launderette, it's a little more expensive, but in terms of hassle, it's like comparing a hover mower to cutting grass with nail clippers.

For a basic TV/VCR combo you're looking at about £10 to £25 a month, including insurance. If you consider what you might otherwise spend on entertainments if you didn't have a TV at home, it can actually be quite a cheap form of amusement (even when you factor in the TV licence, see above). It's cheaper still if you can persuade your housemates to split the cost with you.

You won't need a separate insurance policy for rented stuff if you've already got household contents insurance (see below), but you'll have to take your insurance documents to the hire shop to prove you are covered.

It may, however, turn out cheaper to buy a washing machine or TV (splitting the cost between the house and maybe buying second-hand) rather than renting, particularly if you expect to stay in the same house for two years. This way, you'll have to fork out for any repair costs if a leaky old washing machine breaks (although most new ones come with a warranty – check the small print). But, providing your appliances survive the year, you should be able to recoup a bit of cash by selling them on.

Others

Students do not have to pay council tax, but there may be other expenses such as maintenance costs (for flats) and general household repairs to watch out for.

If you choose to host a party, there's almost always a sacrifice to be made to the great party god. If anyone breaks a window or puts their head through a wall, say, it's down to you to get it fixed and such unexpected costs can be pretty expensive.

BILLS TIPS

If you leave a bill long enough without paying it, it goes red. Well, metaphorically speaking. What usually happens is that a few weeks after you get the first bill, you get a reminder (that often is, literally, printed in red).

They don't warn you again. After that, they cut you off. Phone, electricity, gas, it doesn't matter – someone at head office flicks a switch and you're powerless. Literally.

To get reconnected, you have to pay not only the original bill, but a slap-on-the-wrist charge for being so naughty.

Therefore, it's best not to let the bills go red in the first place.

It's so tempting to ignore bills when you have so many other financial pressures on you, but the best policy is to pay up promptly. Ultimately, it's not just a matter of being cut off – you could be evicted by your landlord for not paying utility bills, or end up with a court summons.

Decide with your housemates who is responsible for which bills. Don't leave it to each other on the assumption that someone will deal with it. Someone rarely does. If a red bill turns up, check what's going on with whoever was supposed to pay it and, if necessary, work something out. But whatever you do, get it paid.

Ideally, keep the bills low in the first place, not just for your benefit but for the environment too.

Switch off lights and don't heat the house when you're not there. That kind of thing makes a big difference (see Chapter 14**).**

Some people like to keep a household kitty which everyone chips into and which you use to pay for communal things like bills and possibly even shopping for food (or for essentials like bread, milk, tea and coffee, at any rate).

In some households, for whatever reason, kitties don't work – they just cause more arguments and friction.

If you all have the same attitude to money, the communal approach is more likely to work and by pooling your resources you could save money and get bills paid on time. **Unfortunately, it's usually only after you've lived with someone for a few months that you realise what a selfish git they really are, how they never wash up and how they never pay up their share on time even though they always seem to have money for their copy of** *Loaded*.

Sometimes, rather than a kitty, a rota for paying bills works out better (and a rota for household chores is usually a good move, too).

Give up beer (only joking). Save coupons (seriously).

Washing, laundry and household sundries

That fateful straw that cripples the poor proverbial camel is not from some super-heavy GM crop.

Likewise, it's the more mundane and easily overlooked costs that can dump you in debt just when you thought you were in the clear. It's a looking-after-the-pennies thing.

Washing powder, cleaning products, toiletries, kitchen towels, toilet paper… again, these are areas where a household kitty could come in handy. They may be little things, but, as anyone who's ever realised they've run out of toilet roll at a critical moment should recognise, they're not expenses you want to skimp on.

You can economise by not using Clinique and designer smellies. To paraphrase L'Oréal, you may be worth it – but you can't afford it. Body Shop was pretty much invented for students (ethically sound, not too expensive), but if you're comfortable making your own soap from the bins out the back of the liposuction clinic (*à la* 'Fight Club'), go ahead.

Laundry costs can be considerable though there is, of course, the option of never washing or doing laundry. It has been known for students to get four days' wear out of their pants through 'quartering' (wear them for a day; turn them back to front, wear them for another day; inside-out, another day; inside-out and back to front… *voilà*, four days' wear). However, this route to cost cutting can mean you need to spend more on your social life to keep any friends.

And, by the way, have you ever experienced the mindless tedium of trying to iron your clothes? In fact, do you even own an iron? (Most university rooms will have a communal ironing board that doesn't stay up, and an iron that doesn't work. In which case you can pick up a perfectly good iron for under £20. Oops, there goes another pony.) Time to go back home for the weekend and tell your mum how much you love her…

Clothes

Two words: charity shops.

They really do give you the best of both worlds – you get to maintain that archetypically scruffy student image for a fraction of the price, while helping out some worthy cause.

But seriously, it's not all tasteless tank tops, corduroy dungarees and flamboyant flares. Just because you're Oxfam's most loyal customer doesn't mean the fashion police will be after you. On the contrary, you'll have more clothes in your wardrobe and more cash in your pocket. You can sashay past the big department stores in your battered old 99p Green Flash trainers with your head held high.

It does matter where you live, however. Not every charity shop is a resting home for retired designer wear, so it's well worth trekking across town to charity shops in the posher or trendier areas to find a better class of old tat.

Two more words: January sales.

If you don't mind risking death by crushing crowds and suffocation, these are often a good bet. The discounts are sometimes unmissable – 75% off, or even more…

Then there are markets and stalls. Most are cheap – well, cheaper than high street shops at any rate. Places like Camden Market in London and the retro shops in the Laines in Brighton are renowned as treasure troves of cheap chic.

Second-hand and cheap gear sellers also often visit students' unions and set up a stall.

Of course, nothing's cheap if you buy more than you need of it, so don't get blinded by the bargains. If necessary, only take a certain amount of cash with you to stop yourself just having to snap up another pair of eight-inch pink glitter knee-high boots – a snip at only £90.

Shopaholism is a recognised ailment in modern society and students are sadly not immune to this terrible affliction.

Students from the 'big cities', especially fashion-conscious London, are particularly susceptible. All their self-control seems to wither away whenever they pass a fashion store. Which is why credit cards and store cards are potentially so dangerous (see **Chapter 9**).

On the whole, new clothes are hardly cheap, although there are plenty of relatively inexpensive fashion stores knocking about on the high street (Top Shop/Top Man, Zara, New Look, Dorothy Perkins, and Miss Selfridge to name but a few) and some will give you discounts if you show them your student union card.

Watch out for the impulse purchase. If you see a bargain, ask yourself: is it really such a good deal? How often will you wear it? But try to buy decent quality – clothes made of good material that'll last longer than the next rinse cycle – you'll want to get a fair amount of wear out of anything you buy.

There are some special occasions when you'll want to splash out (see **Chapter 12**), but as a rule don't buy anything unless you have tried it on first and know you'll be able to wear it regularly for many months before it falls off you in rags.

It's not that you have to give up on image. It's just that you'll need to exercise a bit of imagination to create it.

Don't be tempted to update your wardrobe on a whim every couple of months (or every time you split up with a partner) – learn how to mix and match a few versatile items of clothing to create a range of different looks. Wear layers so that you can get use out of your summer outfit all year round.

Only treat yourself when you can afford to, which means sticking to your budget (see Chapter 14). **Whether you like it or not, clothes represent an area of your spending on which you** *can* **cut back, so it's best to see how finances are going before indulging.**

The average student spends just over £400 a year on clothes. To put this into perspective, Victoria Beckham allegedly spends £2,000 a *day* – but that's probably a smaller percentage of her income than £400 a year would be of yours.

As you can see from the figures above, £400, and certainly anything more, is pushing at the edges of the debt envelope – but you can decide to spend whatever you like so long as when you add it all up, it's within what you can afford. Then you need to stick to it.

Distinguish between wants and needs and prioritise from there.

And how about making your own clothes?

You don't have to be a fashion student to create something unique and wearable (and even stylish). You can always buy something from a second-hand shop and modify it to suit your taste.

You could tie-dye a shirt (*sooo* 90s), embroider some old jeans, hack up a skirt or print your own designs on plain T-shirts. There are a number of books on the market about how to clothe yourself on a budget and you don't have to be Stella McCartney to step out in homemade style.

Supposedly, Lawrence Llewellyn-Bowen makes a lot of his own clothes, but don't let that put you off.

Insurance

Not everybody bothers with insurance, but if you don't it'll probably cost you many times as much in replacing everything or bailing yourself out of whatever crisis you find yourself in.

Basically, if you can't afford to buy everything you currently own, you can't afford not to be insured. There are many different types of policy about and lots of special student packages available.

POSSESSIONS INSURANCE

Don't fall into the trap of thinking, 'I'll be okay, so long as I always lock the door.' Students are notoriously common victims of burglaries. It doesn't matter whether you live in or out, it only takes a minute to grab a hi-fi or walk off with a computer.

Another trap is to think that you don't have anything worth nicking. You'd be surprised what people will take if they can't find anything valuable. If they're stupid enough to go thieving other people's stuff in the first place, they're stupid enough to think your clothes, your homemade music compilations, your books and even your mugs and half-used toiletries are worth taking.

Even students who don't have a computer, a TV or even a stereo are often surprised at how much their combined possessions are worth. Unfortunately, they only usually stop to work it out when it's been pinched and, because they thought insurance was an unnecessary expense, they're now forking out to replace it all.

If you are in halls of residence, you may find that your rent charge includes a comprehensive insurance policy to cover all the students living there. But don't assume that it does.

Failing that, check your parents' home insurance policy. Quite a few of them cover your belongings even though you're living away from home (but sometimes they exclude student residences, so read the small print).

If after checking all these options, it turns out you're not insured, you can get basic personal cover from pretty much any general insurance company or bank.

There are companies that specialise in students, most notably Endsleigh, although other companies such as E&L and Norwich Union often have packages that are just as good, depending on where you're living.

For total possessions up to a value of £3,000, premiums will usually be around £40 to £50, with higher rates for those in private rented accommodation off campus. Three grand isn't actually all that much and if you've got a computer or any expensive bit of kit, you'll need to talk to the insurer about either increased cover or insuring that item separately. (You might also want to cover certain items for accidental loss or damage.)

If you're living out, your landlord should already have building insurance (to cover fire and structural damage), but it won't cover any contents of the building that belong to you.

You'll need to take out either your own policy or a joint policy with your housemates. It's likely to be a little more expensive than if you were living in, depending on the security measures (window locks, alarms and so on) and, most importantly, exactly where you're living.

If you live in a dodgy area and have thousands of pounds worth of stuff in your room, there will be no avoiding a sky-high premium – but it's worth it anyway. It's higher precisely because you're more likely to be robbed.

Generally, possessions insurance shouldn't set you back more than £100 a year tops. If it does, either get another quote or see if you can leave some of your more valuable possessions back at home, especially things like jewellery.

Just because you're insured up to the hilt, don't get complacent about security. Not only is making a claim a real hassle, but replacing stuff takes time and is never 100% satisfactory.

Besides, there'll probably be an 'excess' on your policy – a sort of buffer zone of anything from £50 to £250 to stop you making pathetically small claims. This means that whatever your claim, you have to meet the amount of the excess yourself – you always lose out.

Just taking out insurance isn't enough – be aware, too. Lock doors and windows when you go out (or even when you're in) and if you live on campus and see someone you don't recognise wandering down your corridor in halls, ask them if they need any help (especially if they're carrying anything valuable).

They may just be visiting a friend. On the other hand they could be on their way to your room, to help themselves while you're in the kitchen making a coffee.

WHEELS

Cars

Amazingly enough, quite a few students are car-owners, in spite of the massive costs involved in running a four-wheeled metal monster and the havoc they reek on the planet.

A car may make sense if you're living with your parents, as your other costs are likely to be fairly low and your folks are unlikely to have had proximity to university campus at the top of their list of priorities when choosing the family abode.

The course you do can also tip the balance in favour of keeping a motor. If you've signed up for something that involves a fair bit of to-ing and fro-ing to get to various placements – medicine or teaching, for example – you may find you're wasting hours of each day on public transport or having to walk for miles unless you have your own set of wheels.

After buying the car itself, the biggest expense is the insurance and new drivers under 21 are unlikely to have much luck finding anything that doesn't blow their student income out of the water. The AA reckons annual insurance for the smallest car will set you back £335 a year on average.

Whether your car is shiny and new and sexy or clapped out and rusty, fully comprehensive car insurance for students is likely to be at least £600 a year and more than double that in some cases.

Shop around for the best deal – you can save several hundred quid. It might be cheaper to take out car insurance from your home address rather than your university address or vice versa.

If your car's more than 25 years old, you may qualify for classic car insurance which cuts the cost like a machete through a mango.

Where does it all go?

It's still outrageously expensive, though, and hardly any student who cared about the state of their finances would ever even consider owning a car.

Bicycles

Bike insurance is pretty pricey too, believe it or not. Mainly because the student who doesn't have their bike nicked at some point is probably the student who doesn't own one.

Some of the banks offer good insurance deals also. If you're getting a bike – which, by the way, is a fantastically economical thing to do as a student (so long as you use it) – best to stick with one that doesn't look too flash.

It's also worth splashing out on the most intimidating padlock and chain you can find. (And, by the way, you can buy a metre of saw-proof chain at a hardware store much more cheaply than a tailor-made bike chain). And try to get a bike with a removable saddle.

Bike insurance ranges from about £40 up to £240, although premiums usually take a hike every year. Always check the terms and conditions of your insurance documents very carefully.

Travel insurance

Whether you're travelling in the UK only, around Europe or all over the world, get yourself a good insurance policy. They're not that pricey, and since it's so easy for things to go wrong when you're budget travelling, it's important to know there's a safety net to cover delays, cancellations, theft, lost luggage, medical bills and all your other nightmares.

Every policy's different, however, so make sure you get the right balance of cover for your needs and shop around till you get it at the right price.

If your course includes time abroad, you'll have to manage your finances to cover extra travel expenses (see **Chapter 13**).

Travel

LOCAL TRAVEL

If you live out, you'll probably have to get to campus most days (perhaps every day if you're on a science course). That will almost certainly mean using public transport, for which the operators have an annoying habit of charging fares.

Even if you live in, you'll want to get off campus once in a while, if only to do the shopping – campus life can get a bit like nomination time in the Big Brother House and sometimes getting out and about is the only way to preserve your sanity.

So whichever university you attend and wherever you live, you'll have to put aside a certain amount for local travel, probably anything from a few quid a month up to, in London, potentially £50 or more every week (see below).

Check out the cost and frequency of local buses to and from the university campus, the time of the last bus – perhaps you'll have to fork out for a taxi after midnight – and the safety of the area in which you live. If it's not safe to walk home at night, you'll either be looking at self-imposed house arrest after sun-down or yet more cab fares.

Living on campus obviously cuts your travel costs, but even if you can find somewhere within a mile or two, you will protect your pennies, and what's more you'll keep fit what with all the walking, cycling or even jogging you'll be doing back and forth.

As soon as you get to university, one of your top priorities should be to find out about local travel passes. There'll often be some kind of pass for buses and/or trains for students and/or young people.

Passes are often restricted to a certain number of trips or to a specified period of a day, a weekend, a week, a month, a year – or sometimes even a term – and sorting it out near the beginning of term will ensure that you get the most out of it. They can also cost so much that you'll want to get the expense out of the way before you're too broke.

Travel in London

Most public transport in London makes burning money look like sound investment practice. Thanks to recent price reductions the buses are actually quite reasonable, but they still take forever to get anywhere. The same goes for the whole public transport system, actually, but that's partly because London is just so damn big.

The sheer size of the place also makes walking impractical for a journey even a relatively small way across town. As for cycling, again the distances are a challenge and, if you survive the traffic and the fumes, you may just make it to your destination.

As you probably know, even if you're not a Londoner, public transport consists mainly of the Underground ('the Tube') and red double-decker buses. There are also overground trains and other smaller networks like the Docklands Light Railway, Thameslink and the River buses (which are boats that hardly anyone uses). Students can get 30% off bus passes, travelcards and some DLR fares by flashing a valid photocard.

Using the pre-pay Oyster Card gets you cheaper single fares and cuts down the time you have to spend at congested ticket booths.

There's a whole pack of travelcards for buses, Tubes and trains. They're for different people, for different periods of time and even for different modes of transport (you can, for example, get passes for buses only, which won't set you back more than a few quid).

Most importantly, they're for different zones. Zone-wise, London is split into concentric rings with a circle in the centre. The circle is Zone 1 and the rings going out are Zones 2, 3, 4, 5 and 6. If you only need to travel within a single zone, travel is relatively cheap, but cross the line and prices start climbing. **Unfortunately most of the universities in London aren't in residential areas (or not areas that students can afford) and it can be tough balancing the cost saving of cheaper accommodation with the cost of getting from there to college and back again every day.**

For example, a monthly Travelcard for Zones 1 (where most of London University's buildings are) to Zone 3 (where the rents are more likely to be student-friendly) would set you back £91.40 – or £64 with a Student Card, for which you get an application form from your university.

Don't be tempted to resort to black taxis or minicabs. You could easily blow your weekly travel budget on one trip. Even late at night, you shouldn't have to. The night bus network – although interminably slow and full of drunk teenagers (as well as drunk students) – will get you home eventually.

NATIONAL AND INTERNATIONAL TRAVEL

The further you live from home, the more it's going to cost to get there and back. So either pick a university that's not too far away or give up on the idea of making it back for your mum's Sunday lunch every weekend.

Bus and coach services are usually quite a bit cheaper than the trains, but you may be looking at a much slower journey. Unless, of course, the trains don't get any better over the next few years, in which case you'll be sitting in a stationary carriage for hours anyway.

Either way, you'll want to get either a Student Coachcard (for National Express and other coach services) or a Young Person's Railcard. You could get both, but once you've picked your mode of travel, you might as well stick with it. They charge a one-off fee after which you get big travel discounts – although sometimes you'll find you can only travel on double apex supersaver trains on Tuesdays when there's a 'z' in the month and you've had a rabies shot. The basic deals are as follows:

- **Young Person's Railcard:** a third off most rail fares in the UK. Minimum fares apply before 10am Monday-Friday (except during July and August). You can get a Young Person's Railcard even if you're no longer a young person, so long as you're in full-time education.
- **Student Coachcard:** Full-time students or anyone aged 16-25 can get 30% off National Express fares in England and Wales, plus through fares to Scotland (though not Scottish Citylink journeys entirely within Scotland).

As for travelling abroad, most universities have their own travel bureau on campus. They're usually pretty cheap and specialise in student deals, but if there's either a Campus Travel or STA Travel bureau nearby, you may want to check out fares with them too.

There are discount cards galore for the international traveller – most of which cost money and usually only one of which will be worthwhile (and that not until you need it):

- **The International Student Identity Card (ISIC):** Access to over 25,000 discounts in 100 countries worldwide.
- **Euro under-26 card:** Many perks and benefits for intrepid student travellers.
- **Go 25:** Much the same.

- **YHA Membership (Youth Hostel Association):** Access to budget youth hostels all round the world, plus selected local discounts.

Also available are Inter-rail tickets (cheap tickets for a month's unlimited travel on the railways of Europe).

TRAVEL ALLOWANCES

Students are expected to spend about £500 on travel in a year. But if your expenses are higher and you are lucky enough to fall into one of the following categories, then you can claim more:

- You're disabled, especially if you are unable to use public transport and have to rely primarily on taxis (see **Chapter 13**)
- You need to get to another establishment as part of your medical or dental course
- You're attending an institution abroad as an essential part of your course (see **Chapter 13**).

CARS

Why the hell are you reading a book about student financial survival if you're even contemplating owning a car? You must have money to burn if you think you can afford it. You can't. 'Nuff said.

Oh, alright, we'll say a little more, but only a little.

If you own a car, as we already said, the single biggest cost after the vehicle itself will be the insurance (see above). Then there's petrol, which ain't cheap either (approximately £30 to fill a medium-sized tank), plus you've got road tax (up to £160 annually – more for diesel cars), maintenance and an annual MOT test on top of all that. If (excluding the cost of the car) it doesn't cost you an extra £1,000 a year, you're very lucky or you're using it so little you probably don't need it anyway.

Should you be crazy enough or rich enough to have a car as a student, you could always offer lifts to friends and get them to chip in for the petrol – so long as it's less than the price of a bus or taxi, everyone should benefit.

However, don't set yourself up as a minicab unless you've got a licence. It's illegal and they'll take away your driving licence if they catch you. Then you'll be sorry.

Apart from the expense, possibly the biggest problem with owning a car is that it's always you who has to drive whenever you go anywhere with your mates and that means you can't drink.

Academic costs

You might think that once you've paid your tuition fees, you should get everything provided – exercise books with you name written on them, a pencil, some crayons – just like primary school.

But no – unfortunately, your tuition fees are just the start of it.

For a start, even though we're at the start of the 21st century, books are still a vital element of every degree course.

Strangely enough some students, when confronted with a long reading list of academic titles, get a bit over-excited and rush out and treat it as a shopping list. Don't be tempted. You certainly won't need them all and, even if you do, that's what a library is for.

With any luck, the list will be prioritised. There'll be main texts and secondary texts. You may well want your own copy of the main ones.

If so, your first port of call should be the university's second-hand bookshop (if it has one). If you're lucky, you'll get everything you need for half the usual price – maybe even less. Don't worry if someone's already written notes in the margins or highlighted bits. They may save you a lot of trouble.

Get hold of your reading list as early as possible, so that you can look for pre-enjoyed books before everyone else on your course buys up the complete stock, leaving you to buy your books new.

Whether you buy your books cheap or not, you'll probably spend more on books during the first term of each year than at any other time.

Many students feel they need a computer for typing up essays and for email and internet access. Or for programming or spreadsheets if that kind of thing is part of their course.

All universities have computers available for student use, so you may be able to get by without having your own, but often there aren't really enough to go around or the opening hours don't fit in with your through-the-night attitude to essay crises.

A buzzing, whistling, DVD-playing, CD-rewriting, tea-making state-of-the-art computer will set you back thousands of pounds, but you can get a pretty good second-hand one for a few hundred. Arts students should be able to get away with something more basic, but scientists or design students are probably better off investing in something superfast and superclever to cope with the hi-tech software their courses are likely to use. It's your call whether you really can justify the expense, but if you're going to think about a personal bank loan for anything (see **Chapter 9**), a computer may be the right thing.

Then again, that's what birthdays and Christmases are for. Getting computers as presents.

As we already said back in **Chapter 2**, your choice of course has an impact on what academic costs you're going to face.

Whether it's an easel, oils and canvas or a lab coat, each course has its own cost implications. Art and design courses tend to be most crippling, but most have costs hidden in there somewhere.

Get an idea from your department of what the costs are and whether they know of any help you might be able to apply for (including, for example, bursaries – see **Chapter 8**).

Whatever you study, there are some basics you'll need: piles of notepads, files, folders, pens, paperclips, staples, highlighter pens, printing paper – and lots of dividers so you can spend your time organising your work rather than actually getting on and doing any of it.

Get a part-time job with lots of benefits. Working at a cinema, I got free tickets and popcorn for me and my friends. British Airways sometimes take on students part-time and they get the same discounts on flights as everyone else. At a very minimum, restaurants tend to give staff a free meal.

Eleanor Harris, Durham University.

Make a specific allowance for photocopying. Seriously. You'll have to do that much. If the maintenance and running costs weren't so high and if it weren't for the fact that you'll need to do most of your copying in the library, it would probably be worth buying your own copier.

It isn't, though. We only said that to make you realise quite how much money we're talking about here. Serious bucks.

To limit your academic costs to the £429 listed in the table near the beginning of this chapter, you'll have to take a lot of care.

Your course, however, is obviously pretty damn important. So don't skimp more than you have to. Where possible, buy second-hand. Or better still, borrow.

Entertainment and socialising

Perhaps the only element of your budget that has any more give in it than a frozen pencil is entertainment.

Don't imagine that you can just cut the whole thing, however. You will need to have fun from time to time. Apart from the fact that you'd fairly swiftly go psycho if you didn't go out and kick back occasionally, you'd also miss out on a good chewy chunk of what student life is all about.

But if something's gotta give, it's gotta be the finances for fun.

When you come to work out your budget (see **Chapter 14**), you'll need to allow generously for the cost of everything you can't predict exactly. What's left is what you can allow yourself for entertainment.

With a bit of luck you'll be under budget on other things and therefore be able to loosen up on your own spending restrictions, but it's better to do that *once* you're in the clear, rather than spend first and ask questions later.

Still, if you want to have a good time, but need to do it cheaply, at least it's easier if you happen to be a student.

For a start, if your students' union is affiliated to NUS, you'll get a free NUS card at the beginning of your first year. It'll carry your name, NUS number, the students' union's stamp and an invariably unattractive mug shot.

This is your passport to discounts in clubs, pubs, cinemas, theatres, in fact just about anywhere where students will be welcome bums on seats.

Within your university, too, the students' union will be responsible for putting on ents ranging from regular club nights to hypnotists, from movies to plays – you name it.

As we said in **Chapter 2** (and I'm sure you were paying attention), the quality, quantity and the kind of entertainment varies from place to place – and even if it weren't for those variations, the differences in costs would probably be wider than a hamster eating a frisbee.

As it is, what you spend on entertainments will depend entirely on where you're living, what's available, what tickles your giggle stops and how often you do it.

Taking all this into account, you're probably looking at a good-time budget of around £30 to £40 a week. This is to cover the usual: drinks, entrance to clubs, gigs and concerts, more drinks, movie tickets, eating out (if you don't count it under food, see above), a few more drinks and morning-after painkillers.

Drinking in student bars is almost always cheaper than regular pubs and if you get your drinks in during happy hours, you can squeeze even more alcohol out of your notes.

Always be on the look-out for free entry and cheap deals. If you're a girl, practise your seductive smile and the blokes might just buy your drinks for you. If you're an easily-seduced bloke, try not to get taken in too often.

Miscellaneous expenses

CIGARETTES

If you have a twenty-a-day habit, that's £35 a week on bad breath, smoky hair and a hacking cough. That's more than £1,800 a year. Hardly spare change.

Roll-ups are cheaper, but just as unhealthy and almost as expensive.

Give up the cancer sticks and you can free up that £35 for something healthy and fun, like windsurfing, or Swedish massage.

Loads of students smoke just because it's sociable, but why not get together with a mate who smokes too and resolve to pack it in together?

No more student loan up in smoke (literally). You'll feel better, look better, smell better and save money. What more incentive do you need?

MOBILE PHONES

Pre-pay mobile phones are popular with students and are two-a-penny these days.

Well, not quite that cheap perhaps, but they're an attractive alternative to sharing a single land line with your housemates. You get your own personal number and the cost of calls isn't too high if you don't go crazy (about 5p to 50p per minute, depending on the time of the call, who you're calling and the network you use). It's worth looking into any special deals available – most networks offer discounts if you bulk-buy text messages in advance, for example.

A £50 pre-pay voucher should last you at least an entire term or even longer if you keep your text life under control and avoid peak-rate calls.

Contract mobiles are generally more expensive, even with the free off-peak minutes included in most packages. But keep looking out for special mobile offers advertised in newspapers; sometimes you can get the latest model handset with free connection and other benefits for a very good monthly price.

Whatever deal you opt for, keep an eye on what you actually spend. You may want either to switch tariff or learn to talk quicker.

CHILDCARE

If you have a child in registered day care, you can get some kind of help with the expense. It might not cover all of it, but there are also supplementary grants available to students with dependents. See **Chapter 13** for more guidance for student parents.

And finally...

In **Part 6, The Push Guide to Penny Pinching**, there's even more advice about budgeting and stretching your money till it's a mile long.

Chapter Twelve

Costs from out of the blue

It's all very well planning your finances like a military operation, but sometimes Lady Luck likes to shove an oar in and remind you who's boss. She'll dump an unexpected expense on you that makes all your finely tuned preparation look like doodles in the sand.

Nonetheless, while it may be a contradiction in terms, part of financial planning is to plan for the unexpected.

One way is to get insurance (see **Chapter 11**), but there are also certain seasonal costs you can predict. 'How?' you might ask. Because Push is going to tell you, that's how.

Starting out

FRESHER'S WEEK

One thing about student life can be more or less guaranteed – the first week will the most expensive of your entire university career.

During the first week – or, as it's more commonly known, Freshers' Week (also 'Orientation Week', 'Week One', 'Week Zero', 'Intro Week' and so on) – there aren't usually any academic commitments, just an endless stream of social events and red tape. Some universities make do with just a couple of days, others plump for a whole fortnight, but it'll be an expensive time nonetheless.

There are three functions of Freshers' Week:

- **Social:** to break the ice and establish a social life

- **Environmental:** to get used to the new situation and find your feet (the end of your legs is a good place to start the hunt)
- **Administrative:** to get you to fill out a million more forms and have described to you in tedious detail everything from how your course will be taught and assessed to what to do in the event of a new ice age.

To get the most out of Freshers' Week, it's a good idea to keep all three of these in mind.

And because you're going to be focusing on those three, it's dangerously easy to just spend, spend, spend during the first week.

In fact, it's pretty much impossible not to shell out a quite disturbing proportion of the money that's supposed to last the whole year.

Just for starters, you'll probably have to pay your tuition fees (if you have to pay any), plus your rent for the term or at least your first month's rent and a deposit. That's several tonners down already.

Then there'll be…

- all the clubs, societies and sports teams you want to join (about £3 to £15 a pop)
- drinks to buy – and, believe us, there's a whole lot of drinking going on in Freshers' Week, what with unmissable ents on every night
- pubs and clubs to check out
- people to impress
- new kitchen cupboards to fill up with grub
- plants and posters to make your room feel less like an asylum cell
- books, paper and pens to buy
- endless passport photos to get for all the forms and ID cards.

Allow yourself some extra for Freshers' Week,. At least an extra £50 for entertainments alone (let alone all the one-off expenses like mugs and a hole-punch). Fresher's Week is one of the few times it's okay to push the boat out a bit.

Splashing out is part of settling in, getting to know the people (biblically, in some cases), consuming cheap beer like it's going out of fashion. It's almost an initiation ritual – after a week of binging and parties, you wake up with a hangover, late for a lecture and completely broke. You are now, officially, a student.

Where does it all go?

But after this initial spurt of justifiable madness, it's time to take a chill pill and review your financial status before drinking yourself into a false sense of security.

Even during Freshers' Week there are some reins to pull on. Don't pay out money for anything unless you know you'll benefit from it.

For example, don't join every student society that looks more interesting than belly button fluff – join only those where you think there's a genuine chance you might actually turn up to something they do in the next few years. (But be open-minded – you'd be surprised what strange and perverse pastimes you might find yourself drawn to.)

And don't feel like you have to be a big spender to make friends or impress anyone. If you insist on getting all the rounds in, you'll look like a prat because everyone's in the same boat financially. (In fact, students often don't bother with buying rounds at all.) You'll end up with everyone taking advantage of you for a week and then being too poor to go out again all year.

There are a couple of saving graces about the finances of Freshers' Week.

Firstly the goody bag. The students' union usually organises a plastic bag full of free stuff for new students. The free stuff comes from sponsors desperate to get your custom and includes everything from dog-flavoured Pot Snacks to new guarana and amphetamine drinks.

You'll also be given a whole load of money-off coupons for more of the same which, when you discover the stuff is disgusting, you should throw away rather than waste money.

There should also be some useful stuff in there, like toiletries, condoms, coffee, crisps, chocolate, even beer – you know, the essentials.

`Don't turn the washing machine on unless it's full — anything less is a waste of energy.`

Secondly, there's the stuff you bring from home. Many parents won't object to you raiding the cupboards before setting off to university. Some will even help you load up.

Freshers' Week is also the time parents are most likely to give you some extra cash.

You'll presumably have already worked out between you how the formal parental contributions deal is going to work (see **Chapter 5**) and many parents want to stick rigidly to the formula. Fair enough. However, even they often feel tempted to shove £20 in your hand as they wave you goodbye.

If they can afford it, don't stop them. Just say thanks and tell them you'll see them at Christmas. (You can tell them you love them too, if that's the kind of stuff you do with your folks.)

In fact, if your parents can afford it, you can even tell them from Push that even if they think giving you the odd tenner here, the occasional twenty there, is a bad idea – and we wouldn't disagree with them on that – we think this is the one exception.

Where does it all go?

SETTLING IN

Freshers are particularly susceptible to 'loan arrival frenzy' – when the first instalment of your loan hits your bank account, it's tempting to delude yourself into thinking you're rich. But that apparently huge lump sum has to last the entire term and it won't take much budget planning to see that it'll barely stretch across the bar, let alone across the term.

Budgeting starts from day one. If it doesn't, then that first, reassuringly sizeable stash of cash will disappear like water down a plughole, leaving no more than a few hairs and some gunk behind.

In fact, it's worse than that – even if you do budget, you'll watch as your bank balance after the first week turns into a pale imitation of its former self by week two and after the first or second month the accumulated rent, bills, books, food, drink, taxi fares etc. will almost certainly have beaten it down to minus figures.

In any case, your budget for the first few weeks should be on the high side. For one thing, for several weeks you'll be making one-off payments for stuff you need, like a kettle, washing powder and a second set of underwear.

You'll also need to get the lie of the land. Where's the best place to shop for food, stationery, books and so on, weighing up the pros and cons of distance, price and quality? Where's the nearest laundrette? Where's the best place for new clothes, because your first attempt at the laundrette turned everything pink?

These reconnaissance missions can in themselves become impromptu social events, either as collective outings or as debriefings from various scouting parties.

There are also likely to be some costly abortive attempts at new recipes, unnecessary travel expenses till you find out about the right bus pass and, until you realise why no one else ever goes there, visits to the more expensive kebab shop.

Main events

There are a few events during student life when you will feel the need to spend an obscene amount of money for something really unusual, special or just plain stupid.

University balls, for example. Most of them are basically just a big dinner and a disco – the difference being that you wear posh frocks and pay a posh price tag. Usually, there'll be more by way of entertainments than simply a couple of decks and a few flashing lights. Think ice sculptures and string quartets, cabaret acts and casinos, fun fairs and bouncy castles plus loads of bands – sometimes even has-beens you've heard of.

Some universities go for balls in a much bigger way than others. Some have them once or twice a year – modest affairs at £30 a head.

Other universities (Oxbridge especially) seem to have them almost every week and some of them are outrageously decadent bacchanalias more reminiscent of a Hollywood wedding than a student shindig, whose tickets sell like hot cakes at over a hundred quid each.

Add to the ticket price the cost of far too much alcohol (some will probably be included in the ticket, but usually not enough), obligatory dress or tux hire (or even purchase if you plan to go to several of these jamborees).

The whole thing can end up costing the same as several weeks' rent. At that sort of price, these should be very special occasions. There's no need to go to every ball going. They'll only become mundane.

Then there are job interviews.

Especially in your final year, you'll want to have an outfit that says, 'I scrub up alright and can look professional if I have to'.

Looking dapper is no good if no one gets to see it. Most big graduate employers should offer to pay your train fares (and if they don't, it doesn't hurt to ask), but getting to interviews for postgraduate courses or smaller, impoverished organisations can place a serious toll on your finances.

This is not the kind of worry a budding career-monster needs as they try to impress their way on to the first rung of the ladder. The good news is that you may be able to get some help. In the case of a job interview, your bank will often make allowances and allow you to extend your overdraft (but not by much, mind and don't forget to ask first), so you can buy a suit.

For any other special events, you may just have to ask your parents or put in a few extra hours at your job if you have one – just one extra shift might earn you enough.

Remember that you may need to look smart at quite short notice. You may be able to predict family weddings or christenings a few months ahead of time, but if you have a funeral to attend, you'll probably have other things on your mind than what to wear.

At the end of it all, you may want to look the part for graduation day. Maybe not – plenty of students have collected their scrolls wearing jeans and a T-shirt under their gowns. But even they had to pay to hire the gown and, if they wanted it, the gurning photo for gran's bedside table.

Spoiling yourself

Jewellery, perfume or aftershave, magazines, cosmetics, weekend breaks… now and then you need something to pump up your pecker. So long as you're sensible the rest of the time and when you do take your weekend break you spend it in a youth hostel in the Lake District rather than the Hilton in Hawaii, you should be able to afford the occasional treat.

See how much you have left each week after all the necessities have been paid for. If it's more than nothing, decide if you deserve a treat now or later or just put more into your entertainment budget for next week.

The same goes for holidays. Except you'll need to save up all year. Or better still, make use of the long vacation to earn money in a foreign clime (see **Chapter 7**), although you're likely to need a bit of cash to get you there in the first place.

If you work, you may even be able to put a little aside to save up for something really special, whether it's an air ticket to India, a leather jacket or a scooter.

The secret is learn to recognise a luxury item before you pay for it – distinguish between what you want (the stuff you can live without) and what you need (the things you can't). Shoes are a necessity, for instance. Ten pairs, however, are a luxury.

Prioritising expenditure is a central part of good budgeting sense. Stick luxury items on your Christmas and birthday wish lists and make sure the list does the rounds at the right time.

Gifts

Every now and then (usually when you're down to your last penny), some bastard so-called friend will decide to have a birthday and expect to be bestowed with lavish gifts.

Okay, so if you're all students you know that your mates can barely afford the wrapping paper, let alone anything to put in it. So improvise a bit – give your mate that scratched, battered old CD they gave you for Christmas or make them something 'Blue Peter' style out of an old toilet roll, a cluster of cotton buds, a tub of glitter and some sticky-back plastic.

Better still, convince them that the new Aqualung album is quite simply the best thing since sliced bread and then buy it for them after cheekily recording it for your own collection. That way, you've treated yourself as well as the naturally delighted recipient.

Improvisation is the key here along with, again, a good eye for the bargains.

If it's your mate's birthday, find out what he or she really wants and then club together with some other friends to buy it.

When it comes to family birthdays and anniversaries and Christmas, you'll probably have to use your common sense and maybe a little bit of artistic licence to come up with a novel gift idea.

It's not as if Christmas should come as a surprise. Apart from falling on the same date every year, you may find subtle hints of its approach in shop windows and TV trailers from late September onwards.

Even with a big and demanding family, you should be able to plan and limit the expenditure and the good news is that however many presents you have to give, you'll probably get about the same number back. Make this work for you by putting out the word about what you want good and early.

Also, when the January sales come around, seize the opportunity to buy some reduced Christmas cards and half-price pressies.

Better still, make your own cards – the ones in the shops aren't cheap considering they're just bits of folded card. Making your own will give it that special 'individual' touch, even if you don't have a single creative bone in your body.

After all, it's the thought that counts. Although we've always found that just thinking about buying a present is rarely quite so warmly received. Nevertheless, if you can find something really thoughtful for 50p, it'll often go down better than something impersonal for a lot more.

Oh, and don't forget birthdays. A card on the right day is worth more than a hurriedly bought present three weeks late.

Medical costs

For some people medical costs are an ongoing expense, particularly if you wear contacts or are diabetic or asthmatic. Generally, non-prescription stuff like contact lens solution is just going to have to be part of your budget.

However, all too often, extra medical costs come as a nasty insult added to the injury of being ill or hurt in the first place.

Fortunately the NHS, despite all the complaints, is still both free and offers a pretty high standard of care. A lot better than anything most students could afford in the world of private healthcare, anyway.

Nonetheless, there are charges for prescriptions, eye tests and dental appointments.

Students are no longer automatically exempt from prescription charges and the like, but you may be entitled to help with charges for eye tests, prescriptions and dental treatment through the NHS Low Income Scheme.

Take a look at the booklet HC11, *Are you Entitled to Help with Health Costs?*, available from your local benefits agency and probably from the students' union welfare department and the university's health service. Or you can call the Health Information Service on 0800 66 55 44.

If you're eligible, you will need to fill in an HC1 claim form, which you can get from a Social Security Office or your doctor. Once you've filled that in and sent it off, you'll get an HC2 certificate which entitles you to full help with health costs.

Alternatively, the Prescription Pricing Authority can give more information or an HC1 form – check out www.ppa.org.uk/ppa/low_income.htm or call them on 0845 850 1166.

If you've forgotten to go through all this palaver or you've already had to pay out for treatment or prescriptions, keep your receipts – you might still be able to claim a refund for part of it.

PART 5 5

Finance for real people

Chapter Thirteen

Special interest groups

What about me?

It's easy enough to talk about students as an amorphous collective blob, to say this is how it is if your parents earn this or if you live there – but students are more than case studies. Students – yes, even students – are real people.

And, because they're all individuals and it follows that there are so many exceptions to any rule we might try to describe, it can seem as if the only rule is: there are no rules.

This part of the book, therefore, is dedicated to the exceptions – to the individuals who, one way or another, actually make up about half the student population.

What about postgrads?

As the number of undergraduates has risen over the past ten years, so has the number of postgrads. And it's not just a simple percentage game.

As more people realise the career benefits of having a degree, they rightly assume there are even greater benefits if you distinguish yourself further by having more than one degree.

A higher proportion of graduates in the UK go on to further training than almost anywhere else in the world – second only to Denmark.

Unfortunately, however, more people wanting to take up postgrad studies means more pressure on the sources of funding to support it. New funding possibilities have sprung up, but not enough to make life easy.

To choose to be a postgrad is almost to say: 'I don't mind continuing to be poor for at least another few years' (and quite possibly, if you become an academic, never having a great deal of money).

Costs to consider can be handily split into two main wodges: fees and living costs.

Fees

Those who started an undergraduate degree since 1998 have been gently eased into the idea that you have to pay a bit towards your university education. Postgraduate fees, like undergraduate fees, are usually only a contribution to the total cost, the rest of which is paid for by taxpayers. But the undergraduate fees charged are – for now – peanuts compared to the cost of getting postgrad letters after your name.

Postgrads always have to pay towards their own fees or find someone to pay these for them. Different courses cost different amounts, although the standard going rate is currently £2,870 a year. Quite a few are more expensive – MBAs, for example, can easily cost £10,000 a year.

Living costs

Take a look at Part Four if you're not sure where the cash will go and bear in mind that postgrads' living costs are usually a fair bit higher than undergraduates'.

Postgraduate courses tend to have fewer holidays (a typical masters course lasts 11-12 months) and academic costs (books, computers, periodicals and so on) are likely to take a bigger slice of the budget.

Being a bit older, as a rule, they'll often want somewhere on their own – or less of a dive, at least – and they'll be fed up of living on baked beans and pasta. Living in halls, for example, is hardly conducive to the kind of hard study and long hours most postgrads need (and want) to put in.

SO, HOW DO POSTGRADS PAY FOR IT?

There are a number of sources of funding available to postgrads, but it isn't as, er, *straightforward* as the undergraduate system and the competition is fierce.

By definition, postgraduates are a pretty clever bunch and the myriad of methods of getting funding keeps wannabe boffins on their toes.

The course you want to study and your academic brilliance make a big difference to your chances.

The best odds are in courses that have a clear benefit to the country or to a company. Postgrad courses fall into two categories: taught courses and research degrees. Some funding sources only apply to one type or the other, but taught courses often have a specific use and so whomever it's useful to may be willing to pay.

As a ludicrously broad generalisation, research degrees only get funding if they have a practical application, but if that application makes money for someone other than the student, they may well get support. So science, technology and business courses attract much bigger bucks than, say, research projects on Shakespeare entitled 'To be or not to be: Should Hamlet have phoned a friend?'.

If you're outstanding in your subject area, you're also more likely to get some kind of support, even in the arts (in which case that support may be only a pat on the back and a few luncheon vouchers). This works as a kind of ad hoc filtering system. You should only be doing postgrad study if you're up to the considerable academic challenge. So, the better you are, the more likely you are to get a place on a course (or find a supervisor for your research) and to get funding to do it.

Apply early and apply often is the best way to boost your chances. The postgraduate admissions cycle is more flexible than that of undergraduate courses, with many studentships advertised several months after the UCAS forms had to be in, but it doesn't hurt to start looking a full year before you want to start studying – or even earlier.

Text, don't talk.

Increasingly, postgrads combine their studies (often part-time themselves) with part-time or full-time work.

As for your living expenses, they're your own problem too. Unless you're taking a Postgraduate Certificate in Education (PGCE), you can't apply for a student loan.

Postgrads who got some kind of hardship money when they first came in to higher education might qualify for some emergency funding, but only as a last resort.

Nevertheless, there are funds out there to help pay both fees and the costs of living. The most important are laid out below and your university will also be able to give you advice.

University careers offices often produce leaflets about postgraduate funding and where to get it and most universities publish special postgrad prospectuses.

Talk directly to a tutor in the relevant department where you want to study. They'll tell you more about their work and may be able to give you pointers about raising the readies.

It's also worth taking a look at the 'Gradfund' page on Newcastle University's website (www.newcastle.ac.uk/services/finance/gradfund) and www.studentmoney.org.

You can search for the right source of funding by using pull-down menus to pick the relevant subject, your nationality (some awards are available to all nationalities, but some are specific) and what exactly you intend to do (research, etc.).

The website then searches its database and comes up with suggestions. If you have no luck, you may need to be more general with your criteria.

GOVERNMENT FUNDING

The Government is (indirectly) by far the biggest bill-footer of postgrad study. Its award-making bodies give out funds to students doing masters or doctorates and to full-time students doing professional or vocational training.

These awards might pay for your fees or your maintenance (living) costs, some allowances (for children, for example) or some additional expenses such as travel, but probably not all of them.

You might also be able to wheedle additional funds such as a support grant for research training.

All awards are made on a competitive basis, so it's hardly worth bothering unless you can boast a pretty rocking result in your undergraduate studies – usually a good 2:1 or a 1st.

The awards come in three flavours:

- **A Research Studentship:** Usually a three-year full-time or five-year part-time award for students doing doctorates (PhD or DPhil)
- **A Collaborative Research Studentship:** For example, Cooperative Awards in Science and Engineering (CASE), where a company contributes to the costs of a postgraduate research project and usually offers the student some valuable experience, plus some extra cash on top of the basic award, if they feel like it.
- **Advanced Course Studentships:** For taught courses lasting at least six months (usually for one to two years), usually leading to a masters – MSc, MA – or other qualification.

First check with the university department about how to apply. Sometimes they handle the application themselves – although by no means all courses or departments attract funding. Just because you've been accepted to do a course or research that's eligible for studentships, don't assume that you personally will receive one.

Often you'll need to contact the award-making body directly. There are now seven of them handing out the Government dough, comprising six grant-awarding **Research Councils** and the **Arts and Humanities Research Board** (AHRB), which is expected to become a research council proper in 2005. There are separate arrangements for social work qualifications – the **General Social Care Council** (www.gscc.org.uk) is in charge of bursaries that usually cover tuition fees and include a grant.

Each body gives funding for separate subject areas, so make sure you're going to the right one and if they turn you down, don't bother trying the others.

Before you apply, contact them to check that they cover the right subject and to get full details about all the various strings attached to the money they might or might not give you.

For contact details, turn to the back of the book or surf along to www.rcuk.ac.uk

AHRB

As its name suggests, the AHRB funds arts and humanities students, but it doesn't have as much money as most of the Research Councils (see below) and what it does have tends to be highly sought-after. Even so, if you're lucky and get in there quickly, you might be considered for a grant for large-scale collaborative research projects, an award for research leave or a small grant in the creative and performing arts.

Research Councils

There are six Research Councils, each covering a different subject area – five for sciences and technology, and one for economic and social sciences. You should apply to whichever is most appropriate for whatever you want to study.

*   Biotechnology and Biological Sciences Research Council (BBSRC);
*   Engineering and Physical Sciences Research Council (EPSRC);
*   Economic and Social Research Council (ESRC);
*   Medical Research Council (MRC);
*   Natural Environment Research Council (NERC);
*   Particle Physics and Astronomy Research Council (PPARC).

The Research Councils have to report back to the Office of Science and Technology in the Department for Trade and Industry, which should tell you where the balance lies between education and commerce as far as the funding is concerned.

COMPANIES

Employers sometimes sponsor their staff through courses, especially MBAs.

Alternatively, businesses often fund particular research projects and any postgrads that work on them. Sometimes, this'll be run as a collaborative research studentship through CASE (see above).

TRUSTS AND CHARITIES

Trusts and charities are worth investigating. They will probably not be in a position to offer full financial support, but you may get a small award if you apply early enough. Contact EGAS (see **Chapter 8**) or look in the various directories and registers of charities and grant-making trusts.

'The Grants Register' has over 1,000 pages of information on postgrad grants and professional funding worldwide. It should be in the university careers service or reference library, as should 'The

Directory of Grant Making Trusts' – a comprehensive guide to trusts and foundations that give cash to organisations.

Some charities, for example The Wellcome Trust, may fund particular research in the same way that businesses do.

LEAS

Local education authorities (and their equivalents in Scotland and Northern Ireland) do not have to give any money to postgrads, except those on teacher training courses (see below).

UNIVERSITIES

Many universities have a limited number of studentship awards available, for specific courses, which usually cover fees and maintenance. Criteria and deadlines for applications vary, so do your research well in advance with the admissions officer of the university you want to go to.

Individual university departments may also be able to help in one of two ways.

The first is just to ask – it's a long shot, but if you're a complete star in your chosen subject you might just get lucky.

Your best bet for funding direct from your university or department is having a specific tutor take up your cause individually, which is most likely to happen if you stay in the same department where you've already done an undergraduate or lower postgrad degree.

They'll probably be championing your cause because they want you to become an academic, however, so expect to take on some tutoring responsibilities.

The second option is to get a job within the department more formally as a research assistant. You'll get paid and so long as you write up your research appropriately, it'll be assessed for a qualification.

The jobs are usually advertised in the normal way, although if you're already in a department keep your ear to the ground, just in case you can get in there early and persuade them to look no further. Otherwise, check www.jobs.ac.uk or *The Times*, *The Guardian*, *New Scientist*, *Times Higher Education Supplement*, *Lawyer Magazine* etc.

BANKS

Banks aren't a formal part of the funding mechanism for postgrads, but many students rely on them more than any other source.

Most banks that cater for students extend a warm embrace to postgrads. It's worth shopping around – see **Graduate Packages** in **Chapter 6** to find out what your current bank can offer you and check other deals. The best bank for a pimply fresher may not seem so rosy to a hardened postgrad, although a nice four-figure interest-free overdraft can't hurt. Banks also have special loan packages for postgrads, mostly with a lower than standard rate of interest and repayments deferred till you finish your course.

The Government backs the Career Development Loans scheme, but they're only available to students doing vocational courses. See **Chapter 9** and then phone 0800 585 505 for a booklet about CDLs.

5

What about mature students and part-timers?

MATURE STUDENTS

The definition of a 'mature student' varies, but it doesn't necessarily mean someone who wears a cardigan and slippers and drinks a nice cup of cocoa before a sensible bedtime. For the purpose of student finance, 'mature' means a first-time undergraduate over the age of 25.

Read newspapers online for free.

There's not a great deal of difference in the funding available for mature students and their slightly younger counterparts. Almost any full-time student – mature, youthful or just plain childish – is entitled to the student loan up to the age of 50 (or 54 if they intend to go back to work after qualifying). Mature students starting from 2004 should be eligible for the new higher education grant and may qualify for extra help from the Access to Learning Fund.

Mature students are automatically classed as being independent, which means your parents' income doesn't matter a jot when you are being assessed for loans, grants and fee contributions.

Instead it's your wonga that counts – from 2004, independent students whose income is £10,000 or more will be expected to contribute towards their loans and fees, though they'll get the full HE Grant unless they earn more than £15,200 (see **Chapter 8**).

If you're thinking about going back to studying and becoming a mature student, as a first step you might want to get in touch with your nearest educational guidance and information centre by phoning LearnDirect on 0800 100 900. Alternatively, call in at the local Citizens' Advice Bureau.

PART-TIME STUDENTS

Part-time students doing their first degree course should be entitled to financial help for the duration of their course (up to eight years max). From September 2004, part-time students will be eligible for two grants, one for fees and one for course-related costs.

The grants are means-tested. Those on income-assessed benefits or with incomes of less than £14,600 get the full whack and those on less than £21,487 will get some of the money. Partners' income is taken into account, although the thresholds are slightly higher for those with partners or dependent kids. There's no age limit.

Those on low incomes who are studying the equivalent of at least 50% of a full-time course should get help with fees up to a maximum of £575 as well as a grant of £250 to meet the cost of books, travel and so on. (There used to be a loan scheme instead, but this more generous package has replaced it. Yay!)

Get your application pack from the DfES information line on 0800 731 9133.

Part-time students, including those studying less than 50% of a full-time course, might be able to get help with costs such as childcare through the Access to Learning Fund (see **Chapter 9**).

Part-time students with a disability should be eligible for the Disabled Students' Allowances (see below), as long as they complete the course in no more than twice as long as it would take to do it full-time.

Other than that, part-timers have to pay their own fees and, so the thinking goes, since they've got time to work for a living, they don't need other financial help.

MARITAL STATUS

If you're married or an independent student living with a partner, your husband's, wife's or partner's income will be assessed in the same way as parents' incomes would be assessed for most students (see **Chapter 3**).

What about teachers in training?

The UK needs teachers at the moment like the transport system needs a good kick up the arse. As a result, there's rarely been a better time to give teacher training a whirl.

The Government has been offering greater incentives for trainee teachers, especially for postgrads on PGCEs.

To be a teacher you have to have Qualified Teacher Status (QTS) and a PGCE is the most popular way of getting it. PGCE stands for Postgraduate Certificate in Education and, as the name suggests, you need to be a graduate to do the course, which covers initial teacher training.

PGCEs are normally a year (or two, if you study part-time) and you won't have to pay a penny towards fees. In fact, you'll get a training bursary of £6,000. It's not a loan. It's not means-tested. It's just loot.

And there's more. If you're training to teach a subject at secondary school level where the shortage is particularly severe (i.e. maths, science, modern languages, English, design and technology, ICT, construction, engineering or basic skills), you might get an additional bursary of up to £5,000 (or up to £7,500 if you're over 24), although they'll assess your situation to see how much you need. Even overseas students can apply.

Also, graduates specialising in maths, science, technology, modern languages or English can expect a further £4,000 'golden hello' at the end of their first year working as a teacher. A scheme being piloted means those who start working before June 30 2005 will gradually have their student loans repaid by the Government so long as they stay in teaching. After then, check www.teachernet.gov.uk/teachersloans to see whether the scheme has been extended.

In Wales, this scheme is called the Priority Subject Recruitment Initiative and they add Welsh to the list of shortage subjects. For more info, contact The National Assembly for Wales Education Department on 029 2082 5831.

If you're interested in being a teacher, visit the Graduate Teacher Training Registry at www.gttr.ac.uk or the Teacher Training Agency at www.useyourheadteach.gov.uk.

The Teaching Information Line has full details of money available while you're training: call 0845 6000 991 (the Welsh Language Teaching Information Line is 0845 6000 992).

You can find scintillating stuff about support for Teachers and Trainee Teachers at the following websites: www.teachernet.gov.uk (the full range of relevant government info and sources), www.teacherline.org.uk (free and confidential teacher support network for all teachers and trainees in primary and secondary schools in England and Wales) and www.teachers4london.com (created to try to get people into teaching in London schools).

Details of new training salaries and support for the latest Graduate Teacher Programme are available from the DfES's Public Enquiry Unit on 0870 000 2288 or at www.dfes.gov.uk/go4itnow.

You can also get your QTS by doing a (usually four-year) undergraduate course of teacher training that leads to a first degree – normally a BEd.

But Push doesn't recommend it right now as you or your parents will have to pay the normal fee contributions (subject to assessment) and all you'll get to live on is the normal student loan. Better to spend three years on any old interesting degree and then do a PGCE afterwards. It doesn't take any longer and the demand for teachers is such that the Government is unlikely to drop the sweeteners for a while yet.

What about students with kids and dependants?

If you've got someone who depends on you financially or for care – whether it's your child, someone else's, a husband, wife, parent or some other adult – then you could be eligible for certain extra money, even if you're still dependent on your parents yourself. Contact your LEA or give the DfES a ring on 0800 731 9133 for a copy of 'Childcare Grant and other support for student parents in higher education'.

Childcare Grant

Just like it says on the tin, this is a grant for students with children in childcare (it has to be the real thing, registered and accredited). The idea is that it covers up to 80% of those costs, up to £114.75 a week for one child and £170 a week for two or more.

The DSS won't count this grant when they're working out your social security benefits so there's nothing to lose. There's no point applying if you receive the Lone Parents' Grant or if you claim the childcare element of the Working Tax Credit from the Inland Revenue – you won't be eligible for this as well.

Parents' Learning Allowance

This is to help with course-related costs for student parents who receive the childcare grant or whose dependants (including husband, wife or partner) have a low income. Low, in this case, means a combined income of less than £3,070 for a couple with one child (£4,095 for two or more children) or £4,095 for a single parent with one child (£5,120 for two or more children). The full grant is £1,330. If you earn more than the threshold, it gets gradually reduced to a minimum of £50. Again, it doesn't count as income for benefits purposes.

The Lone Parents' Grant

This has now been replaced by the Childcare Grant (above), but you can still claim up to £1,150 as an extra non-repayable allowance if you began your course in 2000/1 or earlier and don't get the Childcare Grant or parents' learning allowance.

Child tax credit

Students with dependent children up to 16 (or 16-19 in full-time education) should qualify for a child tax credit, regardless of whether they're working, studying or chewing a brick. Call 0800 500 222 or go to www.inlandrevenue.gov.uk/taxcredits to check eligibility and register.

Adult dependants' grant

Up to £2,335 a year is available to those who have a partner or adult family member dependent on them, but what you actually get depends on what your income is and the income of whoever it is that depends on you.

Others

Universities also often have crèches and nurseries – which may be subsidised or just plain cheap – and there may be a student parents support group.

What about students with disabilities?

Just because you have a disability, it doesn't mean you should have any less choice about where and what to study and all universities have a policy statement which outlines the support and facilities they offer, financial or otherwise.

Get a copy of these along with the prospectuses when you're thinking about applying. It's a good idea to check the place out in person if you're serious about studying there, to assess your needs and attend a 'special needs' interview to discuss them with the university's disabilities officer (assuming they have one – if they haven't, well, that tells you something).

Generally, everything we've said elsewhere about fees, loans, blah-de-blah still applies. In fact, even if your disability is severe and is likely to affect your earning potential after graduation, it doesn't affect your right to claim the same student loan as everyone else.

The Student Loans Company will also ignore any benefits you get because of your disability when working out when you should start repaying your loan and how quickly.

Leave your cards at home when you go out and only take cash. And don't buy junk food – it might be cheap but the cost racks up very quickly. After a couple of weeks you'll be off the cola and crisps habit and your teeth will thank you for it.

There are other sources of income you may be able to tap, too.

If you have a disability or a medical condition that directly affects your study (sight impairment, for instance), you might be entitled to a Disabled Students' Allowance (DSA) of up to £1,525 a year basic (£1,140 max for part-timers).

The DSA can be used to pay for a care helper, Braille books, adaptations to accommodation, extra travel costs because of the disability and so on.

In fact, there's up to £4,565 available for specialist equipment over the length of your whole course and up to £11,550 a year to pay for a non-medical helper (£8,670 max for part-timers).

However, the DSA isn't supposed to go towards costs that you'd still have if you weren't at university.

Your need for financial support is assessed on the nature of your disability and what type of course you're studying. There's also usually a bundle of other conditions that might seem like a pointless hassle.

For example, you'll often need to provide medical proof of your disability, such as a letter from your doctor. Or if you're dyslexic, you should get a letter from a recognised specialist.

One way or another, you'll need to convince your LEA that your disability – whether it be physical, mental-health difficulties or a learning difficulty – means you actually need the extra money to study. Ask them what they'll want to see *before* you send in your application, because if you don't make them happy in the first place, they may expect you to undergo the extra hassle and indignity of an independent assessment.

Disabled postgrads can claim a Disabled Students' Allowance (DSA) of up to £5,500 a year, providing they're not receiving bursaries or awards from the research councils, the NHS or General Social Care Council, or a university award that includes support for a disability.

None of the allowances for students with disabilities are means-tested and they don't have to be paid back, but if you're claiming for a particular expense most authorities will want to see a receipt or a quote before they'll pay up.

Although most students can't claim any benefits, if you're getting Incapacity Benefit, say, you'll probably still be allowed to claim while you're studying.

5

For a copy of the DfES's booklet, 'Bridging the Gap', which answers commonly asked questions about DSAs, call their information line on 0800 731 9133 (textphone 0800 328 8988). Handily, the guide is also available in Braille or on audio tape.

There is a free and confidential Benefit Enquiry Line for people with disabilities and their carers. Call 0800 882200 (minicom users call 0800 243355).

It's also a good idea to contact SKILL – the National Bureau for Students with Disabilities. Their free helpline number is 0800 328 5050, though they prefer you to call (020) 7657 2337 if you can afford it. Alternatively, e-mail them via their website, www.skill.org.uk.

Their full contact details can be found in the back of the book, along with those of other relevant organisations. They publish various information booklets, including 'Into Higher Education'.

What about Scottish students?

For starters, you won't be dealing with your LEA, but the Student Awards Agency for Scotland (SAAS) and if you've got any questions, they're the ones to ask.

There are some other significant differences in arrangements too, the most famous of which is that Scottish students studying at Scottish universities don't have to pay tuition fees. At all.

In fact, nor do other EU students studying in Scotland.

However, Scottish students have to pay an 'endowment' when they graduate (which, although the figures are lower, is not dissimilar to how tuition fees will operate in the rest of the UK when top up fees start in 2006). It's £2,092 for people who started in 2003, but it increases by a few quid each year with inflation. Also, it applies only to degree courses, not HNDs or HNCs.

A whole range of people get off scot-free, including mature students, lone parents, part-timers, students with disabilities or those who don't manage to get a degree.

Those feeling flash with their cash can pay endowments off in one lump sum on graduation. Otherwise, they'll be collected along with student loan repayments, which are basically the same as the rest of the UK.

There are loads of ifs and buts to all this – who exactly counts as Scottish and so on – so it's best to check out SAAS's website (www.saas.gov.uk) or get hold of the booklet they produce called 'Student Support in Scotland'.

Even if you won't have to pay tuition fees, it's just as important to apply to the SAAS for support or else, as in the rest of the UK, you could end up paying not only fees, but your entire course costs.

Meanwhile, Scottish students are becoming a rarer sight outside Scotland, where they have to pay tuition fees like everyone else.

There are specific bursaries available to Scottish students whether they're mature students, part-timers or from poorer families (up to two grand for the most needy cases). Being Scottish is also one of the factors that might qualify you for all sorts of charitable scholarships and bursaries.

For more information, SAAS's full details are in the back of the book and we've already given you their website address. If you prefer, you can call them on (0131) 476 8212.

What about students from Northern Ireland?

Basically the system is much the same as England and Wales. The only remotely significant difference is that the things that are known as LEAs in England and Wales are called Education & Library Boards (ELBs) in Northern Ireland.

The Department of Education runs the show and can be phoned on (02891) 279279 or virtually visited at www.deni.gov.uk

What about international (aka overseas) students?

EU STUDENTS

Tuition fees

EU students applying to British universities have to pay tuition fees contributions in the same way as UK students. Starting September

2004, the same rules apply to students from the ten countries that joined the EU in May 2004.

If applying through UCAS, they'll be sent an application form for help with tuition fees when they're offered a place on a course. Forms and other useful information are also available at www.dfes.gov.uk/studentsupport/eustudents for further info.

Living Expenses

EU students can't apply for a UK student loan or the Access to Learning Fund. Well, they can apply but they'll be turned down, so there's not much point.

The SOCRATES-ERASMUS and Leonardo Programmes all splash out grants to promote the exchange of students and academic staff around Europe (see below).

STUDENTS FROM OUTSIDE THE EU

Most students from countries outside the EU will have to pay the full cost of fees, although not for nursing or midwifery courses.

Living expenses are your own problem, too.

Bear in mind that, depending on your status, you may not be allowed to work in the UK to fund yourself – even part-time.

GENERAL ADVICE FOR INTERNATIONAL STUDENTS

Before coming to study in Britain, find out what you're letting yourself in for, particularly costs-wise.

UK course fees may look good value (and most of them are), but the cost of living in Britain may be higher than you're used to – even for Americans and Europeans.

Get the latest advice and guidance from your local British Council office and take a look at **Chapter 16** to see how costs vary from place to place. Your chosen university will probably send you more info on local costs if you want it.

Keep an eye on fluctuations in the exchange rate – they may suddenly make the whole thing unaffordable (or much cheaper, if you're lucky).

Apply for funding and scholarships long before your course starts (at least a year) – deadlines vary and competition is tough, so get organised well in advance.

Look into whether you can get any funding from the UK university you're applying to – some offer scholarships to international students for specific courses and/or from certain countries. Also try the relevant departments of your own government, the British Council in your own country, the European Commission and perhaps even various voluntary organisations.

Don't start a course in the UK until you've calculated all the expenses and can be sure you can still comfortably afford to live. It's both a pain and a challenge to get any financial support once you've left your own country and it can cost a lot just trying.

In order to get into the country, especially if you're from outside the EU, you may need to prove that you'll be able to cover the full costs of your course. It's just one of those immigration things.

Try UKCOSA – The Council for International Education (see www.ukcosa.org.uk or call 020 7226 3762) for more information. Also, visit www.britishcouncil.org/education/index.htm or email education.enquiries@britishcouncil.org

5

What about studying abroad?

If the UK's so expensive (see above), why should even British students study here? Why indeed?

There's a lot to be said for studying abroad, not least if foreign languages play any part in your plans either for your course or your career. (Don't bother going to the USA for the foreign language skills. That particular strange lingo will remain a complete mystery to all Brits however long they spend there.)

In fact, for many students (especially those studying a foreign language) studying abroad is a necessary part of their course.

Living costs in different countries swing like monkeys from a tree – with Japan and Switzerland being among the most expensive – and your financial entitlements will be adjusted accordingly.

You're still entitled to your student loan if you study abroad and if you need to be there for eight weeks or more as part of your course, you may even be able to claim a larger loan, depending on where you are studying.

The SOCRATES-ERASMUS scheme is a European study programme that gives students the chance to live and study somewhere else in Europe for a while – generally a year, or a few months at any rate. If you're interested, you'll need to talk to your course director at your university to find out whether you can apply. Not every course has opted to get into the scheme.

The Leonardo programme (www.leonardo.org.uk) is another EU scheme, again giving students (or graduates) the chance to live in another country for up to a year, but this time the scheme is based around vocational training with an employer.

For details of the UK SOCRATES-ERASMUS Council, ask at your university or take a look at www.erasmus.ac.uk or www.esn.org (Erasmus Student Network).

Individual universities also have bursaries or scholarships to send their students out of the country. Usually it's only the cost of travel that's covered, but occasionally there are awards, bursaries and prizes that fork out for all sorts of strange things like fees at overseas institutions, living expenses or T-shirts that say 'My friend went to Padua and all he got was a few extra CV points'.

You could also try seeking out scholarships not restricted to your university. Or perhaps try contacting the embassy of the country you want to visit – see if there's anything your host country can offer you.

If you want to do your whole degree abroad, there's a book called 'Commonwealth Universities Yearbook', published by Palgrave MacMillan.

What about anyone else?

There's a handful of other Government-backed funds, one of which we detail below – but for any others, try contacting your Local Education Authority as a first step.

Care-Leaver's Grant

This allowance is supposed to help pay anyone who's been in care with their accommodation costs during the summer holidays (up to a maximum of £100 a week) and it's paid by the LEA to the student or their landlord. However, it's now being phased out – the only people eligible are full-time students who were over 16 and in care for at least three months before October 1, 2001 and under 21 at the start of their course. If you left care after this date, you should have a 'pathway plan' and a personal adviser. The LEA responsible for the pathway plan has a duty to help with holiday accommodation costs if necessary and the personal adviser should be able to, well, advise on the matter.

5

Only share accommodation with other poor students, or they'll want to do unreasonable and expensive things like heat the house.

PART 6 6

The Push Guide to Penny Pinching

Chapter Fourteen

A balanced budget

The reason they call it a bank balance is because it's a question of getting the scales to tip the right way.

Ideally, what comes in is heavier than what goes out (unless it's paper coming in, copper going out – but you get the idea). As a student, unfortunately, your expenditure almost invariably squats heavily at one end of the scales as your income is lightly perched at the other. It's like pitting a stick insect against a walrus.

This is not, however, any reason to give up. Indeed, it's all the more reason to put the walrus on a diet and get the stick insect pumping iron.

The two keys to student survival are planning and priorities. Know what you have to spend – even if it's borrowed (which is like borrowing a wombat to join forces with the stick insect). And know what your spending priorities are.

Maximise what comes in. Minimise what goes out. And be extremely pessimistic about both.

To do this you need to work out how much you can afford to spend on any one thing and then stick to it. Or if it's not possible, either make cutbacks elsewhere or somehow get hold of more money.

You can't do this unless you plan, however. You can't know what you can afford until you've worked out what you've got. And you can't make cutbacks until you know the figure you're cutting.

It's all just a matter of balancing the books – a tedious business at first, but once you've done it, the whole being a student thing seems a lot less like living under a rock that hangs by a thread. You can start to enjoy it – student life that is, not balancing the books.

Feeling secure and confident about your finances will boost your overall morale, help your studies (yeah, for real) and although you're unlikely ever to be rich while you're a student, so long as you can make ends meet, you'll have a much more relaxed and stress-free existence.

Just because you're not overdrawn up to your neck, it doesn't mean you're not in trouble. You may have costs round the corner waiting to pounce and planning helps you see round corners.

If the whole lolly lay-out goes doolally, you need to know quickly, before it has a serious detrimental affect on your studies and your health – which it will if you're not able to seek help *before* it gets too serious. There's nearly always a straightforward solution to every problem, if it is dealt with in time, so don't just ignore it and hope it will go away.

Making a budget

So, how do you work out what to spend on what?

Over the next few pages and looking back over the rest of the book, you can work out what you're going to have to spend and what you're going to have to spend it on.

Push has roughed out the range of possibilities but, ultimately, your finances are your own. Not only will your income and costs be unique but, much as we'd love to play the part of personal exchequer to each and every student in the land (yeah, right), it's important to work out your budget for yourself, know it inside out, own it. (Nice cop out on our part, don't you think?) But this chapter will help.

THE RANGE OF INCOMES

Your loan is a big chunk of what comes in, but how big it – and indeed your whole income – is depends largely on your parents. What they're supposed to give you. Whether they give it to you. Whether they give you more.

Beyond that, you need to make the call about what you want out of student life. If you simply want to study and are not too bothered about a social life, you will probably scrape by on your student loan and overdraft without having to supplement your income with work.

But, let's face it, after a fortnight of that, your good intentions will probably pop down to the student bar and take you with them.

Those students with a fiercely independent streak (or a clearly severe shortfall in their budget) will probably seek term-time work as soon as they start their course. It has to be said that earning your own money gives you a greater sense of financial freedom and takes the strain off your parents, while giving you that all-important work experience.

However, it's even more important to ensure that you never compromise on your studies. Maximise your disposable income as much as possible – but if you feel you are taking on too much work, you will have to look at minimising outgoings instead.

This is what budgeting is all about: if you haven't got the funds coming in, you should aim to cut down on what you're spending.

But let's take a look at the range of annual incomes. To hit the highest income outlined in our table below involves having parents in the highest income bracket and doing paid work for 10 to 15 hours a week and/or in vacations.

Bear in mind also that there are so many ifs and buts involved in these figures that they'd read like a stammer if we bothered with them all. They've been dealt with in the other chapters already. Go figure, okay?

Source	Highest (high income families)		Lowest (low income families)	
	London	Elsewhere	London	Elsewhere
Student loan	£3,790	£3,070	£5,050	£4,095
Parental contribution	£4,500	£4,500	£0	£0
LEA award (for fees)	£0	£0	£1,150	£1,150
Higher Education Grant	£0	£0	£1,000	£1,000
Overdraft	£1,000	£1,000	£1,000	£1,000
Paid work (term time)	£2,348	£2,129	£0	£0
Maximum total available	£11,638	£10,699	£8,200	£7,245

Most students won't get either the highest or the lowest – and it won't add up to the maximum total available.

They're more likely to have something around the £5,000 to £8,000 mark (£6,000 to £9,000 in London).

Following the rule about being pessimistic, it's best to work from the bottom up. Take the column on the right and add to it anything extra you know (or at least are pretty sure) you're going to get. For example, if your parents will be giving you an agreed amount each term.

It's best not to count on earnings until you've got a job. At some universities, they're not so easy to come by.

> Volunteer to help at open days. You'll earn brown-nose points with your department plus all the biscuits you can eat.

A sample budget

But how do you put all this into a budget?

Here's one way of doing it. Work out what you have coming in. Work out the costs of essential items. See what's left. Split that appropriately between your other costs – the ones where you could economise if you really have to.

By way of example only, that's what we've done here. It's a budget for a fictional first-year student, whose parents earn £35,000 a year and who intends to study outside London and live in a shared house (for nine-and-a-half months from mid-September to the end of June).

His/her (we haven't filled in too many of the character details here) academic year is made up of three terms of ten weeks each (30 weeks over the year) – the rest of the time, s/he'll go home.

Of course, s/he – let's say he's a she, shall we? In fact, let's call her Penny, er, Penny Pinching – Penny can exercise some control over some of the essential costs and some of the variable costs aren't altogether avoidable, but the breakdown helps.

Part 1: Income	Amount per year	Per term			Per week
		1st	2nd	3rd	
Parental contribution to tuition fees	£1,150	£384	£383	£383	–
Parental contribution to living expenses (LEA's suggestion)	£319	£107	£106	£106	£11
Extra help from parents	£100	£100	£0	£0	–
Student loan	£3,776	£1,259	£1,259	£1,258	£126
Overdraft facility (maximum)	£1,000	£470	£380	£150	£33
Bar work (at £5/hr, 10 hrs/wk)	£1,200	£500	£500	£200	£40
Maximum total available	**£7,545**	**£2,820**	**£2,628**	**£2,097**	**£210**

Part 2: Essential costs	Amount per year	Per term			Per week
		1st	2nd	3rd	
Rent	£2,055	£810	£810	£435	£50
Tuition fees	£1,150	£384	£383	£383	–
Bills	£400	£155	£155	£90	£13
Insurance	£60	£60	£0	£0	–
Food	£1,200	£400	£400	£400	£40
Travel	£450	£150	£150	£150	£15
Laundry /washing	£150	£50	£50	£50	£5
Total essential costs	**£5,465**	**£2,009**	**£1,948**	**£1,508**	**£123**
Maximum remainder	£2,080	£811	£680	£589	–

Part 3: Variable costs		Amount per year	Per term			Per week
			1st	2nd	3rd	
Emergency money	10%	£208	£65	£55	£88	£6.50
Academic costs	12.5%	£260	£100	£100	£60	£8.70
Clothes	10%	£208	£70	£70	£68	–
Entertainment and socialising	50%	£1,010	£400	£350	£260	£34
Freshers' Week extra		£30	£30	–	–	–
Toiletries	5%	£104	£34	£35	£35	£3.50
Phone	7.5%	£156	£56	£45	£55	–
Miscellaneous	5%	£24	£8	£8	£8	£1
Christmas and birthdays		£80	£50	£15	£15	–
Holiday		£0	£0	£0	£0	–
Total variable costs		**£2,080**	**£813**	**£678**	**£589**	**£53.70**

Now, sit back, relax and let Push take you through what Penny did there.

Part 1: Income

This is what she reckons will be her income.

Presumably, she's already applied to her LEA and been told what she can expect by way of a support (no award, just over 90% of the full loan) and what she should expect from her folks.

Presumably, she's also talked to them about it and the amounts she's put down are based on safe assumptions.

That bar work, however, might be a problem. If Penny knows that she's got the job already, then she's safe. If not, then it may be a bit risky to suppose that there'll be any work going.

The amount she's allowed for the bar work – £1,200 – highlights another potential problem that it looks as though she's accounted for. Chances are that there'll be at least a few weeks in the summer term when she can't work at all because she needs to focus on her exams.

She's reckoned on six weeks when she won't be earning. She may make up some of that with vacation jobs or occasional overtime, but she's right not to count on it.

Part 2: Essential Costs

Next, Penny worked out what she'll need for costs that, basically, she can't do much about. Her rent, for example, is just what it will cost. Her travel shouldn't be too bad because she's on campus, but she needs to go into town to do her weekly shopping and, since she's not paying for any rent over the vacations, she'll need to go home at the end of each term.

As it happens, she thinks she won't need that much for food and hopes to keep bills to a minimum – but when making a budget it's best to assume the worst. At least that way you're prepared for it if it happens and, if it doesn't, you've got money to spend on something else (or not to spend at all and therefore end up less far in debt).

She's also spread the costs appropriately. She's allowed more for bills for the first two terms, when the weather's colder and she'll need the heating on more. She's also shoved all the cost of insurance right up the front when she'll actually have to pay it.

Meanwhile, she's spread her rent unevenly between the three terms because she's allowed enough rent money to take her through the short winter and spring vacations too.

Having worked out her costs in Part 2, she's calculated the maximum remainder she'll have left over. Of course, in the income section, she had to factor in an overdraft from the bank of £1,000. If she can get away with it, she'd rather not borrow that much. That's why this is a *maximum* remainder.

Part 3: Variable Costs

The variable costs are the ones where, if necessary, Penny will have to find a way of economising. Even her academic costs may have to be cut. She'll need to spend a certain amount on pens, paper and so on – but if it comes to it, for books, she'll just have to spend longer in the library rather than buy her own or photocopy them.

She's worked out how much to give herself under each heading by allocating a percentage of the remainder to each heading. She's chosen these percentages for herself, based on what they're likely to cost and the priority she puts on them.

By only giving 12.5% to academic costs, it doesn't necessarily mean she'll ignore her studies, just that she thinks they won't cost her as much as, say, entertainments. She's also put most of the costs in the first term when, presumably, she's planning to do most of her book buying.

She's spread out other costs unevenly, too, over the year to reflect when she's actually going to have to shell out. For example, she'll have to do her Christmas shopping at the end of the first term, so she's allowed £35 more than the rest of the year.

She's done something really sensible – that's our Penny for you – by giving herself just over £200 emergency money. She'll try not to touch that, but it means she won't automatically blow the whole schedule if she needs to rush home unexpectedly or loses her job or has her bike stolen and needs to pay an excess on her insurance or aliens land and make her give them her lunch money.

If, at the end of the year, she hasn't used her emergency money, she can put it towards the holiday she clearly wants (after all she's given it a heading even though she seems to have worked out that she can't afford it) or she can just be grateful she didn't have to borrow up to the max that year.

6

CASHFLOW

Under 'Entertainment and socialising', Penny Pinching put a sub-heading for Freshers' Week, where she allowed herself an extra thirty quid to have a good time. (In other words, double her regular weekly ents allowance.)

However, it looked like she hadn't allowed herself anything else for settling in – to cover all the stuff she'll discover she forgot to bring with her (see **Chapter 12**) and for a big splurge at the supermarket to get her kitchen cupboards off to a good start.

That doesn't sound like Penny. Not our Penny who is sensible in a way that only fictional people can be.

Sure enough, she has thought about it. Apart from breaking it down into three terms, Penny has also worked it out for every week of the year. Perversely diligent person that she is, she's even done a spreadsheet on a computer.

Her weekly allowance for food, for example, is £40 average over the year, but if you were to look at her cashflow spreadsheet, you'll see she's allowed herself an extra fiver each week for the first four weeks and one pound less a week for the second two terms.

This weekly breakdown tells her at the end of any week in the year what her bank balance should be. She can then compare it with what it actually is and decide immediately what to do.

If she's over budget on her 'food' heading, say, she either has to just make do on the food she's already laid in for that week – which isn't satisfactory if it means missing meals – or find somewhere else to make a saving – probably one of the variable cost items. In other words, she decides she can't afford to go out tonight.

Alternatively, she can ask her boss at the pub if she can work extra hours.

If, however, she's under budget, she might decide she can afford to treat herself to a takeaway tonight, or put money aside for that holiday. (We understand she intends to go to Switzerland, home of banking – not to mention the cuckoo clock.)

By keeping a check on her cashflow, she's not only counting the money out, but counting it in.

Most students find budgeting very difficult because their money arrives in two or three large chunks during the year, whereas outgoings are roughly constant (and relentless) over every term.

Penny knows when to expect big movements either way and she has an early warning system long before any problems crop up.

FLEXIBILITY

Penny also has a little notebook in which, for the first term at least, she intends to write down every penny she spends. That way she can work out how she's really doing with her budget headings.

Realistically, she knows she won't keep track when she's out for a night on the piss, but that doesn't matter. Just so long as, the next morning, she knows what she spent in total. The whole lot goes down under the entertainments heading as 'night out £9.24'.

Every couple of weeks, she can tot up what she's spent on what and compare it with her budget and cashflow.

Carry your NUS card everywhere and use it religiously.

> **Drop in on friends and try to time it
> just as they're about to eat.**

She knows perfectly well that some of her estimates are going to be way out. By monitoring what she spends closer than a cat watches a tin opener, she'll be able to adjust her budget as she goes along.

Having put so much effort into the budget in the first place, this may seem like sacrilege – but to Penny, it's part of the whole point. If the budget's not working, rather than live a life of misery because you can't afford to go out because you're £5 over on your food, just juggle the figures.

However, Penny shouldn't have to. She even has money for emergencies.

Nevertheless, while you can expect the unexpected, you can't always predict exactly what shape it'll come in. For Penny, as for every student, there are imponderables – and there's no such thing as a typical student budget that will always work for everyone.

If she's over budget, she looks for somewhere where she's under budget. And if she can't find anything, she works out where she can get more money – more hours working at the pub, a heart to heart with the parents or even asking the bank.

If Penny takes her budget and cashflow along to a meeting with the bank, they'll extend her overdraft, no problem. Even if something's gone seriously wrong and she's in a monetary mire, they'll see that she's the kind of person who'll find her way out in the long run through careful financial planning.

Going as far as Penny may seem extreme, but actually, it's not as much work as it looks and it's not so far from what should be basic budgeting procedures.

Even with all her efforts, according to her own calculations she's going to end up more than £14,000 in debt at the end of her three-year course. That's not too far from average at the moment.

At the very least, you should do a budget like Penny's for yourself and keep revisiting it until it works. Then revisit it again every time you get major new information (such as finding part-time work).

And then look at it at least once a month while you're at university to see how you're doing. Stick it on the wall above your desk. If necessary, make changes to keep it current.

It's like a revision timetable, however – it's not just a chart you spend hours colouring in and then ignore prior to last-minute panic. It's a relevant guide to what you can and can't spend if friends, for example, ask you to join them for a drink. If you've spent your weekly entertainment allowance already, the answer is, unfortunately, 'no'. Everyone has to give it a miss sometime. Study instead.

There's nothing crazy in any of this. All we're talking about is looking after your finances.

They're skills that everyone has to acquire sometime – even ridiculously wealthy people. How do you think they became wealthy in the first place?

It's a bit of a deep end experience if you're learning to budget when you're really strapped, but if you want to get anally retentive about the process, it's the best time to do it. And remember, it's better to be anal than sorry.

Priorities

Don't think of budgeting as a negative thing. Think of it as positively expressing your priorities.

It really is worth losing the luxuries and the wild weekends if it means getting by financially in the long run.

It's no fun living on marmite sandwiches and Tesco's Value orange squash for a month after squandering the last of your cash on a couple of over-indulgent Saturday nights. You'll realise with the infallible clarity of hindsight that it just wasn't worth it (however much fun it was at the time).

Doing a preliminary budget is all very well, but sticking to it is the difficult bit. In theory, it's easy – in practice, it's a different matter. Despite your best intentions, you may still find yourself up to your neck in debt, wondering how the hell you got there.

Don't worry about being in debt – that's normal. Worry about being in *too much* debt or being in debt too soon. Some debts are necessary. Others you can do without.

As the debts get bigger, don't panic or give up trying to keep them to a minimum. Even if you find, despite your best efforts (or even because of a lack of any effort), that you're in a debt ditch, there are ways of climbing out. And, for what it's worth, there are thousands of others in exactly the same situation.

However, if you can't pay for tedious but compulsory house-related costs or if you get behind on your rent, your housemates may well start seeing you as a liability. You can't expect others to bail you out or lend you the money to cover your share of the bills.

The key is to *prioritise*. See that the necessities are covered before you get on with the less mundane side of student life.

6

When sharing a house with boys, make sure the phone bill is in their name. (Try saying, 'But you're so much better at numbers than I ever could be.') That way when, inevitably, they don't do any cleaning when you move out and you all lose your deposits, you can just not pay the last phone bill — or the proportion of it you lost.

Thirty Steps to Solvency

1 Work out your budget and get an idea of your cashflow situation before you even pack to go to university. Do it as soon as possible. Preferably sooner.

2 Economise right from the off. If you blow big bucks at the beginning of term your fast and loose spending will only leave you miserable and bored by the end.

3 Don't buy anything you don't need, if you can't afford what you need. Paying your rent on time and having food to eat are more important than anything else.

4 Keep your budget under regular review and make adjustments for any costs you miscalculated.

5 If you need a little extra to tide you over, try to get a job if you can, but don't assume when budgeting that you'll be able to get one immediately.

6 If you've got a job, but you're still feeling the pinch, try to get a few extra shifts but not at the expense of your course.

7 During a 'typical' week at university (or, even better, a whole month or a term), keep a record of everything you buy (by cash, card, direct debit and cheque) and how much it costs – pints, snacks, cab rides, fetish outfits, etc. Cheque stubs, receipts and bank statements can all help you draw up a comprehensive record of total expenditure.

8 It may seem like a hassle, but you can use this information to help you draw up a realistic budget. The little things you don't think twice about buying are often overlooked and after the big birds like fees and rent have flown from the nest egg, they suddenly seem a whole lot bigger.

9 Anyone on a low income should avoid anything with high interest payments. That means you. Big monthly repayments and a high annual percentage rate spell big trouble. Paying off old debts with new ones generates a vicious cycle. You'll end up with mounting mountains of interest and interest on the interest, ad nauseam.

10 Only have the heating on when you really need it – even in winter just a few hours in the morning and a few hours at night will see you alright. Other energy-saving rules: have showers instead of baths, always turn the light off when leaving an empty room, only fill the kettle as much as you need to, don't leave the telly on standby.

6

The Push Guide to Penny Pinching

11 Share cooking and shopping with housemates and split the bills. Don't fuss about who's eating more. You're all subsidising each other anyway because it works out cheaper than buying for one.

12 Buy fruit and veg from market stalls, not the supermarket.

13 You may be covered by insurance, but minimise the risk of having all your precious things nicked in the first place by keeping all expensive-looking items away from the windows and always lock internal doors where you can. Insurance premiums will be lower if you have a personal lock on your bedroom door.

14 Get a friend to cut your hair – preferably one who knows what they're doing. Alternatively, find your nearest hairdresser and ask if they want any models. You'll only pay about £5 and get just about whatever haircut you want. For a bit extra you can get colour and perming too. Toni and Guy always require models so to find your nearest call: 0800 731 2396 or see www.toniandguy.co.uk.

15 Check out 'bargain basement' shops such as Poundland. You can get all sorts of necessities in there – household cleaning products, shampoo, lightbulbs, notepads, novelty pens, etc, etc. All for... er, a pound. Be warned though – these places are full of tat you don't need and not everything's a bargain. Some stuff is actually less than a pound elsewhere.

16 Be on the look-out for special student nights at clubs, pubs, cinemas etc. Carry your NUS card with you everywhere – it can get you so many discounts it could be your most valuable bit of plastic.

17 Pick up free condoms from your local family planning centre or the university health centre. (And use them.)

18 Make calls and surf the net during off-peak times only. Usually after 6 or 7pm and at weekends, but check.

19 If you must have a credit card, choose one that offers money back (instead of points for freebies). And use it as if it were made of glass. Don't use it unless you know you can pay the monthly bill in total. Cut it up if you find you can't.

20 Don't spend all your money on drink and drugs. If going out on the piss, meet up round someone's house first and do most of your drinking there. It's cheaper.

21 Go out in groups of four or five (or more). Get in a round each (or buy your own drinks). Don't take more cash than you're willing to spend and only take your cashpoint card for emergencies. Swap it with one of your friends for safe keeping. (Don't tell them the PIN.) Leave enough money for getting home. When you're all drunk and raucous enough at the end of the night, if you have to catch a taxi, pile in together and split the cost.

22 Where possible, apply for your student loan early and have it put into your account in three instalments throughout the year.

23 Pay regular bills automatically by direct debit or standing order. Not only does this avoid the problem of ignored bills going red and then the electricity strangely cutting out, you also usually get a discount. But keep track of what's coming out of your account each month and when. Take it into account in your budgeting and don't believe the balance the cash machine tells you if a payment's due.

24 Keep a finance file with all your bank statements, bills and letters from the SLC and the bank. That way, you'll know where to find what you need when you need it. Also keep receipts and card payment slips in it and check them off against statements when they arrive.

25 Club together with mates on the same course to buy all the main texts between you and share them on a rota basis. Definitely one to try if your university library is a bit thin on the shelves.

26 In a perfect world, your overdraft facility would only be a last resort. In this world, you'll almost certainly need at least some of it. If you're having trouble sticking to your agreed limit, talk to your bank manager or student adviser immediately. Don't risk getting a snotty letter by going over your limit and hoping nobody will notice – they will notice and that snotty letter will come, complete with fine.

27 Always ask in high street stores, taxis, cinemas, theatres museums – just about anywhere, in fact – if there's a student discount. They'll rarely volunteer the information without being asked.

28 Don't rely on your next loan cheque to pay off what you already owe. You'll need it for your rent and food next term, so what'll you do then?

29 Don't get stressed out over your finances. You'll only make it worse. A calm approach with good planning will see you alright. You'll be in debt, but, hey, so's everyone.

30 The Access to Learning funds exist as a safety net for those who are experiencing problems. Ask if you need help – you shouldn't have to suffer in silence if your situation has got to the stage where you are depriving yourself. Try asking, even if you don't think you'll get anywhere. The worst they'll do is give you free advice.

6

Chapter Fifteen

In the red

Handling debt

Students have always complained about being broke. Chaucer even makes gags about it in *The Canterbury Tales*. Honest (and what a hoot they are too).

But in the last 15 years or so the situation has gone from one where students faced the challenge of merely staying out of the red to one where even the official funding system acknowledges that they're likely to graduate with the worst part of £12,000 in debts.

As it happens, the average debt on graduation is about £14,000, and while there are some who make it through without borrowing anything, there are also plenty who wind up owing closer to £25,000.

And the debts are only going to get deeper. **From 2006, although no new student will have to pay tuition fees while they're at university, they'll have to pay up to £3,000 a year in fees once they graduate.** To cover this and their living costs, they'll get a superloan. There'll be a fair few students graduating more than twenty grand in the red. See **Chapter 4** and **Chapter 10** for more information.

Try moaning about student debt to someone with a mortgage and they probably won't be too impressed – but, if you have a mortgage, you probably have property to show for the hole in your finances. You probably also have a salary to support your repayments.

Most students have neither.

Does this sound a tiny bit negative?

So sorry.

It shouldn't put you off. We've been through that. It's only money, after all, and as the great Bob Dylan once said, 'What's money? A man is a success in life if he gets up in the morning and goes to bed at night and in between does what he wants to do.'

Bloody hippy. Someone go tell him that a degree's an investment.

The good news is that it won't be a problem if you follow the rules.

The key rules: borrow wisely; spend according to need rather than want; keep tabs on your bank balance; don't get behind with bills; tap every available resource; and get yourself a good holiday job.

During holidays, try to get some work so that you can pay off all or part of your overdraft – you will then have the facility available to you once again when you begin the next term. It's not much fun to start term in the red and with your next loan instalment cheque inexplicably delayed in the post. Prepare yourself for the unexpected.

Don't let debt take over your life: it will only become a problem if you let it and ignoring red bills and letters from creditors or applying for more loans when you can't pay off the ones you already have is just asking for trouble.

Don't be complacent and assume it won't happen to you: even the meanest misers, penny-pinchers and prudent puritans are often amazed at the flash with which their bank balance transforms from healthy wealth to black hole.

SAFE AND UNSAFE DEBTS

Your student loan and your overdraft are safe debts, virtually unavoidable, and the cheapest money that money can buy.

Set up an account with a sperm bank and make regular deposits!

Tom Perring, London

The interest on both is very small (the overdraft is usually free while you're a student and if you stay within your limit) and you don't have to worry about paying them back until after you've graduated.

However, any other borrowings are a risk. If possible, avoid taking out other loans altogether. Credit card frivolity, too.

If you run up debts and end up missing or delaying repayments, this will not be good for your future credit rating and you'll end up with pariah status among the entire financial fraternity.

Unauthorised debts – for example, exceeding your overdraft by writing rubber cheques or stretching the debit card a bit far – are also unsafe.

Stick to the safety zone.

`Turn vegetarian.`

Stress-busting tips for the poor and disgruntled

So how do you stop debt becoming a problem?

Debt is undoubtedly a hassle and, in fact, while you're a student one of the main problems with debt is not that you don't have any money, but what worrying about it threatens to do to your head.

Hopefully, after all our wise advice you'll stay in the relative clear, financially speaking – but as Nick Ross would no doubt put it, after all the horrors we've described, 'Don't have nightmares'.

Getting into debt and not getting out is not something you can do much about until you graduate and nor will anyone expect you to. So don't waste nights staring at the ceiling fretting about it.

So long as you can pay your way in the meantime, do what you can and be cool about it.

If you are having difficulties, whatever they are – drawing up your budget, getting by on what you've got, negotiating with your bank, filling in forms to apply for funding, worrying about debt, chasing the SLC for your loan payment – talk to your student welfare officer.

They're usually based in either the students' union welfare department or the university's. Often they'll both have complementary advisors and a specialist debt counsellor or financial adviser too.

They'll offer guidance and, if you need it, sometimes even practical assistance – i.e. they've got the keys to the safe where they keep the access to learning fund.

POMMIE

Where would we be without mnemonics? (Actually Push used to know the answer to that, but couldn't ever come up with a way to remember it.)

The central principles of a stress-free university career (at least as far as money management goes) can be expressed in the almost delightfully uncatchy acronym pommie:

PRIORITISE: Buy what you *need* first (e.g. food and shelter) – what you *want* comes second.
ORGANISE: Plan your budget, check your balance regularly and keep a record of all financial correspondence.
MAXIMISE: Make sure you're getting all the income you're entitled to.
MINIMISE: Keep expenditure to a minimum without depriving yourself unduly.
IMPROVISE: When you can't afford something, be creative about alternatives.
ECONOMISE: Stick to the first five rules and buy cheaply when you can.

For want of a better reminder, stick to the POMMIE principles and remember why you're at university in the first place – to better yourself, to improve your prospects and ultimately to embark on the career you want… money, success, blah, blah, blah. You know the script by know.

The message is, essentially: you don't need money to have a good time.

Students don't stay poor forever and the loudest voices saying that students shouldn't complain are often graduates themselves. A few years down the line, you too will probably wonder what you were so worried about.

Of course, debt and hardship is like a ripe zit on the end of your nose. While it's there, it's horrible – it's as if the world revolves around it – but with the correct procedure, in a shower of pus normality is restored.

Indeed, it's better than that. The money management skills you pick up at university are not only just as useful when you have more money of your own, but in any profession involving any contact with budgets – i.e. almost all of them – they're as useful a skill as being able to suck up to your boss.

If you need help and advice:

Credit Action & Consumer Credit Counselling Service,
www.creditaction.org.uk or www.cccs.co.uk, Helpline 0800 1381111
National Debtline, www.nationaldebtline.co.uk, 0800 808 4000
Department of Work & Pensions, www.dwp.gov.uk,
020 7712 171
Educational Grants Advisory Service, www.egas-online.org,
020 7254 6251
Money Advice Association, www.m-a-a.org.uk, 01476 594970

After university

All good things will come to an end. Falling asleep in nine o'clock lectures, cheap beer, exam stress, being unable to afford a new pair of socks…

Eventually, all being well, you'll get kitted out like Batman with a black square on his head and pick up your scroll.

After that, you might be thinking that all the hard slog is out of the way, but the problem now is that you'll have to earn a living and start to pay back what you owe.

Some debts – such as your overdraft – you won't be able to delay long before you start making repayments. Most banks won't let you swan along indefinitely. They want to see their investment in you start to ripen.

As for others, mainly the student loan, the longer you put off being in a position to start making good, the more interest you'll end up paying.

Besides, after three years of it or more, most people have had quite enough of poverty.

So try to get earning pretty sharpish. If the thought of going straight for a long-term career fills you with dread, try temping or make enquiries about jobs abroad (see what we said about **Filling** the Gap and **Jobs Abroad** in **Chapter 7**). Lots of graduates take a year between finishing university and landing a long-term job, especially if they didn't take the opportunity straight out of school or college.

If you do intend to up sticks and leave or even wait a while before stepping up to the start line of the rat race, check first on what your bank and the Student Loans Company want you to do about your debts. You should be able to defer repayments on your student loan, but your bank may want you to come to some arrangement. In the case of overdrafts, it's probably best to pay off at least part of the negative numbers before you go anywhere drastic. The overdraft facility won't disappear just because you've pulled your account into credit and a nice soft financial cushion can be as much of a lifesaver when you're miles from home as when you were struggling to make ends meet until the end of term.

EMPLOYMENT

Towards the end of your student career, the whole employment issue will raise its short-haired, neatly coiffured head.

Your university's careers service will help. They differ in size, effectiveness and what they'll offer to do for you. You'll want to mastermind the hunt for yourself anyway.

Job Fairs and Graduate Recruitment Fairs will most likely become a regular fixture in your life. Employers have stands where they try to convince you to work for them and you try to convince them to employ you. Despite how it sounds, people and jobs don't pair up quite as easily as you might think.

The name 'fairs' makes them sound like summer fêtes and, sure enough, they're most prolific in June and July, but that's where the similarity ends. There's not a tombola in sight. If you're after a rural metaphor, they're more reminiscent of cattle markets, only most of the livestock are wearing suits.

6

Give blood. You get free tea and biscuits afterwards.

Strangely enough, the cattle theme continues – these fairs and mini-fairs at individual universities are known collectively as the 'milk round'.

There are general fairs for jobs across the board and specialist ones for different industries or fields. Each offers seminars and advice and they provide a unique opportunity to meet hoards of potential employers all in a flock.

Make an irresistible CV and take plenty of copies along with you. Dress up smartly and sell yourself. Be prepared for an interview on the spot.

Even if you don't end up with a job, you can scout the territory, find out about different jobs, different companies and how to get in to what you want to do. You can also network – get names, numbers, contacts – and pick up on the leads later.

You can find out what fairs are where in the Graduate ('Rise') section of *The Guardian* every Saturday, which is also probably the best paper for most graduate vacancies.

After graduating, if you're not walking straight into a job, take the opportunity to pick up some office and IT skills or to improve on what you've got.

If you're not completely sick of education, you could even enrol on a short training course. There may be yet more costs involved, but there are a few schemes to help out. See www.waytolearn.co.uk for more information.

If you're lucky, you may even find an employment agency that's willing to give you some free, basic training – even if it's nothing more than improving your typing speed or introducing you to a software package. Don't knock it. Keyboard skills and computer literacy are often a decider when it comes to getting a job. They also make life easier once you've got one.

PART 7 7

In the back

Chapter Sixteen

The universities

This chapter gives a breakdown of some of the big differences between individual universities – the key costs and the different support on offer. For more details, **The Push Guide to Which University** has a whole bundle of more info about each place. Oh, and by the way, in this chapter, text in italics is Push's opinion – take it or leave it.

....

ABERDEEN UNIVERSITY

The University of Aberdeen, University Office, King's College, Aberdeen, AB24 3FX
Tel: (01224) 272 090/1. Fax: (01224) 272 576. E-mail: sras@abdn.ac.uk
Website: www.abdn.ac.uk
University Students' Association, Luthuli House, 50/52 College Bounds, Old Aberdeen, AB24 3DS
Tel: (01224) 272 965. Fax: (01224) 272 977. E-mail: ausa@abdn.ac.uk
Website: www.ausa.org.uk

DEBTS:
- Ave debt per year: £1,065
- Access fund: £250,000
- Ave payment: £200
- Successful applications/yr: 1,031

Support: There are about 150 endowments, bursaries, external grants and trusts available for school leavers coming to Aberdeen University. *Some are very obscure, for example, for one, applicants must be from Cabrach (a tiny village 40 miles away) and promise not to drink or smoke throughout their degree. As if.*

FEES: *The SA will have chained itself to a good many gates before top up fees hit home.* International fees range from £7,560-£18,570

ACCOMMODATION:
In college:
- Cost of living index: £
- Catered: 8%
- Self-catering: 15%
- First years living in: 14.7%
- Insurance premium: £
- Cost: £75-£94 (32wks)
- Cost: £50-£64 (32-48wks)

Aberdeen:
- Ave rent: £65
- Living at home: 5%

EMPLOYMENT: • Unemployed after 6mths: 3%
Paid work: SA-run JobLink helps students find part-time, vacation and temp work through adverts on their website (www.ausa.org.uk/joblink). Students can sometimes find work in the oil industry, particularly those whose studies are in

some relevant field. *If not, it's time to get out the rod and go fish*.
Careers: The Careers & Appointments Service organises weekly seminars and workshops, sends weekly job update emails and performs *that corporate fad - psychometric testing*. In addition, newsletters, bulletin boards, interview training and job fairs ago-go.

TRAVEL:
National: *Despite being so far north* (the same latitude as St Petersburg), rail connections *are quite good, if expensive*. Among others, services are offered to London (£62.70), Glasgow (£30.70) and Birmingham (£60.45). National Express coach services go to London (£37.50), Glasgow (£20.40), Birmingham (£34.50) among others. Scottish Citylink for coach journeys within Scotland. Stagecoach also run services and there's a ferry service to Lerwick in the Shetlands too.
Local: Good bus services run anywhere in the city from 35p, *useful for getting into the centre from King's*. Taxis are *useful late at night, but expensive* - £5 from the station to King's, £10 from the airport. Despite the heavy traffic and the cold winds, many students take to cycling. Incidentally, bike theft is as rare as any other crime in Aberdeen, which has the lowest crime rate in Britain for a city its size.

ENTERTAINMENTS: • Booze index: £1.82
Aberdeen:	• Pint of beer: £2	• Glass of wine: £2.50
		• Can of Red Bull: £1
University:	• Pint of beer: £1.60	• Glass of wine: £1.50
		• Can of Red Bull: £1

ABERTAY DUNDEE UNIVERSITY
University of Abertay Dundee, Bell Street, Dundee, DD1 1HG
Tel: (01382) 308 080. Fax: (01382) 308 081. E-mail: sro@abertay.ac.uk
Website: www.abertay.ac.uk
University of Abertay Dundee Students Association, 158 Marketgait, Dundee, DD1 1NJ
Tel: (01382) 227 477. E-mail: saadf@abertay.ac.uk
Website: www.abertayunion.com

DEBTS: • Ave debt per year: £2,440
The finance department holds the hardship fund purse-strings. There's a mature students' bursary for Scottish students, sporting excellence fund and a £1,000 centenary scholarship.

ACCOMMODATION: • Cost of living index: £ • Insurance premium: £
In college: • Self-catering: 21% • Cost: £38-58 (36-52wks)
Dundee: • Ave rent: £35-55

EMPLOYMENT:
Paid work: Work in Dundee is *easiest to find out of term*, although the job bureau lends a hand.
Careers: Newsletters, bulletin boards and job fairs. The new student centre has online careers resources.

TRAVEL: see University of Dundee
Local: Dundee station is 10 mins from the University. There's an *extensive* local bus service, which ferries between halls and campus for 80p.

ENTERTAINMENTS: • Booze index: £1.69
Dundee: see Dundee University
University: • Pint of beer: £1.40 • Can of Red Bull: £1

UNIVERSITY OF WALES, ABERYSTWYTH
• **The College is part of the University of Wales.**
University of Wales, Aberystwyth, Old College, King St, Aberystwyth, SY23 2AX
Tel: (01970) 622 021. Fax: (01970) 627 410. E-mail: ug-admissions@aber.ac.uk
Website: www.aber.ac.uk
Urdd Myfyrwyr Aberystwyth Guild of Students, Penglais, Aberystwyth, Ceredigion,
SY23 2AX
Tel: (01970) 621 731. Fax: (01970) 621 701
E-mail: undeb.llywydd@aber.ac.uk/union.president@aber.ac.uk
Website: www.union.aber.ac.uk

DEBTS:
- Ave debt per year: £2,728
- Access fund: £450,000 • Successful applications/yr: 800
- Ave payment: £600

The Student Financial Support Office provides help and advice for all matters fiscal.
There are a good many scholarships available (up to £3,000), plus hardship funds
and bursaries for students from low-income families.

FEES: International students pay either £7,000 or £9,276 depending on whether
their degree is in arts or science subjects. The Welsh Assembly is watching and
waiting on the top up fee issue, so it'll be a while before any decision is made that
will affect Aber students.

ACCOMMODATION: • Cost of living index: £ • Insurance premium: £
In college:
- Catered: 15%
- Cost: £49-72 (30wks)
- Self-catering: 29%
- Cost: £33-63 (30wks)
- First years living in: 98%

Aberystwyth:
- Ave rent: £53 • Living at home: 2%

EMPLOYMENT: • Unemployed after 6mths: 6% • Paid work: term-time 40%;
hols 60%
Paid work: Aberystwyth is too small to offer much in the way of part-time
employment, but prospects improve in the summer, when the tourists are in town.
Aber's Job Link service does its best to find work, mostly bar and cleaning work.
Careers: A *standard* advisory service.

TRAVEL:
National: Aberystwyth station is about ¹/₂ mile from the main campus. London
(£29.55), Birmingham (£21.65) and Manchester (£23.15). Trans Cambria and
National Express coach services: London (£18.25), Birmingham (£15.25), Cardiff
(£14.80).
Local: *Reliable* local buses run until 11pm (50p). There's a free college bus service
running to and from the town throughout the day.

ENTERTAINMENTS: • Booze index: £1.88
Aberystwyth: • Pint of beer: £2.20 • Glass of wine: £1.90
• Can of Red Bull: £1.90
University: • Pint of beer: £1.70 • Glass of wine: £1.70
• Can of Red Bull: £1.60

UNUSUAL COSTS: £25 a year for use of sports facilities.

ANGLIA POLYTECHNIC UNIVERSITY
(1) Anglia Polytechnic University, East Road, Cambridge, CB1 1PT
Tel: (0845) 271 3333. Fax: (01223) 352 973. E-mail: answers@apu.ac.uk
Website: www.anglia.ac.uk
Anglia Students' Union, Victoria Road South, Chelmsford, Essex, CM1 1LL
Tel: (01245) 258 178. Fax: (01245) 267 653. E-mail: ausutc@asu.apu.ac.uk
(2) Chelmsford Campus, Bishop Hall Lane, Chelmsford, CM1 1SQ
Tel: (0845) 271 3333

Chelmsford SU Office, 1st floor, Johnson Building, Bishop Hall Lane, Chelmsford, CM1 1SQ. Tel: (01245) 258 178

DEBTS:
- Ave debt per year: £5,898
- Access fund: £917,813   • Successful applications/yr: 1,483
- Ave payment: £500

Sports scholarships and Anglia Trust scholarships for students doing extraordinary things (previous holders have worked on conservation projects in Tanzania and studied art in Florence). A disability allowance is also available.

ACCOMMODATION: • Cost of living index: ££££ • Insurance premium: £
In college: • Self-catering: 15%   • Cost: £63-68 (40wks)
                  • First years living in: 10%

Housing at the Chelmsford Campus is *good quality but overpriced* (£46-62). The plush new Rivermead development has proved popular despite the costly rooms.
Cambridge: • Ave rent: £70
Chelmsford: • Ave rent: £42-70

EMPLOYMENT: • Unemployed after 6mths: 7.8%
               • Paid work: term-time 50%: hols 95%
Paid work: As Cambridge University forbids its students from working, APU students have a distinct advantage in bagging part-time and summer jobs.
Careers: Only 4 staff to try and get students working. *Alumnus Adam Ant managed to make something of himself, though, so there's hope.*

TRAVEL:
Cambridge: See Cambridge University.
Chelmsford: Chelmsford Station (2 mins from campus) direct to London Liverpool Street (£5). National Express coaches and cars are a regular feature of student travels. Stansted's just down the road for budget flights.

ENTERTAINMENTS: • Booze index: £2.12
Cambridge/Chelmsford: • Pint of beer: £2.30   • Glass of wine: £2.50
                                                  • Can of Red Bull: £1.60
University: • Pint of beer: £1.60   • Glass of wine: £2
                                         • Can of Red Bull: £1.80

7

UNIVERSITY OF THE ARTS LONDON
(1) University of the Arts London, 65 Davies Street, London, W1K 5DA
    Tel: 020 7514 6000. Fax: 020 7514 6131. E-mail: info@linst.ac.uk
    Website: www.linst.ac.uk
    London Institute Students' Union, 2-6 Catton Street, Holborn, London, WC1R 4AA
    Tel: 0207 514 6270. Fax: 0207 514 6284. E-mail: info@lisu.org
    Website: www.lisu.org
(2) London College of Communication, Elephant & Castle, London, SE1 6SB
    Tel: (020) 7514 6569. E-mail: info@lcc.arts.ac.uk
(3) Central St Martin's College of Art and Design, London, WC1B 4AP
    Tel: (020) 7514 7023. E-mail: info@csm.arts.ac.uk
    (4) Chelsea College of Art and Design, enquiries@chelsea.arts.ac.uk
(5) London College of Fashion, 20 John Princes Street, London, W1G 0BJ
    Tel: (020) 7514 7400. E-mail: enquiries@fashion.arts.ac.uk
(6) Camberwell College of Arts, Peckham Road, London, SE5 8UF
    Tel: (020) 7514 6300. E-mail: enquiries@camberwell.arts.ac.uk

DEBTS: • Ave debt per year: £2,321

ACCOMMODATION: • Cost of living index: £££ • Insurance premium: £
In college: • Catered: 209 • Cost: £111 (39-52wks)
• Self-catering: 1,204 • Cost: £58-114 (39-52wks)
London: • Ave rent: £80-100

EMPLOYMENT: • Unemployed after 6mths: 9%
Paid work: Vacancy lists are posted up in the Union, with notices from University of London Union also proving a *goldmine*.
Careers: The Careers Service publishes a monthly job list. Courses at LCC are quite vocational *considering they're so arty. Those who hope to hit the starry heights of fame are no doubt cheered by the glitzy alumni list.*

TRAVEL: see London University
Camberwell: No tube but *plentiful* buses and Peckham Rye station has frequent trains to London Bridge, Victoria and Blackfriars.
Other sites: All fairly central (if widely spread), so well-served by the tube and buses and in some cases the train too.

ENTERTAINMENTS: • Booze index: £2.31
London: • Pint of beer: £2.50 • Glass of wine: £2.80
• Can of Red Bull: £2
University: • Pint of beer: £1.80 • Glass of wine: £1.10

···

ASTON UNIVERSITY
Aston University, The Triangle, Birmingham City Centre, B4 7ET
Tel: (0121) 359 3611. Fax: (0121) 359 4664. E-mail: prospectus@aston.ac.uk
Website: www.aston.ac.uk
Aston Students Guild, Aston University, The Triangle, Birmingham City Centre, B4 7ES
Tel: (0121) 359 6531. Fax: (0121) 333 4218. E-mail: guild.liaison@aton.ac.uk
Website: www.astonguild.org.uk

DEBTS: • Ave debt per year: £2,771
• Access fund: £300,000 • Successful applications/yr: 700
Hardship funds, travel bursaries and an assortment of other prizes, including the Aston bursary (£2,000) are available to those who need them. The access fund provides anything from £50 if you've lost your bank card to large payments for help with rent - it's all decided case by case.
Banks on campus: NatWest, HSBC and Lloyds

FEES: Postgrad fees are £6,000-£17,000. International students pay up to £10,000.

ACCOMMODATION: • Cost of living index: £ • Insurance premium: ££
In college: • Self-catering: 34% • Cost: £53-81 (39wks)
• First years living in: 80%
Birmingham: • Ave rent: £45 • Living at home: 20%

EMPLOYMENT: • Unemployed after 6mths: 5% • Paid work: term-time 60%: hols 85%
The Guild's job shop advertises the *decent* number of local jobs (bars, pubs, clubs, shops and restaurants mostly). The Guild also employs students to help run its facilities and operates a vacation work placement scheme that finds course-related positions paying roughly £160/wk.

TRAVEL: see University of Birmingham
New Street Station is 15mins walk away. Digbeth coach station 5mins by taxi from the campus. The Resident's Association (ACRA) runs a minibus service to local supermarkets so *there's no excuse to go hungry*. Coaches and minibuses take students to the recreation site. Bikes are increasingly common thanks to Birmingham's improved cycle network.

ENTERTAINMENTS: • Booze index: £1.67
Birmingham: • Pint of beer: £2.10   • Glass of wine: £2.20
                                        • Can of Red Bull: £1.70
University: • Pint of beer: £1.75   • Glass of wine: £1.60
                                        • Can of Red Bull: £1.40

UNIVERSITY OF WALES, BANGOR
• **The College is part of University of Wales.**
(1) University of Wales, Bangor, Gwynedd, LL57 2DG
    Tel: (01248) 351151. Fax: (01248) 370451. E-mail: admissions@bangor.ac.uk
    Website: www.bangor.ac.uk
    Undeb Myfyrwyr Bangor Student's Union, Deiniol Road, Bangor, Gwynedd,
    LL57 2TH
    Tel: (01248) 388 000. Fax: (01248) 388 020
    E-mail: undeb@undeb.bangor.ac.uk. Website: www.undeb.bangor.ac.uk
(2) School of Education, University of Wales, Bangor, Gwynedd, LL57 2PX
    Tel: (01978) 316 316
(3) Faculty of Health Studies, Wrexham Technology Park, Wrexham, LL13 7YP

DEBTS: • Ave debt per year: £4,277
           • Access fund: £500,000   • Successful applications/yr: 500
           • Ave payment: £800-2,000
Academic scholarships, various departmental awards and sports opportunity
bursaries of £1,000.
Banks on campus: NatWest.

ACCOMMODATION: • Cost of living index: £££ • Insurance premium: £
In college: • Catered: 24%   • Cost: £74-84 (30wks)
                • Self-catering: 7%   • Cost: £49-66 (30-36wks)
                • First years living in: 100%
Bangor: • Ave rent: £40   • Living at home: 10%

EMPLOYMENT: • Unemployed after 6mths: 8%   • Paid work: term-time 50%:
                                               hols 65%
Paid work: Jobs can be *hard to come by*, although Welsh speakers are *at an
advantage* for office/admin work. GoWales provides 97 paid placements in north-
west Wales during vacations and after graduation. The Portfolio Worker Project
helps develop freelancing abilities.
Careers: The careers service is involved in the GO Wales/Cymru Prosper Wales work
exprerience project, promoting employment for students who live in Wales.

TRAVEL:
National: Trains direct to London (from £40 return). Just about everywhere else
involves a change at Crewe (£17). Coaches to London (£33), Brum (18.25) and
Cardiff (£35.75) among others. Day trips on the ferry to Ireland cost £9.
Local: Buses run around town and all across Gwynedd. *Taxis are cheap, bikes are
even cheaper, if harder work.*

ENTERTAINMENTS: • Booze index: £1.58
Bangor: • Pint of beer: £2.10   • Glass of wine: £1.90
                                       • Can of Red Bull: £1.60
University: • Pint of beer: £1.65 • Glass of wine: £1.50
                                       • Can of Red Bull: £1

7

BATH UNIVERSITY

The University of Bath, Claverton Down, Bath, BA2 7AY
Tel: (01225) 383 019. Fax: (01225) 386 366. E-mail: admissions@bath.ac.uk
Website: www.bath.ac.uk
University of Bath Students' Union, Claverton Down, Bath, BA2 7AY
Tel: (01225) 386 612. Fax: (01225) 444 061. E-mail: union@bath.ac.uk
Website: www.bathstudent.com

DEBTS: • Ave debt per year: £7,471
Students who have to do vacation and field study can apply for special awards.
There's a sports scholarship scheme where exceptional students can take an extra
year for their degrees combined with intensive training. Hardship fund also
available.
Banks on campus: NatWest, HSBC

FEES: The common or garden postgrad fee is £3,400 but it varies. International
students pay £10,100 for lab courses, £7,900 for others.

ACCOMMODATION: • Cost of living index: £££   • Insurance premium: £
In college: • Catered: 1%   • Cost: £77 (35-38wks)
                   • Self-catering: 31%   • Cost: £52-77 (35-38wks)
                   • First years living in: 100%
Bath: • Ave rent: £60

EMPLOYMENT: • Unemployed after 6mths: 4.9%
Paid work: Bath's ever-flowing stream of tourists provides plenty of seasonal work.
SU-run JobLink *is a far cry from the typical tatty Union notice board* and operates
similarly to a council job centre, advertising casual part-time work and keeping to a
strict Code of Practice. On campus, there's work in shops, bars and admin.
Careers: The *ass-kicking* careers service runs a variety of aids for all students
including personal skills workshops, aptitude testing, computer-aided guidance
systems *(nothing to do with missiles)*, job fairs and employer presentations. A lot of
Bath students do work placements while studying, arranged by the careers folk.

TRAVEL:
National: Bath Spa Station roughly 2 miles away has services to London
Paddington, Bristol, Birmingham and beyond. Bath Coach Station has several
National Express and First Group services, including London and Bristol. Bristol
Airport 18 miles away has flights inland and to main European destinations. *Many
students cadge lifts up the hill to the University and the M4's good for thumbing
down to London*.
Local: The SU has negotiated with First Bus to bring about the 'Bright Orange' bus
service, which operates between the town, Bath University and Bath Spa every 6
mins during term. The Union shop sells books of 20 tickets.

ENTERTAINMENTS: • Booze index: £1.75
Bath: • Pint of beer: £2.40   • Glass of wine: £2.60
                                            • Can of Red Bull: £1.70
University: • Pint of beer: £1.75   • Glass of wine: £2

UNUSUAL COSTS: Students living on campus or living privately in BA1 or BA2
postcodes are not eligible for annual parking permits. For others, they cost between
£103 and £155 depending on location.

BATH SPA UNIVERSITY COLLEGE

(1) Bath Spa University College, Newton St Loe, Bath, BA2 9BN
Tel: (01225) 875 875. Fax: (01225) 875 444. E-mail: enquiries@bathspa.ac.uk
Website: www.bathspa.ac.uk
Bath Spa University College Students' Union, Newton Park Campus, Newton
St Loe, Bath, BA2 9BN
Tel: (01225) 875 588. Fax: (01225) 876 156
E-mail: bathspasu@bathspa.ac.uk Website: www.bathspasu.co.uk
(2) Bath Spa University College, Sion Hill, Lansdown, BA1 5SF
Tel: (01225) 875 875
Bath Spa Students Union, Somerset Place, Lansdown, BA1 5SF
Tel: (01225) 875 684

DEBTS:
- Ave debt per year: £5,528
- Access fund: £312,000   • Successful applications/yr: 727
- Ave payment: £293

Hardship loans and grants available.
Banks on campus: NatWest ATMs

ACCOMMODATION: • Cost of living index: ££££ • Insurance premium: £
In college: • Self-catering: 20%   • Cost: £57-84 (38wks)
   • First years living in: 90%
Bath: • Ave rent: £60

EMPLOYMENT: • Unemployed after 6mths: 7.5%
Paid work: The job shop provides part-time work for students – quite literally, since
it employs 3 students itself – and maintains an online job database.
Careers: Bulletin board, careers library, workshops and a host of online resources.

TRAVEL: see Bath University
Local: *Buses are far and away best for the Newton Park-Bath journey*, 2 an hour,
quite reliably, until around 2:30am. Buses run between town, Bath Spa and Bath
University (£2.10 rtn or season ticket) and Newton Park and Sion Hill.

ENTERTAINMENTS: • Booze index: £2.09
Bath: • Pint of beer: £2.40
   • Glass of wine: £2.60
   • Can of Red Bull: £1.70
University: • Pint of beer: £1.80
   • Bottle of wine: £5
   • Can of Red Bull: £1.20

UNUSUAL COSTS: £8 a semester for use of the sports facilities.

BIRKBECK COLLEGE, UNIVERSITY OF LONDON

• **The College is part of <u>London University</u> and students are entitled to use
its facilities.**
Birkbeck College, University of London, Malet Street, Bloomsbury, London,
WC1E 7HX
Tel: (020) 7631 6000. Fax: (020) 7631 6270. E-mail: admissions@bbk.ac.uk
Website: www.bbk.ac.uk
Birkbeck Student's Union, Malet St, Bloomsbury, London, WC1E 7HX
Tel: (020) 7631 6335. Fax: (020) 7631 6349. E-mail: president@bcsu.bbk.ac.uk

DEBTS: • Ave debt per year: £125   • Access fund: £500
Hardship funds and college research funds (which can cover fees and/or
maintenance).

FEES: Fees have been charged at £858, they're still mulling over changes.

ACCOMMODATION: • Cost of living index: £££££ • Insurance premium: ££
In college: • Catered: none • Self-catering: none
For London, see London University.

EMPLOYMENT: • Paid work: term-time 90%: hols 90%
Paid work: Since students generally have work already, there's only ULU's (*admittedly massive*) jobshop and careers service.
Careers: Birkbeck uses London University's careers service. The Graduate Career Resource Centre, the largest in London, is also accessible to students and graduates.

TRAVEL:
National: see London University
Local: Buses *a-plenty* serve the site. Euston and Goodge St stations are both close by for Victoria and Northern line tube travel.

ENTERTAINMENTS: • Booze index: £1.70
London: • Pint of beer: £2.60 • Glass of wine: £2.25
 • Can of Red Bull: £1.50
University: • Pint of beer: £1.70 • Glass of wine: £2
 • Can of Red Bull: £0.95

....

BIRMINGHAM UNIVERSITY

University of Birmingham, Edgbaston, Birmingham, B15 2TT
Tel: (0121) 414 6727. Fax: (0121) 414 7159. E-mail: admissions@bham.ac.uk
Website: www.bham.ac.uk
Birmingham Guild of Students (BUGS), The University of Birmingham, Edgbaston Park Road, B15 2TU
Tel: (0121) 251 2300. Fax: (0121) 251 2301. E-mail: enquiries@bugs.bham.ac.uk
Website: www.bugs.bham.ac.uk

DEBTS: • Ave debt per year: £3,482
 • Access fund: £902,155 • Successful applications/yr: 1,413
 • Ave payment: £100-3,500
A range of bursaries is offered by both the University and Guild for academic success and financial hardship. Amounts vary from £1,000 to full payment of fees and maintenance payments.
Banks on campus: HSBC

FEES: The University will charge new students the full £3,000 top up fee for all courses from 2006.

ACCOMMODATION: • Cost of living index: £££ • Insurance premium: ££
In college: • Catered: 7% • Cost: £85-112 (30-42wks)
 • Self-catering: 17% • Cost: £66-76 (42-50wks)
 • First years living in: 90%
Birmingham: • Ave rent: £48 excluding bills

EMPLOYMENT: • Unemployed after 6mths: 6%
 • Paid work: term-time 30%: hols 30%
Paid work: The Job Zone arranges jobs and placements with the help of the careers centre's services. Loads of opportunities around campus in the kitchens, libraries, bars, alumni office, careers service and so on.
Careers: *Accessible* and *helpful* service with bulletin boards, vacancy lists, employer contacts, web site, skills training, and other events.

TRAVEL:
National: Uniquely, there's a station on campus, connecting to Birmingham New St for mainline links from London (£8.50 single), Manchester (£6.50 single), Edinburgh (£15.50 single) and elsewhere. Coaches to London (£18.50),

Manchester (£8.20), Edinburgh (£26) and all over. Loads of domestic and international budget airlines fly from Birmingham Airport, 9 miles east from the campus. For hitching, *Birmingham is the motorway Mecca of England. Pick a junction and get thumbing.*
Local: The *abundant but busy* bus services run late into the night. *It's easy to get into town, but hard to get around the edge.* Overground trains run around the city – *they're faster than buses, but more expensive and unreliable.* Bikes are *commonplace* on campus and there are cycle lanes and *plenty* of places to lock them up.
College: The University lays on a free bus between Edgbaston and Selly Oak (pass needed) and another from halls to various places around campus with uni ID.

ENTERTAINMENTS: • Booze index: £1.55
Birmingham: • Pint of beer: £1.90   • Glass of wine: £2
                                           • Can of Red Bull: £1.70
University: • Pint of beer: £1.65   • Glass of wine: £1.20
                                           • Can of Red Bull: £1.70

UNUSUAL COSTS: Gym membership costs £131 per year peak, £95 off peak

BOLTON INSTITUTE FOR HIGHER EDUCATION
Bolton Institute for Higher Education, Deane Road, BL3 5AB
Tel: (012904) 903 903. Fax: (01204) 903 809. E-mail: enquires@bolton.ac.uk
Website: www.bolton.ac.uk
Bolton Institute Students Union, Deane Road, BL3 5AB
Tel: (01204) 900 850. Fax: (01204) 900 860. E-mail: bisu@bolton.ac.uk
Website: www.bisu.co.uk

DEBTS: • Ave debt per year: £3,435
             • Access fund: £600,000   • Successful applications/yr: 391
Budget advice, hardship funds, emergency loans and some bursaries available.

FEES: Non-UK or EU students pay £6,025.

ACCOMMODATION: • Cost of living index: £££   • Insurance premium: £££
In college: • Self-catering: 27%   • Cost: £53 (40wks)
                    • First years living in: 100%
Bolton: • Ave rent: £40

EMPLOYMENT: • Unemployed after 6mths: 11%
Paid work: The jobshop at the Student Centre posts part-time vacancies. *Bar, restaurant and supermarket work is fairly common.*
Careers: The Student Centre is *a bit weedy career-wise, but does its best*: newsletters, bulletin boards, careers library, interview training and CV surgery sessions.

TRAVEL:
National: Bolton mainline station is 800m from the Institute and offers connections to Manchester every 15 mins. The coach station (next to the railway) has National Express services to most major cities. *Parking is as easy as a drunken hooker* with plenty of free space at the Institute for student cars. The town is *cheap-ish* for parking too. Manchester Airport (EasyJet) takes 30 mins by car. *The network of main roads means hitching isn't a crazy option.*
Local: Buses *are refreshingly regular*, with many using the *inexpensive* services to get to and from halls until 11.30pm. A nightbus from Manchester chugs in at 1am, 2.30am at weekends.

ENTERTAINMENTS: • Booze index: £1.79
Bolton: • Pint of beer: £1.49   • Glass of wine: £2
                                       • Can of Red Bull: £2

| University: | • Pint of beer: £1.50 | • Glass of wine: £1.50 |
| | | • Can of Red Bull: £1.20 |

BOURNEMOUTH UNIVERSITY

(1) Bournemouth University, Talbot Campus, Fern Barrow, BH12 5BB
Tel: (01202) 524111. Fax: (01202) 702736
E-mail: enquiries@bournemouth.ac.uk. Website: www.bournemouth.ac.uk
The Students' Union at Bournemouth University, Talbot Campus, Fern Barrow,
BH12 5BB
Tel: (01202) 595765. Fax: (01202) 535990. E-mail: subu@bournemouth.ac.uk
Website: www.subu.org.uk
(2) Lansdowne Campus, Christchurch Road and Holdenhurst Road, BH1 3LT

DEBTS: • Ave debt per year: £6,945
• Access fund: £448,490 • Successful applications/yr: 850
A *few* scholarships, but more bursaries
Banks on campus: Barclays with ATMs.

FEES: From 2006, the University plans to charge new students the full £3,000 top up fees for all courses, but not 'unless they are able to', which is, *erm, reassuring.*

ACCOMMODATION: • Cost of living index: £££ • Insurance premium: £
In college: • Self-catering: 25% • Cost: £64-76
• First years living in: 100% • Others living in: 3%
Poole (for main Talbot Campus): • Ave rent: £55-70
• Living at home: 20%

EMPLOYMENT: • Unemployed after 6mths: 7.9%
• Paid work: term-time 54%: hols 87%
During the tourist season, there's a *steady demand* for students in the local hotels, bars, clubs, etc. B&Q and Asda also *lick their lips eagerly* at the start of every academic year. The careers service has a good reputation for getting people into the media, among other things.

TRAVEL:
Trains to London (£17.15), Brighton (£14.70), etc. and Megabus coaches to London (£1.50). *Bike-friendly* terrain.

ENTERTAINMENTS: • Booze index: £2.13
Poole: • Pint of beer: £2
• Glass of wine: £2.50
• Can of Red Bull: £2
University: • Pint of beer: £1.50 • Glass of wine: £2.25
• Can of Red Bull: £1.50

UNUSUAL COSTS: £10 joining fee to use sports facilities.

BRADFORD UNIVERSITY

(1) University of Bradford, Richmond Road, Bradford, West Yorkshire, BD7 1DP
Tel: (01274) 233 081. Fax: (01274) 236 260
E-mail: course-enquiries@bradford.ac.uk. Website: www.bradford.ac.uk/
University of Bradford Union, Communal Building, University of Bradford,
Richmond Road, Bradford, West Yorkshire, BD7 1DP
Tel: (01274) 233300. Fax: (01274) 235530
E-mail: ubu-comms@bradford.ac.uk. Website: www.ubui.co.uk
(2) The School of Management, Emm Lane, Bradford, BD9 4JL
Tel: (01274) 234 393
Fax: (01274) 546 866. E-mail: management@bradford.ac.uk

DEBTS:
- Ave debt per year: £5,898
- Access fund: £420,000 • Successful applications/yr: 969
- Ave payment: £800

Hardship loans (£500); 20 postgrad bursaries (£1,000); travel awards.
Banks on campus: NatWest

ACCOMMODATION: • Cost of living index: £££ • Insurance premium: £££££
In college:
- Self-catering: 100% • Cost: £46-72 (39 wks)
- First years living in: 100%

Bradford: • Ave rent: £35 • Living at home: 26%

EMPLOYMENT: • Unemployed after 6mths: 6.5%
Paid work: The JobShop helps students find part-time work, which *many* do in the cinemas, theatres, SU bars and shops and pubs and restaurants in town.
Careers: Lots of vocational courses, a *well-stocked* careers service with online vacancies and an e-mail advice service to make job-hunting *a little less stressful*.

TRAVEL:
National: Trains to Leeds (£1.45 sgl), London King's Cross (£33), Manchester (£8 rtn), York (£7.55) and Sheffield (£4.60 sgl). Coaches to Leeds (£2.50), London Victoria (£22.50), Manchester (£8 rtn), York (£5) and Sheffield (£6.25). Leeds and Bradford Airport (6$\frac{1}{2}$ miles away) operates flights inland and to Europe, Ireland and North America.
Local: Buses are cheap and convenient for campus, town and the Emm Lane site. West Yorkshire DayRover: a one-day leisure ticket for unlimited travel in West Yorkshire. £3.80 bus only, £4.50 bus and train. £6 family DayRover (covers bus and train).

ENTERTAINMENTS: • Booze index: £1.98
Bradford:
- Pint of beer: £1.60 • Glass of wine: £2.70
- • Can of Red Bull: £2

University:
- Pint of beer: £1.45 • Glass of wine: £1.75
- • Can of Red Bull: £1.50

UNUSUAL COSTS: Parking on campus costs £19, £25 for grads.

7

BRIGHTON UNIVERSITY
(1) University of Brighton, Mithras House, Lewes Road, BN2 4AT
Tel: (01273) 600 900. Fax: (01273) 642 825
E-mail: admissions@brighton.ac.uk Website: www.brighton.ac.uk
University of Brighton Students' Union, Cockcroft Building, Lewes Road, BN2 4GL
Tel: (01273) 642 746. Fax: (01273) 600 649. E-mail: ubsu@bton.ac.uk
Website: ubsu.net
(2) Grand Parade Campus, University of Brighton, Grand Parade, Brighton, BN2 0JY
University of Brighton Students' Union, Main Building, 58-67 Grand Parade, BN2 0JY. Tel: (01273) 643 190
(3) Falmer Campus, University of Brighton, Falmer, BN1 9PH
University of Brighton Students' Union, Friston House, Village Way, BN1 9PH
Tel: (01273) 643 328
(4) Eastbourne Campus, University of Brighton, Trevin Towers, Gaudick Road, Eastbourne, BN20 7SP
University of Brighton Students' Union, Bishopsbourne, 32 Carlise Road, BN20 7SP. Tel: (01273) 643 816

DEBTS:
- Ave debt per year: £2,114
- Access fund: £750,000 • Successful applications/yr: 2,000
- Ave payment: £100-£3,500

Bursary top-ups and scholarships for international students. Fees are temporarily waived for low-income postgrads.

FEES: *Brighton is in favour of top up fees and is likely to charge the full amount for many courses.*

ACCOMMODATION: • Cost of living index: £££ • Insurance premium: £
In college: • Self-catering: 8% • Cost: £58-93 (42wks)
• First years living in: 40%
Brighton: • Ave rent: £50-70 • Living at home: 11%

EMPLOYMENT: • Unemployed after 6mths: 7%
• Paid work: term-time 37%:
Paid work: There are plenty of jobs going in bars, shops and restaurants around town, although many are during the summer vacation.
Careers: 18 staff to help with the job hunt.

TRAVEL:
National: Train connections to London (£6.60), Bristol (£23.75), Sheffield (£38.30) and beyond. National Express coaches to London (£10.50), Bristol (£32), Sheffield (£25) and 23 miles from Gatwick.
Local: The south coast is *better travelled* by train than the *timely but sluggish* bus services. Also a free minibus between Varley Halls of Residence and Falmer campus.

ENTERTAINMENTS: • Booze index: £1.61
Brighton: • Pint of beer: £2.50 • Glass of wine: £3.50
• Can of Red Bull: £2
University: • Pint of beer: £1.80 • Glass of wine: £2
• Can of Red Bull: £1.75

BRISTOL UNIVERSITY

University of Bristol, Senate House, Tyndall Avenue, BS8 1TH
Tel: (0117) 928 9000. Fax: (0117) 925 1424. E-mail: admissions@bristol.ac.uk
Website: www.bristol.ac.uk
University of Bristol Students Union, Queens Road, Clifton, BS8 1LN
Tel: (0117) 954 5800. Fax: (0117) 954 5817
E-mail: communications-ubu@bris.ac.uk. Website: www.ubu.org.uk

DEBTS: • Ave debt per year: £5,767
• Access fund: £500,000 • Successful applications/yr: 676
• Ave payment: £100-4,500
Convocation bursaries (£1,000) to low-income students from schools in Avon. Sports scholarships for the talented.

ACCOMMODATION: • Cost of living index: ££ • Insurance premium: £
In college: • Catered: 16% • Cost: £79-£111 (30-38wks)
• Self-catering: 9% • Cost: £37-£78 (38wks)
• First years living in: 91%
Bristol: • Ave rent: £65 • Living at home: 4%

EMPLOYMENT: • Unemployed after 6mths: 3.4%
• Paid work: term-time 18%: hols 20%
The SU-run employment office helps find the normal limited selection of bar work and restaurants. Meanwhile, an army of staff hawks students around student-hungry long-term employers.

TRAVEL:
National: By train, Bristol Temple Meads is one of the country's centres for mainline routes: London (£27.15), Birmingham (£20.45) and elsewhere. Bristol Parkway for Wales. Also coaches to London (£15), Birmingham (£12.75) and Cardiff (£6.50). Arrow and Bakers Dolphin also offer *cheap* return trips to London. Bristol airport for *low-cost* flights.

Local: Rail stops in and around the city provide a *reliable*, *frequent* and *comprehensive* service *without staggering cost*. Local buses fill in where trains can't go, costing £1 from Temple Meads Station to the Union. StudentLink bus services run in the evening between Stoke Bishop, via Clifton and the Union, down to the city centre, and back. It's 80p a trip and several services visit halls of residence till 11.30pm.

ENTERTAINMENTS: • <u>Booze index: £1.82</u>
Bristol: • <u>Pint of beer: £2.20</u>
                                          • <u>Glass of wine: £2</u>
                                          • <u>Can of Red Bull: £1.80</u>
University: • <u>Pint of beer: £1.30</u>   • <u>Glass of wine: £1.50</u>
                                          • <u>Can of Red Bull: 70p</u>

UNUSUAL COSTS: A Sportspass costs £150 (2 years) or £215 (for 3).

BRUNEL UNIVERSITY
(1) Brunel University, Uxbridge, Middlesex, UB 3PH
    Tel: (01895) 274 000. Fax: (01895) 232 806. E-mail: courses@brunel.ac.uk
    Website: www.brunel.ac.uk
    Union of Brunel Students, Cleveland Road, Uxbridge, Middlesex, UB8 3PH
    Tel: (01895) 462 300. Fax: (01895) 462 300
    E-mail: vp.communications@brunel.ac.uk
(2) Runnymede Campus, Brunel University, Englefield Green, Egham, Surrey,
    TW20 0JZ
    Tel: (01895) 274 000. Fax: (01895) 232 806
(3) Osterley Campus, Brunel University, Borough Road, Isleworth, Middlesex,
    TW7 5DU
    Tel: (0208) 891 0121. Fax: (0208) 891 8211
(4) Twickenham Campus, Brunel University, 300 St Margaret's Road, Twickenham,
    Middlesex, TW1 1PT
    Tel: (0208) 891 0121. Fax: (0208) 891 8270

DEBTS: • <u>Ave debt per year: £2,866</u>
          • <u>Access fund: £570,917</u>   • <u>Successful applications/yr: 441</u>
          • <u>Ave payment: £713</u>
Hardship loans available.
Banks on campus: HSBC Bank/ATM

ACCOMMODATION: • <u>Cost of living index: ££££</u> • <u>Insurance premium: £</u>
In college: • <u>Self-catering: 2,663</u>   • <u>Cost: £57-70 (38-51 wks)</u>
               • <u>First years living in: 66%</u>
Uxbridge: • <u>Ave rent: £68</u>   • <u>Living at home: 15%</u>

EMPLOYMENT: • <u>Unemployed after 6mths: 7.7%</u>
Paid work: There's a jobshop for part-time and vacation work.
Careers: The Careers Service has 9 full-time and 4 part-time staff.

TRAVEL: see <u>London University</u>
National: West Drayton and Hayes (50mins, £8.30 to London Paddington) are the BR stations nearest to the Uxbridge site both a short bus ride away (Uxbridge tube station is closer). National Express and London Country coach services stop at Heathrow Airport (25 mins by bus).
Local: Uxbridge is still within London's local transport network, *which is convenient but expensive*. It's served by buses 207, 222, U3, U4, Express Coach 607 and Night Bus N89 (which goes right into London's West End, though it can take a while). Uxbridge Underground station (a mile from campus) is the last stop on the Metropolitan and Piccadilly Lines *and offers a fast but expensive service into London*. The University runs a bus service between Uxbridge and Runnymede.

ENTERTAINMENTS: • <u>Booze index: £2.30</u>
London: see <u>London University</u>
University: • <u>Pint of beer: £1.50</u>   • <u>Glass of wine: £1.80</u>
                                                   • <u>Can of Red Bull: £2</u>

BUCKINGHAM UNIVERSITY

University of Buckingham, Buckingham, MK18 1EG
Tel: (01280) 814080. Fax: (01280) 822245
E-mail: info@buckingham.ac.uk. Website: www.buckingham.ac.uk
University of Buckingham Students' Union, Tanlaw Mill, Buckingham, MK18 1EG
Tel: (01280) 822522. Fax: (01280) 812791
E-mail: student.union@buckingham.ac.uk
Website: www.buckingham.ac.uk/life/social/su/index.html

DEBTS: • <u>Ave debt per year: £5,270</u> • <u>Access fund: none</u>
The nature of the university as a private institution means student debt figures vary
enormously. Some students owe nothing, some have £25 grand to pay back to the
bank. By shunning Government funding, Buckingham has no access fund, although
there are fee discounts of £4,040 for local students, some hardship funds and
sponsorship deals available from some local organisations – the Rotary Club, for
example. Graduates get discounts off further study based on academic results.

FEES: • <u>Home student fees: £10,920</u>
It's the only university where postgrad fees can be less than undergrads' – although
they range from £7,000-£20,000.

ACCOMMODATION: • <u>Cost of living index: £££££</u> • <u>Insurance premium: £</u>
In college: • <u>Self-catering: 83%</u>   • <u>Cost: £63-104 (40wks)</u>
                • <u>First years living in: 100%</u>
Buckingham: • <u>Ave rent: £115</u>

EMPLOYMENT: • <u>Unemployed after 6mths: 2% (June graduates), 19% (Dec)</u>
Paid work: There are very few opportunities for moonlight occupations at
Buckingham. *Most have plenty of money, thank you, and not enough time to do
much other than study. There are 1 or 2 restaurants, pubs or shops in the town
that might be looking and the Union bar and library night shifts are student-staffed.*
Careers: The careers service is also open to the public – for a small charge, *of
course (all in the best free market tradition).*

TRAVEL:
National: The nearest stations are at Bicester and Milton Keynes (London, £8.20).
Buses take 20 mins to get to MK and National Express services go from there all
over. Also Stagecoach. *Students who can afford Buckingham's fees can often
afford a car as well – there's a thriving used car sale scene in the Union – more
free enterprise. Parking presents few problems and permits are free if students ask
nicely.*
College: The University runs a shuttle service on weekdays between the main
Hunter Street site and the law school at Verney Park for those who find a 10-
minute walk too demanding.

ENTERTAINMENTS: • <u>Booze index: £1.71</u>
Buckingham: • <u>Pint of beer: £2.20</u>   • <u>Glass of wine: ££2</u>
                                                  • <u>Can of Red Bull: £1.80</u>
University: • <u>Pint of beer: £1.60</u>   • <u>Glass of wine: £1.80</u>
                                                  • <u>Can of Red Bull: £1.50</u>

7

In the back

BUCKINGHAMSHIRE CHILTERNS UNIVERSITY COLLEGE

(1) Buckinghamshire Chilterns University College, Queen Alexandra Road, HP11 2JZ
Tel: (01494) 522 141. Fax: (01494) 524 392. Website: www.bcuc.ac.uk
Buckinghamshire Chilterns Students' Union, Queen Alexandra Road, HP11 2JZ
Tel: (01494) 446330. Fax: (01494) 558195. Website: www.bcsu.net
(2) Wellesbourne Campus, Kingshill Road, HP13 5BB
(3) Chalfont Campus, Gorelands Lane, HP8 4AD

DEBTS: • Ave debt per year: £4,164
• Access fund: £160,000
The University has a hardship fund to make emergency loans and a few scholarships.

ACCOMMODATION: • Cost of living index: ££££ • Insurance premium: £
In college: • Self-catering: 18% • Cost: £59.50 (38wks)
High Wycombe: • Ave rent: £40-60

EMPLOYMENT: • Unemployed after 6mths: 8%

ENTERTAINMENTS: • Booze index: £2.34
Locally: • Pint of beer: £2 • Glass of wine: £3.50
• Can of Red Bull: £1.80
University: • Pint of beer: £1.80 • Glass of wine: £2
• Can of Red Bull: £1.90

CAMBRIDGE UNIVERSITY

Cambridge University, Kellett Lodge, Tennis Court Road, Cambridge, CB2 1QJ
Tel: (01223) 333308. Fax: (01223) 366383
E-mail: admissions@cam.ac.uk. Website: www.cam.ac.uk
Cambridge University Students' Union, 11/12 Trumpington Street, Cambridge,
CB2 1QA
Tel: (01223) 356454. Fax: (01223) 323244. E-mail: info@cusu.cam.ac.uk
Website: www.cusu.cam.ac.uk

DEBTS: • Ave debt per year: £1,488
Most financial assistance comes from the colleges and takes the form of hardship funds, academic prizes or *archaic* bursaries from *fetishist* alumni, ranging from cash for Catholic girls whose parents converted from Judaism *to, probably, money for oceanographers who tame wombats. Basically, quite a bit of money floating about, mostly for merit, but there's lots of competition and the individual pay-outs aren't huge.*

FEES: The Vice Chancellor is in agreement with Government top up policies, but there are plans to introduce £4,000/yr Cambridge Bursaries for undergrads who can't afford the fee-hike – the largest undergrad support program in the UK.

ACCOMMODATION: • Cost of living index: £ • Insurance premium: £
In college: • Catered: 95% • Cost: £71-89 (40wks)
• First years living in: 100%
Cambridge: • Ave rent: £66

EMPLOYMENT: • Unemployed after 6mths: 2.7%
• Paid work: term-time 10%: hols 50%
Paid work: Cambridge University authorities officially bar their students from working more than 6hrs a week. Many students ignore them and get bar or baby-sitting jobs around town, and most take on temp holiday work. Life-modelling opportunities with local artists are common and can provide some quick cash for those who don't mind getting their kit off.
Careers: *Although '(Cantab)' after your name might not be the sure-fire guarantee*

of a top job it once was, *a Cambridge education rarely does harm on a CV and, supposedly, employers find Cambridge students more down-to-earth than those from Oxford (who must surely then be space cadets)*. The Careers Service operates a whole houseful of facilities, including weekly email bulletins from the moment a student signs up till the day they die and GradLink, which puts hopefuls in touch with graduates in their chosen professions.

TRAVEL:
National: Cambridge's *smallish* station connects to London King's Cross (3 an hour) and Liverpool Street, Liverpool Lime Street, Birmingham, Bristol and more. The *shabby* outdoor bus station on Drummond Street runs *plenty* of competing coach services. Students aren't allowed to keep cars without a watertight excuse. Stansted Airport, 23 miles down the M11, is on a direct train link and has loads of budget flights.
Local: The *ever-changing* local bus network, Stagecoach, *runs services as regular as prunes* to the surrounding villages, Ely, Huntingdon, the station and the outer colleges. *Cambridge is too small to need much more. Such short distances mean cab companies are comfortable hiking up prices – similar length journeys would be cheaper in larger cities.* Some colleges have free taxi arrangements at night. *Bikes are virtually a prerequisite for living in Cambridge.* There are *ample* racks around town and in the colleges.

ENTERTAINMENTS: • Booze index: £1.53
Cambridge:	• Pint of beer: £2.50	• Glass of wine: £2.50
		• Can of Red Bull: £1.80
University:	• Pint of beer: £1.60	• Glass of wine: £1.50
		• Can of Red Bull: £1

UNUSUAL COSTS: Formal dinners at each college cost around £6 for 3 courses. There's also the Kitchen Fixed Charge (KFC) in most colleges tacked onto the bill (£80-£110). May Balls are luxury affairs and their ticket prices reflect that (up to £200 for a double ticket).

CANTERBURY CHRIST CHURCH UNIVERSITY COLLEGE
(1) Canterbury Christ Church University College, North Holmes Road, Canterbury, Kent, CT1 1QU
Tel: (01227) 767 700. Fax: (01227) 470 442. E-mail: admissions@canterbuy.ac.uk
Website: www.canterbury.ac.uk
Christ Church Students' Union, North Holmes Road, Canterbury, Kent, CT1 1QU
Tel: (01227) 782 416. Fax: (01227) 458 287. E-mail: president@canterbury.ac.uk
Website: www.c4online.net
(2) Thanet Campus, Canterbury Christ Church University College, Northwood Road, Broadstairs, Kent, CT10 2WA. Tel: (01843) 280 600
Canterbury's Students' Union, Room CG13, Northwood Road, Broadstairs, Kent, CT10 2WA. Tel: (01843) 280 600
(3) Salomons Campus, David Salomons Estate, Broomhill Road, Southborough, Tunbridge Wells, Kent, TN3 0TG. Tel: (01892) 515 152
E-mail: enquiries@salomons.org.uk. Website: www.salomonscentre.org.uk

| **DEBTS:** | • Ave debt per year: £3,773 | |
| | • Access fund: £77,059 | • Successful applications/yr: 340 |

ACCOMMODATION:	• Cost of living index: ££	• Insurance premium: £
In college:	• Catered: n/a	• Cost: £57-61 (39wks)
	• Self-catering: n/a	• Cost: £61-74 (39wks)
	• First years living in: 45%	
Canterbury:	• Ave rent: £55-70	

EMPLOYMENT: • Unemployed after 6mths: 5.8%
Paid work: The Jobshop helps find part-time work, including doing up to 15 hours a week for the SU.

Careers: Careers Service. 2nd-year BA/BSc students take part in a Career Development programme during the last three weeks of the academic year, involving advice, work placements or short courses.

TRAVEL: see University of Kent

ENTERTAINMENTS: • Booze index: £1.64
Canterbury: • Pint of beer: £2.40
• Glass of wine: £2.50
• Can of Red Bull: £1.50
University: • Pint of beer: £1.40
• Glass of wine: £1.80
• Can of Red Bull: 70p

UNUSUAL COSTS: For £28 a year students can go for the burn at the St George's Fitness Centre, 5mins from the College.

··

CARDIFF UNIVERSITY
• **The College is part of University of Wales.**
• **Wales College of Medicine was incorporated in August 2004**
(1) Cardiff University, PO Box 921, Cardiff, CF10 3XQ
   Tel: (029) 2087 4839. Fax: (029) 2087 4457
   E-mail: prospectus@cardiff.ac.uk. Website: www.cardiff.ac.uk
   Cardiff university students' Union, Park Place, Cardiff, CF10 3QN
   Tel: (029) 2078 1400. Fax: (029) 2078 1518. E-mail: studentsunion@cf.ac.uk
   Website: www.cardiffstudents.com
(2) Cardiff University, Heath Park Campus, Cardiff, CF14 4XN
   Students Club, Neuadd Meirionnydd, Heath Park, Cardiff, CF14 4YS
   Tel: (029) 2074 2125

DEBTS: • Ave debt per year: £2,089
• Access fund: c£1,000,000
The hardship fund helps out *if things are really tough*. The Oldfield Davies Trust can help women with health problems and there are also short-term loans and small grants for finalists.
Banks on campus: HSBC

FEES: The Welsh Assembly, kinder-hearted than the English lot, has ruled out charging top up fees until 2007.

ACCOMMODATION: • Cost of living index: £   • Insurance premium: £
In college: • Catered: 17%
• Self-catering: 83%
• First years living in: 97%
• Cost: £55-67 (39wks)
• Cost: £39-58 (52wks)
Cardiff: • Ave rent: £50

EMPLOYMENT: • Unemployed after 6mths: 5%
Paid work: The University jobshop employs 700 students a year for up to 15 hours a week in various clerical, administrative, cleaning and catering jobs around campus.

TRAVEL:
National: Direct trains from Cardiff Central: London (£17.15); Birmingham (£13.20); Manchester (£25.10). National Express to most places: London (£18), Birmingham (£14.50) and all over. Cardiff Airport has flights to the Channel Islands, Ireland and even the US, as well as domestic trips. *Hitchers will love the A48 – only 5 mins' walk from the campus and the Welsh are willing.*
Local: Local buses are reliable (average trip, 50p). Everything's *within pedalling distance* and there are sheds at all the halls. *Bike-rustling is a bit of problem, though.*

ENTERTAINMENTS: • <u>Booze index: £2.12</u>
Cardiff: • <u>Pint of beer: £1.90</u>   • <u>Glass of wine: £1.40</u>
University: • <u>Pint of beer: £1.70</u>   • <u>Glass of wine: £1.50</u>

UNUSUAL COSTS: Yearly parking permits for campus cost a hefty £90.

....

CARDIFF INSTITUTE
Llandaff Campus, Western Avenue, PO Box 377, Llandaff, Cardiff, CF5 2SG
Tel: (029) 2041 6070. Fax: 029 2041 6286. E-mail: uwicinfo@uwic.ac.uk
Website: www.uwic.ac.uk
University of Wales Institute, Cardiff Students' Union, Central Union Offices, UWIC,
Cyncoed Road, Cardiff, CF23 6XD
Tel: (029) 2041 6190. E-mail: studentunion@uwic.ac.uk
Website: www.uwicsu.co.uk

DEBTS: • <u>Ave debt per year: £3,061</u>
Hardship funds and sports scholarships have a wee bit o' cash in them.

ACCOMMODATION: • <u>Cost of living index: £</u>   • <u>Insurance premium: £</u>
In college: • <u>Catered: n/a%</u>   • <u>Cost: £81 (39wks)</u>
• <u>Self-catering: n/a%</u>   • <u>Cost: £53-£90 (39wks)</u>
• <u>First years living in: 90%</u>
Cardiff: • <u>Ave rent: £45</u>   • <u>Living at home: 20%</u>

EMPLOYMENT: • <u>Unemployed after 6mths: 6%</u>
Paid work: Many UWIC students work during term time – the Careers Service runs
a jobshop that helps the monkeys find their peanuts. The SU employs bar staff and
shop assistants.
Careers: Careers advisors run a drop-in service on each site one day a week during
term. In addition to many other regular sevices, they have career planning computer
software.

ENTERTAINMENTS: • <u>Booze index: £2.03</u>
Cardiff: • See <u>Cardiff University</u>
University: • <u>Pint of beer: £1.05</u>   • <u>Glass of wine: £1.30</u>
• <u>Can of Red Bull: £1.30</u>

....

UNIVERSITY OF CENTRAL ENGLAND
University of Central England, Perry Barr, Birmingham, B42 2SU
Tel: (0121) 331 5595. Fax: (0121) 331 7994. E-mail: info@ucechoices.com
Website: www.ucechoices.com
Student's Union, University of Central England, Perry Bar, Birmingham, B42 2SU
Tel: (0121) 331 6802. Fax: (0121) 331 6801. E-mail: union.president@uce.ac.uk

DEBTS: • <u>Ave debt per year: £3,720</u>
• <u>Access fund: £778,045</u>   • <u>Successful applications/yr: 2,174</u>
Hardship funds and bursaries for students from low-income or disadvantaged
backgrounds.
Banks on campus: NatWest

ACCOMMODATION: • <u>Cost of living index: £££££</u>   • <u>Insurance premium: ££</u>
In college: • <u>Catered: 2%</u>   • <u>Cost: £60-80 (40wks)</u>
• <u>Self-catering: 24%</u>   • <u>Cost: £44-80 (40wks)</u>
Birmingham: • <u>Ave rent: £35-55</u>

EMPLOYMENT: • <u>Unemployed after 6mths: 3.7%</u>
The University job bureau helps find work on campus, locally, during holidays and
after graduation.

TRAVEL: see <u>University of Birmingham</u>

ENTERTAINMENTS: • Booze index: £1.50
Birmingham: see University of Birmingham
University: • Pint of beer: £1.50 • Glass of wine: £1.25

UNUSUAL COSTS: Sports facilities are charged between 30p and £2 a pop.

UNIVERSITY OF CENTRAL LANCASHIRE

University of Central Lancashire, Preston, PR1 2HE
Tel: (01772) 892400. Fax: (01772) 894959. E-mail: c.enquiries@uclan.ac.ukk
Website: www.uclan.ac.uk
University of Central Lancashire Students Union, Fylde Road, Preston, PR1 2HE
Tel: (01772) 892400. Fax: (01772) 894959. E-mail: s.u.soc@uclan.ac.uk
Website: www.uclan.ac.uk

DEBTS: • Ave debt per year: £5,178
• Access fund: £1,000,000 • Successful applications/yr: 1,600
Hardship fund, postgrad bursary.

FEES: *Despite the vice-chancellor's loud trumpets against top up fees, they're
hardly likely not to charge once they're introduced.*

ACCOMMODATION: • Cost of living index: ££ • Insurance premium: £
In college: • Catered: 1% • Cost: £51 (37wks)
• Self-catering: 8% • Cost: £59-66 (37wks)
• First years living in: 50%
Preston: • Ave rent: £40

EMPLOYMENT: • Unemployed after 6mths: 6%
Paid work: Jobshop (The Bridge). Loads of vacancies round college and in Preston.
Careers: Bulletin boards, jobs fairs, careers library and interview training.

TRAVEL:
National: Trains to London (£28.40), Manchester (£6.55) and beyond; National
Express buses all over and Manchester International for *cheap* flights.
Local: Local buses keep to an exact fare system (no change given). Discounted
Rambler tickets (anywhere in town, £5.20/wk). Bikes are *popular in college, but no
fun in the hills*.

ENTERTAINMENTS: • Booze index: £1.85
Preston: • Pint of beer: £1.60 • Glass of wine: £2
• Can of Red Bull: £2
University: • Pint of beer: £1.25 • Glass of wine: £1.80
• Can of Red Bull: £1.55

UNUSUAL COSTS: Joint membership of Preston Sports Arena and University
facilities costs £28/semester or £45 a year.

UNIVERSITY COLLEGE CHICHESTER

(1) University College Chichester, Otter Bishop Campus, College Lane, Chichester,
West Sussex, PO19 6PE
Tel: (01243) 816 002. Fax: (01243) 816 080
E-mail: studentsunion@ucc.ac.uk Website: www.ucc.ac.uk
University College Chichester's Students' Union, Bishop Otter Campus, College
Lane, Chichester, West Sussex, PO19 7EP
Tel: (01243) 816390. Fax: (01243) 816391. E-mail: studentsunion@ucc.ac.uk
Website: www.uccsu.org.uk/
(2) Bognor Regis, Upper Bognor Road, Bognor Regis, West Sussex, PO21 1HR

DEBTS: • Ave debt per year: £4,015
• Access fund: £263,670 • Successful applications/yr: 234

FEES: Part-time students pay £135 a module. An MA costs £3,000, as does an MSc. Part-time postgrads pay £370 a module. International students cough up £6,300 for classroom-based courses, £7,000 for lab-based ones and £7,000 for postgrad courses.

ACCOMMODATION: • Cost of living index: £   • Insurance premium: £
In college:	• Catered: 100% • Cost: £79-105 (34 wks)
	• First years living in: 35%
Chichester:	• Ave rent: £50-55 • Living at home: 30%
Bognor Regis:	• Ave rent: £45 • Living at home: 30%

EMPLOYMENT: • Unemployed after 6mths: 3.2%
Paid work: Jobshop for internal and external jobs and vacancies board. The careers service *does what it can* to help students find vocational work.
Careers: The Careers Service (2 full-time staff) has bulletin boards, library, teaching fair, job fairs and interview training.

TRAVEL:
National: Chichester Station (15mins walk from campus) has direct services to London Victoria (90mins, £14.55), Portsmouth (45mins, £4.90 sgl), Brighton (55mins, £5.50), Southampton (50mins, £13.95). The coach station (also 15mins) has services to London (£18.40), Southampton (£10.40), Portsmouth and Brighton (£6.40).
Local: Buses and trains from/to campuses cost £5 and £3.40 return respectively. Free college coaches *nip* between sites hourly on weekdays till 9.20pm. Pedal pumpers can get between campuses in 30-40mins.
Sites: Bognor has its own mainline railway station (1$^{1}/_{2}$ hrs direct to London Victoria) and good road links to the rest of the country. Disabled parking available.

ENTERTAINMENTS: • Booze index: £1.70
Chichester:	• Pint of beer: £2.40	• Glass of wine: £1.70
		• Can of Red Bull: £1.60
University:	• Pint of beer: £1.70	• Glass of wine: £1.65
		• Can of Red Bull: £1.20

....

CITY UNIVERSITY
(1) City University, Northampton Square, London, EC1V 0HB
Tel: (020) 7040 5060. Fax: (020) 7040 5070. Website: www.city.ac.uk
City University Students' Union, Northampton Square, London, EC1V 0HB
Tel: (020) 7040 5606. Fax: (020) 7040 5601. E-mail: cusu@city.ac.uk
Website: www.cusuonline.org
(2) Cass Business School, 106 Bunhill Row, London, EC1Y 8TZ
(3) St Bartholomew School of Nursing & Midwifery, London, EC1A 7QN
Tel: (020) 7040 8530

DEBTS: • Ave debt per year: £1,683
The Sir John Cass Foundation offers 14 scholarships a year to undergraduates from London studying computing, engineering, mathematics and actuarial science or nursing and midwifery. These are made to 2nd and 3rd year students and worth £1,000/yr for 3 years. The Reeves Foundation and Finsbury Educational Trust also offer scholarships to Greater London students.

ACCOMMODATION: • Cost of living index: ££££ • Insurance premium: ££
In college:	• Self-catering: 12%	• Cost: £89-96 (35-48wks)
London:	• Ave rent: £80	• Living at home: 20%

EMPLOYMENT: • Unemployed after 6mths: 4.5%
• Paid work: term-time 18%: hols 30%+
Plenty of opportunities for students to find work. The 6-strong careers service is *pretty average*, although the vocational nature of many City courses means that most students are *highly employable* on graduation.

TRAVEL: see <u>London University</u>
Close to several tube stops: Angel (Northern Line), Farringdon and Barbican (Circle, Hammersmith & City, Metropolitan, Thameslink lines). *Loads* of buses rumble past Northampton Square. *Bikes and mopeds are popular with students, but beware – they're also popular with Islington's criminals.*

ENTERTAINMENTS: • <u>Booze index: £1.90</u>
London: • <u>Pint of beer: £2.50</u>
                                   • <u>Glass of wine: £2.80</u>
                                   • <u>Can of Red Bull: £2</u>
University: • <u>Pint of beer: £1.50</u>
                                   • <u>Glass of wine: £2</u>
                                   • <u>Can of Red Bull: £1.50</u>

COURTAULD INSTITUTE OF ART
• **The College is part of <u>London University</u> and students are entitled to use its facilities.**
The Courtauld Institute of Art, Somerset House, Strand, London, WC2R 0RN
Tel: (020) 7848 2645. Fax: (020) 7848 2410
E-mail: ugadmissions@courtauld.ac.uk. Website: www.courtauld.ac.uk
Courtauld Student's Union, Somerset House, Strand, London, WC2R 0RN
Tel: (020) 7848 2717

DEBTS: • <u>Ave debt per year: £2,728</u>
                 • <u>Access fund: £20,000</u>   • <u>Successful applications/yr: 18</u>
                 • <u>Ave payment: £500</u>

ACCOMMODATION: • <u>Cost of living index: ££</u>   • <u>Insurance premium: £</u>
In college: No facilities of its own, but there's <u>London University</u>'s inter-collegiate housing.

EMPLOYMENT: • <u>Unemployed after 6mths: 9%</u>
Normal London chances of getting a job, slightly improved with the help of <u>London University</u>'s *epic* job shop and, despite being arty types, long-term prospects are also abetted by London University's careers centre.

TRAVEL: see <u>London University</u>
Waterloo, Charing Cross and Blackfriars stations are a 10 min stomp away. Tubewise, Covent Garden, Temple, Holborn and Charing Cross are all close. Almost endless buses and cycling's a *popular* way of getting around with bike facilities on site.

7

ENTERTAINMENTS: • <u>Booze index: £2.05</u>
London: see <u>London University</u>
University: • <u>Pint of beer: £1.80</u>   • <u>Glass of wine: £1.80</u>

COVENTRY UNIVERSITY
Coventry University, Priory Street, CV1 5FB
Tel: (0845) 055 5850. Fax: (024) 7688 7845. E-mail: rao.cor@coventry.ac.uk
Website: www.coventry.ac.uk
Coventry University Students' Union, Priory St, Coventry, CV1 5FT
Tel: (024) 7657 1200. Fax: (024) 7657 1239. E-mail: suexec@coventry.ac.uk
Website: www.cusu.org

DEBTS: • <u>Ave debt per year: £3,372</u>
                 • <u>Access fund: £740,427</u>   • <u>Successful applications/yr: 634</u>
There's a small welfare fund for the desperate, short-term loans and arts and sports bursaries, the latter worth up to £750 apiece.

ACCOMMODATION: • Cost of living index: £ • Insurance premium: £££££
In college: • Catered: 5% • Cost: £76-83 (40wks)
• Self-catering: n/a% • Cost: £53-63 (40/50wks)
Coventry: • Ave rent: £40

EMPLOYMENT: • Unemployed after 6mths: 8.4%
Paid work: Coventry Bureau of Employment (CUBE) is run by students, who help each other find all sorts of work from bar work to phone monkeying.

TRAVEL:
National: The station's about a mile from campus and on the main line to London (£11.80) and Birmingham (£2.30). National Express, Bharat and Harry Shaw run loads of coach services, including London (£12), Birmingham (£4) and Manchester (£11).

ENTERTAINMENTS: • Booze index: £1.75
Coventry: • Pint of beer: £1.80 • Glass of wine: £1.80
University: • Pint of beer: £1.45 • Glass of wine: £1.30

DE MONTFORT UNIVERSITY
(1) De Montfort University, Trinity House, The Gateway, Leicester, LE1 9BH
Tel: (0845) 945 4647. Fax: (0116) 257 7533. E-mail: enquiry@dmu.ac.uk
Website: www.dmu.ac.uk
DeMontfort University Students Union, First Floor, Campus Centre Building, Mill Lane, Leicester, LE2 7DR. Tel: (0116) 255 5576. Website: www.mydsu.com
(2) De Montford University Bedford, 37 Lansdowne Road, Bedford, MK40 2BZ
Tel: (01234) 211688
DeMontford University SU, 21 Lansdowne Rd, Bedford, MK40 2BZ
Tel: (01234) 211 688

DEBTS: • Ave debt per year: £2,726
• Access fund: £1.6m • Successful applications/yr: 1,300
• Ave payment: £1,200
Hardship funds are available to cover childcare, travel, accommodation, etc. Academic awards of up to £3,500 dangle invitingly too.
Banks on campus: NatWest, HSBC.

FEES: International undergrads are charged £8,090. Individual modules cost £140 each.

ACCOMMODATION: • Cost of living index: ££ • Insurance premium: £££
In college: • Self-catering: 7% • Cost: £50-70 (32 wks)
• First years living in: 100% • Other years living in: 0%
Leicester: • Ave rent: £43
Bedford: • Ave rent: £42

EMPLOYMENT: • Unemployed after 6mths: 6%
Paid work: Work Bank is a privately run company that caters for all DMU sites and matches local jobs with student needs. Jobs Live is an online vacancy database that allows CV posting so potential employers can check out the talent. The SU employs students in bars and shops.
Careers: *Careers DMU is highly focused on shifting graduates into business.* It has a contract with the local adult guidance network and provides loads of events and back-up.

TRAVEL: see Leicester University
Sites: London is 40mins on the train from Bedford station. Luton Airport takes 17mins for quick getaways.

ENTERTAINMENTS: • <u>Booze index: £1.97</u>
Leicester: • <u>Pint of beer: £2</u>   • <u>Glass of wine: £2.50</u>
                                                     • <u>Can of Red Bull: £1.50</u>
University: • <u>Pint of beer: £1.30</u>   • <u>Glass of wine: £1.50</u>
Entertainment costs aren't substantially different between the two sites.

....

DERBY UNIVERSITY

University of Derby, Kedleston Road, Derby, DE22 1GB
Tel: (01332) 590500. Fax: (01332) 294861. E-mail: admissions@derby.ac.uk
Website: www.derby.ac.uk
University of Derby Student's Union, Kedleston Road, Derby, DE22 1GB
Tel: (01332) 591507. Fax: (01332) 348846. Website: www.udsu-online.co.uk

DEBTS: • Ave debt per year: £3,272
                    • <u>Access fund: £800,000</u>   • <u>Successful applications/yr: 1,000</u>
Students under 21 can apply for an opportunities bursary.
Banks on campus: NatWest and Lloyds

ACCOMMODATION: • <u>Cost of living index: £££££</u> • Insurance premium: £
In college: • <u>Self-catering: 26%</u>   • <u>Cost: £38-71 (39wks)</u>
Derby: • <u>Ave rent: £45-60</u>

EMPLOYMENT: • <u>Unemployed after 6mths: 6%</u>
The Career Development Centre helps students onto the greasy job pole and
doubles as a part-time piggy bank filler, maintaining the online jobs@hand
database. The SU has a number of minimum wage positions available in bars,
shops, admin, gyms, etc.

TRAVEL:
National: Derby station is 2$\frac{1}{2}$ miles from Kedleston Road: London (£23.10),
Sheffield (£4.75) and beyond. National Express coaches to London (£15.75) and
Sheffield (£5), etc. East Midlands is the closest airport, 8 miles south east of town,
good for budget flyers.
Local: *Reliable* buses run every 10mins to the town centre from the main campus.
Multi-ride passes offer a 50% discount. *Regular* buses between sites.

7

ENTERTAINMENTS: • <u>Booze index: £2.21</u>
Derby: • <u>Pint of beer: £1.80</u>   • <u>Glass of wine: £2.60</u>
University: • <u>Pint of beer: £1.20</u>   • <u>Glass of wine: £2</u>

....

DUNDEE UNIVERSITY

(1) University of Dundee, Recruitment & Admissions, Dundee, DD1 4HE
    Tel: (01382) 344160. Fax: (01382) 348150. E-mail: srs@dundee.ac.uk
    Website: www.dundee.ac.uk
    Dundee University Students Association, Airlie Place, Dundee, DD1 4HE
    Tel: (01382) 221841. Fax: (01382) 227124. E-mail: dusa@dusa.co.uk
    Website: www.dusa.co.uk
(2) University of Dundee, Fifie Campus, Fife campus, Kirkcaldy,
    Tel: (01382) 348 585

DEBT: • <u>Ave debt per year: £3,482</u>
Banks on campus: RBS and a cashpoint for Clydesdale

ACCOMMODATION: • <u>Cost of living index: £££</u> • Insurance premium: £
In college: • <u>Catered: 379%</u>   • <u>Cost: £80 (n/awks)</u>
                    • <u>Self-catering: 1362%</u>   • <u>Cost: £57 (n/awks)</u>
Dundee: • <u>Ave rent: £50-60</u>   • <u>Living at home: 22.87%</u>

EMPLOYMENT: • <u>Unemployed after 6mths: 4%</u>
Paid work: *Most people who want a job can get one.* DUSA hires quite a few

people and there's *no end of part-time McJobs* in the city centre. A job shop should have opened by the autumn 2004.

TRAVEL: The Student Association runs a free night bus that takes, um, refreshed students back to halls after a night at the union.

ENTERTAINMENTS:	• Booze index: £1.73	
Dundee:	• Pint of beer: £1.95	• Glass of wine: £2
		• Can of Red Bull: £1.50
University:	• Pint of beer: £1.50	• Glass of wine: £1.50
		• Can of Red Bull: £1.20

UNIVERSITY OF DURHAM

(1) University of Durham, University Office, Durham, DH1 3HP
   Tel: 0191 334 2000. E-mail: admissions@durham.ac.uk
   Website: www.dur.ac.uk
   Durham Students' Union, Dunelm House, New Elvet, Durham, DH1 3AN
   Tel: 0191 334 1777. E-mail: enquiries@dsu.org.uk. Website: www.dsu.org.uk
(2) Queen's Campus, University of Durham, Queen's Campus, University Boulevard, Thornaby, Stockton-on-Tees, Cleveland, TS17 6BH. Tel: (0191) 334 2000

DEBTS:	• Ave debt per year: £2,722	
	• Access fund: £541,054	• Successful applications/yr: 886
	• Ave payment: £100-3,500	

The hardship fund has £50,000/yr to hand out, usually along similar lines to the access fund although payments over £2,000 are exceptional.

FEES: The Union tells students how to get money out of the University, but doesn't offer any themselves. Academic prizes are up for grabs, as are awards for students who want to do some worthy extra-curricular stuff but can't afford it.

ACCOMMODATION:	• Cost of living index: ££££	• Insurance premium: £
In college:	• Catered cost: £106 (28wks)	
	• Self-catering cost: £67 (29wks)	
	• First years living in: 99%	
Durham:	• Ave rent: £53	• Living at home: 4.7%

EMPLOYMENT: • Unemployed after 6mths: 7%
Work can be found in the university bars, libraries or locally and there is a *comprehensive* jobshop to find folk work, *but jobs are still hard to come by*. 20 staff help with the longer term career hunt.

TRAVEL:
Trains: Mainline connections to London King's Cross (£47.50), Newcastle (£2.60) and more. National Express and Blue Line services provide coaches to many destinations: London (£25.50), Newcastle (£3) and so on.

LOCAL: Good buses around town and surrounds, *which lazy students can use to get up the hills*. Fares from 32p and a service between Durham and Queens Campus in Stockton. *Some of Britain's cheapest taxis* (min fare £1, £15 into Newcastle) make it *a worthwhile share*. A bit hilly for bikes.

ENTERTAINMENTS:	• Booze index: £1.70	
Durham:	• Pint of beer: £2.05	• Glass of wine: £2
		• Can of Red Bull: £2.10
University:	• Pint of beer: £1.30	• Glass of wine: £1.50

UNIVERSITY OF EAST ANGLIA

University of East Anglia, Norwich, NR4 7TJ
Tel: (01603) 456161. Fax: (01603) 458553. E-mail: admissions@uea.ac.uk
Website: www.uea.ac.uk
The Union of UEA Students, Union House, University of East Anglia, Norwich,
NR4 7TJ
Tel: 01603 593272. Fax: 01603 250144. E-mail: su.comms@uea.ac.uk
Website: www.stu.uea.ac.uk

DEBTS: • <u>Ave debt per year: £2,407</u>
  • <u>Access fund: £306,755</u>   • <u>Successful applications/yr: 405</u>
Hardship funds and loans, temporary assistance in the event of financial
emergencies and grant aid. Advice also available from the advice centre in the SU.
Banks on campus: Barclays, HSBC

ACCOMMODATION: • <u>Cost of living index: £££££</u> • <u>Insurance premium: £</u>
In college: • <u>Self-catering: 100%</u>   • <u>Cost: £45-70 (n/a wks)</u>
Norwich: • <u>Ave rent: £40-50</u>

EMPLOYMENT: • <u>Unemployed after 6mths: 4%</u>
Paid work: The jobshop is run jointly by the SU and University. There's less
unemployment in East Anglia than most of the country and apart from the usual bar
work, students can get better paid jobs in local government and other areas.
Careers: Interview training, jobs fairs, careers library and an online training service
called Matrix (*unfortunately* no direct brain downloads of job skills or martial arts).

TRAVEL:
National: Trains from Norwich station (across town) to London (£19.95) and the
north via Peterborough. Coach services to London (£15.25) and Glasgow (£42.50).
Local: *Decent* local buses, cheap taxis and a *good* cycle lane network.

ENTERTAINMENTS: • <u>Booze index: £1.93</u>
Norwich: • <u>Pint of beer: £2.10</u>   • <u>Glass of wine: £1.85</u>
University: • <u>Pint of beer: £1.60</u>   • <u>Glass of wine: £1.40</u>

7

UNIVERSITY OF EAST LONDON

(1) University of East London, Longbridge Road, Dagenham, Essex, RM8 2AS
   Tel: (020) 8223 3000. Fax: (020) 8223 4072. E-mail: admiss@uel.ac.uk
   Website: www.uel.ac.uk
   University of London Student's Union, Longbridge Road, Dagenham, Essex
   RM8 2AS
   Tel: (020) 8223 2420
(2) University of East London, Stratford Campus, Romford Road, London, E15 4LZ
(3) University of East London, Docklands Campus, Royal Albert Way, London,
   E16 2RD
   Tel: (020) 8223 3000

DEBTS: • <u>Ave debt per year: £4,443</u>
  • <u>Access fund: £300,000</u>   • <u>Successful applications/yr: 1,000</u>
Loans of up to £500 and payments of £700 to £1,500 are available in cases of
hardship, as are bursaries (apply to the Student Finance Department), *but the
criteria are pretty tough*. Also scholarships for part-time unwaged students and
partial fee-remission schemes.
Banks on campus: Barclays, NatWest

ACCOMMODATION: • <u>Cost of living index: £££</u> • <u>Insurance premium: £</u>
In college: • <u>Self-catering: 8%</u>   • <u>Cost: £49-78 (30wks)</u>
Barking: • <u>Ave rent: £45-80</u>

EMPLOYMENT: • <u>Unemployed after 6mths: 14%</u>

Paid work: Limited work to be had in the various bars and cafes, but the Jobshop helps students to scour locally.
Careers: Lots of potentially useful vocational courses.

TRAVEL:
Tube stops are near most sites. A few buses run between sites, but it requires lots of changing and waiting. Plenty of services run into central London (particularly the City) and back. For Stratford, the nearest rail station is Maryland (10mins from London Liverpool St). Barking station is 13 minutes from London Fenchurch St Station. The Docklands Light Railway Cyprus Station is right at the entrance of the Docklands Campus.

ENTERTAINMENTS: • Booze index: £1.87
London:	• Pint of beer: £1.90	• Glass of wine: £2.00
		• Can of Red Bull: £1.80
University:	• Pint of beer: £1.80	• Glass of wine: £1.80
		• Can of Red Bull: £1.60

EDINBURGH UNIVERSITY

University of Edinburgh, Old College, South Bridge, Edinburgh, EH8 9YL
Tel: 0131 650 1000. Fax: 0131 650 2147. Website: www.ed.ac.uk
Edinburgh University Students Association, EUSA, The Potterow, 5/2 Bristo Square, Edinburgh, EH8 9AL
Tel: 0131 650 2656. Fax: 0131 668 4177. E-mail: eusa.enquiry@ed.ac.uk
Website: www.ed.eusa.ac.uk

DEBTS: • Ave debt per year: £3,360
• Access fund: £742,308 • Successful applications/yr: 750
• Ave payment: £300-2,000
100 bursaries available for undergrads in financial trouble. Postgrad scholarships for Chinese, Canadian, Indian and American students.
Banks on campus: NatWest, Halifax, RBS.

ACCOMMODATION: • Cost of living index: ££ • Insurance premium: £
In college:	• Catered: 9%	• Cost: £101-116 (33wks)
	• Self-catering: 13%	• Cost: £60-77 (38-52wks)
	• First years living in: 90%	• Others living in: 8%
Nearest town (Edinburgh):	• Ave rent: £60-70	• Living at home: 16%

EMPLOYMENT: • Unemployed after 6mths: 4.7%
• Paid work: term-time 40%: hols 80%
Paid work: *Loads* of opportunities to work in the *thriving* city centre, especially showing tourists round in summer. The University/Union-run Student Employment Service helps out.
Careers: The *well-staffed* careers service wheels out a *pretty comprehensive* service. See www.careers@ed.ac.uk

TRAVEL:
National: Direct trains to Glasgow (£4.95) and others to the north and the south (via Newcastle and York) to London (£50.80). Coaches to London (£27.75), Glasgow and all over. Edinburgh (Turnhouse) Airport, 6 miles west of the city centre, has a range of international and internal flights (from £69 return to London).
Local: Bus services are *good* all round the city and *quite cheap* (from 50p). A frequent night bus runs all over the town.

ENTERTAINMENTS: • Booze index: £2.08
Edinburgh:	• Pint of beer: £2.50	• Glass of wine: £2.30
		• Can of Red Bull: £2
University:	• Pint of beer: £1.55	

7

In the back

UNIVERSITY OF ESSEX

(1) University of Essex, Wivenhoe Park, Colchester, Essex, CO4 3SQ
Tel: (01206) 873333. Fax: (01206) 873598
E-mail: admit@essex.ac.uk. Website: www.essex.ac.uk
University of Essex Students' Union, Wivenhoe Park, Colchester, Essex,
CO4 3SQ
Tel: (01206) 863211. Fax: (01206) 870915
E-mail: su@essex.ac.uk. Website: www.essexstudent.com
(2) East 15 Acting School, Hatfields, Rectory Lane, Loughton, Essex, IG10 3RY
Tel: (020) 8508 5983. Website: www.east15.ac.uk

DEBTS:
- Ave debt per year: £3,395
- Access fund: £230,000   • Successful applications/yr: 350
- Ave payment: £300-£750

There are a few things in place to ease financial pain. The University Foundation Alumni Hardship Bursary and Foundation Bursary for Refugees and the Children of Refugees are new funds (that support the students their names suggest). The Sports Bursary scheme is open to athletes who compete at national and international level. It includes financial support, free access to University and local sports facilities (and a bunch of other non-financial perks). The JP Morgan Fleming Bursary is meant for mature students from the local area.
Banks on campus: Barclays and Lloyds.

FEES: Postgrads pay around £2,940, less for part-timers. Non-EU students get charged £7,960-£10,240, depending on the course.

ACCOMMODATION: • Cost of living index: ££   • Insurance premium: £
In college: • Catered: 44%   • Cost: £40-75 (39/50wks)
    • First years living in: 78%
Colchester: • Ave rent: £55   • Living at home: 15.4%

EMPLOYMENT: • Unemployed after 6mths: 3%
Paid work: The University and SU give students paid shop, bar and office work. The Jobshop helps students find work on or off campus.
Careers: The Careers Service has 8 full-time and 6 part-time staff. Services include newsletters, bulletin boards, a careers library, job fairs and interview training.

TRAVEL:
National: The nearest mainline station to the campus is Colchester, 3 miles away (there are 2 other stations in town). Direct services run into London Liverpool Street. National Express coaches run to London, Birmingham and more.
Local: *Buses are expensive, but they're reliable and* tour the local villages, *which is useful for those living there. The University has a late-night minibus.*

ENTERTAINMENTS: • Booze index: £1.70
Colchester: • Pint of beer: £1.50   • Glass of wine: £2
    • Can of Red Bull: £1.60
University: • Pint of beer: £1.50   • Glass of wine: £2
    • Can of Red Bull: £1.60

EXETER UNIVERSITY

University of Exeter, Northcote House, The Queen's Drive, Exeter, EX4 4QJ
Tel: (01392) 661 000. Fax: (01392) 263 108. E-mail: admissions@exeter.ac.uk
Website: www.exeter.ac.uk
Guild of Students, Devonshire House, Stocker Road, EX4 4PZ
Tel: 01392 263540. Fax: (01392) 263 531. E-mail: ask@guild.exeter.ac.uk
Website: www.xnet.exeter.ac.uk

DEBTS:
- Ave debt per year: £3,988
- Access fund: £391,985 • Successful applications/yr: 694
- Ave payment: £469

Sports bursaries available, also short-term Guild loans of £50.
Banks on campus: NatWest.

ACCOMMODATION: • Cost of living index: ££ • Insurance premium: £
In college: • Catered: 50% • Cost: £97-115 (30 wks)
- Self-catering: 50% • Cost: £50-86 (34-50 wks)
- First years living in: 100%
Exeter: • Ave rent: £50-60

EMPLOYMENT: • Unemployed after 6mths: 6.2%
- Paid work: term-time 35%: hols 90%

Paid work: A few local jobs for students in the tourist trade and some bar and clerical work in the Guild. Students can register with a 'job bank' for temping work.
Careers: There's a databank of 500 alumni willing to offer careers advice to current students.

TRAVEL:
National: Trains to London, Bristol, Birmingham and more from Exeter St David's station. Also a Megabus service to London for £1.50 and domestic/European flights from Exeter airport.
Local: *Reliable* but *expensive* local bus services and a free college bus at peak times. *Lots of hills, but pedal-pushing's popular all the same.*

ENTERTAINMENTS: • Booze index: £1.81
Exeter: • Pint of beer: £2.20 • Glass of wine: £2
University: • Pint of beer: £1.50 • Glass of wine: £1.50
- Can of Red Bull: £1.60

UNUSUAL COSTS: Annual sports membership for £20 plus participation fee or £150 for annual membership and unlimited use of gym.

GLAMORGAN UNIVERSITY

(1) University of Glamorgan, Treforest, Pontypridd, Wales, CF37 1DL
Tel: (01443) 480 480. Fax: (01443) 480 558. E-mail: enquiries@glam.ac.uk
Website: www.glam.ac.uk
University of Glamorgan Union, Forest Grove, Treforest, Mid Glamorgan, Wales, CF37 1UF
Tel: 01443 483500. Fax: 01443 483501. E-mail: studunion@glam.ac.uk
Website: www.glamsu.com
(2) Glyntaff Campus, University of Glamorgan, Cemetery Road, Glyntaff, Pontypridd, CF37 4BL

DEBTS:
- Ave debt per year: £4,568
- Access fund: £860,806 • Successful applications/yr: 1,256
- Ave payment: £774

The Union provides short-term hardship loans of £50 in exchange for a post-dated cheque. Help with applications to the Financial Contingency Funds (Welsh Access Fund).
Banks on campus: several ATMs

ACCOMMODATION: • Cost of living index: ££ • Insurance premium: £
In college: • Catered: 2% • Cost: £81 (37wks)
- Self-catering: 8% • Cost: £51-63 (37wks)
- First years living in: 75%
Pontypridd: • Ave rent: £40

EMPLOYMENT: • Unemployed after 6mths: 5%
- Paid work: term-time 60%: hols 85%

Paid work: A handful of jobs available on campus and locally, more for those willing to go to Cardiff or sell their body to medical science. Jobshop.
Careers: There's a job shop and placements scheme: Cymru Prosper Wales. They find relevant work experience for students and also help graduates

TRAVEL:
National: From Treforest station, right outside campus, trains go to Cardiff every 20 minutes (£1.60). Change there for London (£24.60), Swansea (£8.80) and Manchester (£24.60). The last train back from Cardiff is at 11:30pm. National Express coach to London is £18.
Local: Bus services every 20mins to Ponty and every 25 to Cardiff. A free student shuttle within a 10-mile radius of campus runs after 10.30pm.

ENTERTAINMENTS:	• Booze index: £1.68	
Pontypridd:	• Pint of beer: £2	• Glass of wine: £1.50
		• Can of Red Bull: £1.50
University:	• Pint of beer: £1.75	• Glass of wine: £2
		• Can of Red Bull: £1.90

UNUSUAL COSTS: Sports membership ranges between £29-40 a year.

UNIVERSITY OF GLASGOW

(1) University of Glasgow, Glasgow, G12 8QQ
   Tel: (0141) 330 2000. Fax: (0141) 330 4808. E-mail: prospectus@gla.ac.uk
   Website: www.gla.ac.uk
   Student Representative Council, John McIntyre Building, University of Glasgow,
   University Avenue, Glasgow, G12 8QQ
   Tel: (0141) 339 8541. Fax: (0141) 337 3557
   E-mail: the.enquiries@src.gla.ac.uk. Website: www.glasgowstudent.net
(2) Crichton Campus, University of Glasgow, Rutherford McCowan Buildings,
   Dumfires, DG1 4ZL. Tel: (01387) 702 001. Fax: (01387) 702 005

DEBTS:	• Ave debt per year: £3,330	
	• Access fund: £894,508	• Successful applications/yr: 1,584
	• Ave payment: £100-£2,000	

7

The Carnegie Trust pays tuition fees and the mature students bursary helps with childcare costs. The University has a scholarship programme for talented athletes, which pays bursaries of £300-£1,500.
Banks on campus: Bank of Scotland ATMs

FEES: Scottish universities won't be charging top up fees, but the University's opposed to them anyway.

ACCOMMODATION:	• Cost of living index: £££	• Insurance premium: ££
In college:	• Catered: 4%	• Cost: £88-100 (32wks)
	• Self-catering: n/a%	• Cost: £69-94 (32wks)
	• First years living in: 28%	
Glasgow:	• Ave rent: £65	• Living at home: 34%

EMPLOYMENT: • Unemployed after 6mths: 5%
Paid work: Loads of information and training and student advisors to lend a hand. The GU Templine places candidates in temporary jobs and the job centre in Partick is also geared towards students. The SRC posts vacancies too.
Careers: The university's part of the Club 21 scheme, which places students with big graduate employers like AMEC and Deutsche Bank.

TRAVEL:
National: Trains and coaches to national destinations: London (£24 coach, £40 train). *Cheap* flights into Glasgow International airport.
Local: Buses (55p/£1) are *frequent* and *cheap*. Rail services are *pretty good* too,

stopping all over the city. A termly (10-week) pass is £339. The subway, known locally as the Clockwork Orange, is 90p a trip. Strathclyde Public Transport issues a travelcard (£12.10/week) for unlimited weekly travel.

ENTERTAINMENTS:	• Booze index: £1.58	
Glasgow:	• Pint of beer: £2.20	
		• Glass of wine: £2.50
		• Can of Red Bull: £1.50
University:	• Pint of beer: £1.25	• Glass of wine: £1.25
		• Can of Red Bull: £1.50

GLASGOW CALEDONIAN UNIVERSITY

Glasgow Caledonian University, Cowcaddens Road, Glasgow, G4 0BA
Tel: (0141) 331 3000. Fax: (0141) 331 3005. E-mail: rhu@gcal.ac.uk
Website: www.caledonian.ac.uk
Glasgow Caledonian University Student's Association, 70 Cowcaddens Road, Glasgow, G4 0BA
Tel: (0141) 332 0681. Fax: (0141) 353 0029. E-mail: gcusa@gcal.ac.uk
Website: www.caledonianstudent.com

DEBTS:	• Ave debt per year: £2,518	
	• Access fund: £240,000	• Successful applications/yr: 1,000
	• Ave payment: £20-£500	

Emergency loans (£20-£50) are available and the hardship fund will shell out £400-500 at a throw. Scholarships are available for undergrads and grads studying travel and tourism. The university helps with some students' childcare costs.

FEES: It's Scotland, so no top up fees. *Hooray for Scotland!*

ACCOMMODATION:	• Cost of living index: £££	• Insurance premium: £££
In college:	• Self-catering: 5%	• Cost: £65-75 (38wks)
Glasgow:	• Ave rent: £50	

EMPLOYMENT: • Unemployed after 6mths: 8%
Paid work: The Jobshop tries to hawk students around the usual raft of part-time task-masters.
Careers: 7 full-time staff at the careers office to help students find work.

TRAVEL: see University of Glasgow

ENTERTAINMENTS:	• Booze index: £2.04	
Glasgow:	• Pint of beer: £2.20	
		• Glass of wine: £2.50
		• Can of Red Bull: £1.50

UNIVERSITY OF GLOUCESTERSHIRE

(1) University of Gloucestershire, Park Campus, The Park, Cheltenham, GL50 2QF
Tel: (01242) 532 700. Fax: (01242) 532 810. Website: www.glos.ac.uk
University of Gloucestershire Students' Union, The Park, Cheltenham, GL50 2QF
Tel: (01242) 532 848. Fax: (01242) 261 381. E-mail: pksu@glos.ac.uk
Website: www.ugsu.org
(2) Francis Close Hall Campus, Swindon Road, Cheltenham, GL50 4AZ
Tel: (01242) 532 900. Fax: (01242) 532 997
University of Gloucestershire Students' Union (FHC Campus), Swindon Road, Cheltenham, GL50 4AZ. Tel: (01242) 543 439
(3) Pittville Campus, Albert Road, Cheltenham, GL52 3JG
University of Gloucestershire Students' Union (Pitville Campus), Albert Road, Cheltenham, GL52 3JG. Tel: (01242) 532 219
(4) Oxstalls Campus, Oxstalls Lane, Longlevens, Gloucester, GL2 9HW
Tel: (01452) 876600
University of Gloucestershire Students' Union (Oxstall Campus), Oxstalls Lane, Gloucester, GL2 9HW. Tel: (01452) 876 659

DEBTS:
- Ave debt per year: £4,015
- Access fund: £450,000 • Successful applications/yr: 650
- Ave payment: £300

A disabled students' allowance helps buy specialist equipment (up to £4,460) and with other costs.

Banks on campus: Alliance & Leicester ATM

ACCOMMODATION: • Cost of living index: ££££ • Insurance premium: £
In college:
- Self-catering: n/a • Cost: £59-77 (41wks)
- First years living in: 60%

Cheltenham: • Ave rent: £48-55 • Living at home: 34%

EMPLOYMENT: • Unemployed after 6mths: 4%
• Paid work: term-time 65%

Paid work: The SU employs over 100 students and has its own employment agency. UCAS is based in Cheltenham and often employs students, as do other local head offices for Kraft Foods, Bird's Eye, British Energy and many others. Failing that, there's sometimes £6.50 an hour on offer at the Betting Terminal at Cheltenham Racecourse (or you could just put the money on Dead Donkey at 33-1). Gold Cup organisers recruit temp staff at the Jobs Fair.

Careers: 25-min drop-in sessions on a first come first served basis during term-time or by appointment during the summer.

TRAVEL:
Cheltenham: Cheltenham Spa station (a mile from Park Campus) has *rare* direct links to London (£17.80 rtn), Birmingham (£10.30 rtn), Manchester (£10 sgl) and elsewhere. Usually you have to change at Gloucester. National Express, Marchants and Swanbrook coach services to London (£17.25).

Gloucester: Gloucester to London Paddington (£25.55) and Bristol Parkway (under £6). National Express to London Victoria (£38.75).

Local: The University runs a free inter-site bus service between the four campuses, the Halls of Residence, Cheltenham centre and Cheltenham Spa and Gloucester stations.

ENTERTAINMENTS: • Booze index: £1.95
Cheltenham: • Pint of beer: £2.40
- Glass of wine: £2.40
- Can of Red Bull: £1.50
University: • Pint of beer: £1.70
- Glass of wine: £1.30
- Can of Red Bull: £1.05

7

GOLDSMITHS COLLEGE
• **The College is part of London University and students are entitled to use its facilities.**

Goldsmiths College, New Cross, London, SE14 6NW
Tel: (020) 7919 7171. Fax: (020) 7919 7903. E-mail: admissions@gold.ac.uk
Goldsmiths College Student Union, New Cross, London, SE14 6NW
Tel: (020) 8692 1406. Fax: (020) 8694 9789. E-mail: gcsu@gold.ac.uk

DEBTS:
- Ave debt per year: £3,652
- Access fund: £396,548 • Successful applications/yr: 757
- Ave payment: 750

A postgrad scholarship scheme makes payments of up to £1,000. The alumni discounts scheme grants £500 at a time and there's an accommodation bursary with a total fund of £30,000.

Banks on campus: NatWest

ACCOMMODATION: • Cost of living index: £££ • Insurance premium: ££
In college:
- Self-catering: 100% • Cost: £66-90 (39-50 wks)
- First years living in: 95% • Others living in: 10%
New Cross/London: • Ave rent: £75

EMPLOYMENT: • <u>Unemployed after 6mths: 11%</u>
Paid work: Part-time jobs are *easily had* in London and there are *plenty* on campus.
Careers: The careers service provides an e-mail service with vacancies, discussion forums and careers advice.

TRAVEL: see <u>London University</u>
Well-served by buses and trains (New Cross and New Cross Gate go direct into Charing Cross and London Bridge), but not on the tube.

ENTERTAINMENTS: • <u>Booze index: £1.69</u>
London: • <u>Pint of beer: £1.90</u> • <u>Glass of wine: £1.60</u>
University: • <u>Pint of beer: £1.40</u> • <u>Glass of wine: £1.30</u>

GREENWICH UNIVERSITY
(1) The University of Greenwich, Old Royal Naval College, Park Row, Greenwich, London, SE10 9LS
Tel: (020) 8331 8000. Fax: (020) 8331 8145. E-mail: courseinfo@gre.ac.uk
Website: www.greenwich.ac.uk
Student's Union University of Greenwich, SUUG, Cooper Building, King William Walk, Greenwich, SE10 9JH
Tel: (020) 8331 7629. Fax: (020) 8331 7628. Website: www.suug.co.uk
(2) Avery Hill, Avery Hill Road, Eltham, London, SE9 2UG
Students' Union, 1 Boleyn Court, Avery Hill Road, Eltham, London, SE9 2UG
Tel: (020) 8331 9596
(3) Medway, Kent, ME4 4AW
Students' Union, Jellicoe Building, Chatham Maritime, ME4 4AW
Tel: (020) 8331 8053

DEBTS: • <u>Ave debt per year: £3,652</u>
• <u>Access fund: £1.7 million</u> • <u>Successful applications/yr: 2,100</u>
• <u>Ave payment: £100-£2,500</u>

ACCOMMODATION: • <u>Cost of living index: £££</u> • <u>Insurance premium: ££</u>
In college: • <u>Self-catering: 20%</u> • <u>Cost: £66-96 (40wks)</u>
• <u>First years living in: 50%</u>
Locally: • <u>Ave rent: £80</u>

EMPLOYMENT: • <u>Unemployed after 6mths: 7.5%</u>
Paid work: See <u>London University</u>
Careers: The University's service has a *poorly advertised but pretty comprehensive package* to students and recent graduates. Services include: online key skills training; mentoring for ethnic minority students; job shop; job fairs; interview training; careers library; bulletin boards.

TRAVEL: see <u>London University</u>
For Avery Hill Falconwood or New Eltham stations (both 15mins walk). Chatham station for Medway. DLR station (Cutty Sark) at Greenwich. London Bridge is the nearest tube and mainline train station: 15mins from Greenwich, 20mins from Avery Hill and just over an hour from Medway. All sites are served by a wide range of regular London bus services. The University runs free buses between sites.

ENTERTAINMENTS: • <u>Booze index: £2.30</u>
London: see <u>London University</u>
University: • <u>Pint of beer: £1.70</u> • <u>Glass of wine: £1.30</u>

HARPER ADAMS UNIVERSITY COLLEGE

Harper Adams University College, Harper Adams University College, Newport,
Shropshire, TF10 8NB
Tel: (01952) 815000. Fax: (01952) 814783
E-mail: admissions@harper-adams.ac.uk. Website: www.harper-adams.ac.uk

DEBTS:
- Ave debt per year: £1,173
- Access fund: £55,000 • Successful applications/yr: 70
- Ave payment: £500-1,500

An *extensive* range of scholarships and bursaries for new students each year. Prizes
are awarded by key employers to outstanding students. Scholarships available for
Irish rugby players.

FEES: Most courses include a sandwich year during which fees are £550 and
students may well earn some wonga.

ACCOMMODATION: • Cost of living index: ££ • Insurance premium: £
In college:
- Catered: 17% • Cost: £75-90 (32wks)
- Self-catering: 2% • Cost: £45 (32wks)
- First years living in: 98%

Newport:
- Ave rent: £50 • Living at home: 4%

EMPLOYMENT: • Unemployed after 6mths: 4%
Careers: 2 full-time staff at the careers service.

TRAVEL:
National: Train links (Telford) and National Express coaches (Newport) to London
and Birmingham. Low-cost flights from Birmingham International.
Local: *Getting around without a car is nigh-on impossible. A beer bus picks up late-
night revellers, but public transport is an alien concept in the sticks.*

ENTERTAINMENTS: • Booze index: £1.63
Newport:
- Pint of beer: £1.90 • Glass of wine: £2
- Can of Red Bull: £1.50
University:
- Pint of beer: £1.80 • Glass of wine: £1.25
- Can of Red Bull: £1.10

UNUSUAL COSTS: Gym membership costs £20 per semester.

HERIOT-WATT UNIVERSITY

Heriot-Watt University, Edinburgh, EH14 4AS
Tel: (0131) 449 5111. Fax: (0131) 449 5153. E-mail: enquiries@hw.ac.uk
Website: www.hw.ac.uk
Heriot-Watt University Students Association, Edinburgh, EH14 4AS
Tel: (0131) 451 5333. E-mail: hwusa@hw.ac.uk. Website: www.hwusa.org

DEBTS:
- Ave debt per year: £4,355
- Access fund: £360,000 • Successful applications/yr: 569
- Ave payment: £400

In addition to the access fund, several bursaries and scholarships can be
plundered, including a fee waiver for part-timers, living support for students under
25 from low-income families, hardship loans, a hardship fund, sports scholarships
and mature students bursary scheme for married students over 25 who have been
self-supporting for 3 years.

FEES: International students pay £7,060-10,815, postgrads £2,940. Distance
learning modules are available – costs vary.

ACCOMMODATION: • <u>Cost of living index: £££</u> • <u>Insurance premium: £</u>
In college: • <u>Catered: 4%</u> • <u>Cost: £81 (33wks)</u>
                • <u>Self-catering: 8%</u> • <u>Cost: £45-60 (39wks)</u>
                • <u>First years living in: 60%</u>
Edinburgh: • <u>Ave rent: £55-70</u>

EMPLOYMENT: • <u>Unemployed after 6mths: 6.3%</u>
                • <u>Paid work: term-time 75%; hols 85%</u>
Paid work: Jobs on campus are posted by the University jobshop (an offshoot of the Careers Advisory Service).
Careers: The Careers Advisory Service's calendar is *chock-full of* job fairs, recruitment programs, CV clinics and talks. Short and long-term vacancies are posted online and in printed newsletters. The *helpful* Alumni Mentoring Program involves graduates who offer phone and email advice to current students – *particularly useful for international students*.

TRAVEL: see <u>University of Edinburgh</u>
There's a shuttle bus running to the Scottish Borders Campus and back again. It's free but places must be pre-booked.

ENTERTAINMENTS: • <u>Booze index: £1.94</u>
Edinburgh: see <u>University of Edinburgh</u>
University: • <u>Pint of beer: £1.30</u> • <u>Glass of wine: £1.14</u>

UNUSUAL COSTS: 3-banded sports membership tariff, ranging from £18 to £60.

··

UNIVERSITY OF HERTFORDSHIRE

(1) University of Hertfordshire, College Lane, Hatfield, Hertfordshire, AL10 9AB
    Tel: (01707) 284 800. Fax: (01707) 284 870
    E-mail: admissions@herts.ac.uk Website: www.herts.ac.uk
    University of Hertfordshire Students' Union, College Lane, Hatfield, Hertfordshire, AL10 9AB
    Tel: (01707) 285 004. Fax: (01707) 286 151. E-mail: ushu@herts.ac.uk
    Website: www.ushu.herts.ac.uk
(2) Faculty of Law, St Albans Campus, University of Hertfordshire, 7 Hatfield Road, St Albans, Hertfordshire, AL1 3RS

DEBTS: • <u>Ave debt per year: £4,970</u>
                • <u>Access fund: £727,393</u> • <u>Successful applications/yr: 1,974</u>
                • <u>Ave payment: £500</u>
Engineering and some science students with over 280 UCAS points can bag £3,000 scholarships.

FEES: Postgrads pay *a relatively gentle* £2,870 tuition. Internationals shell out £7,600.

ACCOMMODATION: • <u>Cost of living index: ££££</u> • <u>Insurance premium: £</u>
In college: • <u>Self-catering: 21%</u> • <u>Cost: £49-80 (32wks)</u>
                • <u>First years living in: 94%</u>
Hatfield: • <u>Ave rent: £65</u>

EMPLOYMENT: • <u>Unemployed after 6mths: 8%</u>
                • <u>Paid work: term-time 55%; hols 55%</u>
Paid work: Vacancy boards are posted and updated by the recruitment office. Plenty of term-time and vacation opportunities at the Galleria complex and in local supermarkets. The Union has casual work in bars and shops and an online vacancy board. The University Student Ambassador Scheme helps find casual jobs locally.
Careers: The Careers Advisory Service provides vacancy newsletters and bulletin boards, a program of talks, workshops, mock interviews and aptitude testing.

TRAVEL:
National: Hatfield station (1^1/$_2$ miles from the main campus) direct to London King's Cross and Stevenage. Connect to York, Newcastle and Edinburgh. Hertford station is about 30mins from London (£8.90). London Country coaches and Greenline buses to and from London. Luton Airport (Easyjet) is 11 miles northeast.
Local: *Buses aren't the cheapest in the country, but are useful for quick trips into Hatfield.* Also routes to St Albans, Stevenage, Watford and Welwyn Garden City. A regular free University shuttle bus runs between de Havilland site and the main campus and, for 90p, another runs around town (taking in the Galleria, the centre and St Albans).

ENTERTAINMENTS: • Booze index: £2.39
Hatfield:	• Pint of beer: £2.20	• Glass of wine: £1.90
University:	• Pint of beer: £1.80	• Glass of wine: £2.50
		• Can of Red Bull: £2.75

UNUSUAL COSTS: There are charges for sports facilities, but students get *massive* discounts on season or session passes.

HEYTHROP COLLEGE, UNIVERSITY OF LONDON
• The College is part of <u>London University</u> and students are entitled to use its facilities.
Heythrop College, University of London, Kensington Square, London, W8 5HQ
Tel: (020) 7795 6600. Fax: (020) 7795 4200. E-mail: enquiries@heythrop.ac.uk
Website: www.heythrop.ac.uk
Heythrop College Students Union, Kensington Square, London, W8 5HQ
Tel: (020) 7795 4248. Fax: (020) 7795 4248
E-mail: hsupresident@heythrop.ac.uk

DEBTS: • Ave debt per year: £3,681
There is no access fund and support is limited to a few small bursaries.

FEES: • Home student fees: £3,265
Home student fees for undergrads are almost 3 times the norm, *probably because the college is more excited about postgraduate study*, for which students pay a *relatively gentle* £2,905.

ACCOMMODATION: • Cost of living index: ££ • Insurance premium: £
In college:	• Catered: 3%	• Cost: £100 (30wks)
	• First years living in: 100%	
London:	• Ave rent: £100	

EMPLOYMENT: • Unemployed after 6mths: 8%
                     • Paid work: term-time 50%; hols 80%
Paid work: Kensington High Street has plenty of shops, bars, and restaurants that need gruntwork doing.
Careers: See London University

TRAVEL: see London University
Local: Trains nearby, plenty of buses and High Street Kensington tube stop is literally next door. Bicycles: *Kensington is generally quite flat and bike-able and many Heythroppers find it the best way to get around.*

ENTERTAINMENTS: • Booze index: £1.47

LONDON:	• Pint of beer: £2.76	• Glass of wine: £2.76
		• Can of Red Bull: £1.15

UNUSUAL COSTS: The lack of College bar means pennies will mostly be spent in pricier, commercial places.

7

UNIVERSITY OF HUDDERSFIELD

University of Huddersfield, Queensgate, Huddersfield, HD1 3DH
Tel: (01484) 422288. Fax: (01484) 516151. E-mail: prospectus@hud.ac.uk
Website: www.hud.ac.uk
Huddersfield University Union, University of Huddersfield, Queensgate, Huddersfield,
HD1 3DH
Tel: (01484) 538156. Fax: (01484) 432333

DEBTS:
- Ave debt per year: £4,175
- Access fund: £799,000   • Successful applications/yr: 505
- Ave payment: £1,582

Local student bursaries for West Yorkshire students who're the first in their family to
go to university. Some individual course bursaries.

ACCOMMODATION: • Cost of living index: £££££   • Insurance premium: £££
In college:
- Catered: n/a%   • Cost: £69-80 (41-2wks)
- Self-catering: n/a%   • Cost: £54 (41-2wks)
Huddersfield:
- Ave rent: £35-75

EMPLOYMENT:
- Unemployed after 6mths: 6%
- Paid work: term-time 70%: hols 95%
Paid work: The jobshop helps local businesses find student employees. The
University also employs 400 students during vacations.
Careers: 12 staff to try and help students land that dream job.

TRAVEL:
National: Trains to Leeds (£2.80), Manchester (5.80) and London via Wakefield
(£29.60). Coaches all over the country and Manchester airport for *low-cost* flights.
Local: College shuttle bus and *plenty* of cheap taxis.

ENTERTAINMENTS: • Booze index: £1.78
Huddersfield: • Pint of beer: £2
- Glass of wine: £2
- Can of Red Bull: £1.50
University: • Pint of beer: £1.50
- Glass of wine: £1.50
- Can of Red Bull: £1.10

UNIVERSITY OF HULL

(1) University of Hull, Hull, HU6 7RX
   Tel: (0870) 1262000. Fax: (01482) 442290. E-mail: admissions@hull.ac.uk
   Website: www.hull.ac.uk
   Hull University Union, University House, Cottingham Road, Hull, HU6 7RX
   Tel: 01482 445361. Fax: (01482) 466280. Website: www.hullstudent.com
(2) Scarborough Campus, Filey Road, Scarborough, YO11 3AZ
   Hull University Union – Scarborough Campus, Filey Road, Scarborough,
   YO11 3AZ. Tel: (01723) 367258

DEBTS:
- Ave debt per year: £3,917
- Access fund: £902,513   • Successful applications/yr: 718
- Ave payment: £1,125 (range £100-3,500)

Financial assistance is available in the form of hardship funds, emergency funds,
bursaries for books and a postgraduate teaching support scheme.
Banks on campus: HSBC

ACCOMMODATION: • Cost of living index: £££   • Insurance premium: ££
In college:
- Catered: 9.6%   • Cost: £75-95 (31wks)
- Self-catering: 11%   • Cost: £56-73 (31-50wks)
- First years living in: 90%
Hull:
- Ave rent: £35-42   • Living at home: 10%

EMPLOYMENT: • <u>Unemployed after 6mths: 4%</u>
  • <u>Paid work: term-time 50%: hols 80%</u>
Paid work: The town employs *large numbers* of students and the Union has facilities for helping them find work: e-mail service; links with local businesses; jobs fairs; NASE membership; vacancy board.
Careers: The careers service has 2 full-time and 4 part-time careers officers and *enough resources* to help students on their way in the real world.

TRAVEL:
Direct rail links to London, Newcastle and Leeds. Hull is flat and *suited to pedal power*, although local bus services are a *less thigh-burning alternative*.

ENTERTAINMENTS: • <u>Booze index: £1.84</u>
Hull: • <u>Pint of beer: £1.80</u> • <u>Glass of wine: £2</u>
  • <u>Can of Red Bull: £2</u>
University: • <u>Pint of beer: £1.65</u> • <u>Glass of wine: £1.50</u>
  • <u>Can of Red Bull: £1.50</u>

IMPERIAL COLLEGE, LONDON
• **The College is part of <u>London University</u> and students are entitled to use its facilities.**
(1) Imperial College London, South Kensington Campus, London, SW7 2AZ
   Tel: (020) 7594 8014. Fax: (020) 7594 8004. E-mail: info@imperial.ac.uk
   Website: www.imperial.ac.uk
   Imperial College Union, Prince Consort Road, London, SW7 2BB
   Tel: (020) 7594 8060. Fax: (020) 7594 8065. E-mail: president@imperial.ac.uk
   Website: www.union.imperial.ac.uk
(2) Wye Campus, Imperial College London, Wye, Ashford, Kent, TN25 5AH
   Tel: (020) 7594 2754
   Imperial College Union at Wye, Wye Campus, Wye, Ashford, Kent, TN25 5AH
   Tel: (020) 7594 2660

DEBTS: • <u>Ave debt per year: £5,582</u>
  • <u>Access fund: £440,721</u> • <u>Successful applications/yr: 403</u>
Many, many scholarships and sponsorships are available.

FEES: International students have to cough up five figures, starting at £13,250, but some courses charge premium *sell-your-granny* rates.

ACCOMMODATION: • <u>Cost of living index: ££</u> • <u>Insurance premium: ££</u>
In college: • <u>Catered: 10%</u> • <u>Cost: £81-128 (30/34/38wks)</u>
  • <u>Self-catering: 36%</u> • <u>Cost: £43-102 (34/38/51wks)</u>
  • <u>First years living in: 94%</u>
London: • <u>Ave rent: £90-100</u>

EMPLOYMENT: • <u>Unemployed after 6mths: 5.8%</u>
Paid work: Imperial students can appeal to the firms constantly vying for their talents for vacation work or there's Imperial's UROP scheme where they help lecturers with their research work and can expect to earn cash *and many brownie points*. The Careers Service advertises *any part-time job opportunities that come its way.*
Careers: The careers service offers *just about everything you could want (bar a foot massage)* and *potential employers, particularly in scientific and technical areas, regard Imperial as a goldmine.*

TRAVEL: see <u>London University</u>

ENTERTAINMENTS: • Booze index: £2.21
London: • Pint of beer: £2.50
• Glass of wine: £2.80
• Can of Red Bull: £2.00
University: • Pint of beer: £1.50
• Glass of wine: £1.60

KEELE UNIVERSITY

Keele University, Keele University, Keele, Staffordshire, ST5 5BG
Tel: (01782) 621111. Fax: (01782) 632343. E-mail: undergraduate@keele.ac.uk
Website: www.keele.ac.uk
Keele University Students' Union, KUSU, Keele University, Staffs, ST5 5BJ
Tel: (01782) 583700. Fax: (01782) 712671. E-mail: sta15@kusu.keele.ac.uk
Website: www.kusu.net

DEBTS: • Ave debt per year: £4,653
• Access fund: £302,258 • Successful applications/yr: 615
• Ave payment: £100-3,500
Hardship loans and opportunity bursaries (for students from low-income families)
and mature student bursaries, as well as other help for students with children. The
SU and chaplaincy have further arrangements for small loans and grants.
Banks on campus: NatWest

ACCOMMODATION: • Cost of living index: ££££ • Insurance premium: £
In college: • Self-catering: 85% • Cost: £50-82.40 (33/37/42wks)
• First years living in: 90%
Newcastle-under-Lyme: • Ave rent: £35-40 • Living at home: 5%

EMPLOYMENT: • Unemployed after 6mths: 6.4%
Paid work: The SU pretty much has a monopoly on employment, *everything else is
too far away. Luckily*, it employs about 500 students and has a job bureau.
Careers: The careers service website has vacancies and news plus the Windmills
Programme, a virtual career coach.

TRAVEL:
National: The nearest train station is 5 miles away at Stoke (London, £28.70;
Manchester, £7.20). Coaches also stop in Stoke. London by National Express takes
5 hours (£21.50).
Local: From Stoke-on-Trent station, no 29 bus leaves every 15mins to the campus.
A college safety bus runs between the campus, halls of residence and surrounds.
Taxis take about 15-20mins from Stoke Station, costing about a fiver. Bikes are
handy on campus but everything else is too far away and way too hilly.

ENTERTAINMENTS: • Booze index: £1.53
Keele: • Pint of beer: £2
• Glass of wine: £1.75
• Can of Red Bull: £2
University: • Pint of beer: £1.60
• Glass of wine: £1.30
• Can of Red Bull: £1.50

UNUSUAL COSTS: There's a small charge for some sports facilities if not organised
through the sporting clubs.

UNIVERSITY OF KENT

University of Kent, The Registry, Canterbury, Kent, CT2 7NZ
Tel: (01227) 764 000. E-mail: recruitment@kent.ac.uk. Website: www.kent.ac.uk
University of Kent Students' Union, Mandela Building, Canterbury, Kent, CT2 7NW
Tel: (01227) 824 200. E-mail: union@kent.ac.uk. Website: www.kentunion.co.uk

DEBTS: • Ave debt per year: £3,608
• Access fund: £160,000
Some music, art and sport bursaries available to those with talent.
Banks on campus: HSBC, Barclays.

ACCOMMODATION: • <u>Cost of living index: £££££</u>   • <u>Insurance premium: £</u>
In college: • <u>Catered: 20%</u>   • <u>Cost: £69 (31wks)</u>
             • <u>Self-catering: 20%</u>   • <u>Cost: £61 (38wks)</u>
Canterbury: • <u>Ave rent: £50-75</u>

EMPLOYMENT: • <u>Unemployed after 6mths: 4%</u>
Paid work: The Union jobshop has vacancy boards, newsletters and advice. In the summertime, the Garden of England needs harvesting and there are hop- and fruit-picking jobs going. *A foreign language can be helpful for dog-walking some of the millions of tourists.* There's bar and admin work in the Union and similar stuff in the city.
Careers: The Careers Advisory Service caters for Kent students as well as a variety of smaller local colleges.

TRAVEL:
Although Canterbury West is closer, Canterbury East is the station for London (£17.30 single) and Dover and connections to Edinburgh, Birmingham and Bristol. Canterbury Bus Station in the town centre for National Express (London Victoria, £16rtn). Also *regular* Stagecoach buses to campus; annual student bus pass is £170-£290. A term-time late night university minibus goes to and from the town centre. Plenty of car parks around the University.

ENTERTAINMENTS: • <u>Booze index: £2.30</u>
Canterbury: • <u>Pint of beer: £2</u>   • <u>Glass of wine: £3.50</u>
                                    • <u>Can of Red Bull: £1.80</u>
University: • <u>Pint of beer: £1.60</u>   • <u>Glass of wine: £1.50</u>
                                    • <u>Can of Red Bull: £1.50</u>

UNUSUAL COSTS: £40 annual membership of sports facilities.

KING'S COLLEGE, LONDON
• **The College is part of <u>London University</u> and students are entitled to use its facilities.**
(1) King's College London, University of London, The Strand, London, WC2R 2LS
  Tel: (020) 7836 5454. Fax: (020) 7836 1799. E-mail: ceu@kcl.ac.uk
  Website: www.kcl.ac.uk
  King's College London Students' Union, Macadam Building, Surrey Street, London, WC2R 2NS
  Tel: (020) 7836 7132. Fax: (020) 7379 9833
  E-mail: enquiries@kclsu.org. Website: http://www.kclsu.org
(2) Guy's Campus, King's College London, Guy's, King's and St Thomas's Schools of Medicine, Dentistry & Biomedical Sciences, London, SE1 1UL
  Tel: (020) 7848 6000
  KCLSU, Guy's Campus Student Union, Boland House, London, SE1 1UL
  Tel: (020) 7955 5000 xt 3990

DEBTS: • <u>Ave debt per year: £4,703</u>
             • <u>Access fund: £651,686</u>   • <u>Successful applications/yr: 593</u>
             • <u>Ave payment: £1,500</u>
Support: 100 bursaries are available for applicants in addition to other scholarships, bursaries and hardship funds for internationals.
Banks on campus: Several on the Strand

FEES: International students can pay up to £23,070 for clinically based degrees. For postgrads, it's between £2,940 (arts) and £4,298 (nursing)

ACCOMMODATION: • <u>Cost of living index: ££</u>   • <u>Insurance premium: £</u>
In college: • <u>Catered: 3%</u>   • <u>Cost: £95 (39wks)</u>
             • <u>Self-catering: 13%</u>   • <u>Cost: £53-91 (39-41wks)</u>
             • <u>First years living in: 73%</u>

London: • <u>Ave rent: £55-90</u>

EMPLOYMENT: • <u>Unemployed after 6mths: 7%</u>
Paid work: see <u>London University</u>. Some paid work is available with the SU, mainly bar work.
Careers: *The Grad Club, as they call it, provides the full Monty (only with their clothes on), from newsletters to career consultations on each campus.*

TRAVEL: see <u>London University</u>
All sites are well served by London bus and train routes and, in most cases, the tube. A bus is provided for medical students travelling between Guy's Hospital and St. Thomas's Hospital. *Bicycles are still the fastest way of getting around, despite congestion and traffic fumes.*

ENTERTAINMENTS:	• <u>Booze index: £1.80</u>	
London:	• <u>Pint of beer: £2.20</u>	• <u>Glass of wine: ££2.80</u>
		• <u>Can of Red Bull: £1.20</u>
University:	• <u>Pint of beer: £1.60</u>	• <u>Glass of wine: £1.30</u>
		• <u>Can of Red Bull: £1.25</u>

KINGSTON UNIVERSITY
Kingston University, Student Enquiry and Applicant Services, Cooper House, 40-46 Surbiton Road, Kingston upon Thames, Surrey, KT1 2HX
Tel: (020) 8547 2000. Fax: (020) 8547 7080
E-mail: admissions-info@kingston.ac.uk. Website: www.kingston.ac.uk
Kingston University Students Union, Penrhyn Road, Kingston upon Thames, Surrey, KT1 2EE
Tel: (020) 8547 8868. Fax: (020) 8547 8862. E-mail: president@kingston.ac.uk

DEBTS:	• <u>Ave debt per year: £3,457</u>	
	• <u>Access fund: £627,000</u>	• <u>Successful applications/yr: 627</u>
	• <u>Ave payment: £1,200-1,500</u>	

Hardship loans available.

ACCOMMODATION:	• <u>Cost of living index: £££££</u>	• <u>Insurance premium: ££</u>
In college:	• <u>Self-catering: 13%</u>	• <u>Cost: £85 (32wks)</u>
	• <u>First years living in: 33%</u>	
Kingston:	• <u>Ave rent: £85</u>	• <u>Living at home: 30%</u>

EMPLOYMENT: • <u>Unemployed after 6mths: 6%</u>
• <u>Paid work: term-time 60%; hols 90%</u>
Paid work: There's *no need* to go job-hunting in London when there are *plenty of opportunities on the doorstep.* Shopping centres, Union bars, Uni admin, tutoring, office temping, bar work – *it's all there for the taking.*
Careers: *Adequate resources to avert a crash-landing onto the runway of the real world.*

TRAVEL: see <u>London University</u>
National: *Kingston's quite convenient for Heathrow.*
Local: Trains into Waterloo (£3.40); Uni buses from station to halls; loads of taxis and a good cycle lane network.

ENTERTAINMENTS:	• <u>Booze index: £2.09</u>	
London:	• <u>Pint of beer: £2.20</u>	• <u>Glass of wine: £2.50</u>
		• <u>Can of Red Bull: £1.75</u>
University:	• <u>Pint of beer: £1.65</u>	• <u>Glass of wine: £2.25</u>
		• <u>Can of Red Bull: £1.65</u>

UNIVERSITY OF WALES, LAMPETER
• **The College is part of the University of Wales.**
University of Wales, Lampeter, Ceredigion, SA48 7ED
Tel: (01570) 422 351. Fax: (01570) 423 423. E-mail: recruit@lamp.ac.uk
Website: www.lamp.ac.uk
University of Wales, Lampeter, Students' Union, Lampeter, Ceredigion, SA48 7ED
Tel: (01570) 422 619. Fax: (01570) 422 480. E-mail: ents@lamp.ac.uk
Website: www.lamp.ac.uk/su

DEBTS:
• Ave debt per year: £2,608
• Access fund: £185,241   • Successful applications/yr: 420
• Ave payment: £500

Aside from rugby scholarships, there are accommodation bursaries, awards for mature students and an assortment of cash pots available via application or academic achievement, from £20-£500.

FEES: International undergrads are looking at £6,500, postgrads at £2,940. It'll be 2007 before top up fees hit.

ACCOMMODATION: • Cost of living index: ££   • Insurance premium: £
In college: • Self-catering: 26%   • Cost: £42 (36wks)
• First years living in: 85%
Lampeter: • Ave rent: £40   • Living at home: 10%

EMPLOYMENT: • Unemployed after 6mths: 12%
The Employability Unit is a job centre and career guidance facility. Some jobs in the Union and the bar. Local pub and shop work isn't out of the question, but besides that and the organic food packing centre, there's not a lot about.

TRAVEL:
National: No immediately local mainline trains, but from Carmarthen it's direct to London (£27.70), Cardiff (£10.30) and Birmingham (£24.25). Aberystwyth station is better for northbound journeys. Lampeter is on a National Express coach route to London via Cardiff (£30.60), Cardiff (£12.10) and Birmingham via Swansea (£26.15). *A car – or failing that, a rocket pack – makes a big difference to the quality of life. Day trips and shopping become feasible for a start.*
Local: The buses stick to the timetables, hourly till about 5.30pm. It's £3.50 return to Carmarthen with a similar service to Aberystwyth. The University occasionally organises trips to Swansea, Cardiff and Aberystwyth.

ENTERTAINMENTS: • Booze index: £1.68
Lampeter: • Pint of beer: £2   • Glass of wine: £2
• Can of Red Bull: £2
University: • Pint of beer: £1.70   • Glass of wine: £1.50
• Can of Red Bull: £1.50

UNUSUAL COSTS: £25 a year to get into the *stark* modern sports hall.

LANCASTER UNIVERSITY
Lancaster University, Lancaster House, Lancaster, LA1 4YW
Tel: (01524) 65 201. Fax: (01524) 846 243. E-mail: ugadmissions@lancs.ac.uk
Website: www.lancs.ac.uk
Lancaster University Students' Union, Bailrigg, Lancaster, LA1 4YW
Tel: (01524) 593 765. Fax: (01524) 846 732. Website: www.lusu.co.uk

DEBTS:
• Ave debt per year: £3,920
• Access fund: £448,323   • Successful applications/yr: 558
• Ave payment: £100-3,500

Nearly £75,000 in bursaries, mainly aimed at mature students, students with kids and postgrads.

Banks on campus: Several nearby.

FEES: International students pay £8,000.

ACCOMMODATION: • <u>Cost of living index: ££</u> • <u>Insurance premium: £</u>
In college: • <u>Self-catering: 59%</u> • <u>Cost: £42-71 (31-51wks)</u>
• <u>First years living in: 92%</u>
Lancaster: • <u>Ave rent: £44</u>

EMPLOYMENT: • <u>Unemployed after 6mths: 8.4%</u>
Paid work: The SU keeps a notebook of term-time vacancies and runs a jobshop. Tourist-related jobs *abound* in the summer.
Careers: *Pretty comprehensive* careers services.

TRAVEL:
Lancaster station (3 miles away) direct to London, Manchester, Birmingham and other places. National Express and local buses have a coach stop on campus. Buses are £1.10 into town or £120 for a yearly pass (plus online discounts). There's a special hitch-hiking shelter on campus and an established point in town for pick-ups for trips to and from the University *although most students don't use it since the University and the Union have been telling hitching horror stories.*

ENTERTAINMENTS: • <u>Booze index: £1.32</u>
Lancaster: • <u>Pint of beer: £1.70</u> • <u>Glass of wine: £1.50</u>
• <u>Can of Red Bull: £2</u>
University: • <u>Pint of beer: £1.47</u> • <u>Glass of wine: £1.40</u>
• <u>Can of Red Bull: £1.50</u>

LEEDS METROPOLITAN UNIVERSITY
Leeds Metropolitan University, Calverley Street, Leeds, LS1 3HE
Tel: (0113) 283 3113. Fax: (0113) 283 3114
E-mail: course-enquiries@leedsmet.ac.uk. Website: www.leedsmet.ac.uk
Leeds Metropolitan University Students Union, Calverley Street, Leeds, LS1 3HE
Tel: (0113) 2098400. Fax: 01633 432688. E-mail: enquiries@lmusu.ac.uk
Website: www.lmusu.org.uk

DEBTS: • <u>Ave debt per year: £4,339</u>
• <u>Access fund: £990,000</u> • <u>Successful applications/yr: 800</u>
Debt counselling is available from the Budget Advisor and 2 part-timers. There's an emergency fund for overseas students.
Banks on campus: Lloyds

ACCOMMODATION: • <u>Cost of living index: ££££</u> • <u>Insurance premium: ££££</u>
In college: • <u>Catered: n/a</u> • <u>Cost: £79-£89 (32wks)</u>
• <u>Self-catering: n/a</u> • <u>Cost: £44-£58 (41-43wks)</u>
• <u>First years living in: 60%</u>
Leeds: • <u>Ave rent: £43</u>

EMPLOYMENT: • <u>Unemployed after 6mths: 8%</u>
Paid work: The job shop has filled well over 2,000 vacancies and is now online.
Careers: *Friendly, welcoming and reassuringly busy* careers service.

ENTERTAINMENTS: • <u>Booze index: £2.05</u>
Leeds: • <u>Pint of beer: £2.50</u> • <u>Glass of wine: £2.60</u>
• <u>Can of Red Bull: £1.50</u>
University: • <u>Pint of beer: £1.70</u> • <u>Glass of wine: £1.25</u>
• <u>Can of Red Bull: £1.10</u>

LEEDS UNIVERSITY

The University of Leeds, Leeds, LS2 9JT
Tel: (0113) 243 1751. Fax: (0113) 233 3991. E-mail: prospectus@leeds.ac.uk
Website: www.leeds.ac.uk
Leeds University Students' Union, PO Box 157, Leeds, LS1 1UH
Tel: (0113) 380 1234. Fax: 0113 380 1205. E-mail: comms@union.leeds.ac.uk
Website: www.luuonline.com

DEBTS:
- Ave debt per year: £4,188
- Access fund: £875,000
- Successful applications/yr: 1,000
- Ave payment: £875

The Union offers emergency loans up to £100, the usual bursaries and welfare funds and there's a range of budgeting advice, debt counselling and even, in a sign of the times, help with bankruptcy.
Banks on campus: Lloyds

FEES: Part-time students £570 for arts programmes, £774 for science programmes. Postgrads pay £2,940.

ACCOMMODATION:
- Cost of living index: £££££
- Insurance premium: £££££

In college:
- Catered: 11%
- Cost: £64-119 (31wks)
- Self-catering: 28%
- Cost: £51-101 (40wks)

Leeds:
- Ave rent: £43

EMPLOYMENT:
- Unemployed after 6mths: 5.5%

Paid work: The usual bar work and stewarding at Union ents and vacancies advertised online by the SU on a noticeboard and online. Also a job bureau.
Careers: *Huge and highly efficient* careers service (27 full-time and 19 part-time staff). Performing Arts students get an in-house casting service and those interested in becoming self-employed have a dedicated service called 'Spark'.

TRAVEL:
Leeds station is the centre of the *very efficient* West Yorkshire metro train network serving all the local Yorkshire towns (Bradford, Wakefield, Sheffield and York). Also direct services to London (£38.30), Manchester (£9.10) and elsewhere. National Express and Blueline coaches to London (£16.75), Manchester (£7), Edinburgh (£22.50), etc. Leeds/Bradford Airport.
Local: Buses trips are 80p and a monthly student Metrocard (bus and train) is £39.50. Student First travel card (£34 per month) is valid on bus routes from the uni through to the city centre.

ENTERTAINMENTS:
- Booze index: £1.89

Leeds:
- Pint of beer: £2.50
- Glass of wine: £2.60
- Can of Red Bull: £1.50

University:
- Pint of beer: £1
- Glass of wine: £1
- Can of Red Bull: £1.10

LEICESTER UNIVERSITY

University of Leicester, University Road, Leicester, LE1 7RH
Tel: (0116) 252 2522. Fax: (0116) 252 2200. E-mail: admissions@le.ac.uk
Website: www.le.ac.uk
University of Leicester Students' Union, Percy Gee Building, University Road, Leicester, LE1 7RH
Tel: (0116) 2231111. Fax: (0116) 2231112. E-mail: lusu@le.ac.uk
Website: www.leicesterstudent.org

DEBTS:
- Ave debt per year: £3,747

Numerous hardship funds exist, some for specific groups (mature students, overseas students, etc.), scholarships for physics, engineering and sports bursaries. The SU

gives hardship loans up to £100 and special needs students are given priority.
Banks on campus: NatWest, HSBC

ACCOMMODATION: • Cost of living index: ££ • Insurance premium: £££
In college: • Catered: 9% • Cost: £75-104 (30wks)
• Self-catering: 3% • Cost: £50-95 (39-52wks)
• First years living in: 90%
Lecicester: • Ave rent: £45-50 • Living at home: 12%

EMPLOYMENT: • Unemployed after 6mths: 8%
• Paid work: term-time 45%
Paid work: The Union-run jobshop matches students with casual jobs and, failing that, there's always the Walkers Crisps factory. The University runs a student employment centre allowing local companies to recruit directly from the student body.
Careers: The *thorough* careers service not only gives careers a good servicing, doing all the normal stuff, but also offers students advice on how to start their own business – *anything from double-glazing sales to porn empires.*

TRAVEL:
National: Trains from Leicester Station, National Express coaches, planes from East Midlands Airport (16 miles away) and Birmingham International (45-min drive). *Excellent* hitching for London or Birmingham.
Local: *Buses are reliable, cheap (60p from campus to town), well used and run until 11pm.*

ENTERTAINMENTS: • Booze index: £1.95
Leicester: • Pint of beer: £2 • Glass of wine: £2.80
• Can of Red Bull: £1.90
University: • Pint of beer: £1.40 • Glass of wine: £1.50

UNUSUAL COSTS: A Sports Card, giving access to all facilities, costs £45 for the year. 2 halls of residence require £35 parking permits.

....

UNIVERSITY OF LINCOLN
University of Lincoln, Brayford Pool, Lincoln, LN6 7TS
Tel: 01522 882000. Fax: 01522 882088. E-mail: enquiries@lincoln.ac.uk
Website: www.lincoln.ac.uk
ULSU Co-operative, University of Lincoln, Brayford Pool, Lincoln, LN6 7TS
Tel: 01522 886142. E-mail: sureception@lincoln.ac.uk

DEBTS: • Ave debt per year: £4,157
• Access fund: £500,000 • Successful applications/yr: 1,500
The University waives fees for part-time undergraduates on income support.

ACCOMMODATION: • Cost of living index: £££££ • Insurance premium: £
In college: • Catered: 2% • Cost: £60-65 (38wks)
• Self-catering: 15% • Cost: £53 (38wks)
For Hull, see Hull University
Lincoln: • Ave rent: £35

EMPLOYMENT: • Unemployed after 6mths: 11%
Paid work: SU-run Job Exchange provides details of sits vac for those trying to get into the job queue.
Careers: 4 staff to get students out of college and into the daily grind.

TRAVEL:
National: Lincoln has train services to London (£27.70), Birmingham (£16.65), Edinburgh (£51.30) and more.
Local: *Flat beyond your dreams. Get pedalling.*

ENTERTAINMENTS: • Booze index: £2.23
Lincoln: • Pint of beer: £1.90 • Glass of wine: £2
• Can of Red Bull: £1.95
For Hull, see University of Hull
University: • Pint of beer: £0.99 • Glass of wine: £2.30
• Can of Red Bull: £1.95

....

LIVERPOOL UNIVERSITY
University of Liverpool, 150 Mount Pleasant, Liverpool, L69 3GD
Tel: (0151) 794 2000. Fax: (0151) 794 5602. E-mail: ugrecriutment@liv.ac.uk
Website: www.liv.ac.uk
University of Liverpool Guild of Students, 160 Mount Pleasant, Liverpool, L69 7BR
Tel: (0151) 794 4128. Fax: (0151) 794 4174. E-mail: gensec@liv.ac.uk
Website: www.liverpoolguild.org.uk

DEBTS: • Ave debt per year: £3,583
• Access fund: £607,227 • Successful applications/yr: 935
• Ave payment: £930
The University offers financial advice and assistance to students with holes in their
piggy banks. A large number of bursaries and scholarships are available, including
the Alumni Scholarship (which pays out £2,000 for academic achievement), the
John Lennon Memorial Scholarship (£1,200) for Merseyside residents with
environmental interests and several hardship funds.
Banks on campus: Royal Bank of Scotland

ACCOMMODATION: • Cost of living index: £££ • Insurance premium: £
In college: • Catered: 18% • Cost: £81-94 (32 wks)
• Self-catering: 8% • Cost: £60 (38-40 wks)
• First years living in: 81%
Liverpool: • Ave rent: £35-50

EMPLOYMENT: • Unemployed after 6mths: 4.3%
• Paid work: term-time 65%: hols 90%
Paid work: PULSE is run through the Careers Service and sources part-time and
temp jobs and advertises them by email and txts. The Business Bridge scheme
helps find placements locally. Liverpool itself has a high unemployment rate, but the
tenacious job-seeker should be able to find bar, shop or restaurant work.
Careers: *Excellent* Careers Service.

TRAVEL:
National: Liverpool Lime Street (10mins walk) to London, Manchester, Leeds,
Birmingham and loads of other cities. National Express coaches (800m) to Leeds,
Birmingham, London, and hourly to Manchester (£6 rtn). Liverpool Airport (8 miles)
has budget flyers easyJet and Keen. Liverpool's a main ferry port for Belfast and
Ireland. *Edge Lane is a top spot for hitching just before it hits the motorway and the
M57's not a bad option either.*
Local: Various *useful and reliable* bus services (£1 or so, but yearly or termly
passes are *cheaper and less faffy*). Passes are also available for the University bus
service which runs between the Guild and halls of residence.

ENTERTAINMENTS: • Booze index: £1.55
Liverpool: • Pint of beer: £1.50 • Glass of wine: £1.50
• Can of Red Bull: £1.50
University: • Pint of beer: £1 • Glass of wine: £1.25
• Can of Red Bull: £1.45

UNUSUAL COSTS: The Athletics Union asks £24 a year of its members.

LIVERPOOL JOHN MOORES UNIVERSITY

Liverpool John Moores University, Student Recruitment, Roscoe Court, 4 Rodney Street, Liverpool, Merseyside, L1 2TZ
Tel: (0151) 231 5090. Fax: (0151) 231 3194. E-mail: recruitment@livjm.ac.uk
Website: www.livjm.ac.uk
Liverpool John Moores Student Union, The Haigh Building, Maryland Street, Liverpool, Merseyside, L1 9DE
Tel: (0151) 794 1900. Fax: (0151) 708 5334. E-mail: studentsunion@livjm.ac.uk
Website: www.l-s-u.com

DEBTS: • Ave debt per year: £5,225
Some local businesses sponsor students through their courses. Various bursaries, scholarships, hardship fund and emergency loans are kicking around.
Banks on campus: Barclays and Link ATMs on several sites.

FEES: Tuition costs for international students average out at £7,000.

ACCOMMODATION: • Cost of living index: ££   • Insurance premium: ££
In college: • Cost: £65 (40wks)
                   • First years living in: 100%   • Others living in: 8%
Liverpool: • Ave rent: £55   • Living at home: 18%

EMPLOYMENT: • Unemployed after 6mths: 9.1%
                • Paid work: term-time 68%: hols 92%
Paid work: The relaxed academic atmosphere allows more than 2/3 of students to work for their dosh during term. The Haigh contains Workbank (helps students find work during or between semesters) and several other schemes are in place, like 'Business Bridge', which assists students in finding work relevant to their course with local businesses.
Careers: 7-staff Career Development Service.

TRAVEL: see University of Liverpool
LJMU operates a shuttle bus between various sites get students and staff around campus.

ENTERTAINMENTS: • Booze index: £1.69
Liverpool: • Pint of beer: £1.50   • Glass of wine: £1.80
                                          • Can of Red Bull: £1.65
University: • Pint of beer: £1.65   • Glass of wine: £2.25
                                           • Can of Red Bull: £1.80

LONDON METROPOLITAN UNIVERSITY

London Metropolitan University, 166-220 Holloway Road, London, N7 8DB
Tel: (020) 7133 4200. E-mail: admissions@londonmet.ac.uk
Website: www.londonmet.ac.uk
London Metropolitan University Students Union, MG48, Tower Building, 166-220 Holloway Road, London, N7 8DB. Tel: (020) 7133 2769
E-mail: su@londonmet.ac.uk Website: www.londonmetsu.org.uk

DEBTS: • Ave debt per year: £4,475
              • Access fund: £2,500,000   • Successful applications/yr: 3,000+
              • Ave payment: £750
A range of bursaries and scholarships is available.
Banks on campus: Barclays

FEES: International students pay £6,840. Postgrads pay £3,000-3,400.

ACCOMMODATION: • <u>Cost of living index: ££££</u> • <u>Insurance premium: ££</u>
In college: • <u>Catered: 1%</u> • <u>Cost: £90 (40wks)</u>
  • <u>Self-catering: 5%</u> • <u>Cost: £76 (40wks)</u>
London: • <u>Ave rent: £70-120</u>

EMPLOYMENT: • <u>Unemployed after 6mths: 11%</u>
Paid work: The Careers Development and Employment Service advertises part-time
temp/vacation work, work experience and placements. Lots of Met students are
employed during term and the University itself has a large number of clerical
positions.
Careers: Careers library, newsletters, 1-to-1 guidance, interview practice, workshop
training, bulletin boards and job fairs.

TRAVEL: see <u>London University</u>

ENTERTAINMENTS: • <u>Booze index: £2</u>
London: • <u>Pint of beer: £2</u> • <u>Glass of wine: £2.90</u>
  • <u>Can of Red Bull: £1.20</u>
University: • <u>Pint of beer: £1.50</u> • <u>Glass of wine: £1.80</u>
  • <u>Can of Red Bull: £1</u>

UNUSUAL COSTS: Sports cards for use of the facilities can vary between £30-42 a
year. Beer prices in the bars rocket to £1.80 after 8pm – *get pissed by sundown,
then*.

LONDON SOUTH BANK UNIVERSITY
(1) London South Bank University, 103 Borough Road, London, SE1 0AA
 Tel: (020) 7928 8989. Fax: (020) 7815 8273. Website: www.lsbu.ac.uk
 London South Bank University Students Union, Keyworth Street, London,
 SE1 6NG
 Tel: (020) 7815 6060. Fax: (020) 7815 6061. E-mail: su.general.@lsbu.ac.uk
 Website: www.lsbu.org
(2) Essex Campus, Faculaty of Health and Social Care, Harold Wood Road Hospital,
 Gubbins Lane, Romford, Essex, RN3 0BE

7

DEBTS: • <u>Ave debt per year: £1,703</u>
  • <u>Access fund: £1m</u> • <u>Ave payment: £250-400</u>
Lots of sports scholarships (£3,000); Governers Charitable Fund; Lawrence Burrow
scholarship (£1,000 grants for 10 Asian/West Indian students); Minerva
Scholarship offers £20,000 for Built Enviroment Students.
Banks on campus: HSBC.

ACCOMMODATION: • <u>Cost of living index: £££££</u> • <u>Insurance premium: ££</u>
In college: • <u>Self-catering: 100%</u> • <u>Cost: £71-89 (40wks)</u>
  • <u>First years living in: 12%</u>
South London: • <u>Ave rent: £55-80</u>

EMPLOYMENT: • <u>Unemployed after 6mths: 5%</u>
  • <u>Paid work: term-time 60%: hols 75%</u>
Vacancy lists are published in the Union and at the Jobshop (10 staff) which also
arranges placements.

TRAVEL: see <u>London University</u>
Mainline trains from Waterloo or London Bridge, Zone 1 on the tube - the Bakerloo
and the tube's Northern Line pass through Elephant & Castle station (100m from
college), as do Thameslink trains. *Buses galore.*

ENTERTAINMENTS: • <u>Booze index: £2.17</u>
London: • <u>Pint of beer: £2.20</u> • <u>Glass of wine: £2.60</u>
  • <u>Can of Red Bull: £1.80</u>

| **University:** | • Pint of beer: £1.60 | • Glass of wine: £2.50 |
| | | • Can of Red Bull: £1.50 |

UNUSUAL COSTS: There's a £30 annual fee to use the facilities and sport clubs charge £5 yearly subs.

LONDON UNIVERSITY

• *The information which follows refers to London University as an amorphous blob. The colleges and individual unions of the University vary considerably and Push covers these differences in the individual college profiles. Similarly, the general comments about London apply on the whole to central London, particularly the areas close to ULU itself. They are broadly relevant to the many institutions which are in the city but not part of London University itself.*

University of London, Senate House, Malet St, London, WC1E 7HU
Tel: (020) 7862 8000. Fax: (020) 7862 8358. E-mail: enquiries@lon.ac.uk
Website: www.lon.ac.uk
University of London Union, Malet St, London, WC1E 7HY
Tel: (020) 7664 2000. Fax: (020) 7436 4604. E-mail: general@ulu.ucl.ac.uk
Website: www.ulucube.com

FINANCE:
Any cash going is distributed by the colleges.
Banks on campus: Barclays and Halifax banks/ATMs.

FEES: All fees depend on individual colleges, there are no set rates. Imperial plans to charge maximum top up fees, Royal Holloway plans to charge minimum.

ACCOMMODATION:	• Cost of living index: £££££
	• Insurance premium: ££
In intercollegiate housing:	• Catered: 2%	• Cost: £92-121 (36-39wks)
	• Self-catering: 0.5%	• Cost: £60-217 (50wks)
London:	• Ave rent: £100

EMPLOYMENT: • Unemployed after 6mths: 14%
Paid work: Vacancy lists are posted up in the Union and ULU usually has vacancies itself. There are more opportunities in London for part-time work than anywhere else, but there are also more people trying to get those jobs. Students find work *quite easily* in all the usual places like bars and restaurants and also in theatres, offices and shops.
Careers: See www.careers.lon.ac.uk for vacancies and general information. The main office is at Golden Square in Soho, but there are also facilities at nine of the colleges, which vary according to subject/professions.

TRAVEL:
National: London is the centre of the rail network: Birmingham (£24.30 rtn, 1hr 45); Manchester (£34.40 rtn, 2hr 40); Leeds (£43.70 rtn, 2hr 45); Bristol Parkway (£28.50 1hr 25); Glasgow (£57.50 rtn, 6hrs). London is also the centre of the National Express system and a whole variety of other national bus services (Green Line, Blue Line and so on), letting you ride to Birmingham (from £33, 2hr 45), Manchester and so on.
Local: The 'tube' is the largest underground train system in the world, and generally *it's okay and takes you most places you might want to go (except in east and south-east London). On the down-side, it's often crowded, shuts down around midnight during the week, is often disrupted by strikes and breakdowns and is expensive.* Nearest tube to Senate House/ULU Building: Goodge St (Northern Line), Warren St (Victoria) or Russell Sq (Piccadilly) – all zone 1. *Buses, just as efficient as the Tube, offer even more destinations and are cheap (£1 for any journey).* After midnight, buses come into their own – Night Buses are London's only form of all-night public transport and *if you don't mind how long it takes,* you can go almost anywhere within 10 miles of the centre. *Trains are often the best bet south of the river. The*

east of the city is covered by the tube/train hybrid, the DLR (Docklands Light Railway) which covers places like Canary Wharf, Mile End and East Ham. Students in full-time education are entitled to a 30% discount on travelcards for bus/local rail/tube travel.

ENTERTAINMENTS:

London:	• Pint of beer: £2.50
	• Glass of wine: £2.50
	• Can of Red Bull: £2
University:	• Pint of beer: £1.80
	• Glass of wine: £2
	• Can of Red Bull: £1.50

LOUGHBOROUGH UNIVERSITY

Loughborough University, Loughborough, Leicestershire, LE11 3TU
Tel: (01509) 223 522. Fax: (01509) 223 905. E-mail: admissions@lboro.ac.uk
Website: www.lboro.ac.uk
Loughborough Students' Union, Loughborough, Leicestershire, LE11 3TT
Tel: (01509) 635 000. Fax: (01509) 635 003. E-mail: union@lufbra.net
Website: www.lufbra.net

DEBTS:
- Ave debt per year: £3,767
- Access fund: £400,000
- Successful applications/yr: 673
- Ave payment: £650

International scholarships, music tuition scholarships and bursaries, some dept scholarships, student prizes, some sponsored courses.
Banks on campus: HSBC, Barclay's, NatWest

ACCOMMODATION:
- Cost of living index: £
- Insurance premium: £

In college:
- Catered: 25%
- Cost: £79-108 (31wks)
- Self-catering: 17%
- Cost: £45-66 (34-38wks)

Loughborough:
- Ave rent: £45

EMPLOYMENT: • Unemployed after 6mths: 11%
Paid work: *A very successful* employment exchange with a job database for students.

TRAVEL:
National: Loughborough Station (2 miles away) is on the mainline north from London St Pancras (£20.45) to Edinburgh (£61.45). Also served by local coach company Paul Winson and National Express.
Local: Buses run between campus and town.

ENTERTAINMENTS:
Loughborough:
- Booze index: £1.60
- Pint of beer: £1.65

University:
- Pint of beer: £1.20
- Glass of wine: £1.75
- Can of Red Bull: £1.60

UNUSUAL COSTS: Limited £48 parking available for 2nd and 3rd years.

LONDON SCHOOL OF ECONOMICS (LSE)

• **The College is part of <u>London University</u> and students are entitled to use its facilities.**
The London School of Economics & Political Science, Houghton Street, London, WC2A 2AE
Tel: (020) 7405 7686. Fax: (0207) 955 6001.
E-mail: stu.rec-admissions@lse.ac.uk. Website: www.lse.ac.uk
LSE Students Union, East Building, LSE, Houghton Street, London, WC2A 2AE
Tel: (020) 7955 7158. Fax: (020) 7955 6789. E-mail: su.gensec@lse.ac.uk
Website: www.lsesu.com

DEBTS:
- Ave debt per year: £2,763
- Access fund: £108,611
- Successful applications/yr: 112
- Ave payment: £1,200

Limited scholarships, bursaries and special awards in cases of academic excellence or extreme hardship.

FEES: Fees for postgrads are rising above the rate of inflation. *There's not much doubt that LSE will rake in as much from top up fees as every other elite university in the country.*

ACCOMMODATION:
- Cost of living index: £££
- Insurance premium: £

In college:
- Catered: 19%
- Cost: £57-120 (30wks)
- Self-catering: 7%
- Cost: £86-122 (30wks)
- First years living in: 95%

London:
- Ave rent: £100
- Living at home: 10%

EMPLOYMENT:
- Unemployed after 6mths: 5.9%
- Paid work: term-time 50%; hols 70%

Paid work: Work going in the SU services. Jobshop tries to set students up with part-time work online.

Careers: Lots of LSE's graduates go on to further training or another degree – *more through naked ambition than addiction to the lie-in lifestyle.*

ENTERTAINMENTS:
- Booze index: £1.74

London:
- Pint of beer: £2
- Glass of wine: £2
- Can of Red Bull: £2

University:
- Pint of beer: £1.20
- Glass of wine: £2
- Can of Red Bull: £1.50

LUTON UNIVERSITY

University of Luton, Park Street, Luton, LU1 3JU
Tel: (01582) 734111. Fax: (01582) 743 400. E-mail: admissions@luton.ac.uk
Website: www.luton.ac.uk
University of Luton Students' Union, Europa House, Vicarage Street, Luton, LU1 3HZ
Tel: (01582) 743 286. Fax: (01582) 457 187. Website: www.ulsu.net

DEBTS:
- Ave debt per year: £4,127
- Access fund: £497,588
- Successful applications/yr: 853
- Ave payment: £583

Some local businesses offer £500 handouts – *but be warned, they'll probably want something in return at some point.* Specific funds are available for members of specific groups: locals, ethnic minorities, mature students etc.

FEES: International undergrads pay £6,700-£7,400. UK postgrads pay around £4,000. Luton will *probably end up charging top up fees in one form or another –* the University plans to charge a variety of different fee levels, with flagship courses, like those in the highly-regarded Media department, going the whole hog.

ACCOMMODATION:
- Cost of living index: £££££
- Insurance premium: £

In college:
- Self-catering: 26%
- Cost: £45-66 (30wks)
- First years living in: 100%

Luton:
- Ave rent: £35-60

EMPLOYMENT:
- Unemployed after 6mths: 8%
- Paid work: term-time 90%; hols 95%

Paid work: Jobshop posts vacancies, gives CV advice and finds voluntary work for *selfless do-gooders.* Several companies in Luton (the Airport, the council) employ students.

Careers: The Student Centre Careers Service. Several big businesses in the area offer Graduate Apprenticeship Schemes to Luton students.

TRAVEL:
National: Luton station (5mins walk) to London King's Cross (£21), Bedford, Milton Keynes and east coast mainline services all the way to Edinburgh (£58.90). Green Line coaches and National Express (London £8, Birmingham £12). Luton Airport is the home of budget airline easyJet and offers domestic and international services to Europe, Ireland and the USA.
Local: 'Hopper' buses scuttle round the town every 30mins till 11pm, around 60p a trip from the outskirts to Park Square. Free university shuttle bus from Park Square to Putteridge Bury and back again (9am-5pm daily).

ENTERTAINMENTS:	• Booze index: £1.94	
Luton:	• Pint of beer: £2	• Glass of wine: £2.50
		• Can of Red Bull: £1.50
University:	• Pint of beer: £1.60	• Glass of wine: £2.20
		• Can of Red Bull: £1.50

UNUSUAL COSTS: The sports facilities at the Vauxhall Recreation Centre cost either £60 a year or are charged on a per session basis.

MANCHESTER UNIVERSITY

University of Manchester, Oxford Road, Manchester, M13 9PL
Tel: (0161) 2752 000. E-mail: ug.admissions@man.ac.uk
Website: www.manchester.ac.uk
University of Manchester Union, Steve Biko Building, Oxford Road, Manchester, M13 9PR
Tel: (0161) 275 2930. Fax: (0161) 275 2936. Website: www.umu.man.ac.uk

DEBTS: • Ave debt per year: £1,454
Some short-term loans and helpful handouts from both the Union and the University.
Banks on campus: Barclays and Halifax ATMs.

FEES: For international students, fees are £8,300 a year for Arts courses, £10,750 for scientists and almost twenty grand for wannabe doctors and dentists.

7

ACCOMMODATION:	• Cost of living index: £	• Insurance premium: £££££
In college:	• Catered: 14%	• Cost: £59-87 (38wks)
	• Self-catering: 35%	• Cost: £42-74 (38wks)
	• First years living in: 86%	
Manchester:	• Ave rent: £43	

EMPLOYMENT: • Unemployed after 6mths: 8%
Paid work: The University runs a fully-staffed jobshop in the foyer of the Union building, where the Careers service posts part-time and vacation vacancies. *Because Manchester's such a big centre for entertainment there are lots of part-time jobs in bars, clubs, shops and restaurants.*
Careers: Manchester has the second biggest careers service in the country. It has over 50 staff in all *and is rather brilliant*. They help students find both work placements and life-long careers, arranging around 120 companies-worth of employer presentations. See the dedicated Website: www.graduatecareersonline.com.

TRAVEL:
National: Not 1, but 2 mainline stations, Manchester Piccadilly for London and the South, and Manchester Victoria for just about everywhere else. All sorts of coach services to, among most other places, London, Birmingham, Edinburgh and beyond. Manchester Airport's one of the UK's big ones – flights all over the world as well as inland. *Hitching's not possible from central Manchester, but quite good on arterial routes out of the city.*
Local: Manchester has a major bus network, running all over town, especially up

and down Oxford Road. Trains are a *quicker alternative, especially for the outskirts*. The Metrolink tram service trundles around helpfully.

ENTERTAINMENTS: • Booze index: £1.85
Manchester: • Pint of beer: £1.90   • Glass of wine: £2.20
                                          • Can of Red Bull: £2
University: • Pint of beer: £1.35   • Glass of wine: £2
                                          • Can of Red Bull: £1.65

MANCHESTER METROPOLITAN UNIVERSITY
Manchester Metropolitan University, All Saints, Oxford Road, Manchester, M15 6BH
Tel: (0161) 247 2000. Fax: (0161) 247 6390. E-mail: enquiries@mmu.ac.uk
MMU Students' Union, MMU Students' Union, 99 Oxford Road, Manchester,
M1 7EL
Tel: (0161) 273 1162. Fax: (0161) 273 7237. E-mail: mmsu@mmu.ac.uk

DEBTS: • Ave debt per year: £3,654
          • Access fund: £1,449,561   • Successful applications/yr: 2,431
The SU can give loans of up to £75 (or higher in exceptional circumstances) but they'd like to stress that that's 'loan', not gift.
Banks on campus: Barclays and Link ATMs.

ACCOMMODATION: • Cost of living index: £   • Insurance premium: £££££
In college: • Catered: 4%   • Cost: £70 (34wks)
                • Self-catering: 10%   • Cost: £45-60 (40-44wks)
Manchester: • Ave rent: £40-55

EMPLOYMENT: • Unemployed after 6mths: 11%
Paid work: The university jobshop 'Steam' has close links with local job networks. See Manchester University.

ENTERTAINMENTS: • Booze index: £1.61
Manchester: • Pint of beer: £1.90   • Glass of wine: £2.20
                                          • Can of Red Bull: £2
University: • Pint of beer: £1   • Glass of wine: £1.30
                                          • Can of Red Bull: £1.65

MIDDLESEX UNIVERSITY
(1) Middlesex University, North London Business Park, London, N11 1QS
    Tel: (020) 8411 5898. Fax: (020) 8411 5649
    E-mail: admissions@mdx.ac.uk. Website: www.mdx.ac.uk
(2) Middlesex University Students' Union, Trent Park, Bramley Road, London,
    N14 4YZ
    Tel: (020) 8362 6450. Fax: (020) 8440 5944

DEBTS: • Ave debt per year: £4,193
Chancellor's scholarships are awarded for academic or sporting excellence or community achievements.

ACCOMMODATION: • Cost of living index: ££   • Insurance premium: ££
In college: • Self-catering: 100%   • Cost: £72.17-81.62 (40wks)
Locally in London: • Ave rent: £60

EMPLOYMENT: • Unemployed after 6mths: 17%
Paid work: There's some work to be found at the University and SU, which employ students to marshal carparks, steward at balls, help at Open Days and suchlike. The JobsOnline website has an online vacancy service.
Careers: 4 full-time and 3 part-time staff provide *all the usual gubbins including* alumni mentors, computer-based guidance and seminars.

TRAVEL: see <u>London University</u>
Nearest rail/tube stations are Finsbury Park, Seven Sisters and Tottenham Hale (all Victoria line), Oakwood for the Piccadilly line. The University sites are in zones 3-5. Local buses operate and the University minibus runs from Oakwood station to campus every 15 mins in term-time (useful for Cat Hill and Trent Park). Free and paid-for parking at or near most sites, *but finding a space can mean a bit of bunfight*. Permits required to park on campus.

ENTERTAINMENTS: • <u>Booze index: £2.38</u>
London: see <u>University of London</u>
University: • <u>Pint of beer: £1.70</u>   • <u>Glass of wine: £2</u>
                                              • <u>Can of Red Bull: £1.60</u>

NAPIER UNIVERSITY

(1) Napier University, Merchiston Campus, 10 Colinton Road, Edinburgh, EH10 5DT
   Tel: 0500 35 35 70. Fax: 0131 455 2885. E-mail: info@napier.ac.uk
   Website: www.napier.ac.uk
   Napier Students Association, 12 Merchiston Place, Edinburgh, EH10 4NR
   Tel: 0131 229 8791. E-mail: nsa@napier.ac.uk
   Website: www.napierstudents.com
(2) Craighouse Campus, Craighouse Road, Edinburgh, EH10 5LG
(3) Craiglockhart Campus, 219 Colinton Road, Edinburgh, EH14 1DG
(4) Canaan Lane Campus, 74 Canaan Lane, Edinburgh, EH10 4TB
(5) Comely Bank Campus, Crewe Road South, Edinburgh, EH14 2LD
(6) Sighthill Campus, Sighthill Court, Edinburgh, EH11 4BN

DEBTS: • <u>Ave debt per year: £1,040</u>
                 • <u>Access fund: £300,000</u>   • <u>Successful applications/yr: 1,900</u>
                 • <u>Ave payment: £100-1,200</u>
Young student's bursary (non-repayable grant of £2,100/yr for under-25s from low-income families), mature student's bursary, hardship loans (up to £500/yr) and a childcare fund which grants up to £200 per child per month.

ACCOMMODATION: • <u>Cost of living index: £££££</u> • <u>Insurance premium: £</u>
In college: • <u>Self-catering: 100%</u>   • <u>Cost: £65 (38wks)</u>
                    • <u>First years living in: 75%</u>
Edinburgh: • <u>Ave rent: £65</u>

EMPLOYMENT: • <u>Unemployed after 6mths: 5%</u>
Paid work: NSA runs a JobBank and a net-based job bank.
Careers: 8 full-time careers staff on hand to try and get students working.

ENTERTAINMENTS: • <u>Booze index: £2.20</u>
Edinburgh: • <u>Pint of beer: £2.50</u>   • <u>Glass of wine: £2.30</u>
                                                 • <u>Can of Red Bull: £2</u>
University: • <u>Pint of beer: £1.75</u>   • <u>Glass of wine: £1.70</u>
                                                 • <u>Can of Red Bull: £1</u>

NEWCASTLE UNIVERSITY

University of Newcastle upon Tyne, 6 Kensington Terrace, Newcastle upon Tyne, NE1 7RU
Tel: (0191) 222 5594. Fax: (0191) 222 8685. E-mail: enquiries@ncl.ac.uk
Website: www.ncl.ac.uk
The Union Society, King's Walk, Newcastle upon Tyne, NE1 8QB
Tel: (0191) 239 3900. Fax: (0191) 222 1876. E-mail: union.society@ncl.ac.uk
Website: www.unionsociety.co.uk

DEBTS: • Ave debt per year: £1,362 • Access fund: £598,166
There are up to 200 £2,000 bursaries for financially disadvantaged but academically talented students. The South African Scholarship provides funds for a South African student to study at Newcastle.

ACCOMMODATION:	• Cost of living index: £££	• Insurance premium: ££
In college:	• Catered: 10%	• Cost: £42-74 (39wks)
	• Self-catering: 16%	• Cost: £66-91 (39wks)
Newcastle:	• Ave rent: £45-50	• Living at home: 14%

EMPLOYMENT: • Unemployed after 6mths: 4%
Paid work: The Union runs a jobshop which also monitors conditions and pay and gives students an introduction to job-related issues. In 2004 it posted over 1,000 vacation and term-time vacancies, many in bars, shops, the theatres and *no end of soul-destroying* work at the Metro Centre.
Careers: The careers service attracts some *fairly big* players to *trawl its graduates*.

TRAVEL:
National: Newcastle station (10mins walk from the city centre, 2mins by Metro) to London, Sheffield, Edinburgh and all over the country. Several coach companies, including Clipper, Blue Line and National Express
Local: Bus routes through the city are regular, *reliable and cheap*. A University minibus (50p, priority for women) takes students home from the library, school and Union building. The Metro (undergound) is *clean, cheap, reliable and easy to use. It's noisy but serves all the essential student areas and has now been extended to Sunderland (£4 rtn)*.

ENTERTAINMENTS:	• Booze index: £1.93	
Newcastle-upon-Tyne:	• Pint of beer: £2.10	• Glass of wine: £1.90
		• Can of Red Bull: £2
University:	• Pint of beer: £1.60	• Glass of wine: £2.25
		• Can of Red Bull: £1.40

UNUSUAL COSTS: Range of sports memberships from £28-£83 depending on facilities used.

NEWPORT, UNIVERSITY OF WALES
• **The College is part of the University of Wales.**
University of Wales, Newport, Caerleon Campus, PO Box 179, Newport, South Wales, NP18 3YG
Tel: (01633) 432 432. Fax: (01633) 432 850. E-mail: uic@newport.ac.uk
Website: www.newport.ac.uk
Students' Union, Caerleon Campus, College Crescent, Caerleon, NP18 3YG
Tel: (01633) 432 076. Fax: (01633) 432 688
E-mail: students.union@newport.ac.uk. Website: www.newportunion.com

DEBTS:	• Ave debt per year: £4,362	
	• Access fund: £461,442	• Successful applications/yr: 624
	• Ave payment: £200-2,000	

Total of £33,000 in bursary funding available each year (68 awarded in 2003). An emergency loan scheme slips skint students a few notes in sticky situations.

FEES: Postgrads pay around £3,300 a year in tuition fees, internationals closer to £6,700. The University has a firm policy of widening access and thinks top up fees won't help.

ACCOMMODATION:	• Cost of living index: £££	• Insurance premium: £
In college:	• Self-catering: 16%	• Cost: £50 (39wks)
	• First years living in: 32%	
Newport:	• Ave rent: £40	• Living at home: 35%

EMPLOYMENT: • Unemployed after 6mths: 5%
Many work part-time both in term and out. The University job bureau is essentially the *admirable* Careers Service in a different hat. The rest of the time it helps graduates with the long-term. A temp agency visits the Freshers' Fair each year *to hunt down fresh meat*. Some SU work's to be had – bar, library, shop, IT suites, marketing – and locally, it's mainly shops, pubs, clubs and call centres.

TRAVEL:
National: Newport station is on the Cardiff-Birmingham line and is directly linked to London. The coach station has local and National Express services. Cardiff International Airport is 30 miles away and has cheap flights (Ryanair and BMI Baby).
Local: From the bus station, plenty of buses take the 15-20min trip to campus (£1.65 rtn). An hourly college shuttle bus runs between the Caerleon Campus and Allt yr Yn campus, 20mins away.

ENTERTAINMENTS: • Booze index: £1.85
Newport:	• Pint of beer: £2	• Glass of wine: £1.80
		• Can of Red Bull: £2
University:	• Pint of beer: £1.70	• Glass of wine: £1.40
		• Can of Red Bull: £1.70

UNUSUAL COSTS: Membership of the sports facilities sucks £45 out of student pockets, in addition to charges of £1.10 per session. Parking permits cost £40 (£10 if sharing). And, the Link ATM on campus ain't free, neither.

UNIVERSITY COLLEGE NORTHAMPTON

University College Northampton, Park Campus, Boughton Green Road, Northampton, NN2 7AL
Tel: (01604) 735 500. Fax: (01604) 722 083
E-mail: study@northampton.ac.uk. Website: www.northampton.ac.uk
University College Northampton Students' Union, Park Campus, Bougton Green Road, Northampton, NN2 7AL
Tel: (01604) 892 818. Fax: (01604) 719 454. Website: www.ucnu.org

DEBTS: • Ave debt per year: £2,897
• Access fund: n/a • Ave payment: £100-3,500
There's an emergency loan of £150 available when things get tight. Also bridging loans of £200 and opportunity bursaries for undergrads with low-income families of up to £2,000.
Banks on campus: NatWest and Co-op ATMs

ACCOMMODATION: • Cost of living index: £££££ • Insurance premium: £
In college:	• Self-catering: 100%	• Cost: £33-66 (40wks)
	• First years living in: 90%	
Northampton:	• Ave rent: £45	

EMPLOYMENT: • Unemployed after 6mths: 7%
• Paid work: term-time 75%: hols 80%
Paid work: The SU and the University's Student Services unit between them run Jobs Junction with local employer links. Jobs going in the Union and in local bars and shops. Students get the odd pittance here and there acting as student ambassadors, *or, in English, university tour guides*.
Careers: Careers service facilities available until 3 years after graduation.

TRAVEL: see Northampton University
Northampton Station and the coach station are 4 miles from Park Campus. The bus station is *utterly horrid, but services are reliable enough*. Trips between town and College cost 90p each way. There's a free college bus for students and staff between the main campus and the town's bus and train stations.

ENTERTAINMENTS: • <u>Booze index: £1.90</u>
Northampton: • <u>Pint of beer: £2</u> • <u>Glass of wine: £2</u>
• <u>Can of Red Bull: £2</u>
University: • <u>Pint of beer: £1.50</u> • <u>Can of Red Bull: £1.40</u>

UNUSUAL COSTS: The Park Campus sports hall charges £20 a year. Parking permits are £120 yearly.

NORTHUMBRIA UNIVERSITY

(1) Northumbria University, Newcastle City Campus, Ellison Place, Newcastle upon Tyne, NE1 8ST
Tel: (0191) 232 6002. Fax: (0191) 227 4017
Website: www.northumbria.ac.uk
Northumbria University Students' Union, Newcastle City Campus, 2 Sandyford Road, Newcastle upon Tyne, NE1 8SB. Tel: (0191) 227 4757
(2) University of Northumbria, Coach Lane Campus, Coach Lane, Benton, Newcastle upon Tyne, NE7 7XA. Tel: (0191) 215 6000. Fax: (0191) 215 6015

DEBTS: • <u>Ave debt per year: £3,577</u>
Apart from the access fund (*which runs out quickly*), there's *not a great deal of extra support* apart from a few loans for those in need.

ACCOMMODATION: • <u>Cost of living index: £</u> • <u>Insurance premium: £</u>
In college: • <u>Catered: 2%</u> • <u>Cost: £74-81 (36wks)</u>
• <u>Self-catering: 10%</u> • <u>Cost: £56-86 (36wks)</u>
Self-catering rooms in Carlisle cost £53.50 (20 or 40 weeks).
Newcastle: see <u>University of Newcastle</u>
Carlisle: • <u>Ave rent: £50</u>

EMPLOYMENT: • <u>Unemployed after 6mths: 4.8%</u>
Paid work: 20% of the students are registered with the job shop, which employs 2 full-time staff and some casual student assistants during term-term. They pass on CVs to employers looking for cheap, *exploitable – sorry, flexible, enthusiastic –* labour.
Careers: The careers service (7 full-time staff) has limited outposts at Coach Lane and Carlisle but zilch at Longhist, *but they try to plug the gap with their website*.

TRAVEL: see <u>University of Newcastle</u>
Carlisle: The mainline train station is 20mins walk from campus, as is the Stagecoach bus station.
Sites: The University operates its own *infrequent* bus service between the Newcastle and Longhirst campuses with a last bus after midnight.

ENTERTAINMENTS: • <u>Booze index: £2</u>
Newcastle upon Tyne: see <u>University of Newcastle</u>
University: • <u>Pint of beer: £1.80</u> • <u>Glass of wine: £2.20</u>

UNIVERSITY OF NOTTINGHAM

(1) The University of Nottingham, University Park, Nottingham, NG7 2RD
Tel: (0115) 951 5151. Fax: (0115) 951 1573
E-mail: undergraduate-enquiries@nottingham.ac.uk
Website: www.nottingham.ac.uk
University of Nottingham Union, Portland Building, University Park, NG7 2RD
Tel: (0115) 935 1138. Fax: (0115) 935 1101
Website: www.students-union.nottingham.ac.uk
(2) University of Nottingham, Sutton Bonington, Nr Loughborough, Leicestershire, LE12 5RD. Tel: (0115) 951 515
(3) The University of Nottingham Malaysia Campus, www.unim.nottingham.ac.uk

DEBTS:
- Ave debt per year: £3,300
- Access fund: n/a
- Ave payment: £100-3,500

Various bursaries and scholarships are up for grabs, including sporting bursaries for the superfit.

Banks on campus: NatWest and HSBC

FEES: Postgrad fees are around £3,020. International students have to pay between £8,350 and £11,020.

ACCOMMODATION:
- Cost of living index: £
- Insurance premium: ££

In college:
- Catered: 20%
- Self-catering: 10%
- Cost: £52.60
- Cost: £124.80

Nottingham:
- Ave rent: £55

EMPLOYMENT: • Unemployed after 6mths: 1.7%
The Union runs a job agency, 'Nucleus'. Apart from the usual money scrambles, students have been known to sell themselves as guinea pigs at the medical school. There's a Careers Service for long-term prospects.

TRAVEL:
National: Nottingham Midland and Beeston stations to London, Birmingham, Manchester and Edinburgh. National Express coaches.
Local: Free University shuttle bus between the 3 campuses. Reasonable taxi rates. The University is *flat with a major network of cycle lanes connecting the city centre, University Park and Jubilee campuses. Laxity with locks can leave legs with little to lever.*

ENTERTAINMENTS: • Booze index: £2.01

Nottingham:
- Pint of beer: £1.80
- Glass of wine: £2.50
- Can of Red Bull: £2

University:
- Pint of beer: £1.55
- Glass of wine: £2.20
- Can of Red Bull: £1.70

NOTTINGHAM TRENT UNIVERSITY

(1) The Nottingham Trent University, Burton St, Nottingham, NG1 4BU
   Tel: (0115) 941 8418. Fax: (0115) 848 6503. E-mail: marketing@ntu.ac.uk
   Website: www.ntu.ac.uk
   The Nottingham Trent University Union of Students, Byron House, Shakespeare Street, NG1 4GH
   Tel: (0115) 848 6200. Fax: (0115) 848 6201. E-mail: empstore@su.ntu.ac.uk
   Website: www.su.ntu.ac.uk
(2) Clifton Campus, Clifton, Nottingham
(3) School of Land-based Studies, Brackenhurst, Southwell, Nottinghamshire, NG25 0QF
   Tel: (01636) 817 000. Fax: (01636) 815 404. Email: enquiries.lbs@ntu.ac.uk

DEBTS:
- Ave debt per year: £5,012
- Access fund: £1,013,556

As well as the Access fund there are opportunity bursaries, Learning and Skills Council Learner Support Funds, hardship loans and TTA bursaries.

Banks on campus: HSBC

ACCOMMODATION:
- Cost of living index: £
- Insurance premium: ££

In college:
- Catered: 0%
- Self-catering: 10%
- First years living in: 42.8%
- Cost: £58 (39wks)

Nottingham:
- Ave rent: £38-50

EMPLOYMENT: • Unemployed after 6mths: 3.2%
Paid work: Job bureau on campus.

Careers: The careers service employs a shed-load of people itself and has bulletin boards, library and advice.

TRAVEL: see <u>Nottingham University</u>
Nottingham station's a mile from the City site, buses cost between 50-80p (or a quid return) from the City Centre to Clifton, with several companies running regular services. There's also an inter-campus bus service which covers late-night antics and a new tram service running between the University, the station and elsewhere.

ENTERTAINMENTS: • <u>Booze index: £2.43</u>
Nottingham: see <u>Nottingham University</u>
University: • <u>Pint of beer: £1.50</u> • <u>Glass of wine: £1.45</u>

UNUSUAL COSTS: £5 annual fee for sports facilities, plus additional small charges.

OPEN UNIVERSITY

The Open University, Walton Hall, Milton Keynes, MK7 6AA
Tel: (01908) 653231. Fax: (01908) 655072.
E-mail: general-enquiries@open.ac.uk. Website: www.open.ac.uk
Open University Students' Association, PO Box 397, Walton Hall, Milton Keynes, MK7 6BE
Tel: (01908) 652026. Fax: (01908) 654326. E-mail: ousa@open.ac.uk
Website: www.open.ac.uk/ousa

DEBTS: • <u>Access fund: £13,000,000</u> • <u>Successful applications/yr: 21,351</u>
• <u>Ave payment: £640</u>
The average access fund payment would cover the cost of almost 1$\frac{1}{2}$ 60-point OU modules (an honours degree requires 360 points). OUSET hands out assistance and looks at cases on individual merit. There are £500/yr loans available for students on benefits or low incomes and a hardship fund (average payment £290) for help with course and living costs. Last year 1,800 students benefitted.

FEES: A BA/BSc degree costs about £4,400. *Compared to the cost of a degree in a conventional university, it's starting to look like pretty good value, especially if it's your boss that's forking out.*

EMPLOYMENT: Most OU students already have jobs, but the university lays on workshops, newsletters and bulletin boards *to keep employer-hunters' options open.*

OXFORD UNIVERSITY

University of Oxford, University Offices, Wellington Square, Oxford, OX1 2JD
Tel: (01865) 288000. Fax: (01865) 270708
E-mail: undergraduate.admissions@admin.ox.ac.uk. Website: www.ox.ac.uk
Oxford University Student Union, Thomas Hull House, New Inn Hall Street, Oxford, OX1 2DH
Tel: (01865) 288450. Fax: (01865) 288453. E-mail: enquiries@ousu.org
Website: www.ousu.org

DEBTS: • <u>Ave debt per year: £3,356</u>
• <u>Access fund: £1,500,000</u> • <u>Ave payment: £100-3,000</u>
Bursaries available to anyone who's exempt from paying tuition fees. The University pays £1,000 in the 1st year and £500 for each year afterwards.

FEES: Oxford's keeping tight-lipped over the dreaded top up fees. *That shouldn't fool anyone – if anyone charges them, it'll be Oxbridge.*

ACCOMMODATION: • <u>Cost of living index: £££££</u> • <u>Insurance premium: £</u>
In college: • <u>Catered: 87%</u>
• <u>First years living in: 100%</u>
Oxford: • <u>Ave rent: £55</u>

EMPLOYMENT: • <u>Unemployed after 6mths: 7%</u>
Paid work: Students are banned from working during term-time (*not that most of them would be able to find time*). That's not to say that no-one does and Oxford has *plenty* of shops and bars around to take students on. The Careers Service has a vacation employment service and a wide range of jobs and internships are available.
Careers: *Forget any romantic notions of being headhunted straight out of Oxford into the City, the BBC or the Foreign Office.* Oxford grads have to *scrap it out with the rabble* nowadays. So it's a *good job* the careers service has vacancy lists, careers library, talks and counselling.

TRAVEL:
Oxford Station to London (£11.20), Bristol (£17.80) and so on. *Cheap* coaches go to London 24/7. Several local bus companies with *frequent and cheap services* (40p to get as far as digs in Jericho), but not really worth it for shorter trips. *Taxis are pricey, bikes are cheap. Go figure which is more popular.*

ENTERTAINMENTS: • <u>Booze index: £1.53</u>
Oxford: • <u>Pint of beer: £2.50</u> • <u>Glass of wine: £2.60</u>
• <u>Can of Red Bull: £2.50</u>
University: • <u>Pint of beer: £1.20</u> • <u>Glass of wine: £1.20</u>

OXFORD BROOKES UNIVERSITY
(1) Oxford Brookes University, Headington Campus, Oxford, OX3 0BP
Tel: (01865) 484848. Fax: (01865) 483616. E-mail: query@brookes.ac.uk
Website: www.brookes.ac.uk
Oxford Brookes University Students Union, Helena Kennedy Student Centre,
Headington Hill Campus, Oxford, OX3 0BP
Tel: (01865) 484750. Fax: (01865) 484799. E-mail: obsu@brookes.ac.uk
Website: www.thesu.com
(2) Harcourt Hill Campus, Oxford, OX2 9AT
(3) Wheatley Campus, Wheatley, Oxford, OX33 1HX

7

DEBTS: • <u>Ave debt per year: £3,003</u>
• <u>Access fund: £255,000</u> • <u>Successful applications/yr: 445</u>
John Henry Brookes bursary scheme is a limited fund to provide bursaries for hardship cases.

FEES: Nothing official on top up fees, *although the vice-chancellor signed an advertisement in* The Guardian *supporting them and it's an open secret that Brookes will charge fees at the highest amount.*

ACCOMMODATION: • <u>Cost of living index: £££</u> • <u>Insurance premium: £</u>
In college: • <u>Catered: 11%</u> • Cost: £74 (42wks)
• <u>Self-catering: 29%</u> • Cost: £57 (42wks)
Oxford: • <u>Ave rent: £75</u>

EMPLOYMENT: • <u>Unemployed after 6mths: 3%</u>
Paid work: The SU runs a jobshop with specialist staff filling over 1,500 vacancies a year. Unlike their <u>Oxford University</u> counterparts, Brookes students are allowed to take part-time jobs and lots of them do.
Careers: The careers service provides bulletin boards, job fairs, library and interview training.

TRAVEL: see <u>Oxford University</u>

Local: OBSU's late night minibus runs from 9pm-3am anywhere within the ringroad for a £1 donation. A University bus runs around the various sites. A pass costs £150 and is automatically included in halls fees. Some students are *less than overjoyed* at this, particularly those in the halls right next to the campus.

ENTERTAINMENTS:	• Booze index: £2.42	
Oxford:	• Pint of beer: £2.50	• Glass of wine: £2.60
		• Can of Red Bull: £2.50
University:	• Pint of beer: £1.80	• Glass of wine: £2
		• Can of Red Bull: £2

PAISLEY UNIVERSITY
• **Formerly Paisley College**

(1) University of Paisley, Paisley, PA1 2BE
Tel: (0141) 848 3000. Fax: (0141) 848 3333
E-mail: uni-direct@paisley.ac.uk. Website: www.paisley.ac.uk
Paisley University Students Association, Paisley Campus Union, Storie Street, Paisley, PA1 2HB
Tel: (0141) 849 4157. Fax: (0141) 848 3333. Website: www.upsa.org.uk
(2) University Campus, Ayr, Beech Grove, Ayr, KA8 0SR. Tel: 01387 702060
University of Paisley Student's Association. Tel: (0141) 849 4169
(3) Crichton University Campus, University of Paisley, Crichton University Campus, Maxwell House, Dumfries, DG1 4UQ

DEBTS:	• Ave debt per year: £1,846	
	• Access fund: £185,000	• Successful applications/yr: 627
	• Ave payment: £100-2,500	

Loans (but not grants) from the access fund available in as little as 48 hours. There's help (from £1,000-2,000) with childcare and housing from a total Mature Students Bursary Fund of £399,000. The welfare service provides bursaries and support from a hardship fund (£10,000) to those who wouldn't get other help and can refer students to a host of external trusts and scholarships.
Banks on campus: Royal Bank of Scotland cashpoint

ACCOMMODATION:	• Cost of living index: ££££ • Insurance premium: £	
In college:	• Catered: 0%	
	• Self-catering: 10%	• Cost: £45
	• First years living in: 35%	
Paisley:	• Ave rent: £55	

EMPLOYMENT: • Unemployed after 6mths: 9.5%

TRAVEL:
Trains: Regular direct train services to Glasgow (£2.60 return), London (£50.80) and elsewhere. Scottish Citylink coaches go nationwide via Glasgow (London, £27; Glasgow, £1.70).
Local: *Buses for easy short hops:* at 85p, a single fare to Glasgow is cheaper than the train and good till 3am.

ENTERTAINMENTS:	• Booze index: £1.91	
Paisley:	• Pint of beer: £2	• Glass of wine: £2.30
		• Can of Red Bull: £1.50
University:	• Pint of beer: £1.80	• Glass of wine: £1.50
		• Can of Red Bull: £1.50

SCHOOL OF PHARMACY, UNIVERSITY OF LONDON

• **The College is part of <u>London University</u> and students are entitled to use its facilities.**

The School of Pharmacy, University of London, 29-39 Brunswick Square, London, WC1N 1AX
Tel: (020) 7753 5831. Fax: (020) 7753 5829. E-mail: registry@ulsop.ac.uk
Website: www.ulsop.ac.uk
The School of Pharmacy Student's Union, 29-39 Brunswick Square, London, WC1N 1AX
Tel: (020) 7753 5809. E-mail: student.union@lisa.ulsop.ac.uk

DEBTS:
- Ave debt per year: £3,405
- Access fund: £42,000 • Successful applications/yr: 70
- Ave payment: £100-1,000

ACCOMMODATION: • Cost of living index: ££££ • Insurance premium: ££
In college:
- Catered: 13% • Cost: £105-110 (30wks)
- First years living in: 50%
London, locally: • Ave rent: £120 • Living at home: 50%

EMPLOYMENT: • Unemployed after 6mths: 1%
Paid work: Students are expected to take work placements in the holidays.
Careers: The careers service is threadbare, but as the only subject taught is pharmacy, all students have a good idea what they want to do anyway and can do it.

ENTERTAINMENTS: • Booze index: £1.94
London: • Pint of beer: £2.30 • Glass of wine: £2
• Can of Red Bull: £2.25
University: • Pint of beer: £1.00 • Glass of wine: £1.50
• Can of Red Bull: £1.10

UNUSUAL COSTS: Postgrads pay 'bench fees' on top of the £2,940 basic rate.

PLYMOUTH UNIVERSITY

7

(1) University of Plymouth, Drake Circus, Plymouth, PL4 8AA
Tel: (01752) 232 232. Fax: (01752) 233 984
E-mail: prospectus@plymouth.ac.uk. Website: www.plymouth.ac.uk
University of Plymouth Students' Union, University of Plymouth, Drake Circus, PL4 8AA
Tel: (01752) 663 337. Fax: (01752) 251 669
E-mail: presplymouth@plymouth.ac.uk. Website: www.upsuonline.co.uk
(2) University of Plymouth, Faculty of Arts & Education (Exeter Campus), Earl Richards Road North, Exeter, EX2 6AS. Tel: (01392) 475 010
(3) University of Plymouth, Faculty of Arts & Education (Exmouth Campus), Douglas Avenue, Exmouth, EX8 2AT. Tel: (01395) 355 522

DEBTS:
- Ave debt per year: £6,077
- Access fund: £1.2m • Successful applications/yr: 1,300
- Ave payment: £300-700
Mature students have a better chance of scooping large sums from the access fund. Some small loans and start-up awards for non-stereotypical students.
Banks on campus: HSBC

ACCOMMODATION: • Cost of living index: £££££ • Insurance premium: £
In college:
- Self-catering: 8% • Cost: £60-125 (39wks)
- First years living in: 35%
Plymouth: • Ave rent: £48-55

EMPLOYMENT: • Unemployed after 6mths: 7.6%
Apart from the usual bar work and all that, a few tourist and maritime-based jobs.

SU's employment register can be *fruitful* as can Plymouth Careers Service for long-term prospects.

TRAVEL:
National: Plymouth's (5mins away) to London, Bristol, etc. Most stop at Exeter (on the same line). National Express and Western National coaches from Plymouth's Bretonside Bus Station (10mins) to London and beyond.
Local: Bus from the popular student area of Mutley to the city centre (£1.10).

ENTERTAINMENTS: • <u>Booze index: £2.47</u>
Plymouth: • <u>Pint of beer: £2.10</u>   • <u>Glass of wine: £1.45</u>
University: • <u>Pint of beer: £1.45</u>   • <u>Glass of wine: £1.15</u>

UNIVERSITY OF PORTSMOUTH

University of Portsmouth, University House, Winston Churchill Avenue, PO1 2UP
Tel: (02392) 848484. Fax: (02392) 843082. E-mail: admissions@port.ac.uk
Website: www.port.ac.uk
University of Portsmouth Students' Union, The Student Centre, Cambridge Road, PO1 2EF
Tel: (02392) 843640. Fax: (02392) 843667. Website: www.upsu.net

DEBTS: • <u>Ave debt per year: £6,077</u>
  • <u>Access fund: £830,668</u>   • <u>Successful applications/yr: 1,114</u>
The Union's Student Finance Centre dishes out advice, while the University doles out the occasional bursary cash-bucket.
Banks on campus: ATMs on campus

FEES: International students pay between £6,940 and £8,050 depending on their course. Postgrads pay £2,940. The University isn't keen on top up fees and is concentrating on improving access to grants for students.

ACCOMMODATION: • <u>Cost of living index: ££££</u> • <u>Insurance premium: £</u>
In college: • <u>Catered: 5%</u>   • <u>Cost: £100 (36wks)</u>
  • <u>Self-catering: 18%</u>   • <u>Cost: £87 (36wks)</u>
  • <u>First years living in: 80%</u>
Portsmouth: • <u>Ave rent: £55-70</u>

EMPLOYMENT: • <u>Unemployed after 6mths: 4%</u>
Paid work: The job shop in the Union does its bit to help cash-hunters and with all the bars, ferries, shops and tourists, chances of finding work are above average.
Careers: The *electronically stonky* careers service offers loads of online resources. *Luddites might be more comfy with* the one-on-one discussion sessions, CV surgeries, job fairs and the careers library.

TRAVEL:
National: Portsmouth & Southsea station to London Waterloo, Southampton and Liverpool, among others. National Express coach station is a mile from Guildhall. *Plentiful Portsmouth parking provision*, but use of University spaces (around 850 at each site) costs £25 a year. Regular ferries to the Isle of Wight, Spain and France (St Malo, Cherbourg, Caen, Le Havre) and the Isle of Wight hovercraft.
Local: Buses and local trains are *reliable* (around £2) *but most distances are walkable*. A free student shuttle bus service runs between Langstone Halls and Guildhall between 7.30am and 11pm.

ENTERTAINMENTS: • <u>Booze index: £2.33</u>
Portsmouth: • <u>Pint of beer: £2</u>
  • <u>Glass of wine: £3.50</u>
  • <u>Can of Red Bull: £2</u>
University: • <u>Pint of beer: £1.60</u>
  • <u>Glass of wine: £2</u>
  • <u>Can of Red Bull: £1.50</u>

UNUSUAL COSTS: Membership of the sports centre costs £97 a year. Gym use is £3 a session.

....

QUEEN MARGARET UNIVERSITY COLLEGE
(1) Queen Margaret University College, Corstorphine Campus, Edinburgh, EH12 8TS
Tel: 0131 317 3000. Fax: 0131 317 3248
E-mail: admissions@qmuc.ac.uk. Website: www.qmuc.ac.uk
Queen Margaret Student Association, Clerwood Terrace, Edinburgh, EH12 8TS
Tel: 0131 317 3401. Fax: 0131 317 3402
E-mail: union@qmuc.ac.uk
(2) Leith Campus, Duke Street, Leith, Edinburgh, EH6 8HF. Tel: (0131) 317 3353
(3) The Gateway, Gateway Theatre, Leith Walk, Edinburgh. Tel: (0131) 317 3900

DEBTS: • Ave debt per year: £1,953
• Access fund: £124,000 • Successful applications/yr: 180
The College has £16,000 to hand out each year in hardship loans as well as
£86,372 for hardship grants and £71,873 worth of mature students' bursaries.

ACCOMMODATION: • Cost of living index: £ • Insurance premium: £
In college: • Catered: 6% • Cost: £67 (31wks)
• Self-catering: 14% • Cost: £42-51 (38wks)
Edinburgh: • Ave rent: £55

EMPLOYMENT: • Unemployed after 6mths: 4%
As well as careers, the Jobshop helps students find part-time or vacation work and
vocational employment related to their degree (*good amount* of these jobs around
Edinburgh Festival time, but that's during the summer break).

TRAVEL: see Edinburgh University

ENTERTAINMENTS: • Booze index: £2.09
Edinburgh: • Pint of beer: £2.50 • Glass of wine: £2.30
• Can of Red Bull: £2
University: • Pint of beer: £1.70 • Glass of wine: £1.40
• Can of Red Bull: £1

7

....

QUEEN MARY, UNIVERSITY OF LONDON
• **The College is part of London University and students are entitled to use
its facilities.**
(1) Queen Mary, University of London, Mile End Road, London, E1 4NS
Tel: (020) 7882 5555. Fax: (020) 7882 5556. E-mail: admissions@qmul.ac.uk
Website: www.qmul.ac.uk
Queen Mary Students' Union, Mile End Site, 432 Bancroft Road, London,
E1 4DH
Tel: (020) 7882 7670. Fax: (020) 8981 0802. E-mail: su-genoff@qmul.ac.uk
Website: www.qmsu.org
(2) Barts & the London School of Medicine & Dentistry, Turner Street, London
E1 2AD
Tel: (020) 7377 7611. Fax: (020) 7377 7612
E-mail: medicaladmissions@qmul.ac.uk
Barts & the London Students' Association, Stepney Way, London E1 2JJ
Tel: (020) 7377 7640. Fax: (020) 7377 7641.
E-mail: president@bartslondon.com. Website: www.bartslondon.com/assoc

DEBTS: • Ave debt per year: £2,390
• Access fund: £260,0000 • Successful applications/yr: 641
Undergraduate bursaries of £1,500pa *for a lucky few*.

ACCOMMODATION: • Cost of living index: £££££ • Insurance premium: ££
In college: • Self-catering: 100% • Cost: £79-106 (38wks)
• First years living in: 35%
London: see London University

EMPLOYMENT: • Unemployed after 6mths: 17%
• Paid work: term-time 35%: hols 50%
Paid work: QMSU and the College run jobshops advertising opportunities for students. There's a part-time work website, notice boards and workshops.
Careers: The Careers Service (5 staff) provides a library, interview training, bulletin boards and job fairs.

TRAVEL: see London University
Local: Several buses and the tube from Mile End (Central, District, Jubilee, Hammersmith & City lines) and Stepney Green (District, Hammersmith & City lines, peak times only). Whitechapel (District, East London Line, Hammersmith & City) for the London Hospital, St Paul's or Barbican for Bart's.

ENTERTAINMENTS: • Booze index: £2.20
London: • Pint of beer: £2.40 • Glass of wine: £2.60
• Can of Red Bull: £2.25
University: • Pint of beer: £1.70 • Glass of wine: £2
• Can of Red Bull: £1.60

....

QUEEN'S UNIVERSITY OF BELFAST

(1) The Queen's University of Belfast, University Road, Belfast, BT7 1PE
Tel: (028) 9024 5133. Fax: (028) 9024 7895
E-mail: comms.office@qub.ac.uk. Website: www.qub.ac.uk
Queen's University of Belfast Students' Union, University Road, Belfast, BT7 1PE
Tel: (028) 9027 3106. Fax: (028) 9023 6900. Website: www.qubsu.org
(2) Queen's University Armagh, 39 Abbey Street, Armagh, BT61 7EB
Tel: (028) 3751 0678. Fax: (028) 3751 0679. E-mail: qua@qub.ac.uk
Website: www.armagh.qub.ac.uk

DEBTS: • Ave debt per year: £1,111
• Access fund: £762,250 • Successful applications/yr: 901
Various scholarships including the Guinness sports bursaries.
Banks on campus: Bank of Ireland.

ACCOMMODATION: • Cost of living index: ££££ • Insurance premium: £
In college: • Catered: 7% • Cost: £54-62 (32wks)
• Self-catering: 13% • Cost: £39-50 (50wks)
Belfast: • Ave rent: £35-40

EMPLOYMENT: • Unemployed after 6mths: 3.5%
Paid work: 250 bar jobs at the university every year. Plenty of part-time work in town. 10-week work placements are a part of many courses and the careers service can also set students up with companies for part time work, work experience, a year out etc.
Careers: A mixture of full-time staff and student assistants offer advice, services and work placements.

TRAVEL:
National: All of Ireland's main cities and towns, north and south, are just a train journey away, including Derry (£7.20) and Coleraine. A *nippy* train service, the Enterprise (boldly going where it went yesterday), does Dublin for £21. Translink coaches serve most destinations throughout Ireland, but a direct coach from Britain is difficult to catch (what with the Irish Sea and all). National Express runs a service to London (£60). Ferry services to Stranraer, Holyhead and Liverpool and a fast Sea Cat service.
Local: Frequent buses provide a 10-min journey into the city centre for around 50p.

ENTERTAINMENTS: • Booze index: £1.57
Belfast: • Pint of beer: £1.80   • Glass of wine: £1.80
University: • Pint of beer: £1.50   • Glass of wine: £2
                                          • Can of Red Bull: £1

UNIVERSITY OF READING

(1) University of Reading, Whiteknights, PO Box 217, Reading, RG6 6AH
  Tel: (0118) 378 6586. Fax: (0118) 378 8924
  E-mail: schools.liaison@reading.ac.uk. Website: www.reading.ac.uk
  University of Reading Students' Union, Whiteknights, University of Reading,
  PO Box 230, Reading, RG6 6AZ
  Tel: (0118) 986 0222. Fax: (0118) 975 5283. E-mail: rusu@rusu.co.uk
  Website: www.rusu.co.uk
(2) Bulmershe Campus, Bulmershe Court, Early, RG6 1HY. Tel: (0118) 987 5123

DEBTS: • Ave debt per year: £2,694
          • Access fund: £400,000   • Successful applications/yr: 600
          • Ave payment: £100-3,500
Food Science scholarships and chemistry bursaries. Other small academic bursaries
for freshers include an English book award for A level work and three full
scholarships for International Baccalaureate holders.
Banks on campus: Lloyds TSB

ACCOMMODATION: • Cost of living index: £££   • Insurance premium: £
In college: • Catered: 70%   • Cost: £78-£119 (30wks)
                • Self-catering: 30%   • Cost: £48-£85 (30/39wks)
                • First years living in: 96%
Reading: • Ave rent: £65

EMPLOYMENT: • Unemployed after 6mths: 5%
Paid work: Jobshop only advertises vacancies of more than 16hrs a week. Many
students find work in local shops.
Careers: With 20 staff, this is a hefty careers service.

TRAVEL:
National: Trains direct to London, Oxford and the west. National Express leads
magical mystery (*guess how late the bus will arrive*) tours all over and Heathrow is
45 mins away by coach.
Local: Buses connect town to campus, £1 each way. There's a free college night
bus too.

ENTERTAINMENTS: • Booze index: £2.39
Reading: • Pint of beer: £2.60   • Glass of wine: £2.50
                                        • Can of Red Bull: £2.50
University: • Pint of beer: £1.50   • Glass of wine: £1.50
                                        • Can of Red Bull: £2.50

ROBERT GORDON UNIVERSITY

The Robert Gordon University, Schoolhill, Aberdeen, AB10 1FR
Tel: (01224) 262 728. Fax: (01224) 262 728. E-mail: admissions@rgu.ac.uk
Website: www.rgu.ac.uk
The Robert Gordon University Student Association, 60 Schoolhill, Aberdeen,
AB10 1JQ
Tel: (01224) 262 262. Fax: (01224) 262 268. E-mail: rgusa@rgu.ac.uk
Website: www.rgunion.co.uk

DEBTS: • Ave debt per year: £1,510
Hardship/mature student funds, bursaries, disabled students allowance,
dependant's grant.

ACCOMMODATION: • Cost of living index: £ • Insurance premium: £
In college: • Self-catering: 15% • Cost: £64-75
Aberdeen: • Ave rent: £65

EMPLOYMENT: • Unemployed after 6mths: 1.8%
Paid work: Job Bureau on hand to get students working.
Careers: 6 staff at the careers service.

TRAVEL: see Aberdeen University
A free shuttle bus runs between the Garthdee and City Centre sites every 15 mins *when it runs on time*.

ENTERTAINMENTS: • Booze index: £1.76
Aberdeen: see University of Aberdeen
University: • Pint of beer: £1.50 • Glass of wine: £1

ROYAL ACADEMY OF MUSIC
• **The College is part of <u>London University</u> and students are entitled to use its facilities.**
Royal Academy of Music, Marylebone Road, London, NW1 5HT
Tel: (020) 7873 7373. Fax: (020) 7873 7374. E-mail: registry@ram.ac.uk
Website: www.ram.ac.uk
Royal Academy of Music Students Union, Marylebone Road, London, NW1 5HT
Tel: (020) 7837 7337. Fax: (020) 7873 7334

DEBTS: • Ave debt per year: £3,613
• Access fund: £37,000 • Successful applications/yr: 47
• Ave payment: £1,000
A *whopping* 250 different bursaries to be seized, ranging from £20 to £10,000.
Banks on campus: ATM on campus

ACCOMMODATION: • Cost of living index: ££££ • Insurance premium: ££
In college: • Self-catering: 0% • First years living in: 10%
London: • Ave rent: £100 • Living at home: 2%

EMPLOYMENT: • Unemployed after 6mths: 4%
• Paid work: term-time 75%: hols 90%
Paid work: The Woodhouse Centre offers paid performance opportunities. There's also regular opera and concert stewarding and occasional admin work to be fought over.
Careers: RAM has the Career Surgery (a job-centre for the musical), tutor advice, newsletters and support for graduates, including fellowships for the promising. Many go on to be freelance musicians, which *means work varying from none to world-famous*.

TRAVEL: see London University

ENTERTAINMENTS: • Booze index: £2.11
London: • Pint of beer: £2 • Glass of wine: £2.50
• Can of Red Bull: £2
University: • Pint of beer: £1.80 • Glass of wine: £1.60
• Can of Red Bull: £1.40

ROYAL AGRICULTURAL COLLEGE
Royal Agricultural College, Stroud Road, Cirencester, Gloucestershire, GL7 6JS
Tel: (01285) 652531. Fax: (01285) 650219. E-mail: admissions@rac.ac.uk
Website: www.royagcol.ac.uk
RAC Students' Union, Cirencester, Gloucestershire, GL7 6JS
Tel: (01285) 652531. Website: www.royagcol.ac.uk/document/union.htm

DEBTS:
- Ave debt per year: £3,113
- Access fund: £90,000   • Successful applications/yr: 40

£40,000 available in hardship fund/scholarships. Sports Scholarships and Outstanding Achiever Scholarships (for students who've attained academic excellence or who have overcome hardship such as handicap or deprivation) are available. Also student bursaries and hardship awards.

ACCOMMODATION: • Cost of living index: ££££ • Insurance premium: £
In college: • Catered: 260   • Cost: £70-£150 (30wks)
   • First years living in: 95%
Nearest town (Cirencester):   • Ave rent: £60   • Living at home: 10%

EMPLOYMENT: • Unemployed after 6mths: 8%
   • Paid work: term-time 20%; hols 30%
Paid work: *Very difficult* to find work during term-time but during holidays there's always lambing and harvesting.
Careers: The Careers Service do all the usual stuff in terms of advice etc., but an extra advantage for RAC students is that they can put you in touch with the old boy (and occasional girl) network scattered around the globe. There's also a networking organisation in the college called 'The 100 Club' which puts students in touch with the big names of agribusiness.

TRAVEL:
National: From London it's £16.15 by train from Paddington to nearby Kemble station or £17.25 to Cirencester by coach from Victoria. From Cheltenham it's £8.85 return on the train and from Bristol it's £9 return.
Local: Local transport is limited, you can get a cab from Kemble Station to the campus but that's an extortionate £9 for a 3-mile journey. Or they will let you park your helicopter in front of the main building if you ask nicely (no really, they will).

ENTERTAINMENTS: • Booze index: £1.90
Cirencester: • Pint of beer: £2   • Glass of wine: £2.40
   • Can of Red Bull: £1.40
University: • Pint of beer: £2   • Glass of wine: £2
   • Can of Red Bull: £1.50

7

ROYAL COLLEGE OF MUSIC
• **The College is part of <u>London University</u> and students are entitled to use its facilities.**
Royal College of Music, Prince Consort Road, London, SW7 2BS
Tel: (020) 7589 3643. Fax: (020) 7589 7740. E-mail: info@rcm.ac.uk
Website: www.rcm.ac.uk
The Students Association, Royal College of Music, Prince Consort Road, London, SW7 2BS
Tel: (020) 7589 3643. E-mail: aredpath@rcm.ac.uk

DEBTS:
- Ave debt per year: £1,757
- Access fund: £30,000   • Successful applications/yr: 48
- Ave payment: £150-£2,000

Scholarships, study support grants, instrument loan fund, hardship money available ranging from £150 to £1,500. *On the whole, quite a soft cushion relatively.*

ACCOMMODATION: • Cost of living index: £   • Insurance premium: ££
In college: • Self-catering: 66%   • Cost: £50-87 (47wks)
   • First years living in: 66%
London: • Ave rent: £70-150

EMPLOYMENT: • Unemployed after 6mths: 1.8%
   • Paid work: term-time 80%: hols 80%
Paid work: The Woodhouse Centre finds paid performances, stewarding and admin

work as well as teaching spotty school-kids to play musical instruments.
Careers: The Woodhouse Centre does the funky advice/newsletter/bulletin board thang, teaches Alexander Technique and arranges visits and even lessons from key figures in the profession.

TRAVEL: see <u>London University</u>

ENTERTAINMENTS: • <u>Booze index: £1.43</u>
London: see <u>London University</u>
University: • <u>Pint of beer: £1.80</u>
• <u>Glass of wine: £1.60</u>
• <u>Can of Red Bull: £1.40</u>

ROYAL HOLLOWAY, LONDON
• **The College is part of <u>London University</u> and students are entitled to use its facilities.**
(1) Royal Holloway, Egham Hill, Egham, Surrey, TW20 8BL
  Tel: (01784) 477 003. Fax: (01784) 477 003. E-mail: Liaison-office@rhul.ac.uk
  Website: www.rhul.ac.uk
  Royal Holloway Students' Union, Egham Hill, Egham, Surrey, TW20 0EX
  Tel: (01784) 443 979. Fax: (01784) 471 381
(2) Bedford Square, 2 Gower Street, London. Tel: (020) 7307 8600

DEBTS: • Ave debt per year: £5,800
• <u>Access fund: £217,344</u>
• <u>Successful applications/yr: 335</u>
• Ave payment: £630
There are a few bursaries on offer *for the crème de la crème*. Bedford Entrance Scholarships give £1,000 and guaranteed accommodation to *the cleverest undergrads*. Bioscience Entrance Scholarships dish up *the same goodies* to students of that subject. Choral, Organ and Instrumental Scholarships give guaranteed accommodation and between £100-£300 to the musically gifted. Sporty students who compete at national or international level may get up to £750, guaranteed accommodation, discounted physio and free access to local sports centres under the Student Talented Athlete Recognition Scheme (STARS). Separate scholarships are available for international students, particularly those from India.
Banks on campus: NatWest

FEES: International undergrads have to stump up between £7,975 and £11,750 a year.

ACCOMMODATION: • <u>Cost of living index: £</u>
• <u>Insurance premium: £</u>
In college: • <u>Catered: 15%</u>
• <u>Cost: £60-85 (30-38wks)</u>
• <u>Self-catering: 20%</u>
• <u>Cost: £60-85 (30-50wks)</u>
• <u>First years living in: 51%</u>
London: • Ave rent: £55-70

EMPLOYMENT: • <u>Unemployed after 6mths: 6%</u>
Paid work: *Plenty* of job opportunities on campus or locally *for those in need of an extra bob or two*. The College and the SU provide vacancy boards and there's a job file and 2 members of staff *to make job-hunting that bit easier*.
Careers: Services run by <u>London University</u>.

TRAVEL:
Local: Trains to Waterloo from Egham every 15mins. Buses are *infrequent and expensive*, but there's a College service to the station every 15mins or so and an SU bus late at night. *A car is obviously handier than at other London sites but parking's tricky on campus*

ENTERTAINMENTS: • <u>Booze index: £1.68</u>
London: • <u>Pint of beer: £1.80</u>
• <u>Glass of wine: £2.30</u>
• <u>Can of Red Bull: £1.55</u>

University: • Pint of beer: £1.70   • Glass of wine: £1.20
                                        • Can of Red Bull: £1

ROYAL SCOTTISH ACADEMY OF MUSIC AND DRAMA
The Royal Scottish Academy of Music and Drama, 100 Renfrew Street, Glasgow,
G2 3DB
Tel: (0141) 332 4101. Fax: (0141) 332 8901. E-mail: registry@rsamd.ac.uk
Website: www.rsamd.ac.uk
RSAMD Students Union, 100 Renfrew Street, Glasgow, G2 3DB
Tel: (0141) 270 8296. Fax: (0141) 270 8371
Email: supresident@rsamd.ac.uk. Website: www.rsamd-su.org.uk

DEBTS: • Ave debt per year: £2,199
Some bursaries are available for new students and married students over 25 can
be eligible for a Mature Student's Bursary, mainly for childcare. Entrance
scholarships ranging from £100-£1,000 are awarded on the basis of admittance
auditions. Plus loads of other awards and scholarships, most of them aimed at
promoting exceptional talent.

FEES: Costs vary widely, depending on the size of the course's practical element,
but international undergrad fees start at £9,975.

ACCOMMODATION: • Cost of living index: ££   • Insurance premium: ££
In college: • Self-catering: 68%   • Cost: £72 (35-50wks)
                  • First years living in: 80%
Glasgow: • Ave rent: £55   • Living at home: 25%

EMPLOYMENT: • Unemployed after 6mths: 3%
Paid work: *Despite hectic schedules, most students work during and out of term.*
The Union keeps notice boards of vacancies, mainly relating to the arts, but with
the odd wallet-top-up job in sales or call centres. Ushering work is available in the
Academy.
Careers: Students have the option of using Glasgow University's careers resources
but most don't need to. RSAMD receives regular visits from professionals (from the
BBC, Scottish Symphony Orchestra etc), who offer advice on performance, business
planning and self-promotion. Students get practical help with career management,
including assistance with CVs, headshot photos and auditions, graduate mentors
and a yearly job fair and careers day.

TRAVEL: see University of Glasgow
Bus routes 40, 41 and 61 are handy for halls. Fares around £1.15.

ENTERTAINMENTS: • Booze index: £2.11
Glasgow: see University of Glasgow
University: • Pint of beer: £1.80   • Glass of wine: £2
                                          • Can of Red Bull: £1.50

ROYAL VETERINARY COLLEGE
• **The College is part of London University and students are entitled to use
its facilities.**
(1) The Royal Veterinary College, Royal College Street, London, NW1 OTU
    Tel: (020) 7468 5000. Fax: (020) 7388 2342. E-mail: registry@rvc.ac.uk
    Website: www.rvc.ac.uk
(2) Hawkshead, Hawkshead Lane, North Mimms, Hatfield, Herts, AL9 7TA
    Tel: (01707) 652090
    Royal Veterinary College Students' Union Society, Hawkshead Campus,
    Hawkshead Lane, North Mimms, Hatfield, Herts, AL9 7TA
    Tel: (01707) 666310. Fax: (01707) 652090

FINANCE: Hardship funds available. Prizes for excellence are awarded on merit.
Fees: International undergrads pay nearly £15,000 for courses.

ACCOMMODATION: • Cost of living index: ££   • Insurance premium: ££
In college: • Catered: 75%   • Cost: £82 (50wks)
    • First years living in: 63%
London: • Ave rent: £95   • Living at home: 5%

EMPLOYMENT: • Unemployed after 6mths: 3%
Students are expected to spend time on animal placements (e.g. lambing) so there
isn't much time for other work.

TRAVEL: see London University
Hawkshead: see University of Hertfordshire

ENTERTAINMENTS: • Booze index: £1.51
London: see London University
University: • Pint of beer: £1.30

··

SALFORD UNIVERSITY
The University of Salford, The Crescent, Salford, Greater Manchester, M5 4WT
Tel: (0161) 295 5000. Fax: (0161) 295 5999
E-mail: course-enquiries@salford.ac.uk Website: www.salford.ac.uk

DEBTS: • Ave debt per year: £3,545
Banks on campus: Various ATMs

ACCOMMODATION: • Cost of living index: ££   • Insurance premium: ££££
In college: • Catered: 3000+   • Cost: £82-93 (33wks)
    • Self-catering: 1777   • Cost: £46-58 (39-50wks)
Salford/Manchester: • Ave rent: £40-55

EMPLOYMENT: • Unemployed after 6mths: 5%
Careers: The careers service provides help for graduates starting their own
business as well as placements with local industry and part-time work for current
students.

TRAVEL: see Manchester University

ENTERTAINMENTS: • Booze index: £1.94
Salford: • Pint of beer: £2.20
    • Glass of wine: £2.40
    • Can of Red Bull: £2
University: • Pint of beer: £1.35
    • Glass of wine: £2
    • Can of Red Bull: £1.65

UNUSUAL COSTS: Access to a whole range of sports facilities costs £95 a year.

··

UNIVERSITY OF SHEFFIELD
University of Sheffield, 8 Palmerston Road, Sheffield, S10 2TE
Tel: (0114) 222 8031. Fax: (0114) 273 9826. E-mail: study@sheffield.ac.uk
Website: www.shef.ac.uk
The University of Sheffield Union of Students, Western Bank, Sheffield, S10 2TG
Tel: (0114) 222 8500. Fax: (0114) 275 2506. E-mail: union@sheffield.ac.uk
Website: www.sheffieldunion.com

DEBTS: • Ave debt per year: £3,433
    • Access fund: £730,287   • Successful applications/yr: 1,031
Some bursaries/hardship funds and support to cover childcare.
Banks on campus: Co-op, NatWest.

7

In the back

FEES: Postgrads' research degrees are charged at £2,940. International fees vary considerably (£7,650-£18,800) depending on the course. There are no plans to charge top ups yet, *but it's likely to be the full Monty when they do hit.*

ACCOMMODATION: • Cost of living index: £££££ • Insurance premium: £
In college: • Catered: 6%   • Cost: £79-114 (30-37wks)
              • Self-catering: 12%   • Cost: £58-77
              • First years living in: 96%
Sheffield: • Ave rent: £48

EMPLOYMENT: • Unemployed after 6mths: 4.6%
Paid work: Potential in bars and shops on campus and in town. Also some departmental envelope-stuffing type daywork and the OpUS section of the Careers Service acts as a job shop for voluntary, vacation and part-time vacancies.
Careers: The *extensive* service includes a careers library, interview training, job fairs, employer presentations and graduate workshops. The Student Directions website is *stuffed with helpful advice and job-hunting aids.* OpUS is a subdivision that focuses on finding work experience opportunities and promotes work-based learning in academic departments.

TRAVEL:
National: Sheffield Station, less than a mile from the University, offers services to London (£32.55), Birmingham (£18.60), Edinburgh (£47.15) and more. The Sheffield Interchange, also less than a mile, runs National Express and Stagecoach Express services (London £16.50). University parking involves a permit (£78.60), not generally available to undergrads.
Local: Local buses run all day and night and are *frequent, reliable and quite cheap. Local minibuses are even better because they go everywhere. The Supertram is best of all, though, 'cause it's fun and cheap* (£1.90 all-day pass, Megarider 7-day pass £6.30) and the University is on the Yellow Line. The SU provides the Union Safety Bus for women (runs at night till 2.15am, SU to halls, £1).

ENTERTAINMENTS: • Booze index: £2.30
Sheffield: • Pint of beer: £1.75   • Glass of wine: £1.85
University: • Pint of beer: £1.69   • Glass of wine: £1.89

7

....
SHEFFIELD HALLAM UNIVERSITY
Sheffield Hallam University, City Campus, Howard Street, Sheffield, S1 1WB
Tel: 0114 225 5555. Fax: 0114 225 3398. E-mail: enquiries@shu.ac.uk
Website: www.shu.ac.uk
Sheffield Hallam University Union of Students, Nelson Mandela Building, City Campus, Sheffield, S1 2BW
Tel: 0114 255 411. Fax: 0114 255 4140. E-mail: hallam-union@shu.ac.uk

DEBTS: • Ave debt per year: £2,829
          • Access fund: £1.25m   • Successful applications/yr: 1,691
Hillsborough Trust memorial bursaries, international prize, scholarships and hardship funds. Also a loan of £50 cash or food vouchers is available in extreme emergencies to be repaid as soon as possible.
Banks on campus: Nationwide

ACCOMMODATION: • Cost of living index: £££££ • Insurance premium: £
In college: • Catered cost: £74-77 (39wks)
              • Self-catering cost: £51-58 (39wks)
              • First years living in: 80%
Sheffield: • Ave rent: £40

EMPLOYMENT: • Unemployed after 6mths: 11%   • Paid work: term-time 62%
Paid work: Network job fairs circulate CVs around prospective employers.
Careers: 13 full-time staff try to hawk students out of college and into jobs.

TRAVEL: see <u>University of Sheffield</u>
Local: Public transport links make getting around the uni a *doddle*. Sheffield Station stop on the Super tram goes into centre of the city campus.

ENTERTAINMENTS: • <u>Booze index: £2.41</u>
Sheffield: see <u>University of Sheffield</u>
University: • <u>Pint of beer: £1.70</u>   • <u>Glass of wine: £1.95</u>
                                                        • <u>Can of Red Bull: £1</u>

UNUSUAL COSTS: For £40-110 a year students have access to some or all of the University's *excellent* sporting facilities. Non-members can pay as they go.

SOAS (SCHOOL OF ORIENTAL & AFRICAN STUDIES)
• **The College is part of <u>London University</u> and students are entitled to use its facilities.**
(1) School of Oriental & African Studies, Thornhaugh Street, Russell Square, London, WC1H 0XG
Tel: (020) 7898 4038. Fax: (020) 7898 4039. E-mail: study@soas.ac.uk
Website: www.soas.ac.uk
School of Oriental & African Studies SU, Thornhaugh Street, Russell Square, London, WC1H 0XG
Tel: (020) 7637 2388. Fax: (020) 7637 2388. E-mail: study@soas.ac.uk
Website: www.soasunion.org
(2) Vernon Square Campus, Vernon Square, Penton Rise, WC1X 9EL
Tel: (020) 7637 2388

DEBTS: • <u>Ave debt per year: £2,444</u>
            • <u>Access fund: £141,000</u>   • <u>Successful applications/yr: 181</u>
            • <u>Ave payment: £6,000</u>
There are a number of funds, such as the hardship fund for EU/Overseas students, and bursaries, such as from the Zoroastrian Studies Fund.

FEES: Full-time fees for international students are £9,500.

ACCOMMODATION: • <u>Cost of living index: ££££</u> • <u>Insurance premium: ££</u>
In college: • <u>Self-catering: 25%</u>   • <u>Cost: £95-108 (30-50wks)</u>
London: • <u>Ave rent: £81</u>

EMPLOYMENT: • <u>Unemployed after 6mths: 3.1%</u>
                • <u>Paid work: term-time 25%: hols 50%</u>
Paid work: Students use <u>London University</u>'s facilities. *In any case, London's a fiesta of part-time work opportunities.*
Careers: SOAS's 'Grad Club' is run by <u>London University</u>'s Careers Service. It has a careers library, bulletin boards, interview training and weekly seminars.

ENTERTAINMENTS: • <u>Booze index: £1.91</u>
London: • <u>Pint of beer: £1.60</u>   • <u>Glass of wine: £1.50</u>
University: • <u>Pint of beer: £1.80</u>

SOUTHAMPTON INSTITUTE
Southampton Institute, East Park Terrace, Southampton, SO14 0YN
Tel: (023) 8031 9039. Fax: (023) 8033 4161. E-mail: enquiries@solent.ac.uk
Website: www.solent.ac.uk
Southampton Institute Students' Union, Students Union Building, East Park Terrace, SO14 0YN
Tel: (023) 8023 2154. Fax: (023) 8023 5248. E-mail: suadmin@solent.ac.uk
Website: www.sisuonline.co.uk

DEBTS:
- Ave debt per year: £5,667
- Access fund: £566,763 • Successful applications/yr: 850
- Ave payment: £100-3,500

Opportunity bursaries, bridging loans, emergency loans, part-time fee waivers, postgrad bursaries and start-up bursaries. Also scholarships for business, media, arts and society students (£1,000 a year). Sports scholarships help with equipment, training etc.
Banks on campus: Barclays/NatWest ATMs

ACCOMMODATION: • Cost of living index: ££££ • Insurance premium: £
In college:
- Self-catering: 29% • Cost: £44-85 (39-46wks)
- First years living in: 60%

Southampton: • Ave rent: £45-75

EMPLOYMENT: • Unemployed after 6mths: 7.8%
- Paid work: term-time 65%: hols 75%

Paid work: The SU street team employs students to do promos for the Union. The Jobshop e-mails and advertises vacancies to students.
Careers: Lots of vocational subjects and 9 staff trying to get students into work.

TRAVEL: see Southampton University
Local: A coach service run by the Institute connects the main campus with Warsash.

ENTERTAINMENTS: • Booze index: £2.07
Southampton: • Pint of beer: £2.20
- Glass of wine: £2.50
- Can of Red Bull: £2

University: • Pint of beer: £1.65
- Glass of wine: £1.75
- Can of Red Bull: £1.50

UNIVERSITY OF SOUTHAMPTON
(1) University of Southampton, Highfield Campus, Southampton, SO17 1BJ
Tel: (02380) 595 000. Fax: (02380) 593 037. E-mail: prospenq@soton.ac.uk
Website: www.soton.ac.uk
Southampton University Students' Union, University of Southampton, Highfield, Southampton, SO17 1BJ
Tel: (02380) 595 233. Fax: (02380) 595 252. E-mail: susu@soton.ac.uk
Website: www.susu.org
(2) University of Southampton, Boldrewood Campus, Biomedical Sciences Building, Bassett Crescent East, SO16 7PX
(3) University of Southampton, Avenue Campus, Highfield Road, Southampton, SO17 1BJ
(4) Southampton Oceanography Centre, University of Southampton, Waterfront Campus, European Way, SO14 3ZH. Tel: (02380) 596 666
(5) Southampton General Hospital, Tremona Road, SO16 6YD
Tel: (02380) 777 222
(6) Winchester School of Art, Park Avenue, SO23 8DL. Tel: (02380) 596 900
Winchester School of Art Students' Union, Park Avenue, SO23 8DL
Tel: (01962) 840 772

DEBTS:
- Ave debt per year: £4,360
- Access fund: £672,000 • Successful applications/yr: 1,458

In addition to the access fund, the University runs a hardship fund for people whose circumstances change mid-course. SUSU also gives short-term emergency loans.
Banks on campus: Barclays, HSBC, Lloyds, NatWest banks/ATMs

ACCOMMODATION: • Cost of living index: ££££ • Insurance premium: £
In college:
- Catered: 4% • Cost: £81-120 (32wks)
- Self-catering: 31% • Cost: £50-103 (35-51wks)
- First years living in: 85%

Southampton: • Ave rent: £50-60

EMPLOYMENT: • Unemployed after 6mths: 8%
               • Paid work: term-time 60%; hols 70%
Paid work: As well as the *usual gamut* of bar and shop slog, students can *rake in the cash* at the boat show in the summer. The job shop's Openings service matches students to taskmasters.
Careers: Careers service does fairs, vacancy lists, psychometric tests, etc.

TRAVEL:
National: Trains to London (£15.45), Bristol (£19.80), Manchester (£38.60) and others. Coaches to London (£9.50), Manchester (£26.50) and all points beyond.
Local: Buses are *cheap and reliable, but infrequent*. Local trains are *regular* with connections all over Hampshire and 7 stations around the city, but it's *not the cheapest or most practical way of getting around*. Bikes are *best* on a budget.

ENTERTAINMENTS: • Booze index: £1.97
Southampton: • Pint of beer: £2.20   • Glass of wine: £2.10
                                       • Can of Red Bull: £2.40
University: • Pint of beer: £1.80   • Glass of wine: £1.20
                                       • Can of Red Bull: £1.50

UNUSUAL COSTS: A SportRec card (£45) gives year-long sporting access.

UNIVERSITY OF ST ANDREWS

University of St Andrews, Education Liaison Office, Admissions Reception, Butts Wynd, St Andrews, Fife, KY16 9AJ
Tel: (01334) 462245. Fax: (01334) 463330. E-mail: ed-liason@st-andrews.ac.uk
Website: www.st-andrews.ac.uk
The University of St Andrews Students' Association, St Mary's Place, St Andrews, Fife, KY16 9UZ
Tel: (01334) 462700. Fax: (01334) 462740. E-mail: union@st-andrews.ac.uk
Website: www.yourunion.net

DEBTS: • Ave debt per year: £2,681
         • Access fund: £180,000   • Successful applications/yr: 522
         • Ave payment: £350-£500
In addition to the access fund, bursaries and scholarships, the university can provide interest-free loans in extreme cases through the Director of Student Support Services. Mature students have a stab at special bursaries and there's an emergency grant or two for internationals.
Banks on campus: RboS, HboS, Clydesdale, Lloyds TSB

FEES: International undergrads are looking at upwards of £9,000 in fees. UK or EU postgrads need to cough up around £2,940.

ACCOMMODATION: • Cost of living index: ££   • Insurance premium: £
In college: • Catered: 26%   • Cost: £49-117 (31-50wks)
         • Self-catering: 18%   • Cost: £29-75 (36-50wks)
         • First years living in: 100%
St Andrews: • Ave rent: £77   • Living at home: 7%

EMPLOYMENT: • Unemployed after 6mths: 5%
Paid work: The university job bureau advertises local vacancies – *mainly involving gimping for golfers (caddying) and other tourist-related hotel and bar work*.
Careers: Fully kitted-out careers centre provides a regular newsletter and has a bundle of resources accessible online.

TRAVEL:
National: Leuchars station (5 miles from the main group of the University buildings)

direct to London (£53.45), Dundee and Edinburgh. Otherwise change at Edinburgh or Dundee. National Express coaches run from Dundee, 13 miles away, see Dundee University.
Local: *Infrequent buses, specially at night, but quite cheap* (£1.40). *In general, St Andrews is small enough for legs, either walking or cycling.* The university runs a late night minibus on Friday nights.

ENTERTAINMENTS: • Booze index: £1.93
St Andrews: • Pint of beer: £2.20
                                   • Glass of wine: £2.50
                                   • Can of Red Bull: £2
University: • Pint of beer: £1.50
                                   • Glass of wine: £2
                                   • Can of Red Bull: £1.70

UNUSUAL COSTS: There's a small charge per use of sports facilities.

··

ST GEORGE'S HOSPITAL MEDICAL SCHOOL, LONDON
• **The College is part of London University and students are entitled to use its facilities.**
St George's Hospital Medical School, University of London, Cranmer Terrace, Tooting, London, SW17 0RE
Tel: (020) 8672 9944. Fax: (020) 8725 2734. E-mail: medicine@sghms.ac.uk
Website: www.sghms.ac.uk
The School Club, St Georges Hospital Medical School, Cranmer Terrace, Tooting, London, SW17 0RE
Tel: (20) 8725 5201. Fax: (020) 8767 0841. E-mail: stuuni@sghms.ac.uk
Website: www.students.sghms.ac.uk

DEBTS: • Ave debt per year: £4,753
             • Access fund: £90,000   • Successful applications/yr: 51
             • Ave payment: £1,500
Bursaries and scholarships available, some from the NHS, plus a fistful of prizes and awards.
Banks on campus: NatWest

FEES: International students can expect £10,825 in fees. *Things are looking bad for home students too*, with plans to charge the top whack top up fees despite mass student protest.

ACCOMMODATION: • Cost of living index: ££££ • Insurance premium: £
In college: • Catered: 1.4%
                               • Cost: £97 (39wks)
             • Self-catering: 12%
                               • Cost: £59 (40wks)
             • First years living in: 50%
                               • Others living in: 13%
London: • Ave rent: £65-100

EMPLOYMENT: • Unemployed after 6mths: 5%
                 • Paid work: term-time 33%: hols 50%
Being a vocational institution, a careers service *is largely unnecessary,* although facilities are accessible at London University. A med school employee is on hand for vocational advice. Medicos don't usually have time for part-time work.

TRAVEL: see London University
Tooting Broadway tube (Northern Line) and the many buses are the main way of getting around, but Tooting also has a train station. Car: Outside the Congestion Charging Zone, but very limited parking on or around campus. Most students live within 10mins of the hospital, so bikes *are particularly popular.*

ENTERTAINMENTS: • Booze index: £2.41
London: • Pint of beer: £2.66
                               • Glass of wine: £2.70
                               • Can of Red Bull: £2.60

7

University: • Pint of beer: £1.55   • Glass of wine: £1.50
                                             • Can of Red Bull: £1.25

STAFFORDSHIRE UNIVERSITY
(1) Staffordshire University, College Road, Stoke-on-Trent, ST4 2DE
Tel: (01782) 294000. Fax: (01782) 745422. E-mail: admissions@staffs.ac.uk
Website: www.staffs.ac.uk
Staffordshire University Students Union, Staffordshire University, College Road,
Stoke-on-Trent, ST4 2DE
Tel: (01782) 294629. Fax: (01782) 295736. E-mail: theunion@staffs.ac.uk
(2) Staffordshire University, Beaconside Campus, Stafford, ST18 0AD
Tel: (01785) 353253
Staffordshire University Students Union, Beaconside Campus, Stafford,
ST18 0AD. Tel: (01785) 353311

DEBTS: • Ave debt per year: £3,898
           • Access fund: £75,000   • Successful applications/yr: 1,385
           • Ave payment: £634
Up to 30 Ashley scholarships are awarded to local applicants who face particular
difficult circumstances (financial, social or physical). Also hardship loans.
Banks on campus: Lloyds TSB; NatWest; Co-op.

FEES: The University is likely to charge full top up fees.

ACCOMMODATION: • Cost of living index: ££   • Insurance premium: £
In college: • Self-catering: 15%   • Cost: £51-64 (38wks)
                 • First years living in: 100%
Stoke-on-Trent: • Ave rent: £37-43   • Living at home: 15%

EMPLOYMENT: • Unemployed after 6mths: 14.7%
Paid work: Bar and shop work available in both towns. The workbank *helps
students find it.*
Careers: The careers service is there to help out - *but judging from the graduate
unemployment rate, they could do better.*

TRAVEL:
National: Trains on the Manchester-Mersey line go through both Stafford and
Stoke, as do National Express coaches to most of the country.
Local: *Cheap* local buses and free inter-campus university buses. *Taxis don't cost a
fortune, but bikes are even less.*

ENTERTAINMENTS: • Booze index: £1.42
Stoke-on-Trent: • Pint of beer: £1.80   • Glass of wine: £2.75
                                 • Can of Red Bull: £2.50
University: • Pint of beer: £1.45   • Glass of wine: £1.80
                                 • Can of Red Bull: £1.50

UNUSUAL COSTS: *Top* sports facilities, but they cost £90 a year to use.

STIRLING UNIVERSITY
(1) University of Stirling, FK9 4LA
Tel: 01786 467046. Fax: 01786 446800. E-mail: recruitment@stir.ac.uk
Website: www.stir.ac.uk
Stirling University Students Association, The Robbins Centre, University of
Stirling, Stirling, FK9 4LA
Tel: 01686 467166. Fax: 01786 467190. E-mail: susa-president@stir.ac.uk
Website: www.susaonline.org.uk
(2) Highland Campus, University of Stirling, Department of Nursing and Midwifery,
Highland Campus, Old Perth Road, Inverness, IV2 3SG
(3) Western Isles Campus, University of Stirling, Department of Nursing and Midwifery,
Western Isles Hospital, Macaulay Road, Stornaway, Isle of Lewis, HS1 2AF

7

In the back

DEBTS:
- Ave debt per year: £1,990
- Access fund: £139,900
- Ave payment: £200-500
- Successful applications/yr: 370

The University distributes hardship loans or non-repayable bursaries to students who have received their full loan but are still finding it difficult to make ends meet. These are administered by SISS (the Student Information and Support Service) which also provides financial advice. Certain students may also be eligible for the Lone Parent Grant or the Disabled Students Grant. There are a wide range of University scholarships for international, local and UK/EU students.
Banks on campus: Royal Bank of Scotland

FEES: No fees payable for Scottish and EU full-time students not from the UK. Non-Scottish UK full-time undergraduate degrees £1,150. International full-time undergraduates: £7,660 classroom-based; £9,500 lab-based.

ACCOMMODATION:
- Cost of living index: £
- Insurance premium: £

In college:
- Self-catering: 47%
- Cost: £53-68 (30-50wks)

Nearest town (Stirling):
- Ave rent: £50+
- Living at home: 30%

EMPLOYMENT:
- Unemployed after 6mths: 5.3%
- Paid work: term-time 40%; hols 90%

Paid work: Students work in both the Library and the Robbins Centre bars. Plenty of pubs and restaurants in nearby Bridge of Allan employ students. Jobs in Stirling are limited, but during vacations, try Glasgow and Edinburgh, a train journey away. The University Job Shop is a useful resource with all the latest vacancies.
Careers: The Careers Advisory Service has a careers library, newsletter and bulletin boards and provides guidance interviews with careers advisors, CV and application form assistance, practice aptitude tests covering verbal, numerical and diagrammatic reasoning, and an Insight into Management Course (a prestigious 4-day course which gives students the opportunity to discover what a career in management is really like).

TRAVEL:
Stirling Station, 2 miles from campus, has half-hourly direct services to London (£93.50) and the main cities in Scotland, including Glasgow (£8.30) and Edinburgh (£9.40) in under an hour. National Express runs services to all the major cities in Scotland and the UK. Ferguson Coaches go from campus to Stirling train station. It's 1hr 20mins to Glasgow International Airport and 45mins to Edinburgh's for budget operators such as easyJet and Britannia Direct.
Local: First Buses operate between campus and the town centre (75p-£1.20). Taxis are easy to find (£2.50-3 from town to campus; late-night trip back £5). Bikes increasingly popular on campus.

ENTERTAINMENTS:
- Booze index: £1.42

Stirling:
- Pint of beer: £1.50
- Glass of wine: £1.80
- Can of Red Bull: £1.20

University:
- Pint of beer: £1.50
- Glass of wine: £1.10
- Can of Red Bull: £1.50

UNIVERSITY OF STRATHCLYDE
(1) University of Strathclyde, 16 Richmond Street, Glasgow, G1 1XQ
Tel: (0141) 552 4400. Fax: (0141) 552 5860. E-mail: scls@mis.strath.ac.uk
Website: www.strath.ac.uk
University of Strathclyde Students' Association, 90 John Street, Glasgow, G1 1JH
Tel: (0141) 567 5000. Fax: (0141) 567 5050
E-mail: admin@theunion.strath.ac.uk. Website: www.strathstudents.com
(2) Jordanhill Campus, University of Strathclyde, 76 Southbrae Drive, Glasgow, G13 1PP
University of Strathclyde Students Association, Jordanhill Campus, 76 Southbrae Drive, Glasgow, G13 1PP. Tel: (0141) 950 3256

DEBTS:
- Ave debt per year: £3,372
- Access fund: £8,000
- Ave payment: £400
- Successful applications/yr: 1,000

Sports bursaries of up to £1,000 from the University (with Glasgow City Council). The Royal & Ancient Golf Club awards £1,500 bursaries to rising golf stars. The Mature Students' Bursary fund helps with childcare costs. Also other hardship funds and short-term loans available.

Banks on campus: NatWest.

ACCOMMODATION:
- Cost of living index: £££
- Insurance premium: £

In college:
- Catered: 3%
- Self-catering: 9%
- Cost: £51 (37-50wks)
- Cost: £47-73 (37wks)

Glasgow:
- Ave rent: £55

EMPLOYMENT: • Unemployed after 6mths: 3%

A Government Charter mark for the past 5 years is quite a recommendation of the careers service. It also has a database of part-time and vacation opportunities. There are several jobs going in the University doing bar work and the like. The Union keeps its own vacancy board.

TRAVEL: see University of Glasgow

Strathclyde is 5mins walk from Queen Street Station and 10mins from Central Station. The University shuttle bus links John Anderson Campus and Jordanhill 8 times a day till 5pm.

ENTERTAINMENTS: • Booze index: £1.99

Glasgow: see University of Glasgow

University:
- Pint of beer: £1.50
- Glass of wine: £1.25
- Can of Red Bull: £1.50

UNUSUAL COSTS: One-off £20 payment for sports membership.

SUNDERLAND UNIVERSITY

(1) The University of Sunderland, Edinburgh Building, Chester Road, Sunderland, SR1 3SD
Tel: (0191) 515 2000. E-mail: student-helpline@sunderland.ac.uk
Website: www.sunderland.ac.uk
University of Sunderland Students' Union, Wearmouth Hall, Chester Road, Sunderland, SR1 3SD
Tel: (0191) 514 5512. Fax: (0191) 515 2441
Website: www.sunderlandsu.ac.uk

(2) St. Peters Campus, Chester Road, Sunderland, SR6 0DD
Students' Union, Wearbank House, Charles Street, Sunderland, SR6 0AN
Tel: (0191) 515 3583. Fax: (0191) 515 2499

DEBTS: • Ave debt per year: £3,215

ACCOMMODATION:
- Cost of living index: ££
- Insurance premium: £££££

In college:
- Self-catering: n/a%
- First years living in: 35%
- Cost: £41.72-44.20 (50wks)

Sunderland:
- Ave rent: £40
- Living at home: 51%

EMPLOYMENT: • Unemployed after 6mths: 6%

Paid work: The Union bars all employ students but the local area isn't a job hotbed. Jobshop/careers centre is run by 5 full- and 2 part-time staffers, who'll help with part time work, cv-boosting voluntary stuff and graduate employment

TRAVEL:
Sunderland station (10mins walk from Chester Road) direct to Newcastle, Middlesbrough (£3.95) and London (£47.50). Metro Link in Newcastle runs to

Sunderland (and back again) taking in Gateshead (£4). Several stops around Sunderland itself including a designated 'University Park' stop. Blueline and National Express coaches to London (£25.50) and Manchester (£17.50). Local buses are *cheap* (from 20p) *and quite reliable*. A free campus bus service runs between all key University buildings and halls of residence. Sunderland is small, so taxi fares are pretty cheap.

ENTERTAINMENTS:	• Booze index: £1.89	
Sunderland:	• Pint of beer: £2.10	• Glass of wine: £2
		• Can of Red Bull: £1.80
University:	• Pint of beer: £1.80	• Glass of wine: £1.60
		• Can of Red Bull: £1.50

SURREY INSTITUTE OF ART & DESIGN

(1) The Surrey Institute of Art & Design, University College, Farnham Campus, Falkner Road, Farnham, Surrey, GU9 7DS
Tel: (01252) 722441. Fax: (01252) 892616. E-mail: registry@surrart.ac.uk
Website: www.surrart.ac.uk
Students' Union, Farnham Campus, Falkner Road, Farnham, Surrey, GU9 7DS
Tel: (01252) 710263. Fax: (01252) 713591. E-mail: su@surrart.ac.uk
(2) The Surrey Institute of Art & Design University College, Epsom Campus, Ashley Road, Epsom, Surrey, KT18 5BE
SIAD Students' Union, Epsom Campus, Ashley Road, Epsom, Surrey, KT18 5BE

DEBTS:
• Ave debt per year: £3,668
• Access fund: £144,000   • Successful applications/yr: 366
Hardship Loans of up to £500 for students in trouble and part-timers under 55. The Institute offers a small number of bursaries and research studentships for postgrads, to be used as a contribution to fees.

ACCOMMODATION: • Cost of living index: ££££ • Insurance premium: £
In college: • Self-catering: 24%   • Cost: £37-82 (38wks)
• First years living in: 70% (Farnham) 32% (Epsom)
Farnham: • Ave rent: £75-90

EMPLOYMENT: • Unemployed after 6mths: 15%
Paid work: The jobshop has a noticeboard it updates regularly. *Supermarket, pub and bar work are the best bets.* The Institute also employs students as cleaners and security staff and SU takes them on for bar work.
Careers: Staff and services are split equally between sites.

TRAVEL:
National: Farnham station is just under a mile from the College, on the line to London (£6.65) and Guildford. Epsom station is 5 mins walk from the Institute site – a return trip to London costs a *mere* £3.05. Coach services to London (£8.50), Birmingham (£20.75) and Manchester (£27.50) and Heathrow/Gatwick *within spitting distance*.
Local: *Regular* buses in Farnham and Epsom and *a bikers' paradise*.

ENTERTAINMENTS:	• Booze index: £1.92	
Farnham:	• Pint of beer: £2.10	• Glass of wine: £1.80
		• Can of Red Bull: £2
University:	• Pint of beer: £1.55	• Glass of wine: £1.20
		• Can of Red Bull: £1.60

7

SURREY UNIVERSITY

University of Surrey, Guildford, Surrey, GU2 7XH
Tel: (01483) 300800. Fax: (01483) 300803. E-mail: information@surrey.ac.uk
Website: www.surrey.ac.uk
University of Surrey Students' Union, Union House, University of Surrey, Guildford, Surrey, GU2 7XH
Tel: (01483) 689223. Fax: (01483) 534749. E-mail: comms@ussu.co.uk
Website: www.ussu.co.uk

DEBTS:
- Ave debt per year: £2,665
- Access fund: £233,850 • Successful applications/yr: 715
- Ave payment: £1000 is available for undergraduates and mature students.

Banks on campus: NatWest plus an ATM for Barclays.

FEES: The University supports fees, saying the new system will allow them to increase participation from 'traditionally excluded groups' by offering scholarships and bursaries.

ACCOMMODATION: • Cost of living index: ££££ • Insurance premium: £
In college:
- Self-catering: 40% • Cost: £39.20-77.35 (28-53wks)
- First years living in: 80%

Guildford: • Ave rent: £62

EMPLOYMENT: • Unemployed after 6mths: 2.3%
There's a job bureau for paid work and the University has links with various local stores (Tesco, Debenham's, House Of Fraser). There's plenty of bar work in the area.

TRAVEL:
National: Guildford is on the main London (Waterloo) to Portsmouth line, £5.55 single. Coaches from London (Victoria) are £8.50 return.
Local: Buses from the Friary Bus Station to the campus (50p or £100 Travelcard for a year, £50 for 3 months – £400 without student discount).

ENTERTAINMENTS: • Booze index: £1.94
Guildford:
- Pint of beer: £1.89 • Glass of wine: £1.85
- Can of Red Bull: £1.45

University:
- Pint of beer: £1.80 • Glass of wine: £3
- Can of Red Bull: £2

UNUSUAL COSTS: For £70 a year students can use all of the University's *extensive* sports facilities.

UNIVERSITY OF SUSSEX

University of Sussex, Sussex House, Falmer, BN1 9RH
Tel: (01273) 678 416. Fax: (01273) 678 545
E-mail: ug.admissions@sussex.ac.uk. Website: www.sussex.ac.uk
University of Sussex Students' Union, Falmer House, Falmer, BN1 9RH
Tel: (01273) 678 152. E-mail: ussu-coms@sussex.ac.uk. Website: www.ussu.info

DEBTS:
- Ave debt per year: £1,806
- Access fund: £455,000 • Successful applications/yr: 877
- Ave payment: £200-3,000

Sports bursaries, 10 postgrad bursaries of £2,000 and a hardship fund.
Banks on campus: Barclays, HSBC.

ACCOMMODATION: • Cost of living index: ££££ • Insurance premium: £
In college:
- Self-catering: 35% • Cost: £44-76 (31-42wks)
- First years living in: 95%

Brighton: • Ave rent: £60

EMPLOYMENT: • Unemployed after 6mths: 5%
                • Paid work: term-time 40%: hols 70%
The Careers Development & Employment Centre dredges through the local employment scene and points students in the direction of part-time or vacation work. It also hosts career workshops, interview training, job fairs and employer presentations.

TRAVEL: *see* University of Brighton
Falmer station is 200m from the campus (Brighton, £1.50). Car parks around campus, but not enough space for everyone. Permits cost £300 a year or £1 a day. Weekly bus passes cost £10.

ENTERTAINMENTS: • Booze index: £2.37
Brighton: see University of Brighton
University: • Pint of beer: £1.90   • Glass of wine: £2
                                   • Can of Red Bull: £1.30

UNUSUAL COSTS: £18.50 for annual membership of the 2 sports centres.

SWANSEA, UNIVERSITY OF WALES
• **The College is part of the University of Wales.**
University of Wales, Swansea, Singleton Park, Swansea, SA2 8PP
Tel: (01792) 205 678. Fax: (01792) 295 157
E-mail: admissions@swansea.ac.uk Website: www.swansea.ac.uk
Swansea Students' Union, Singleton Park, Swansea, SA2 8PP
Tel: (01792) 295 466. Fax: (01792) 206 029
E-mail: president@swansea-union.co.uk. Website: www.swansea-union.co.uk

DEBTS: • Ave debt per year: £1,523
           • Access fund: £201,339   • Successful applications/yr: 882
Scholarships worth £1,000 a year and bursaries worth £350 a year are offered to students outstanding in sport or the arts. Awards of £1,000 are available to cover the cost of tuition fees for students with disabilities, special needs, those of outstanding academic ability and mature students.
Banks on campus: Several ATMs

7

FEES: The Welsh Assembly has ruled out top up fees before 2007.

ACCOMMODATION: • Cost of living index: £   • Insurance premium: £
In college: • Catered: 8%   • Cost: £63-77 (31wks)
           • Self-catering: 19%   • Cost: £44-65 (40-51wks)
           • First years living in: 97%
Swansea: • Ave rent: £42

EMPLOYMENT: • Unemployed after 6mths: 8%
                • Paid work: term-time 60%: hols 80%
Worklink's services include: duty careers advice sessions; specialist follow-up sessions; CV and application workshops; skills workshops; psychometric testing workshops; employer talks programme; careers fair; 6 jobs and placements advisers. There's also a *well-organised and friendly* jobshop for part-time money-spinning.

TRAVEL:
National: Direct trains from Swansea station, 3 miles from campus, to Cardiff (£9.05) and London (£23.70), book at least a week early to avoid the price doubling. Coach services to London (£22.75), Cardiff (£5.50), Manchester (£27.50).
Local: Free taxi phone on campus for students with flammable cash. *Not as expensive as in some towns. Bikes are a better choice* between campus and town. *The local hills and scenery are gorgeous* in the right weather and *full of bikeable* trails.

ENTERTAINMENTS: • <u>Booze index: £1.49</u>
Swansea: • <u>Pint of beer: £1.95</u>   • <u>Glass of wine: £1.20</u>
                                            • <u>Can of Red Bull: £1.75</u>
University: • <u>Pint of beer: £1.40</u>   • <u>Glass of wine: £1.20</u>

UNUSUAL COSTS: £3 a year *pittance* for sports amenities.

UNIVERSITY OF TEESSIDE
University of Teesside, Middlesbrough, Tees Valley, TS1 3BA
Tel: (01642) 218121. Fax: (01642) 342067. E-mail: recruit@tees.ac.uk
Website: www.tees.ac.uk
University of Teesside Students' Union, Middlesbrough, TS1 3BA
Tel: (01642) 342234. Fax: (01642) 342241. E-mail: enquiry@utsu.org.uk
Website: www.utsu.org.uk

DEBTS: • <u>Ave debt per year: £3,938</u>
          • <u>Access fund: £650,000</u>   • <u>Successful applications/yr: 1,150</u>
          • <u>Ave payment: £100-3,500</u>
Bursaries are available to cover a range of circumstances, including short-term
emergency loans.

ACCOMMODATION: • <u>Cost of living index: £££</u> • <u>Insurance premium: £££££</u>
In college: • <u>Head tenancy: 9%</u>   • <u>Cost: £32-36 (37wks)</u>
                • <u>Self-catering: 12%</u>   • <u>Cost: £31-35 (38wks)</u>
Middlesbrough: • <u>Ave rent: £35</u>

EMPLOYMENT: • <u>Unemployed after 6mths: 7.8%</u>
Paid work: The Student Job Centre helps students find part-time work and the SU
employs more than 150 students every year.
Careers: The careers service *ticks all the right boxes.*

TRAVEL:
National: Middlesbrough station direct to Newcastle (£5.15), Manchester
(£18.15) and other major interchanges. For London (£42.25) change at
Darlington. Coach services by Blue Line, City Link, Swiftline and National Express to
London (£21), Manchester (£11.75), etc.
Local: Buses are *cheap* (50p max) and fairly *regular* (until 11pm). Trains run
regularly all over the Teesside conurbation.

ENTERTAINMENTS: • <u>Booze index: £1.84</u>
Middlesbrough: • <u>Pint of beer: £2.05</u>   • <u>Glass of wine: £2</u>
                                                    • <u>Can of Red Bull: £1.60</u>
University: • <u>Pint of beer: £1.70</u>   • <u>Glass of wine: £1.45</u>
                                                • <u>Can of Red Bull: £1.50</u>

UNUSUAL COSTS: £40 buys an 'all-in' sports ticket for Teesside's *excellent*
facilities.

THAMES VALLEY UNIVERSITY
(1) Thames Valley University, St Mary's Road, Ealing, London, W5 5RF
    Tel: (0800) 036 8888. Fax: (020) 8566 1353
    E-mail: learning.advice@tvu.ac.uk. Website: www.tvu.ac.uk
    Thames Valley Students Union, Thames Valley University, St. Mary's Road,
    Ealing, London, W5 5RF
    Tel: (020) 8231 2573. E-mail: student.services@tvu.ac.uk
    Website: www.tvu.ac.uk/student-services
(2) Thames Valley University, Wellington Street, Slough, Berkshire, SL1 1YG
    Tel: (01753) 534 585
(3) Thames Valley University, King's Road, Reading, Berkshire, RG1 4HJ
    Tel: (0118) 967 5000

7

In the back

DEBTS:
- Ave debt per year: £5,009
- Access fund: £1,000,000   • Successful applications/yr: 596
- Ave payment: £100-£3,500

Various trusts and charitable donations can be had and scholarships are available through the faculties (aka academic departments).

ACCOMMODATION: • Cost of living index: ££   • Insurance premium: £
In college: • First years living in: %   • Others living in: %
Reading: • Ave rent: £85

EMPLOYMENT: • Unemployed after 6mths: 9%
• Paid work: term-time 96%: hols 97%

Paid work: The Job Bureau hands out various opportunities including bar work, marketing, IT support, office admin, retail, translation, marketing and charity work.
Careers: A *well-stocked* careers service, with career planning and management, appointments, workshops, student-employer meetings and employer presentations.

TRAVEL: see London University
Local: Tube stations at Ealing Broadway, Ealing Common and South Ealing. Also lots of local bus services and limited parking at £5 a day.

ENTERTAINMENTS: • Booze index: £2.05
London: • Pint of beer: £2.40
• Glass of wine: £2.50
• Can of Red Bull: £2
University: • Pint of beer: £2.40
• Glass of wine: £1.75
• Can of Red Bull: £2

UNUSUAL COSTS: £20 a year to use the *less than ideal* sports facilities.

UNIVERSITY OF ULSTER

(1) University of Ulster, Cromore Road, Coleraine, Co Londonderry, BT52 1SA
Tel: 08 700 400 700. Fax: (028) 7034 0947. E-mail: online@ulster.ac.uk
Website: www.ulster.ac.uk
Students' Union, University of Ulster, Cromore Rd, Coleraine, BT52 1SA
Tel: (028) 7032 4319. Fax: (028) 7033 24915. Website: www.uusu.org
(2) The University of Ulster, Jordanstown, Shore Road, Newtonabbey, Co Antrim, BT37 0QB. Tel: (028) 9036 5131. Fax: (028) 9036 2817
(3) The University of Ulster, York Street, Belfast, BT15 1ED. Tel: (028) 9032 8515
(4) The University of Ulster, Magee College, Northland Road, Londonderry, BT48 7JL
Tel: (028) 7137 1371

7

DEBTS:
- Ave debt per year: £528
- Access fund: £1,045,500   • Successful applications/yr: 2,070
- Ave payment: £100-3,500

Financial help is available through the hardship fund, endowment awards, disabled student allowance and sports bursaries.

ACCOMMODATION: • Cost of living index: £   • Insurance premium: £
In college: • Catered: 69%   • Cost: £35-61 (37wks)
• Self-catering: 9%   • Cost: £38-45 (37-50wks)
• First years living in: 65%
Coleraine: • Ave rent: £40-60   • Living at home: 35%

EMPLOYMENT: • Unemployed after 6mths: 9%
Paid work: The SU employs around 100 people throughout the year. There's plenty of part-time/vacation work to be had in local bars, cafes and other tourist traps.
Careers: The Jordanstown, Coleraine and Magee sites all have their own services. Coleraine's looks after students up to 2 years after graduation.

TRAVEL:
National: Direct trains from Coleraine to Belfast and (London)Derry and from Belfast to Dublin. Coachwise, Goldline Express and Ulsterbus link Belfast, (London)Derry and Coleraine. Flights to Belfast have come down, pricewise, thanks to the budget airlines.
Local: *Comprehensive and expensive local buses,* but half-price for students around Coleraine. Ulsterbus does an all day rambler ticket for a fiver.
Sites: *It's rare to have to travel between the sites, rarer still because of a video conferencing facility.*

ENTERTAINMENTS: • Booze index: £1.36
Coleraine: • Pint of beer: £1.80 • Glass of wine: £2.20
• Can of Red Bull: £1.20
University: • Pint of beer: £1.50 • Glass of wine: £1.20
• Can of Red Bull: 80p

UNIVERSITY COLLEGE, LONDON

• **The College is part of <u>London University</u> and students are entitled to use its facilities.**
University College London, Gower Street, London, WC1E 6BT
Tel: (020) 7679 3000. Fax: (020) 7383 3937. E-mail: degree-info@ucl.ac.uk
Website: www.ucl.ac.uk
University College London Union, 25 Gordon Street, London, WC1H 0AY
Tel: (020) 7387 3611. Fax: (020) 7387 3937. E-mail: uclu-personnel@ucl.ac.uk
Website: www.uclunion.org

DEBTS: • Ave debt per year: £2,866
Hard-up students have been able to get up to £1,320 from the access fund. Cash from other funds, eg. the Friend's Trust, is occasionally available – notices are posted by the Registry department.

ACCOMMODATION: • Cost of living index: £££££ • Insurance premium: ££
In college: • Catered: 12% • Cost: £79-102 (38 wks)
• Self-catering: 20% • Cost: £53-84 (38 wks)
London: See <u>London University</u>

EMPLOYMENT: • Unemployed after 6mths: 16%
Paid work: *The Union-run Workstation is invaluable in finding flexible, part-time work. A bunch of student entrepreneurs make money from their IT skills, running website companies and the like.*
Careers: As well as <u>London University</u>'s, UCL has its own *sizeable* careers service (11 full-time staff), complete with job fairs, careers library and interview training.

ENTERTAINMENTS: • Booze index: £2.11
London: see <u>London University</u>
University: • Pint of beer: £1.80 • Glass of wine: £1.80

UNUSUAL COSTS: There's an annual charge for the Bloomsbury Fitness Centre.

UWE, BRISTOL

(1) UWE, Bristol, Frenchay Campus, Coldharbour Lane, BS16 1QY
Tel: (0117) 332 8333. Fax: (0117) 328 2810. E-mail: admissions@uwe.ac.uk
Website: www.uwe.ac.uk
UWE Students Union, Frenchay Campus, Coldharbour Lane, BS16 1QY
Tel: (0117) 328 2577. Fax: (0117) 328 2986. E-mail: union@uwe.ac.uk
Website: www.uwesu.net
(2) Glenside Campus, UWE, Bristol, Blackberry Hill, BS16 1DD
Tel: (0117) 328 8534. SU Tel: (0117) 328 8514
(3) St Matthias Campus, UWE, Bristol, Oldbury Court Road, Fishponds, BS16 2JP
Tel: (0117) 965 5384. SU Tel: (0117) 328 4435

(4) Bower Ashton Campus, Kennel Lodge Road, Bristol, BS3 2JT
   Tel: 0117 328 4716. SU Tel: 0117 328 4725

DEBTS:
- Ave debt per year: £5,215
- Hardship fund: £1,065,877 • Successful applications/yr: 1,200
- Ave payment: £100-3500

Hardship and NHS bursaries, LEA/NHS allowances, pre-entry bursaries and short-term loans all available to help out if things get tight.
Banks on campus: NatWest

FEES: *No official decision yet but top up fees likely to be charged at the full whack.*

ACCOMMODATION: • Cost of living index: £££££ • Insurance premium: £
In college:
- Self-catering: 7%
- Head tenancy: n/a% • Cost: £50-60 (46wks)
- First years living in: 70% • Cost: £41-61 (46wks)
Bristol:
- Ave rent: £55 • Living at home: 10%

EMPLOYMENT: • Unemployed after 6mths: 9.1%
- Paid work: term-time 60%: hols 80%
Paid work: 2 staff and *reasonable* facilities at the Job Bureau.
Careers: 12 staff doing their best to push students into the big bad world of work.

TRAVEL: see University of Bristol
There's a free inter-campus bus every 30 mins. Hourly student shuttle bus to/from
city centre student accomodation to Frenchay campus for £1 (sgl).

ENTERTAINMENTS: • Booze index: £2.03
Bristol:
- Pint of beer: £1.80 • Glass of wine: £2.50
- Can of Red Bull: £2
University:
- Pint of beer: £1.60 • Glass of wine: £1.80
- Can of Red Bull: £1.50

UNIVERSITY OF WARWICK
University of Warwick, Coventry, CV4 7AL
Tel: (02476) 523523. Fax: (02476) 461606. E-mail: ugoffice@warwick.ac.uk
Website: www.warwick.ac.uk
Students' Union, University of Warwick, Coventry, CV4 7AL
Tel: (02476) 572777. Fax: (02476) 572759
E-mail: sunion@sunion.warwick.ac.uk. Website: www.sunion.warwick.ac.uk

7

DEBTS:
- Ave debt per year: £3,473
- Access fund: £400,000 • Successful applications/yr: 300
- Ave payment: up to £2,000

There are 50 or so Graduate Association bursaries each year, worth about £2,000
each, plus music scholarships and a hardship fund.
Banks on campus: 4 major banks.

FEES: Internationals fork out between £7,950 and £10,350 depending on whether
their course is classroom or lab-based. Part-timers can take individual modules for
£280 a throw. *Top up fees will hit Warwick as hard as possible and they'd probably
charge even more if they could.*

ACCOMMODATION: • Cost of living index: £ • Insurance premium: ££
In college:
- Catered: 3% • Cost: £86 (30wks)
- Self-catering: 40% • Cost: £50-78 (30-39wks)
- First years living in: 95%
Coventry:
- Ave rent: £50-70

EMPLOYMENT: • Unemployed after 6mths: 5%

Paid work: Unitemps on campus gives advice and posts vacancies. With such a conference-heavy vacation agenda, there's always plenty of work to be had looking after visitors. The SU itself employs 300 students.
Careers: The *full-fat* Careers Advisory Service has newsletters, bulletin boards, a full careers library and arranges job fairs and interview training.

TRAVEL: see University of Coventry
The closest mainline station is 2 miles away in Coventry, but a line runs through Leamington Spa and Warwick. There's room for 1,000 cars on campus (*useful, given that the campus is off the beaten track*) but first years aren't allowed to bring their wheels anywhere near. It's 10 miles to Birmingham Airport. Several buses stop on campus en route to Coventry centre via the train station every 15 mins until 11pm (80p-£1). Similar services to Leamington and Kenilworth. Late-night university bus services during term. *It's almost inevitable that students will need a late-night cab occasionally*: Coventry's around £6, Leamington can be over a tenner. *Bikes are helpful for getting around campus* (racks and lanes), *but few fancy 7 miles to Leamington twice a day unless they want big calves.*

ENTERTAINMENTS: • Booze index: £1.55
Leamington: • Pint of beer: £1.70
 • Glass of wine: £1.40
 • Can of Red Bull: £1.50
University: • Pint of beer: £1.60
 • Glass of wine: £1.50
 • Can of Red Bull: £1.80

UNUSUAL COSTS: Annual campus parking permits are £250.

UNIVERSITY OF WESTMINSTER
University of Westminster, 309 Regents Street, London, W1B 2UW
Tel: (020) 7911 5000. Fax: (020) 7911 5858. E-mail: admissions@wmin.ac.uk
Website: www.wmin.ac.uk
University of Westminster Students' Union, 32-38 Wells Street, London, W1T 3UW
Tel: (020) 7911 5738. Fax: (020) 7911 5192. E-mail: supresi@wmin.ac.uk
Website: www.uwsu.com

DEBTS: • Ave debt per year: £2,537
 • Access fund: £924,000 • Successful applications/yr: 902
 • Ave payment: £1,000
All students are assessed for scholarships on arrival. There are also opportunity bursaries and hardship funds.

FEES: International undergraduates pay £7,735-£8,110 depending on course. The University is keen to embrace top up fees.

ACCOMMODATION: • Cost of living index: ££££ • Insurance premium: £
In college: • Self-catering: 6% • Cost: £64-125 (38wks)
 • First years living in: 26%
London: • Ave rent: £87

EMPLOYMENT: • Unemployed after 6mths: 11.5%
Paid work: The SU runs a job shop (external jobs and employment within the SU).
Careers: CaSE covers all aspects of employment during and after study, everything from job fairs to CV advice – *the whole nine yards.*

ENTERTAINMENTS: • Booze index: £2.06
London: • Pint of beer: £2
 • Glass of wine: £2.50
 • Can of Red Bull: £2
University: • Pint of beer: £2.10
 • Glass of wine: £1.70
 • Can of Red Bull: £1.50

UNIVERSITY OF WOLVERHAMPTON

University of Wolverhampton, Wulfruna Street, Wolverhampton, WV1 1SB
Tel: (01902) 322222. Fax: (01902) 322680. E-mail: enquiries@wlv.ac.uk
Website: www.wlv.ac.uk
University of Wolverhampton Student's Union, Wulfruna Street, Wolverhampton,
WV1 1LY
Tel: (01902) 322021. Fax: (01902) 322020. E-mail: UWSU@wlv.ac.uk
Website: www.wolvesunion.org

DEBTS: • Ave debt per year: £4,268
• Access fund: £3,000,000 • Ave payment: £50-£1,000
The university provides hardship loans and bursaries. There's a fund for black South
African students.
Banks on campus: Nationwide

FEES: Top up fees will be charged.

ACCOMMODATION: • Cost of living index: £££ • Insurance premium: ££
In college: • Self-catering: 15% • Cost: £45-62 (37wks)
Wolverhampton: • Ave rent: £35-40

EMPLOYMENT: • Unemployed after 6mths: 7.8%
• Paid work: term-time 75%: hols 80%
Paid work: Wolves work is *easy to come by*, with *loads* of pubs, bars and
restaurants in town. The university jobshop helps out if students get stuck.
Careers: *Comprehensive* service with newsletters, bulletin boards, a careers library,
job fairs, interview coaching, psychometric testing, vacancy database and so forth.

TRAVEL: see University of Birmingham
The supertram Metro links Wolves to Brum. It's £2.30 into Brum on the train, or the
ever-popular night special is £1.40 (last train at 3am). There's also a 50p night bus
from Brum to Walsall. Intersite shuttle buses (free with NUS ID). Late-night safety
bus that does doorstep drop-offs within a 3-mile radius of college events. Women
get first dibs.

ENTERTAINMENTS: • Booze index: £1.91
Birmingham: • Pint of beer: £1.85   • Glass of wine: £2
                                          • Can of Red Bull: £2
University: • Pint of beer: £1.65   • Glass of wine: £1.70
                                          • Can of Red Bull: £1.50

UNIVERSITY OF YORK

University of York, Heslington, York, North Yorkshire, YO10 5DD
Tel: (01904) 430 000 / 433 533. Fax: (01904) 433 538
E-mail: admissions@york.ac.uk. Website: www.york.ac.uk
York University Students Union, The Daw Suu Centre, Goodricke College,
Heslington, York, North Yorkshire, YO10 5DD
Tel: (01904) 433724. Fax: (01904) 434664. E-mail: su-enquiries@york.ac.uk
Website: www.yusu.org

DEBTS: • Ave debt per year: £2,474 • Access fund: £506,000
The SU can provide a hardship loan of £100 on the spot. Some bursaries and
sponsorships available, particularly for international or mature students.
Banks on campus: Several major banks in Heslington village. NatWest ATM on
campus.

FEES: Fees for non-EU nationals vary between £7,842 and £10,365 depending on
the course. Postgrads: £2,940 a year.

ACCOMMODATION:

In college:	• Cost of living index: £ • Insurance premium: £
	• Self-catering: 49% • Cost: £60 (33-38 wks)
	• First years living in: 100% • Others living in: 12%
York:	• Ave rent: £55 • Living at home: 4%

EMPLOYMENT: • Unemployed after 6mths: 6%

Paid work: The thriving tourist industry means lots of jobs for students in high season. Museum, tearoom, restaurant and pub work is *easy to find*. Unijobs is a helpful agency that links students up with local businesses. Target assists first and second years in finding vacation or gap year work in all corners of the globe.

CAREERS: Careers service has bulletin boards, interview practice, a careers library and a program of employer presentations.

TRAVEL:

National: From York Station in the city centre (2 miles from campus) to many destinations, mostly via Leeds. National Express coaches from the rail station. Leeds Bradford Airport is 24 miles away, budget airlines include Ryanair, BMI, Jet2 and British European.

Local: Buses from the campus to the city centre (£1.20 sgl, £2.20 day ticket). SU minibus service between front doors and campus at 18.30 and 21.45. The late-late night bus runs only between the campus and halls at a rough approximation of 00.15, for which a 20p donation is appreciated. Taxis are *cheap and easy enough to find*.

ENTERTAINMENTS: • Booze index: £1.86

York:	• Pint of beer: £2	• Glass of wine: £2.50
		• Can of Red Bull: £1.60
University:	• Pint of beer: £1.50	• Glass of wine: £1.75
		• Can of Red Bull: £1.70

Chapter Seventeen

Useful contacts and further info

PUSH BOOKS AND SERVICES

If you find this book helpful, try these…

* *The Push Guide to Which University* 2005, £15.95 – details of every aspect of student life at every university in the UK.
* *The Push Guide to Choosing a University*, £5.00 – how to choose the right university for you and how student life should affect your choice.
* Push Online at www.push.co.uk – the online guide to choosing a university, with interactive search facilities to find the right university for you.

GENERAL ADVICE AND INFORMATION

Department for Education & Skills

www.dfes.gov.uk

'Financial Support for Higher Education Students in 2004/05' plus other useful guides and forms and a veritable host of funding information available to download at www.dfes.gov.uk/studentsupport.

0800 731 9133 – free information line or to order free copies of the guides.

www.dfes.gov.uk/hegateway for the latest higher education news.

www.aimhigher.ac.uk – government portal particularly useful for those starting university after 2006.

For **Scottish students:** Student Awards Agency for Scotland (SAAS): www.saas.gov.uk. Loads of useful information, online support application facility and forms and guides available to download. Alternatively, contact them on 0845 111 1711 or e-mail saas.geu@scotland.gsi.gov.uk.

Their address: SAAS
Gyleview House
3 Redheughs Rigg
Edinburgh EH12 9HH.

For students from **Northern Ireland:** The Department for Education can be contacted on (02891) 279279 or virtually visited at www.deni.gov.uk.

Their address: Rathgael House
43 Balloo Road
Bangor
Co Down
BT19 7PR

Their specialist funding site, www.student-support.org.uk, is also worth a click.

Welsh students: Different arrangements for some bursaries exist in Wales and the Welsh Assembly is hoping to get more control over tuition fees and student support arrangements from 2006. See www.learning.wales.gov.uk or call (029) 2082 5831.

Their address: Higher Education Division
National Assembly for Wales
Cathays Park
Cardiff CF10 3NQ.

The National Union of Students (NUS) produces a series of information sheets on student finance, all of which are available at their website: www.nusonline.co.uk.

NUS addresses:

NUS, Nelson Mandela House, 461 Holloway Road, London, N7 6LJ. Telephone: 020 7272 8900. E-mail: nusuk@nus.org.uk.

NUS Scotland, 29 Forth Street, Edinburgh, EH1 3LE. Telephone: 0131 556 6598. E-mail: nus-scot@dircon.co.uk.

National Union of Students-Union of Students in Ireland, 29 Bedford Street, Belfast, BT2 7EJ. Telephone: 028 9024 4641. E-mail: info@nistudents.org.

NUS Wales (Undeb Cenedlaethol Myfyrwyr Cymru), Windsor House, Windsor Lane, Cardiff, CF10 3DE. Telephone: 029 2037 5980. E-mail: office@nus-wales.org.uk.

EU students (non-UK) should visit www.dfes.gov.uk/studentsupport/eustudents.

You can contact The European Team at the Department for Education and Skills, 2F - Area B, Mowden Hall, Staindrop Road, Darlington, DL3 9BG, United Kingdom. Telephone: 01325 391199 or e-mail: EUTeam@dfes.gsi.gov.uk (you may have to wait up to 20 days for a response).

UCAS General enquiries: 01242 222444.
Applicant enquiries: 0870 112 2211. Website: www.ucas.com.
Address: UCAS Enquiries, UCAS, PO Box 28, Cheltenham GL52 3LZ.
E-mail enquiries@ucas.ac.uk for an automated response with general information and guidance on the UCAS procedures.

Department of Social Security (freephone helpline): 0800 666555

Money Advice Association: 020 7236 3566

National Association of Citizens Advice Bureaux: 020 7833 2181

Credit Action and Consumer Credit Counselling Service:

www.creditaction.org.uk and www.cccs.co.uk. Joint helpline: 0800 138 1111

www.lifelonglearning.co.uk

Local Government Agency: www.lga.gov.uk

www.support4learning.org.uk/money/index.htm

BURSARIES, SCHOLARSHIPS AND SPONSORSHIPS:

The Student Money website at www.scholarship-search.org.uk has a free search facility for all undergraduate and postgraduate students. You can search by subject, type of award or region. Postal address: Student Money, Hotcourses Ltd, 150-152 King Street, London, W6 9JG.

Also try www.freefund.com for info on all types of educational assistance. Check your own eligibility with the search facility.

The Windsor Fellowship runs undergraduate personal and professional development programmes (such as sponsorships, community work and summer placements) – this is primarily for gifted black and Asian students. Their address: The Stables, 138 Kingsland Road, London E2 8DY. Telephone: (020) 7613 0373. Website: www.windsor-fellowship.org.
E-mail office@windsor-fellowship.org.

Education Grants Advisory Service (EGAS): 501-505 Kingsland Road, London E8 4AU. (Enclose a stamped addressed envelope with you enquiry letter). Telephone: 020 7254 6251. Website: www.egas-online.org.

ARMED FORCES

Army - www.army.mod.uk/careers. Telephone: 0345 300111.

Royal Air Force - www.rafcareers.com. Telephone: 0345 300100.

The Royal Navy and Royal Marines Careers Service - www.royal-navy.mod.uk. Telephone: 08456 075555.

NHS-FUNDED STUDIES

NHS courses in England and Wales. Telephone: 0845 6060655, website: www.nhscareers.nhs.uk

The NHS Student Grants Unit, 22 Plymouth Road, Blackpool, FY3 7JS. Telephone: 01253 655 655.

NHS Bursaries in Wales: Student Awards Unit, 2nd Floor Golate House, 101 St Mary Street, Cardiff CF10 1DX. Telephone: 029 2026 1495.

NHS bursaries in Scotland: The Student Awards Agency for Scotland, 3 Redheughs Rigg, South Gyle, Edinburgh EH12 9YT. Telephone: 0131 4768 212.

NHS bursaries in Northern Ireland: The Department of Higher and Further Education Training and Employment, Student Support Branch, 4th Floor Adelaide House, 39-49 Adelaide Street, Belfast, BT2 8FD. Telephone: 028 9025 7777.

POSTGRADUATES: SOURCES OF FUNDING

The UK Research Councils

Biotechnology and Biological Sciences Research Council (BBSRC)
Polaris House
North Star Avenue
Swindon SN2 1UH
Telephone: 01793 413200
Website: www.bbsrc.ac.uk

Economic and Social Research Council (ESRC)
Address as above (Postcode SN2 1UJ)
Telephone: 01793 413000
Website: www.esrc.ac.uk

Engineering and Physical Sciences Research (EPSRC)
Address as above (Postcode SN2 1ET)
Telephone: 01793 444000
Website: www.epsrc.ac.uk

Natural Environment Research Council (NERC)
Address as above (Postcode SN2 1EU)
Telephone: 01793 411500
Website: www.nerc.ac.uk

Particle Physics and Astronomy Research (PPARC)
Address as above (Postcode SN2 1SZ)
Telephone: 01793 442000
Website: www.pparc.ac.uk

Medical Research Council (MRC)
20 Park Crescent
London W1B 1AL.
Telephone: 020 7636 5422
Website: www.mrc.ac.uk

Arts and Humanities

The Arts and Humanities Research Board (AHRB), Whitefriars, Lewins Mead,
Bristol, BS1 2AE. Telephone: 0117 987 6543 (Postgraduate Awards
Division). Website: www.ahrb.ac.uk

Council for the Central Laboratory of the Research Councils (CCLRC)
Rutherford Appleton Laboratory
Chilton
Didcot
Oxfordshire OX11 0QX
Telephone: 01235 445000
Website: www.cclrc.ac.uk

Further Postgraduate Sources:

The Association of Graduate Careers Advisory Service (AGCAS), AGCAS
Administration Office, c/o the Careers Service, Sheffield University, 8-10
Favell Road, Sheffield, S3 7QX. Telephone: 0870 7703310. Website:
www.agcas.org.uk

Royal Society Research Fellowships
Research Appointments Department
6 Carlton House Terrace
London SW1Y 5AG.
Telephone: 020 7451 2547
Website: www.royalsoc.ac.uk

Charities:

The Wellcome Trust
183 Euston Road
London NW1 2BE.
Telephone: 020 7611 8888
Website: www.wellcome.ac.uk

Association of Medical Research Charities (AMRC), 61 Gray's Inn Road, London WC1X 8TL. Telephone 020 7269 8820. An organisation that represents almost 90 charities. Visit www.amrc.org.uk for further info.

STUDENTS WITH DISABILITIES

SKILL - National Bureau for **Students with Disabilities**: www.skill.org.uk

Their address: Chapter House, 18-20 Crucifix Lane, London SE1 3JW.

For the DfES leaflet *Bridging the Gap: A guide to the disabled students' allowances* and information about the Disabled Students' Allowances, call the DfES information line on 0800 731 9133. See also the recommended reading list for the book 'Higher Education and Disability'.

Action for Blind People, Grants Officer, 14-16 Verney Road, London SE16 3DZ. Telephone: 020 7635 4821. Website: www.afbp.org.

Association for Spina Bifida and Hydrocephalus, ASBAH House, 42 Park Road, Peterborough, PE1 2UQ. Telephone: (01733) 555988. Website: www.asbah.org.uk. E-mail: info@asbah.org.

The Dyslexia Institute Bursary Fund, 133 Gresham Road, Staines, Middlesex. TW18 2AJ. Telephone 01784 463851. Website: www.dyslexia-inst.org.uk/di_bursary_fund.htm

Snowdon Award Scheme, 22 City Business Centre, 6 Brighton Road, Horsham, West Sussex RH13 5BB. Helps disabled students aged 17-25 in further, higher or adult education. Website: www.snowdonawardscheme.org.uk. Telephone: 01403 211252. E-mail: info@snowdonawardscheme.org.uk.

For **disabled students looking for work**: See www.opportunities.org.uk.

PAID WORK

If you're looking for a **job**, check out www.summerjobs4students.co.uk, which despite the name has suggestions for all seasons.

Also: www.work-experience.org or the student section of www.loot.com, both of which offer excellent info and details of companies who offer student placements. There is also a site called www.hotrecruit.co.uk and this has student-specific jobs nationwide.

www.jobpilot.co.uk/content/channel/student is another one to try and don't forget that *The Guardian* newspaper has student and graduate opportunities advertised regularly (especially in Saturday editions) or try www.guardian.co.uk/jobs

www.dti.gov.uk/er/pay.htm tells you about the national minimum wage and hours of employment and also has a 'young worker' section. Minimum wage national helpline: 0845 600 0678

www.tiger.gov.uk

TAKING A YEAR OUT

Getting started: www.yearoutgroup.org/organisations.htm and www.gap–year.com.

The **Year in Industry** scheme – see www.yini.org.uk for further information, contact details of regional offices or to apply online.

Visit www.yearoutgroup.org for a full list of organisations, including:

Africa and Asia Venture: four to six-month schemes offering great scope for cultural and interpersonal development in Kenya, Tanzania, Uganda, Malawi, Botswana, Mexico, India and Nepal. Teaching, sports coaching and conservation work, with extensive travel and safari opportunities. Telephone: 01380 729009. Website: www.aventure.co.uk

BUNAC (British Universities North America Club) offers an extensive range of work/travel programmes worldwide, varying from a few months to a whole year, depending on destination and programme. Telephone: 020 7251 3472. Website: www.bunac.org

Community Service Volunteers (CSV) – full-time voluntary placements throughout the UK last 4-12 months. Allowance, accommodation and food provided. Freephone 0800 374 991. Website: www.csv.org.uk.

Buy Christmas cards and other festive fripperies in the January sales. You're a student. Have no shame.

Council on International Educational Exchange Work, language learning and internship programmes abroad. Internships in North America, teaching in Asia, work in Australasia and many more. Programmes range from a few months to more than a year. Telephone: 020 7478 2020. Website: www.councilexchanges.org.uk.

Gap Activity Projects (GAP) Ltd: an independent educational charity founded in 1972, which organises voluntary work overseas in 30 different countries. Telephone: 0118 959 4914. Website: www.gap.org.uk

Gap Challenge/World Challenge Expeditions: Varied schemes for students 18-25, from voluntary conservation projects to paid hotel work in many different countries. Telephone 020 8728 7200. Website www.world-challenge.co.uk

i-to-i: International volunteer work and teaching placements in 19 different countries. Placements include English teaching, community development, journalism, business, conservation and care work. Telephone: 0870 333 2332. Website: www.i-to-i.com

Raleigh International: Charity-run scheme offering 3-month expeditions all over the world for environmental, adventure and community project work. Over 20,000 young people have taken part in a total of 168 expeditions in 35 countries since 1984. Telephone 020 7371 8585. Website www.raleigh.org.uk

Students Partnership Worldwide: 4-9 month health education and community resource projects in Africa and Asia. Telephone 020 7222 0138. Website: www.spw.org

Teaching & Projects Abroad: Foreign travel and experience in teaching English, conservation work, medicine and business among others. Countries include China, Ghana, India, Thailand, Mexico and South Africa. Telephone 01903 859911. Website: www.teaching-abroad.co.uk

VSO runs special overseas youth programmes for under 25s. There is the **World Youth** programme, for people between 17 and 25. Participants are paired with another young person from the exchange country and spend six months on a practical project (three months in the UK, three months in the exchange country). The **Youth for Development** programme is aimed at young people aged 18-25 or undergraduates with an interest in overseas development who are able to spend a summer vacation abroad. Applications can be made through the participant's university. Placements are in areas such as education, HIV and AIDS-awareness work, participation and governance, disability or secure livelihoods.

Contact VSO Enquiries: 020 8780 7200 or e-mail enquiry@vso.org.uk

You can apply online at www.vso.org.uk.

SUMMER WORK ABROAD

AIESEC – International Exchange Programme. Many types of placements and traineeships for students and recent graduates. Some universities have a branch on campus. If not, contact them at: AIESEC UK, 29-31 Cowper Street, London EC2A 4AT. Telephone: 020 7549 1800. Website: www.uk.aiesec.org. E-mail: national@uk.aiesec.org.uk.

If you fancy working on a **kibbutz**, contact: Kibbutz Representatives, 16 Accommodation Road, London NW11 8ED. Telephone: 020 8458 9235. E-mail: enquiries@kibbutz.org.uk. See www.kibbutz.org.il for more information about kibbutzim.

A number of organisations can arrange work on summer camps in the USA, either as a counsellor or as a member of support staff. In addition to BUNAC (details in Gap year section), try **Camp America**: Dept YO, 37a Queens Gate, London SW7 5HR. Telephone: 020 7581 7373. Website: www.campamerica.co.uk. BUNAC and CIEE (details as above) also offer Work America programmes. Read one of the specialised books in 'Recommended Reading' for further info. For example, the 'Vacation Work' series (website www.vacationwork.co.uk)

For international students or UK students studying overseas:

7

www.britishcouncil.org/education/index.htm and www.ukcosa.org.uk – info about UK courses and qualifications available and also those in the home country of international students.

Erasmus website: www.erasmus.ac.uk. Erasmus Student Network: www.esn.org

Student Travel: www.studentflights.co.uk

www.statravel.co.uk – branches on many university campuses

INSURANCE

Endsleigh Insurance: branch locator and more details of policies available at www.endsleigh.co.uk. A number of universities have branches on campus. For a quote, call free on: 0800 028 3571.

CAREER DEVELOPMENT LOANS

DfES's Career Development Loan Helpline: 0800 585505 or see www.lifelonglearning.co.uk/cdl

Banks offering career development loans:

Barclays Bank: www.barclays.co.uk. Telephone: 0845 609 0060 (option2) for information, 0845 607 0080 for an application form.

Co-operative Bank: www.co-operativebank.co.uk. Telephone: 08457 212 212.

Royal Bank of Scotland: www.rbs.co.uk. Telephone: 0800 121127.

STUDENT LOANS

For information about your **student loan**:

Student Loans Company

100 Bothwell Street

Glasgow G2 7JD

General Enquiries about the loan scheme or when you will receive your loan: 0800 40 50 10

Queries about your loan account:

General enquiries: 0870 24 222 11

Deferment Enquiries: 0870 60 60 70 4

If you are in arrears with your loan repayments: 0870 24 23 22 0

Disabled helpline: 0870 60 60 70 4

www.slc.co.uk or www.studentfinancedirect.co.uk

Birth Certificates for Student Loans

To get hold of copies of Birth or Adoption Certificates, which you need for Student Loan Applications, contact:

For England and Wales: General Register Office, PO Box 2, Southport, Merseyside PR8 2JD. Telephone: 0870 243 77 88. Apply online (birth certificates only) at www.statistics.gov.uk.

For Scotland: The Registrar General, New Register House, 3 West Register Street, Edinburgh, EH1 3YT. Telephone (0131) 314 4411. www.gro-scotland.gov.uk.

7

In the back

For Northern Ireland: The Registrar General, Oxford House, 49/55 Chichester Street, Belfast BT1 4HL. Telephone (028) 90252000. www.groni.gov.uk

For the Republic of Ireland: The Registrar General, Joyce House, 8/11 Lombard Street East, Dublin 2. Telephone (035 31) 635 40 00. www.groireland.ie.

BOOKS

University Scholarships and Awards 2003, Brian Heap (Trotman). All the info you'll need, plus information for overseas students and a list of charitable and other awards. Each university is broken down with a list of awards they offer.

The Educational Grants Directory, Sarah Harland (Directory of Social Change). Lists all sources of non-statutory help for students in financial need.

Sponsorship and Funding Directory (Hobsons), available in most schools, colleges and public libraries.

Students' Money Matters, Gwenda Thomas (Trotman). A reference book with details on just about everything concerning student finance, plus student case studies and 'thrift tips' throughout.

Balancing your Books (ECCTIS/CRAC).

Into Higher Education 2004 (SKILL). Information and advice for disabled people planning to apply to university, updated annually. One of many publications available from www.skill.org.uk or (020) 7450 0620, reduced prices for disabled students.

Student Life – A Survival Guide, Natasha Roe (Lifetime Careers).

Everything you need to know about going to University, Sally Longson (Kogan Page).

Summer Jobs Abroad 2004 and *Summer Jobs USA* and *Summer Jobs Britain 2004*, three titles from a selection of useful books geared primarily at students and young people, published by Vacation Work. They also publish comprehensive and authoritative guides called *Working Your Way Around the World* and *Taking a Gap Year*. For students interested in the **voluntary** sector, there's *The International Directory of Voluntary Work* and *The Directory of Work and Study in Developing Countries*, plus several more titles. Telephone 01865 241978 or order online at www.vacationwork.co.uk for a discount of £2 per title.

The Gap-Year Guidebook 2004/05, Susannah Hecht (John Catt Educational).

Before you Go: the Ultimate Guide to Planning Your Gap Year, Tom Griffiths (Bloomsbury).

Taking a Year Off, Val Butcher (Trotman).

A Year Off…A Year On?, Doe, Evans and Steel De'ath (Lifetime Careers Publishing).

Working Holidays (Central Bureau for Educational Visits and Exchanges); if you can't find a copy in your local library contact the Bureau on 020 7389 4004.

Other Useful Websites

The Liberal Democrats' petition regarding fees: www.scraptuitionfees.com.

The NUS's student funding campaign site: www.stopfeesnow.com.

The Times Higher Education Supplement is the UK's most authoritative source of information about higher education: www.thes.co.uk.

www.studentuk.com – a general guide plus money section.

www.studentmoneynet.co.uk – this website offers some sound advice and general financing info.

www.hotbeast.com – designed to help students and graduates build networks.

www.studentsgetoff.com – providing discounts on books, booze, clubs, haircuts, mobiles, movies, travel…all a student could need. Except for winning lottery numbers, unfortunately.

www.studentswapshop.co.uk – speaks for itself.

www.uniservity.net – academic, social and financial web resources.

www.uniserveuk.com – offering lots of sound advice to students, with a great money section.

Other useful student websites: www.student123.com and www.uni4me.com.

7

In the back

Give your money to me and I'll look after it for you.

Kate Berry, South Tyneside College

Index

7

7

7